Being Shelley

P. B. Shelley
Sketched from life
by E. E. Williams
Pisa. Nov.ᵗ 27
1821

BEING SHELLEY

The Poet's Search for Himself

Ann Wroe

JONATHAN CAPE
LONDON

First published by Jonathan Cape in 2007

2 4 6 8 10 9 7 5 3 1

First published in Great Britain in 2007 by
Jonathan Cape
Random House, 20 Vauxhall Bridge Road,
London SW1V 2SA

Random House Australia (Pty) Limited
20 Alfred Street, Milsons Point, Sydney
New South Wales 2061, Australia

Random House New Zealand Limited
18 Poland Road, Glenfield
Auckland 10, New Zealand

Random House (Pty) Limited
Isle of Houghton, Corner of Boundary Road & Carse O'Gowrie,
Houghton 2198, South Africa

Random House Publishers India Private Limited
301 World Trade Tower, Hotel Intercontinental Grand Complex,
Barakhamba Lane, New Delhi 110 001, India

The Random House Group Limited Reg. No. 954009
www.randomhouse.co.uk

A CIP catalogue record for this book is available from the British Library

ISBN 9780224080781

Papers used by Random House are natural,
recyclable products made from wood grown in sustainable forests.
The manufacturing processes conform to the environmental
regulations of the country of origin

Typeset in Bembo by Palimpsest Book Production Limited,
Grangemouth, Stirlingshire

Printed and bound in Great Britain by
William Clowes Ltd, Beccles, Suffolk

Contents

List of Illustrations

p. 341 Comet and 'Thou wert the Morning Star'(1821): from BSM e. 9 p. 317

p. 383 The boat appearing (1822): from BSM vol. 1, 'Triumph of Life', f. 53v

All Bodleian material is reproduced with permission. For guide to abbreviations please see Notes on page 393.

Introduction

This book is an experiment. It is an attempt to write the life of a poet from the inside out: that is, from the perspective of the creative spirit struggling to discover its true nature. It is a book about Shelley the poet, rather than Shelley the man. The distinction was one he himself was sure of. 'The poet & the man', he wrote in 1821, 'are two different natures; though they exist together they may be unconscious of each other, & incapable of deciding on each other's powers & effects by any reflex act.'

The man who was Shelley is not neglected. He was the dragging shadow with which the soul had to live. But the usual priorities of biography are reversed. Rather than writing the life of a man into which poetry erupts occasionally, my hope is to reconstruct the world of a poet into which earthly life keeps intruding. This, I believe, is how things were for Shelley. The lives of great writers and thinkers are not principally a succession of ordinary events in the day-to-day world. They live, and often move, elsewhere.

Sheer astonishment at Shelley's poems made me write this book; astonishment, and regret that his spiritual force seems to have been largely forgotten. In the twentieth century his biography was rewritten to recover, rightly, his political radicalism. As a result he has been brought severely to earth, as if this is the only way to make him strong, sharp and relevant to us. But if the life of the spirit is man's most vital resource and means of change — as Shelley believed it is — he has truly revolutionary things to suggest to us. To dwell on his metaphysics does not blunt his challenge or still his urgency at all.

My sources have been almost entirely Shelley's own words: in poetry, prose, letters, recorded conversations, and especially his notebooks, preserved in the Bodleian Library at Oxford and the Huntingdon Library in San Marino, California. Of the mountain of literary criticism on Shelley I have read what seems best. But his is the only mind whose labyrinths I want to explore – through his confident, flowing essays, his scratched-out, stumbling efforts to describe his visions, and also in his pauses.

This book does not proceed chronologically. It takes seriously Shelley's statement that a poet 'participates in the eternal, the infinite and the one; as far as relates to his conceptions, time and place and number are not'. Its narrative track is the poet's quest for truth through the steadily rarefying elements of earth, water, air and fire. It is an adventure story of Shelley's search to discover, in his words, 'whence I came, and where I am, and why'.

These questions enthralled and obsessed him. Everything Shelley proposed and pursued had its basis in his search for the meaning of life and the truth of his being. His friends and lovers – Byron, Mary, Leigh Hunt – complained about his devotion to 'mystifying metaphysics' and wished he could be weaned away from it, but Shelley's emphasis made perfect sense. No revolution in the moral and social order could take place until he, and all men and women, knew themselves for what they were and could unlock the true power they possessed.

Some readers may complain, as Shelley's friends did when they read his works, that this book is not about 'real life'. I would disagree. And, more to the point, so would he.

Prelude: The voyage out

In the morning he set sail. The high sun beat on the water, and the wind was soft. A push from the shore set him rocking across the shallows, above his own shadow on the rippled sand. The keel dipped, and the ink on it began to blur and run. But it did not yet ship water, and he was safe.

The whole craft juddered, from stem to stern, as it breasted the continuous waves that formed and swelled before him. His ballast, a halfpenny piece, held him steady; beneath it lay the hull, porous and slowly softening, inscribed with the words *Your most Obt. Servant*. He was not most obedient, but bold and exploring. He bucked and circled, skimming the surface of the dim tremendous deep.

Wind filled every part of him, though invisibly. The pinched white peaks of his sails were swollen and crinkled with the pressing air. At the stern the wind was a rough god, buffeting him. The whole world was motion and breath; stirring his hair, playing over his skin, blowing in every nerve and vein of him, a shell of woven paper intrepidly and madly on the sea.

Time could not touch him. On land perhaps an hour passed, as impatient friends waited for the game to end. On the water he essayed a full Odyssey, or a voyage of the Argonauts that might stretch out for years. He passed Charybdis and the isle of the Sirens, dipping danger-ously close. Sea monsters rose with the plop of a trout, and the wide concentric ripples rocked and disoriented him. Glittering wavelets almost swallowed him in the dazzle of the sunlight they reflected. At all times the contest went on between his desire and the wind's control, at vari-ance or at one, as long as his substance lasted.

To the casual eye he was on shore, a tall, stooped young man with tangled hair and yet more boats in his pockets. He was, as his friend Hogg once said, the Demiurgus of Plato's *Timaeus*, constantly creating both men and the lower gods, equipping them with star-souls and setting them afloat. The remark made him laugh like the giant he seemed to be, filling the horizon of his little fleet with cataclysmic splashings. Yet in reality he was out on the huge sea adventuring, one of them.

The end was still unknown. After years the tiny boat might reach the other side, all obstacles triumphantly circumnavigated, to be swept up joyfully in the Demiurgus's arms and crammed inside his jacket. Or the wind would take him, twirl him and overset him. Water would soak his body, and with a rapturous rush of cold he would go down into the unimagined depths.

His vanishing would be so swift and silent that scarcely anyone would notice. The evening would draw in; supper would beckon; passers-by would saunter past, lighting their pipes as the last rays of sun faded across the water. His body would go on falling through the blue deep, softly, like paper. He had once told a small boy, watching with him, that this would be his favourite of all deaths.

Earth

I
Substance

In later life, Charles MacFarlane recalled the moment more or less exactly. He was standing in the Royal Bourbon Museum in Naples in February 1819, admiring a statue assumed to be of Agrippina, when someone at his shoulder murmured words. The remark had something to do with the statue's gracefulness, little enough in itself, though it seemed 'that sort of commonplace which is not heard from the vulgar'. MacFarlane remembered rather the voice, soft and strangely touching. The speaker was a gentleman of twenty-five or twenty-six, English, thin, with a delicate and negligent, even wild, appearance. They had not been introduced.

Falling in together, they wandered from statue to statue for the rest of the afternoon. His new escort talked avidly of Beauty, Justice, the Venus di Medici ('all over a goddess!'), love of the Ideal and the astonishments of modern archaeology. At the end he shook MacFarlane's hand, thanked him heartily, and disappeared. MacFarlane realised that he still had no idea who his 'unknown friend' had been. No name had been proffered, no visiting card. Instead he was left with fragments of deep thought, like leaves from a private notebook.

His mysterious companion had a past. You could learn from his acquaintances that he was Percy Bysshe Shelley, born at Field Place, Horsham, Sussex, in 1792, the first son of Timothy Shelley, landowner, sometime MP for New Shoreham and, since 1815, a baronet. The family was large: Shelley had four younger sisters and a brother 14 years his junior. He had been schooled at Syon House Academy and Eton, where he excelled in Latin composition; and at University College, Oxford, where after one term, in March 1811, he had been expelled with his best friend, Thomas Jefferson Hogg, for writing a pamphlet entitled *The Necessity of Atheism*. He had eloped the next August, aged nineteen, with a schoolgirl of sixteen, Harriet Westbrook; and then, that marriage having failed, had run off in 1814 with the almost-as-young Mary Godwin, daughter of William Godwin, the philosopher, and Mary Wollstonecraft, a champion of the rights of women. With Mary and her sixteen-year-old step-half-sister, Jane (later Claire) Clairmont, he had journeyed for six weeks through France and Germany in a sort of *ménage à trois*, and had set up a household with the girls on returning. As a result of this extraordinary behaviour his father had severed all connection with him, leaving Shelley for a time almost destitute; and despite his eventual marriage to Mary Godwin, the Lord Chancellor in 1817 had deprived him, on the double grounds of immorality and atheism, of the two infant children of his first marriage.

From boyhood he had written poems, as well as political tracts and the odd romantic novel. According to taste these were tedious, blasphemous or immoral, though a few saw beauty and genius in them. For a while, fearing that he had Jacobin tendencies and meant to revolutionise England in the style seen so recently in France, the government watched him, but most of his writings proved too obscure to be subversive. Disheartened and discredited, and convinced (for he had never retracted either his atheism or his singular notions of morality) that his two children by Mary Godwin would also be taken from him, he had left England in March 1818 for Italy. And there he seemed likely to remain.

MacFarlane later learned a little of this, including Shelley's name, from mutual friends who formally introduced them. On a subsequent day they drove out in a carriage as far as Pompeii, hurtling crazily along to the ruins and back, and visited a macaroni factory where his companion, like a schoolboy, exulted in the giant levers that pressed out the pasta and, as he left, gave his small change to beggars. Of his life, condition and history he continued to provide no details. Much of the afternoon was spent sitting by the sea on curious lava rocks, watching until sunset the tranquil waves breaking on the sand, in the sort of enforced intimacy in which English gentlemen may sometimes feel induced to talk of schooldays or love affairs. In all that time, Shelley said nothing. MacFarlane, looking at his sad, lined face, concluded that he should not break the silence.

Shelley's past seemed hateful to him. For most of his life he looked passionately forward, taking, as his friend Hogg observed at Oxford, 'no pleasure in the retrospect'. He read history occasionally, but out of duty rather than pleasure; his historical dramas were aberrations in his career. The 'record of crimes & miseries' that men had left on earth was testimony merely to the worst of human nature. Facts, Shelley wrote, in poetry or history or in the lives of men, 'are not what we want to know'. Sometimes he used the word 'cered' of memories, to imply that he had coated them, like corpses, with impermeable wax.

A few stories only he told frequently and with zest. One was of stabbing a boy in the hand with a knife (sometimes a fork) at Eton, pinning him viciously to his desk on some noble and desperate impulse; another was a fight, related at the highest pitch of horror, with an intruder in Wales who had tried to murder him. Neither may have been true. 'His imagination', one friend recalled, 'often presented past events to him as they might have been, not as they were.' Hogg's view was less poetic and more blunt: 'He was altogether incapable of rendering an account of any transaction whatsoever, according to the strict and precise truth, and the bare naked realities of actual life.' Again, imagination was to blame. Indulgently, two of Shelley's sisters remembered his boyhood account of a visit to some ladies in the village, their conversation, his wanderings in their garden along a winding turf bank and a filbert walk, when he had never been there.

In 1814, when they eloped and fled to France, Shelley and Mary Godwin began a joint journal. Very quickly his entries dwindled, then stopped. The few he made gave the doings of 'S.' in the third person, at one remove from himself. In 1816, Mary tried to persuade him to write a story based on his early life; he started, but could not keep it up, any more than he could follow her desire to put more human interest in his poems. Whatever he had been since birth he endeavoured to leave behind. He could not help it that his mother had a miniature of him, sweet and bright-eyed, with three rows of buttons on his best jacket; or that his four younger sisters were full of stories of him, the adored and bullying elder brother, with his terrifying tales and his rough garden games. His friend Edward Trelawny once told him that he had met two of his sisters at an evening party. Shelley, after giving him a hard, cold stare, walked away from him and out of the room.

His writings gave few more clues. Experiences of boyhood made a line here and there: shells found on the beach, a breathless run in the night woods, hard-boiled eggs and radishes stowed in his pockets, and a walk at school beside a mossy fence with a boy he thought 'exquisitely beautiful', their arms round each other's shoulders. But such memories were no sooner found than they were suppressed again. All that mattered to him of his childhood he seemed to commit to a notebook in 1820, in several strongly underlined verses of the Wisdom of Solomon in the Apocrypha:

> *I myself also am a mortal man, like to all, & the offspring of him that was first made of the Earth.*
>
> *And in my mothers womb was fashioned to be flesh in the time of ten months, being compacted in blood, of the seed of man and the pleasure that came with sleep.*
>
> *And when I was born I drew in the common air, & fell upon the earth which is of like nature, & the first voice which I uttered was crying, as all others do*
>
> *I was nursed in swaddling clothes & that with cares.*
>
> *For there is no King that had any other beginning of birth.*

★   ★   ★

His own beginning was as a Sussex boy. He had been pushed into existence in a first-floor bedroom at Field Place near Horsham, a red-brick Tudor house with Georgian attachments nestled in a snug dip of copses and lawns. There was no view, save of near slopes or outbuildings; his child's world was circumscribed and close as a womb. A Sussex nurse with a flat, burring accent rocked him in her arms. He was embraced by Established Anglicanism in the nearby church at Warnham, crouched among yews and tombs. His ancestors lay there under slabs of black stone engraved with three whelk shells, the family arms, or were commemorated on marble plaques in the small, drab Shelley chapel, where those of his family who cared to could say their prayers.

Until the age of ten he was schooled in Warnham vicarage, a country education, though reams of Latin verses rang already in his head. He could put on rustic clothes and act the yokel for fun, toting a truss of hay on his shoulder and riding in farmers' carts. Around him and into St Leonard's Forest stretched Shelley fields, farms and stands of timber that would one day be his.

Here and there in his poems he placed Sussex touches: shadows outracing the wind on the long grass slopes of the Downs, a dog herding sheep to the corner of a field, spiders' webs in hayrick and hedge, bats beating against the wired window of a dairy. Grey moths fluttered out of heaps of new-mown, still-moving grass; over the woods, a flock of rooks rose at the crack of a farmer's gun. Small clouds in the sky were 'crudded', like a dish of curds, or scattered out quietly like sheep grazing. Several poems carried memories of water and flowers observed at Warnham pond through a grille of reeds, branches and his own small fingers locked against the sun. A nightingale's song, too, might suddenly catch him,

> And now to the hushed ear it floats
> Like field smells known in infancy,
> Then failing, soothes the air again.

At times he thought himself a countryman. In 1811, on his first marriage to Harriet Westbrook, he described himself in the register as 'farmer, Sussex'. He told friends that he meant to manage his estates efficiently. When he later satirised the placid working folk of England he made them Sussex pigs in low-thatched sties, munching on rutabaga and red oats, while the government sharpened its knives to flay their bristled hides and make sausages from their spilling blood and guts.

In his first conversation with Hogg at Oxford (late, cold, the fire burning down), Shelley glowed with enthusiasm for agricultural chemistry. Breathlessly, he expatiated on the mystery of how some lands were fertile, others barren, when a spadeful of soil from one appeared the same as the other; on how food, so readily reduced to carbon, might be made from new, surprising substances; and on how, if water could be manufactured, the deserts of Africa might be transformed into 'rich meadows and vast fields of maize and rice'. Later he read eagerly the lectures of Humphry Davy, the greatest chemist of the day, who believed that almost all soil could be made better. ('Manure is useful', Shelley noted, 'and may be converted into organised bodies . . . Chemistry a correct instrument for agricultural improvement.')

Pages of an 1819 pocketbook were also filled with notes on the yield per acre of potatoes and rutabaga, the chow of the pigs; to feed people on these would be more economical and more moral, he had concluded, than feeding them on meat. The regenerated earth Shelley dreamed of was covered with wheatfields, an image so captivating to him that he applied it also to the 'pastured' sea, newly reclaimed from Chaos:

> like plains of corn
> Swayed by the summer air.

At the deepest level, earth and himself were not so different. Their substance was shared. All matter, as he knew from his eager reading of Lucretius at school, was made of minute, permanent, primordial atoms, 'first-beginnings' of 'single solidness'. These moved in a void, struck by random blows of Fate until they aggregated as minerals, or grasses, or inky-fingered boys. Water and air were made of far finer *primordia*, and aether, or subtle fire, of the smallest atoms there could be. But all were composed of the same 'fixed seeds', hard and indestructible, eternally gathering and dispersing. Shelley told classmates that he was never so delighted as to discover that there were no such chemical elements as earth, air, water and fire. As Lucretius put it, the same elements, changed only a little in their relations and combinations, made up both *lignis . . . et ignis*, trees and flame. And Shelley, such as he was.

Evidently, the seeds and their structures could never be seen with his naked eye. Yet as closely as was feasible, he stared at things. He got right down beside the plate to study pink fatty slabs of bacon or the jutting crag of a teacake. Pressed against fir trees, he inspected and licked the oozy runnels of resin. He read with his face only inches from the page, and watched tiny insects in the palm of his hand with fervent dedication.

Some friends thought he was short-sighted, with his large and slightly protuberant eyes. Mary in Italy ordered a gold-rimmed spyglass with a number 10 lens for myopia, perhaps for him. Yet Trelawny thought all his faculties 'marvellously acute', and Shelley himself sometimes complained not of dim vision but the reverse. Under 'unnatural and keen excitement', he once explained, 'I find the very blades of grass & the boughs of distant trees present themselves to me with microscopical distinctness.' Each object, somehow, had 'being clearer than its own could be'. Yet after that clarity and intensity he would take for hours to the sofa, lethargic and miserable without knowing why.

His senses, supposedly, were the ultimate and only source of knowledge about the world. So taught Locke, Hume, Helvetius and a whole procession of later, mostly French, philosophers. Shelley had no other reference point on which he could depend; what he could neither see nor feel, he could not trust. To negate, as the immaterialists did, 'that actual world to which our senses introduce us' seemed absurd. The earth into which he had fallen crying – real, tangible and beautiful as it seemed – thrust itself at him, demanding to be believed.

One of his most treasured possessions, from boyhood onwards, was a solar microscope in a heavy mahogany box that projected, on a sheet or a wall, giant images of the animalculae that wriggled in vinegar, or the overlapping plates of a fly's wing, or the mites entombed in cheese. In 1812, at the age of nineteen, he declared this instrument essential for his studies in 'a branch of philosophy'. As he viewed his specimens, lining them up in the shaft of light thrown through a window-shutter, he was taking apart the tiny bits of a solidly material universe: entangling his swift wings in atoms, as he wrote of Lucretius later. And he himself was nothing else. Laid under a lens, he too would swarm and flicker as the *primordia* moved in him.

He believed with Erasmus Darwin, whose books on science and Nature he also devoured as a schoolboy, that the minute worlds he saw suffered and felt as he did. All Nature was animated and, with even bigger and better microscopes, would doubtless be shown to be 'but a mass of organized animation'. In *Queen Mab*, his first visionary poem of a perfected world, written in 1812, the Fairy Queen herself also saw to the hidden pulse of microscopic things.

> 'I tell thee that those viewless beings,
> Whose mansion is the smallest particle
> Of the impassive atmosphere,
> Think, feel and live like man . . .
> And the minutest throb
> That through their frame diffuses
> The slightest, faintest motion,
> Is fixed and indispensable . . .'

From his earliest years of scientific enquiry Shelley pictured Nature as one concurring whole, with an iron chain of Necessity binding the smallest to the mightiest. He himself was in this chain, a mere agglomeration of responding atoms. He did not choose to act well or badly, just as he could not choose whether to believe or disbelieve in any notion or system put before him. 'Motive is to voluntary action in the human mind', he wrote in his notes to *Queen Mab*, 'what cause is to effect in the material universe.' Liberty, in Hume's words, was merely 'a false sensation'. 'It is impossible to deny,' he had told a correspondent in 1811, 'but that the turn which my mind has taken, originated from the conquest of England by William of Normandy.'

What had set this system going in which he moved and lived? Clearly not the Jewish-Christian God, for Hume had abolished all respectable arguments for such a belief, and Pliny had drawn an irresistible picture of 'God' as impersonal power, '*the existing power of existence*', as Shelley termed it. Until he could 'REALLY feel' the being of a God, he explained in 1811, 'I must be content with the substitute reason.' Whatever unknown power or imperative lay behind the material universe, it was not an organism and had no personal connection with human beings. Prayers were made to it in vain.

The fact that something *was*, as Shelley argued in *The Necessity of Atheism*, did not demand a designer and a cause. The fact that *he* existed did not demand that he had been created, beyond the basic generative act by his father and his mother. If you found a watch lying on the ground, never having seen a watch before, you would not automatically assume (unless you were Shelley's father or his father's favourite theologian, Paley) that a Great Designer had made it. It might be merely 'a thing of Nature', a combination of matter not encountered before. Any 'miracle' was either this, or a plain lie. Besides, a creator would himself need creating, and so on *ad infinitum* and *ad absurdum*.

The universe had probably always existed, and would go on operating eternally, according to the laws of its own nature. Shelley pressed that argument too into *Queen Mab*, the earliest repository of his atheism and his hopes.

'   . . . let every seed that falls
In silent eloquence unfold its store
Of argument; infinity within,
Infinity without, belie creation . . .'

Nil posse creari/ de nilo, as Lucretius said. Nothing could be made of nothing, or return to nothing. Instead the primordial seeds, following their fixed laws and limitations, constantly grouped into forms, resolved to singleness and merged into new forms again. Shelley's notion of 'creation' was arrangement and organisation of this sort, nothing more. Unending mutability was the nature of existence. Around these forms, in the infinite void – the 'intense inane' in his words – free play was allowed to the blows of blind Necessity, or whatever force held sway there. And that was all there was in the world, or in him.

Chance atoms came together: Shelley lived. He would die when by some stroke they dispersed again, into the waiting grave of the Earth around him. In the small space of time intervening he was 'a mass of electrified clay'. No act or thought or transgression was truly his own, but marked the operation of eternal and immutable laws. Reason told him this was so. A high, remote spirit-voice mocked him as 'Atom-born!', and laughed at any presumption to think otherwise.

★   ★   ★

Instinctively, though, he hated earth to sully him. On long Sussex walks with his sisters, when the heavy blue-brown Wealden clay had smeared their shoes and stockings, he would carry the little girls home in his arms but forbid their feet to touch his clothes. At Eton he roared with pain when leather footballs, caked and soaked from the field, were kicked deliberately and hard against the boy who would not play games. Near Oxford once, in the finery of a new blue coat, he became incensed when a farmyard mastiff forced him into cow dung and deep black mud. 'Clogs' and 'clods' of earth jammed the fine mechanism of thinking minds, his own and others'. 'Filth' was almost the strongest word in his lexicon, a spasm of horror.

Earth was not his element, either in its substance or its society. He did not belong. The point was made in a notebook fragment of 1821:

> I would not be, that which another is—
> I would not be equal below above
> Anything human. I would make my bliss
> A solitude! . . .
>   And though my form might move
> Like a ~~vain cloud~~ through a wilderness
> Of mountains, o'er this world; I am not of
> Its shadows or its sunbeams—

Beside his half-hidden child-self there always walked another boy. Like him, this child had been born to wealth, but he was neither happy nor comfortable. Mocked, misunderstood, touched already with divine inspiration, he was a Poet-child who lingered and dreamed alone. When Shelley read Byron's *The Lament of Tasso*, a romanticised verse-life of Italy's sixteenth-century heroic poet, the sixth canto made his head 'wild with tears'. This boy of 'delicate susceptibilities and elevated fancies', was too much like another he knew. Byron's lines were the history of himself.

> And then they smote me, and I did not weep,
> But cursed them in my heart, and to my haunt

13

> Return'd and wept alone, and dream'd again
> The visions . . .

Shelley said he had been beaten too, by boys as well as masters, though they could not tame him. He told friends that he had been twice expelled from Eton, already a fighter for liberty and equality against the system of 'fagging', or doing chores, for the senior boys. Contemporaries remembered no expulsions, but instead a prankster and a brawler, a tall, slovenly looking boy (though also like 'a girl in Boy's clothes'), who flailed around with his fists and was fearsomely violent when thwarted. Yet in his mind he was the quiet, trembling youth at the edge of the playing field, already dedicated to his calling, listening to the elements as though these alone had truth to impart to him.

At Eton one tutor alone, Dr James Lind, had befriended him. The old gentleman, tall, white-haired and with 'supernatural spirit' in his eyes, had talked to him for hours, nursed him through a fever and introduced him to Plato, Herschel and Erasmus Darwin, opening his mind to wonders of Socratic philosophy, natural science, steam-power and the stars. In Lind's library Shelley first read William Godwin's *Political Justice*, the dense treatise on equality and practical philanthropy that most keenly developed his urge to reform the world. Teacher and pupil cursed George III as they drank their tea together.

From these beginnings, Dr Lind entered the Poet-child's life. In *Prince Athanase*, an unfinished poem of 1817 that tracked Shelley's imagined history, he became the philosopher Zonoras, 'the last whom superstition's blight/ Had spared in Greece', tutoring the young prince in a flame-lit tower from which light streamed across the sea. One 'rainy even' they read Plato's *Symposium* together, perhaps for the first time. Shelley then deleted that English, Eton rain, inserting instead a beach where they walked, talking Plato, as the moon set.

In his idealised past, his childhood contained no school or family. At times even Dr Lind was dismissed. All teachers were 'tyrants'. 'I have known no tutor or adviser not excepting my father', Shelley told Godwin, 'from whose lessons and suggestions I have not recoiled with disgust.' His hero-self grew up alone in some glen, or mountain, or wood. His teachers and playmates were the trees, the wind, the waves and the stars. 'Solemn vision and bright silver dream' were all the instruction he needed or received.'

In his preface to *The Revolt of Islam*, his epic 1817 poem of idealised

14

French Revolution-making, Shelley described his own education as a Poet. No desks or canes were mentioned. Instead,

> I have been familiar from boyhood with mountains and lakes and the sea, and the solitude of forests: Danger, which sports upon the brink of precipices, has been my playmate . . . I have been a wanderer among distant fields, I have sailed down mighty rivers, and seen the sun rise and set, and the stars come forth . . . I have seen populous cities, and have watched the passions which rise and spread, and sink and change, amongst assembled multitudes of men.

Of all those childhood experiences, real or imagined, one had marked him above all others. This was his sudden awakening, on one particular morning, to the shadow of the Spirit of Beauty in the world. After this he became a fighter for Liberty and an insatiate seeker after Beauty, Love and Truth, obsessions that never left him. He was made aware, in a moment, of what his purpose was.

He had not dreamed this. Several of his poems described the moment of conversion, but enclosed it in details too vague to pinpoint where or when it had occurred. Again, facts were unimportant. Shelley mentioned only 'a fresh May-dawn', 'glittering grass', harsh voices from a nearby schoolroom. In one draft, he was wandering among meadows and trees while shouting schoolmates pushed past him. Whether this was Syon House or Eton, he was indifferent. The visitation had happened despite teachers and despite school. Nothing mattered except the 'bright shadow' that had fallen on him and his own boyish promise, spoken aloud, to love and to obey.

> And then I clasped my hands and looked around—
>   —But none was near to mock my streaming eyes,
> Which poured their warm drops on the sunny ground—
>   So, without shame, I spake: '—I will be wise,
>   And just, and free, and mild, if in me lies
> Such power, for I grow weary to behold
>   The selfish and the strong still tyrannise
> Without reproach or check.' I then controlled
> My tears, my heart grew calm, and I was meek and bold.

In later poems the tears and ecstasy happened under 'the breathless heavens', on the sea-shore, or among night ruins. Beauty's shadow visited him not once, but often, in 'visioned wanderings' quite removed from earthly things:

> far aloft,
>> In the clear golden prime of my life's dawn,
>> Upon the fairy isles of sunny lawn,
>> Amid the enchanted mountains, and the caves
>> Of divine sleep, and on the air-like waves
>> Of wonder-level dream . . .

In other writings Beauty's shade was not to be retrieved. In 'Una Favola', an unfinished story written in Italian in 1820–21, Shelley described a young man awakened by love at the age of fifteen and led by veiled female figures through a hidden sexual labyrinth of pines, cypresses, cedars and yews, 'whose shadows begot a mixture of delight and sadness'. He lost his heart first to Life, then to Death, but neither was the love he sought, and both deceived him.

Shelley once blundered with Hogg into an incarnation of this scene, a secret garden near Oxford encircled by tall trees. The trim paths were overhung with laurel, the flower-beds bare in the dereliction of winter. Shelley took it for an enchanted grove, an Eden ruled by some absent spirit of Beauty or ideal Love, before swiftly plunging back through the hedge in embarrassment. He had trespassed into his other life, as into a waking dream.

Wandering naturally led him to such places, from which Beauty had gone and where melancholy closed round him. This was his Poet's condition. Like the sad young man of Gray's *Elegy Written in a Country Church-Yard*, the poem he most loved at Eton, he would loiter on certain hillsides, or by certain streams, until sleep lured him to the deep shade. Then, in Gray's words,

> 'Hard by yon wood, now smiling as in scorn,
> Muttering his wayward fancies he would rove;
> Now drooping woeful-wan, like one forlorn,
> Or crazed with care, or crossed in hopeless love.'

Sometimes his two lives converged. In the summer of 1811 Shelley tried to recover, at Cwm Elan in the Welsh mountains, from the collapse of all his adolescent hopes. That spring he had been expelled from Oxford for atheism; a little before, he had been forsaken by his first love, his cousin Harriet Grove, a pretty, provincial girl who lived not far from the Shelley seat at Field Place. They had been informally engaged, but her parents had discouraged their friendship because of his radical opinions. Now he was alone.

Under the storm-blasted oaks he flung himself down, the river roaring in his ears, in a state of despair. He had wandered in the mountains, watched the sunset, and now he longed to die. Uncaringly, the great rocks observed him, and Earth, his unfeeling parent, crushed him to her cold, hard breast. The boy Shelley would eventually scramble up, hungry, and make his way back to the fine white villa owned by the Groves beside the river. But the Poet lay cold, still, comfortless.

Earthly parentage was in other ways unbearable. He had learned, taking his cue from Godwin's *Political Justice*, that no human being was to be preferred over another simply because they were sister or mother or father to him. Those ties, though underlined by frequent, rigid filial bows, meant nothing. His Poet-self did without them, subsisting on Nature and on visions. He fled to Wales because by mid-1811, at eighteen, he had more or less rejected his family, and they him.

He nursed no strong feelings for his mother, whom he thought mildly ineffectual and 'narrow-minded'. Towards his father he came to feel nothing but loathing and defiance. From his Eton days onwards he hated him, and could draw an appreciative audience with his strident cursings of 'Killjoy' and 'the Old Buck' until he collapsed in laughter. There seemed no reason for his hate, back then, except his father's eager militarism, too-feeble Whiggism, and religion. After Shelley's expulsion from Oxford, reasons accumulated on both sides. Timothy Shelley was appalled that his son should have written a tract called *The Necessity of Atheism*. He was startled by his son's self-righteousness and high-handedness, and outraged by Shelley's demand that he should be allowed to keep corresponding with Hogg, his partner in unbelief ('Fine fellows these to presume to offer Proposals'). But most of all he was profoundly shocked by his son's decision, in April 1811, to give up the entail on his grandfather's estate, exchanging a secure landed inheritance for £200 yearly in cash.

Shelley's life had been mapped out for him as his father meant him to pursue it. Education once completed at his father's old college, he would probably go into politics. Clientism, patronage and borough-

17

mongering already ran in the family. His grandfather was a client of the Duke of Norfolk, to whom he owed his baronetcy. His father also owed Norfolk his seat in Parliament, and the duke – unkempt, odoriferous, uncouth, but a Whig and thus, in theory, a reformer – could have secured a seat for young Shelley too, probably Horsham, if he had wanted it. He did not want it. He had heard too many people talk party politics round Field Place, 'and hated it and them'. Indeed, he desired nothing his father could provide for him.

He knew very well what he could own, if he chose to claim it. He could enumerate the farms and timber leases, track land sales from the estate since 1792, his birth-year, and juggle with income figures in the thousands of pounds. In several pointed letters to William Whitton, his father's London solicitor, over the business of the entail and the £200 a year, he explained that he knew what he was doing. 'I will not listen', he snapped, 'to the suggestions of family pride, to interest to fortune I am indifferent.' He also desired 'that when I am addressed again, a less authoritative manner be used, or subsequent letters are returned unopened.'

Shrewdly, Timothy Shelley realised that all his son's rejections were connected. 'To cast off all thoughts of his Maker,' he sighed to Whitton, 'to abandon his Parents, to wish to relinquish his Fortune, and to court Persecution all seems to arise from the same source.' The source was Shelley's longing to be free. The son saw in the father a composite symbol of all tyranny, yet horrifically personal and close. The 'old fellow's' blood ran in him, sluggish and inescapable: as if he too could be a complacent Sussex landowner, in outmoded hat and frock coat, taking breakfast in his London hotel.

In January 1812 Shelley began, in some awe, a correspondence with Godwin, who had become his model and guide in political matters. He told him, angling for sympathy as one radical to another, that his father had always regarded him as 'a blot, a defilement of his honor', that 'he wished to induce me by poverty to accept of some commission in a distant regiment' (hoping, too, that he would die in the Peninsular Wars against the French), and meant to proclaim him an outlaw. It was stirring stuff. None of it was true.

Through the spring of 1811 letters continued between Shelley and his father in terms of pained politeness ('yr affect. Dutyful Son', 'My Dear Boy'). After 14 April, however, they had dealings only through Whitton. From 28 August, when Timothy Shelley heard of his son's elopement with Harriet Westbrook, the annuity was cut off and civil correspondence ceased. Shelley from his side, desperate for money but utterly unbending, continued to pour out incandescent letters to the 'Shelley' he refused to be.

> *Obedience* is in my opinion a word which should have no existence— you regard it as necessary. —
> Yes, you can command it. The institutions of society have made you, tho' liable to be misled by passion and prejudice like others, the *Head of the family*; and I confess it is almost natural for minds not of the highest order to value even the errors whence they derive their importance.
> Adieu, answer this. —

Timothy Shelley chose not to. At Field Place his son's name, always 'Bysshe' to them, could not be mentioned. With infinite coldness, at one of their last meetings, Shelley had watched his father weep and lecture him; as he scolded, the wild son – suddenly seeing Timothy Shelley as Jehovah with a handkerchief – fell off the edge of his chair, laughing like a demon. He had already floated in several letters, including one to his mother, a made-up story of his father being cuckolded by the family's music master, with two horns growing from his forehead. Beneath the scorn was a sadder, simpler conviction, confided to Godwin, that his father could not separate his welfare from 'certain considerations of birth; and feeling for these things was not feeling for me.' In short, the Old Buck had never loved him, but only the continuation of name, property and status he represented, like a house or a field.

In the last of his regular letters to his father, written on 15 October 1811, he cried that he had been treated '*ill, vilely*'. But he would not go away. The rejected and rejected son would go on erupting horribly into his father's life, reminding him again and again of the physical bond he himself so hated.

> if *you* will not hear my name, *I* will pronounce it. Think not I am an insect whom injuries destroy—had I money enough I would meet you in London, & hollow in your ears Bysshe, Bysshe, Bysshe—aye Bysshe till you're deaf.

★ ★ ★

To put aside Shelley, gentleman of Horsham, was always harder than he supposed. Breeding went deep. People clustered to 'the magic' of his 'unmeaning name'; a handshake, a turn of phrase, a shudder of distaste could give him immediately away.

His clothes, too, proclaimed him. As a baby he had been wrapped in the best Japan muslin and Valenciennes lace, at a cost of almost £200, and had teethed on a golden rattle impressed with his initials. As a schoolboy he wore beautifully fitting pantaloons of silk; at Field Place he would stand in them before the fire, warming his tails like a young patrician, while his sisters silently admired him.

'Almost every one', he wrote later, 'remembers the wry faces which the first glass of port produced.'

At Eton he bought cakes, oranges and dancing gloves. He ordered his shooting jacket sent from home, as well as his pistols. Back at Field Place, surrounded by 'Provincial Stupidity', aristocracy seemed ordinary. 'I wander about this place, walking all over the grounds,' he wrote to the middle-class Hogg, unaffectedly. 'Excuse the shortness of this as the s[ervan]t waits.' 'The Post fellow wants the letter.' 'I have rung the bell for the horse.'

'My object in writing', he informed Longman & Co., potential publishers, at the age of sixteen,

> ... was not *pecuniary*, as I am independent, being the heir of a gentleman of large fortune in the County of Sussex, & prosecuting my studies as an *Oppidan* at Eton ...

'Jock' Robinson, who eventually published Shelley's first novel, *Zastrozzi*, was 'a dog', loathsome but useful. 'We will all go [then] in a posse to the booksellers in Mr. Groves barouche & four,' Shelley suggested to a friend in 1810; '—shew them we are no grub street gareteers'.

In March 1811, a tailor's bill revealed the Oxford wardrobe of the budding young champion of equality and philanthropy:

A Superfine Olive Coat Gilt Buttns.	4. 8 0
A Pair Rich Silk Knitt Pantaloons	3 8 0
. . .	
Two Stripd. Marcela Waistcoats Double Breastd	2 0 0
. . .	
1. Pair Patent Silk Braces	0 8 0
A Superfine Blue Coat Velvett Collr. & Gilt Buttns.	4. 12. 0

The blue coat was fresh-ordered. Obsequiously, with many bowings, the tailor fitted it to him: shoulders, lapels, cuffs. Shelley bore this with impatience. He dismissed him, grabbed his hat and cried 'Let us go!' He did not pay him, or not then. Salesmen could be made to wait.

He knew he was someone, said the Dean of College: wore extraordinary clothes, put on airs, paraded in the quad with his friend Hogg 'as much as to say "We are superior to every body"'. To Godwin he admitted it: 'Oxonian society was insipid to me, uncongenial with my habits of thinking. —I could not descend to common life.' No wonder he had come to grief.

In 1811 – freshly expelled from Oxford and with no obvious means of employment – Shelley boasted that he could live on £50 a year. By 1817 friends thought him as poor as Pythagoras, living philosophically on crusts and book-reading. Yet his upholsterers that year were Beck & English, the smartest firm in fashionable Bath, to whom he eventually owed £1,192 1s. 10d. for furnishing a house at Marlow, in Buckinghamshire. (Again, he ignored their 'fatuous claims', departing for Italy in 1818 without leaving a forwarding address.) His beverage of choice was the best green tea, subsequently shipped to Italy from London ('Townley tea', Mary reported, 'was tried and found wanting'). His jewellery repairs were done in Bond Street, his piano ordered from Novello's. And his wayward brown locks were tamed, at least sometimes, with tortoiseshell combs from Floris's in Jermyn Street and a good shake of Brewster's Russia Oil, by appointment to princes.

For much of his adult life he kept horses and a carriage. The carriage came from Charters of New Bond Street, expensively accoutred, sprung and upholstered, and never paid for. He claimed it was his wife Harriet's caprice, like the silver plate he also bought, but he continued to use it long after she had gone. Charters sent their bills in vain. In Italy, having emptied his pockets of farthings for mendicants, the *milord* in his *calesso* pronounced that they were happier than he was.

In February 1818, a rare month of hectic socialising just before his Italian exile, he was seen in style at the London opera, in a blue coat and white waistcoat. Leigh Hunt, the radical writer and magazine editor who became his most devoted friend, imagined him in retrospect at the theatre, 'a thin patrician-looking cosmopolite' leaning from his box. He was not out of place there. 'We all laughed', another friend wrote later, 'at S's little occasional aristocratical sallies, but we agreed that in general it is the aristocracy of superior with regard to inferior intellect.'

With Byron, his greatest poet-rival, to whom he first diffidently introduced himself in Geneva in 1816, he was exquisitely aware of the gradations of class. 'My dear Lord Byron' each letter began, even when their friendship was easy. Shelley, countered Byron, 'was as perfect a Gentleman as ever crossed a drawing room; when he liked—& where he liked. —'

But the status of gentleman bothered him. In principle and essence, he believed all men were equal. When he read in Diogenes Laertius that Plato thought wealth, health and good birth desirable for happiness, as well as virtue, Shelley scribbled 'very bad' in the margin of his old, brown, battered copy. He preferred, and jotted down in Greek, the assessment of Plato by Diogenes the Cynic: 'He would consider good birth and fame and all such distinctions as showy ornaments of vice.'

Aristocrats, Shelley wrote, were 'gilded flies', or 'drones', kept in idle comfort by the worker-bees who were the labouring poor. Though he stressed to Hunt that the word 'aristocratical' had no 'ill signification', and that land-owning gentry were slightly more tolerable than the 'pelting wretches' newly ennobled from banking, stockjobbing and commerce, perhaps they should all give up their land and earn their living. ('But this Paradise is all visionary!' people would cry. 'Why is it visionary, have you tried?' he would cry back.) No man, he wrote in his own French-flavoured *Declaration of Rights*, in 1812,

22

. . . has a right to be respected for any other possessions but those of virtue and talents. Titles are tinsel, power a corrupter, glory a bubble, and excessive wealth a libel on its possessor.

No man has a right to monopolise more than he can enjoy . . .

Queen Mab, his first full vision of an egalitarian earthly paradise, was printed on fine paper 'to catch the aristocrats', as if he were not one himself. Often, he wished he was not. He railed against '*mahogany* tables, silver vases', and was mortified when a beggar to whom he had given money, sprinting impulsively downstairs from dressing, upbraided him for his rich clothes. 'In me,' he told an acquaintance in 1811, 'although as it were a living outcast from my parent's bosom, the same machinery of oppression is preparing, in order that I also in my turn may become an oppressor.'

A friend once pointed out, delicately enough, the difference of class between them. Shelley replied with almost incoherent passion:

You remind me of what I hate despise & shudder at, what willingly I would not, & the part from which I can emancipate myself from, in this detestable coil of primaeval prejudice, that will I free myself from—Have I not foresworn all this, am I not I [a] worshipper of equality—

If he could not prove his sincerity, he would give possessions up. Property acquired by labour, skill or 'genius' he could accept; that obtained by violence, usurpation or 'imposture' he abhorred. His own inheritance, he supposed, fell under the second head; he therefore strove to disown it. To shed property would leave him unencumbered. Among true and real friends, moreover, 'all is common'. From his expulsion onwards he dreamed of establishing remote, radical communes of his 'brothers' and 'sisters' in which by natural right everything would be shared: 'chairs tables beds glasses plates and food', and love.

The dream remained, but came no closer. Equality of possessions, Shelley confessed in 1819, was unrealistic for the moment, 'a system of . . . absolute perfection . . . unattainable perhaps by us'. Yet politics based on that distant vision was the only sort he claimed to care for. Property, as Godwin had written in *Political Justice*, rightly belonged to those who needed it. It was the duty of the rich man to give and the right of the poor man to demand. On that principle, Shelley gave away his shoes (arriving at a neighbour's barefoot), his money, and Mary's clothes, continuing to hand out spontaneous charity until the last weeks of his life. On the same principle he took other men's books, and raided Hunt's wardrobe for waistcoats and handkerchiefs he might need himself. To take as well as give – though sometimes blushing 'not a little', Hunt said, in doing it – was proper redistributive justice.

Yet charity had its limits. The struggling lace-workers of Marlow, to whom Shelley handed out soup and money in 1817, were given blankets with 'PBS Esq., Marlow, Bucks' worked in the corner, in case they tried to sell them on. The 'industrious poor' only, of whom he kept a list, received an allowance on Saturday evenings from the bag of silver on his desk. His brushes with the truly destitute – in France in 1814, in the rubble of their burnt-out houses, where they encircled him silently as he ate their 'sour bread' and 'stinking bacon' – were disgusting and horrific to him. Unlike Malthus, whose *Treatise on Population* was a topic of hot debate round dinner tables, Shelley did not believe the numbers of the poor were sensibly reduced by starvation; he loathed that argument. Yet most men, he was convinced, lived in a state of 'squalid ignorance, & moral imbecility' from which he foresaw no swift improvement. And some, it seemed clear, would never rise out of the mud and slime of their incarnation: smoking Germans, demobilised soldiers, crass Swiss *voituriers*, or the 'filthy people' who, in one Italian way-station, covered his letter with oil.

He himself was pure. The word was a favourite, used often and with no false modesty. His virtue raised him above the common herd; he considered himself just, good, and unflinching in opinions for which the world would lacerate him. If others thought him 'a blot', he was a bright one. 'A certain degree & a certain kind of infamy is to be borne,' he told Mary, alluding in 1821 to the rumours of affairs and bastards that were being spread about him by their servants,

> & in fact is the best compliment which an exalted nature can receive from the filthy world of which it is it's Hell to be a part—

★   ★   ★

Pure as he was, Shelley felt no esteem or fondness for his body. It was a simple machine that would run for a while until worn out by age and disease. The human organism was a repository of dust and foulness, like the charnel-house at Warnham where he had plotted to linger

24

as a boy, dry-mouthed, waiting for ghouls to emerge from their stone boxes. From body, to coffin, to tomb, to the earth, each covering was heavier and darker than the last.

He had probably seen corpses rotting as a child, on the gibbets on Horsham Common and Hounslow Heath. Death was handed out routinely by the authorities, even for petty stealing. 'Zeinab and Kathema', written when he was seventeen, described the chains creaking and the movement of maggots in the ruins of a face. Worms bred even in the young, fresh body of his little son William, his favourite child, born to Mary in 1816: a child who could run and skip and cry, 'Che bella!', and whose beauty drew Italian neighbours to watch him as he slept. Gamboge, aloes and wormwood were all tried, but the vermin multiplied. His lot was human.

—We decay
Like corpses in a charnel; fear and grief
Convulse us and consume us day by day,
And cold hopes swarm like worms within our living clay.

The link between political oppression, moral evil and physical degradation was all too obvious to him. The common folk of Dublin were 'one mass of animated filth', the Austrian-occupied Italians 'stupid & shrivelled slaves'. He observed with horrified fascination the goitred and crooked children of Nernier on Lake Geneva, diseased, as he supposed, by the 'blighting mischiefs' of their rulers, and noticed as he crossed into the Kingdom of Sardinia that the tyrannised inhabitants had scratched into the very rocks the story of their miseries.

Evil was infectious. From the poor of Marlow he caught ophthalmia, which stopped him reading; sitting opposite a fat old woman in a stage-coach he risked elephantiasis, indeed believed he had it, and obsessively pinched and searched his skin for the swelling signs of contagion. In 1821 something in the Pisan earth, air or water made his face erupt, like Job's, with boils. Writing a little broadside once against a visiting bore, he threw down the words that most disgusted him:

Spurt phiz vomit, sweat, whine,
Caper, squalid, squalling, red

His images were not only of the sick body and its secretions, but of human birth.

He could find no innate stain in human beings, no stupidity of Adam,

25

Eve and apple, but instead the 'wrong impressions' stamped on the young by nurses and parents and, if they grew older, by the barbarity of schools and systems of government. Evil, in Shelley's view, was a strong, autonomous power in the world, constantly at war with the power of good, invading and overwhelming whichever mind or body gave it admittance. The tenderest were most at risk. Baby Ianthe, his first child by Harriet, born with *Queen Mab* in 1813, sucked milk from a wet-nurse he loathed and who, he was sure, would infect her; in despair he snatched her away one day, tore open his shirt and forced the tiny mouth to his own unsullied breast.

His body was tall, vigorous and strong-limbed, like that of 'a young Indian' to his sailor-friend Edward Trelawny, who often saw him naked when they bathed together in Italian rivers and seas. He could row and tow boats, outwalk and outclimb his friends and deck, with one punch, a stupid Swiss who took his seat in the Laufenburg *diligence*. At Marlow once he was seen hauling the womenfolk up a steep bank and hurtling down to fetch others, shooting past in explosions of dust. In his note-books he drew himself naked and muscle-bound, often with weapons in his hands.

Yet his Poet-body was much frailer. Pestered and wounded by thoughts that snapped at his heels like hounds, he stumbled through life as through a forest of thorns that tore his pale, exhausted flesh. Hence the strange combination, which Hogg noted at Oxford, of superhuman strength with 'weakness less than human'. Though Shelley seemed careless of his body, he saw it as graphically as he did the rest of Nature: his heart a rubbed stone, his nerves stretched like catgut, his whole frame 'shaken to pieces' by the ceaseless round of the claret bottle at Byron's dinner parties. Obsessively – since Eton days, Trelawny thought – he worried his head with Thornton's *Medical Extracts*, Trotter's *View of the Nervous Temperament*, Lambe's *Reports on Cancer*, and much else. Week by week, every fault in the machine was reported to his friends:

My head is rather dizzy today on account of not taking rest, & a slight attack of Typhus . . .

I have been ill with an inflammatory fever . . . I feard to write to you with a hand unsteady, & a head disordered with illness . . .

I have experienced a decisive pulmonary attack . . .

I was seized last night with symptoms of irritable fever . . .

I am weak & with much nervous irritability. My spirits are by no means good . . .

26

I am a feeble, wavering, feverish being, who requires support and consolation, which his energies are too exhausted to return.

In the joint journal he started with Mary in 1814 – for the short time that he bothered to contribute – he made more notes, as if observing from a curious distance. 'S. very ill.' 'S . . . feverish & fatigued', 'unwell', 'agitated'. Mary, in the journal and in letters, added to the list:

Shelley has suffered very much . . . his health is so very delicate . . .
Shelley is somewhat but not much better . . .
Shelley of course is not well . . .

Few of these troubles were common coughs, colds or infections. They were 'the contagion of the world's slow stain', so easily fatal to poets, the sort of languors and vapours and excessive sensibilities that made young men throw themselves into chairs with their handkerchiefs pressed to their faces. The Poet, Shelley wrote, 'is more delicately organized than other men and sensible to pain and pleasure, both his own and that of others, in a degree unknown to them'. Dragged back to the life of a man, 'abandoned to the sudden reflux of the influences under which others habitually live', he could feel his strength draining out of him.

Most of all he was the victim of mysterious 'spasms' in his side, possibly caused by kidney stones and aggravated by nervous strain. When they struck him he would fall to the floor and scream, drumming his heels and pulling down cushions to cover him. ('I have the elephant-iasis,' he once explained.) Doctors gave different diagnoses. One considered cutting him for the stone; another, supposing liver trouble, prescribed mercury and Cheltenham salts. He tried Scott's vitriolic immersions, poultices of caustic, warm baths and Mesmerism. Leeches were applied, their 'lubricious round rings' swelling to little red bags as they fastened on him. But he could not be cured by anything.

He often assumed, sometimes hoped, that it would all end painfully and soon. His impetuous marriage to Harriet Westbrook, he confided once, was contracted 'thinking he was dying'. He told Godwin that his doctor had diagnosed consumption and abscesses of the lungs (though the consumption vanished as soon as his doctor was replaced). At intervals he feared that latent syphilis would strike him with horrible ulcerations, leprosy, blindness and, ultimately, madness. His hair was touched with grey prematurely, a syphilitic symptom that filled him with foreboding. Both *Alastor* in 1815 and *The Revolt of Islam* in 1817 – poems that summed up his searchings so far for ideal Beauty and for moral revolution – were written as last testaments, with 'Death and Love . . . contending for their prey'. In September 1817 his doctor forbade him to strain himself by writing poetry. Visiting friends, however, sometimes thought nothing would do him more good than a brisk constitutional, a thick veal chop and a pint of ale; and he, from his bed, faintly, would tend to half agree with them.

* * *

In November 1817, Mrs Ford drew up the bill for her temporary lodger at 2 Brick Street, Covent Garden:

Shelley Esqre

22 [November] Rolls Milk & Butter—		1.5
23	Errand Milk	1.8½
24	Rolls & Milk	7

He seemed to eat little else. There was no need, for bread was almost all-sufficing. Chunks in his pockets, crumbling into pellets to be thrown to the winds or flicked at passers-by. Loaves fresh-bought, torn up and devoured, crust and dough still chewy and warm, in the street. Thick slices steeped in milk, soaked in hot water. Embellishments were few: pudding raisins, honey, shavings of sugar. The machine was kept going mostly with tea and bread.

Bouts of gluttony were not unknown to him. Two years into his Italian exile, in 1820, he summoned up English feasts:

> Yet let's be merry: we'll have tea and toast;
> Custards for supper, and an endless host
> Of syllabubs and jellies and mince-pies . . .
> Feasting on which we will philosophize!

Yet the body did not need such things. Even butter was an indulgence. Shelley watched with horror as it was slathered on penny buns, and was appalled, when he visited Robert Southey at Keswick in 1811, to see thick butter glistening on the fruit-stuffed teacakes served up by the poet's wife. (Tasting them himself, however, he quickly surrendered,

28

devouring them by the plate-load.) Exceptional shows of frugality were what his friends remembered: a crust dipped in whey for supper, days of grim subsistence on packets of powdered lemonade, a dinner of raisins eaten from one particular china plate. His hero Verezzi, in his youthful Gothic novel *Zastrozzi*, was saved from starving by a plate of raisins. In general, though, his hero-selves ate nothing, living on the exaltation of their thoughts.

Books, too, replaced food. Lost in them, he was unaware whether he had eaten or not. With a book in his pocket, under his arm, in his hand, he had no need of breakfast or supper. He gobbled words and thoughts as greedily as others cleared their plates of pudding. Books were brought open to table, laid face down on the tablecloth, then slyly taken up again, his face pressed to the pages while his fork made pretence of eating.

From at least the age of nineteen he was a practising vegetarian. The 'use of dead flesh', he believed, made men barbarous. If evil was not an intrinsic part of the Chain of Being, and was unnecessary in Nature, the eating of meat by human beings must have introduced it, and with it every sort of tyranny, disorder and disease. 'Who will assert', he wrote, thinking of the Terror that in 1793 had followed the French Revolution,

> that had the populace of Paris drank at the pure source of the Seine and satisfied their hunger at the ever-furnished table of vegetable nature, that they would have lent their brutal suffrage to the proscription list of Robespierre?

When Shelley wanted to pile on horror he described the eating of flesh, usually human, dwelling on its warm fibrous feel between his teeth and the rust or salt 'bitterness' of blood (his own arm bitten, his own chains licked). His prisoners *in extremis* ate 'strange flesh', grimly unspecified; his hero-self Laon, locked up for revolution-making in *The Revolt of Islam*, chewed on a hanged corpse that dangled on the other side of the bars. It was not, after all, so different from any butcher's rack in Whitechapel.

Use of 'spiritous liquors' he equally condemned. Pure water only passed the lips of the virtuous man. He had tried 'the genial bowl' at Oxford, holding wine and poetry parties in his rooms and whiling away the evenings with sherry and hot water, but he could do without it. Alcohol seemed to upset him, tipping him yet further into wildness, especially in the febrile, defiant weeks after his expulsion. A glass or two of wine, offered by his mother in June 1811, sent him 'raving', making him write to Hogg of Love and flowers and immortality and Death; a tumbler of brandy and water, ordered up in the tap-room of the Swan in Horsham, led to a fearsome argument about religion, reason and the proposed adoption of two small girls as an educational experiment. He had enough such notions sane and sober. Only once, in 1817, did he muse aloud that he meant to take 'a great glass of ale' every day to deaden his feelings. Laudanum usually did that job for him.

A diet of vegetables and distilled water seemed a guarantee of longevity, but length of years was not the point. 'The very sense of being', Shelley wrote, was then 'a continued pleasure', like the bright, rare moments of abandon he had known and felt as a child.

In October 1816, just before the move to Marlow, he determined to keep a note of the weight of his intake of food every day.

> Sunday 27th B[reakfast]. 3oz 12 gr. L[unch]. 3 oz . . . D[inner]. 13 oz. T[ea]. 4 oz. 4. g in all . . . =24. oz

This regime lasted only until the Tuesday, but he clung to the principle. Sobriety of body and mind was 'necessary to those who would be free'. Indeed, as Christ taught, the man who had fewest bodily wants 'approaches nearest to the Divine Nature'. Vegetarianism drew him because it made more frequent – or should have made more frequent – such moments of release.

Yet his resolution wavered. He was found demolishing bacon ('Bring more bacon!') and feasting on veal chops, well peppered. Cold meat was discovered on his luncheon plate in Italy. He caught fish, too, among the rocks near Lerici where he spent his last weeks, though he had once chided Wordsworth for describing the beauty of dead, hooked trout. By then he had long ceased to shoot birds for sport; but his holidays from school had seen him hunting snipe on the lakes at Field Place, killing three with successive shots, and he had been found on the towpath at Eton hobbled by a duck-spear that had been meant to spill, not his own blood, but that of a mallard rising swiftly out of the river.

In general, however, the diet and the scruples were observed. He ate bread and medlars on the road in France, oranges and figs at Pompeii, rejoicing in his rations among the slender ruins. He filtered his water through a stone in Italy, or stuck to the 'alcalescent' sort that did not disagree with him. When he could, he missed meals. Byron feared that if his illegitimate daughter Allegra was brought up by the Shelleys, as they proposed, she would 'perish of Starvation, and green fruit'. Friends agreed that Shelley's vegetarianism made him nervous, weak and fanciful, but for him this was partly the point: lightness of being, escape from the flesh.

★   ★   ★

Over all this hung the tinge of madness. As early as Syon House, his first school, he had been judged 'out of step' by his masters. At Eton he was 'Mad Shelley', wild and odd. He was once sent home suffering from brain fever; a servant, so he said, overheard his father musing whether he should be sent to a private madhouse. Dr Lind intervened, and he was saved.

After the collapse of his informal engagement to his cousin Harriet Grove, almost revelling in his misery and his status as an outcast, he was often 'mad' at Field Place, or told others he was. 'A strange melange of maddened stuff', 'nonsense' and 'ravings' flowed from his pen to Hogg, who seemed his only friend. ('Am I not mad? Alas I am . . . Ohe! Jam satis dementiae I hear you exclaim.') He fled to Wales in 1811 as a 'maniac-sufferer' with 'venomed snakes' stifling every impulse to high, poetic thoughts. The 'sallies of Folly and Madness' surrounding his ejection from Oxford – his father's words – were part of a long practice of what seemed, to Timothy Shelley, deliberate lunacy.

Deliberate or not, Shelley seemed proud of it. 'If madness 'tis to be unlike the world', he accepted the charge, and might play up to it. Acquaintances noted his odd starts, peculiar gestures and sudden fixed attitudes, as if frozen in abstraction. Charles MacFarlane, who had at least read *Queen Mab* when he first heard Shelley's soft words beside him at the Naples Museum, thought that 'both the verse and the prose savoured of insanity'. The *Literary Gazette* agreed, proclaiming in 1821 that it had never doubted that Shelley, denying God and defying all social mores, was 'essentially mad'.

This madness was always of the same kind: seeing what others could not see, yearning for what others could not fathom, not belonging. In 1818, Shelley noted down his feelings among the wooded hills at Bagni di Lucca:

31

I know not the internal constitution of other men, or even thine whom I now address. I see that in some external attributes they resemble me, but when, misled by that appearance I have thought to appeal to something in common & unburthen my inmost soul to them I have found my language misunderstood like one in a distant & savage land.

He and his hero-selves sought for absolutes not to be found, and asked questions that could not be answered, anywhere on earth. 'Your mind is not fitted for the reception of truth!' he cried out to Hogg once, furiously wanting to know it too, but also implying he had truth to give. In *Alastor*, his account of his own search for ideal Beauty, the distracted young Poet – wraith-like and prematurely grey – could no longer speak words that made sense to others. But his wild eyes blazed with love and desperation.

Books were often to blame, or too much remembering. The mind of Prince Athanase, the tormented young aristocrat who was also Shelley, had been disturbed by obscure dreams and longings:

> There was a youth who, as with long toil & travel,
> Had grown quite weak & gray before his time,
> Nor any could the restless griefs unravel
>
> Which burned within him, withering up his prime
> And goading him like fiends . . .

The Prince himself, Shelley wrote, readily engaged in discussion about his own case, wittily canvassing opinions 'as if its theme might be/ Another, not himself'. But Shelley abandoned the poem in 1818 with what seemed to be a note of embarrassment as much as explanation.

> The Author was pursuing a fuller development of the ideal char-
> acter of Athanase, when it struck him that in an attempt at extreme
> refinement & analysis, his conceptions might be betrayed into the
> assuming a morbid character. —The reader will judge whether he
> is a loser or gainer by his diffidence.

At other times he slid into morbidity with no compunction, letting 'ideal melancholy' suffuse him as he wrote. He was the young idealist Lionel in his 'Modern Eclogue' *Rosalind and Helen*, drained and weak-ened by selflessness and the world's incomprehension until he died, transported by music, in his lover's arms. In one of Shelley's notebook 'scraps' of 1821, a made-up critic flippantly discussed him:

A strange fellow that Lionel—but there is a kind of method in his madness—which I should be glad to ~~find~~ see unravelled. —

In *Julian and Maddalo*, a bantering exposition of his ideological differences with Byron, Shelley played two characters made odd, or mad, by their dreams. He was both the serious, idealistic Julian ('an Englishman of good family, passionately attached to those philosophical notions which assert the power of man over his own mind') and a Maniac in a madhouse, demented by lost love, who still sang by moments his beautiful unbidden songs. Julian, visiting him, noted the Maniac's 'sad meek face', his eyes 'lustrous and glazed' and the tokens of his former gentility that lay uselessly about him: statues, flowers, a piano. 'I knew one like you,' Maddalo–Byron told Julian,

> '. . . and he
> Is now gone mad, —
> . . .
> But he was ever talking in such sort
> As you do—'

The Maniac left behind poems, blotted with tears, whose theme was naturally the same as those by Shelley, or Prince Athanase, or the sad young Poet of *Alastor*, or Lionel, dropping his verses listlessly to the earth:

> How am I changed! my hopes were once like fire:
> I loved, and I believed that life was love.
> How am I lost!

As he stood in that madhouse apartment, listening unnoticed to the Maniac's grief, Julian wept. 'I think I never was impressed so much,' he wrote. Going quietly out, he left his madman-self to fitful sleep on the sofa, murmuring 'some familiar name'.

Shelley insisted that he did not know him. This character, he told Hunt, was 'in some degree a painting from nature, but, with respect to time & place, ideal'. Whether this madman was him – whether he was any of these sad, similar souls – had no importance to the poem as he saw it. 'Of the Maniac', he wrote,

I can give no information . . . He was evidently a very cultivated and amiable person when in his right senses. His story, told at length, might be like many other stories of the same kind: the unconnected exclamations of his agony will perhaps be found a sufficient comment for the text of every heart.

One fact, however, lay at the core of all these histories: a fact so intrinsic to Shelley, and so precious, that he was unable ever to describe it. Each Shelley-character held a memory – disturbed, but not eclipsed, even by stark grief – of a blissful, momentary, controlling presence both within and beyond himself. This was what had made him mad, if he was truly so: that he had glimpsed this presence while on earth, and could not bear the rift between that reality and his existence.

Under its influence, Shelley had made his boyhood vow – stumblingly, but devotedly – to Truth, Beauty, Liberty and Love. These seemed the closest approximation to the message he had been given, without words. He did not know to whom, or what, he made this promise. For years he could not even try to name what it was that had so moved him. But his search for it became his history, and his life. All else was secondary.

2
Chains

In 1816 Shelley toured the dungeons at the Castle of Chillon, near Geneva. They were dug below the lake, where the water, he was told, was 800 feet deep. The columns that supported the ceilings were fitted with iron rings and scratched with prisoners' names. One loftier dungeon, further in, was spanned by a rotting beam on which captives had been hanged in secret. 'I never saw', he wrote, 'a monument more terrible of that cold & inhuman tyranny, which it has been the delight of man to exercise over man.'

Wherever he went, he mused on prisons: the jail at Bonneville, a vast white pile dominating the town, or the Torre del Fame at Pisa, 'a spectre wrapped in shapeless terror' that soaked up the light of the sunset. When he could he went inside them, exploring the wells in the Doge's palace in Venice, where captives had been kept waist-deep in stinking water, and the gloomy subterranean chambers of the palace of the Cenci in Rome, where Beatrice Cenci in the sixteenth century had been confined for parricide. Tenderly he pored over her prisoner's portrait: 'her head ... bound with folds of white drapery from which the yellow strings of her golden hair escape, and fall about her neck'. In Tasso's low damp cell at Ferrara, several feet below the ground, he picked tiny slivers of wood from the door and sent them, like relics, to his friend Thomas Love Peacock in England.

He himself had known prison as a boy, merely by going to school. At Syon House the boys were released from class, starving on their diet of bread and butter and thin blue milk, into a play-yard of patchy grass surrounded by stone walls. It contained one battered elm tree, with a bell hung in the branches that would call them to their desks again.

Shelley would range along the southern wall, to and fro, to and fro, rehearsing his forbidden thoughts. Or, when he knew himself alone, he would weep there.

His time in prison proper was limited to two nights, for debts outstanding of around £1,500, at Marlow in 1817. He found it 'most annoying'. (He had had a narrow brush in 1812, arrested at Carnarvon in Wales for a debt of £60, and was glad the local surgeon bailed him out.) Yet he often imagined his radicalism would put him in jail, 'confined in a damp cell, without a sixpence, without a friend' and inevitably 'starved to death'. Lovers and friends were enjoined to pity him, though he promised he would suffer with defiance: as proudly as his hero Verezzi, weighed down with chains that were stapled to the bare rock.

If he could, he succoured prisoners. At Oxford in March 1811 he published a 'Poetical Essay' to be sold on behalf of Peter Finnerty, imprisoned under the Libel Acts for exposing British military blunders. His *Letter to Lord Ellenborough* of 1812 defended Daniel Isaac Eaton, the publisher of part of a work by Tom Paine, who was closely associated with the revolutions in both America and France. In the same year Shelley tried to save a young man in Ireland from the press gang, petitioning a member of Parliament on his behalf. He sent £20 to Leigh Hunt and his brother John, jailed for two years under the Sedition Acts for publishing in the *Examiner* a piece on the stoutness and stupidity of the Prince Regent, besides trying to start a subscription to pay their enormous fines. In 1819 from Italy he filled five double sheets with a defence of Richard Carlile, a Deist imprisoned for reprinting Paine and for 'some inexplicable crime, which his prosecutors call blasphemy'. Even creatures were set free: he released a caged squirrel in France, which bit him, and ordered his servant to slip bought crayfish back to the Thames at Marlow.

Yet another prison loomed around him, 'Whose chains and mossy walls/ We feel, but cannot see'. Against such a wall, made of fallen rocks entwined with roots and ivy, the hopelessly seeking Poet of *Alastor* leaned his head and died. Plato in the *Republic* had depicted the human condition as a dark cave in which men were chained, their backs to the light, unable to glimpse more of Reality than shadows on the wall before them. Thus, on earth, Shelley was compelled to live.

In his view slavery pervaded life, even the otiose and disgusting lives of emperors, priests and kings. He drew them on iron thrones, weighed under iron sceptres, heavily dragging their carcasses to feast and shackled to the very systems they imposed on others. Under them, the people groaned. In England in particular, bonds of debt for foreign wars bound the whole population, and ties of superstition and deference to 'Church-craft and State-craft' kept the masses powerless. Reinforcing these were laws, customs and social duties that forbade, chief among other things, the free expression of sexual love. If man was a slave, woman was his 'bond-slave'. Shelley saw young women downtrodden and dishonoured by convention   models of his favourite heroine, Antigone, destroyed for her love and pity by the Theban laws – while young men like himself were forced to visit prostitutes by 'monkish' rules of chastity that spread disease and despair.

The imprisonment of the human condition seemed cruellest to Shelley in the case of children. Their spirits should have been freest and closest to his own, yet he saw them everywhere restrained by parental discipline, church, school, and worse. He was especially shocked to read, in Southey's *Letters from England*, that child-workers in the factories of Manchester were deprived not only of rest and instruction but also of daylight and air.

Often he tried to intervene. He dreamed of buying a Sussex waif who did tumbling tricks at the back door of Field Place, and of carrying off in his carriage a little girl he met in France. In Dublin in 1812 he 'rescued' an urchin, found hiding in 'unutterable filth and misery' with his mother, and was about to teach him to read when the boy was arrested and pressed into military service. Another little girl, hungry and half frozen, came for a few hours under his wing; he persuaded her to go with him to the nearest cottage where, kneeling on one knee in front of her, he fed her carefully from a wooden bowl with spoon-fuls of warm milk. Such simple things, he wrote later, were the neces-sary basis of freedom in England:

> clothes, and fire, and food
> For the trampled multitude—

Yet he meant to feed them also with visions of true, transcendent freedom, drop by insistent drop.

His most spectacular rescue was of Harriet Westbrook, in August 1811, from Mrs Fenning's school at Clapham. She attended with Shelley's sisters, Mary and Hellen; that was how he had first seen her, some time in the winter of 1810–11, confined with them behind the railings. On Sundays, chaperoned by her watchful sister Eliza, he could walk with her on Clapham Common. Allowed to visit one summer day he showed off wildly, upsetting the port on the tray-cloth and cavorting in the garden to spite their rules. Harriet helped his sisters to calm him. He sent her letters, said to have been stuffed full of devils and liberty and atheism; at least one was torn in pieces by the headmistress. But he persuaded her to flee with him from London on a stage-coach as far as Edinburgh, and she was free.

And what then? She was sixteen and ravishingly pretty, a coffee-house-keeper's daughter with simple, pleasing manners, thick auburn hair and skin as soft as roses. He was nineteen, cast out of Oxford, alienated from his family and flattered by her affection – and in love, though as late as that July he had assured Hogg otherwise. ('If I know anything about *Love* I am *not* in love.') He supposed, he told Hogg later, that Harriet had thrown herself upon him as a liberator and protector.

In fact he had determined for months to rescue her, even if she resisted. His *Poetical Essay*, written to get a radical journalist out of jail, had been dedicated to Harriet five months before her escape. He was now involved in an illicit union neither her parents nor his could tolerate, and was forced to flee to Scotland, where they could marry with no questions asked.

But he had not intended to marry her. Matrimony revolted him. As a husband, to adopt Godwin's view, he would become the oppressive monopoliser of his wife. 'Yes *marriage* is hateful detestable,' he told Hogg in May 1811,

—a kind of ineffable sickening disgust seizes my mind when I think of this most despotic most unrequired fetter which prejudice has forg'd to confine it's energies.

He could not bear the idea of restricting love to one person, one object, 'one chained friend' by law and superstition. Love could not be a matter of coercion. But earthly existence made it so, or had done in his case. In childhood, he told Godwin – his Poet's childhood, bullied and sad – 'I was required to love because it was *my duty* to love'. Duty had also kept him subservient to, and dependent on, his father. He could not offer Harriet this mockery of love.

Nonetheless, he persuaded himself to marry her. On 29 August 1811 he signed the register in Edinburgh. He accepted that young women suffered unequally from the stigma of cohabitation and that, in the present state of morals, the fetters of the law were necessary. In any case, under his 'superintending mind', Harriet would still tread the path to a higher, freer state. As they set up house together, moving constantly round the country, she was his pupil as much as his wife. He began at once to teach her Latin, just the nouns and verbs at first, dispensing with tricky grammar; she progressed to Horace and Virgil. Obedient to his dictates, she served up cabbage and apples rather than 'murdered chicken'. By listening to him day after day as he argued for men's equality and inveighed against religion, she absorbed so many of his words that her long, neat letters were full of his own indignation. She copied out his poems with the same eager diligence, and even helped him organise his campaigns for liberty in Ireland. Yet her mind was in fetters of another kind, bound by propriety, seemliness and fashion as tightly as ribbons on a bonnet, and Shelley could neither change her nor, in the end, save her.

Only months into the marriage the bars came down around him. In short order he acquired furniture, crockery, linen, a carriage and an older, ugly sister-in-law, Eliza Westbrook, who by October 1811 had moved in with them. Eliza brought censoriousness and rectitude, scolding and 'nerves', while endlessly brushing her long black hair. At home and on the road Harriet read aloud in her pleasant, clear, unvarying voice the second-rate writers of the day, ramparts and battlements and portcullises of words, while Shelley paced desperately round and round the room. ('Is it necessary to read all that, Harriet dear?') On one northern journey Hogg found the fugitive husband on the sea wall at Berwick in the drizzling rain, watching the wild and dreary sea 'with looks not less wild and dreary'.

Love was free. Shelley wrote as much in the notes to *Queen Mab*, the year after his marriage:

> Love withers under constraint: its very essence is liberty: it is compatible neither with obedience, jealousy, nor fear: it is there most pure, perfect, and unlimited, where its votaries live in confidence, equality, and unreserve.
>
> . . . to promise for ever to love the same woman is not less absurd than to promise to believe the same creed: such a vow, in both cases, excludes us from all inquiry.

Yet his love was now confined, numb, tranquillised. 'Love seems inclined to stay in the prison,' he told a friend, and for a time it was true. He bound himself with Harriet's bright hair like a rope, let her smiles gild the 'rivets' driven into him, and made her words and glances a cage around his heart. When Hogg in October 1811 attempted to seduce her, Shelley was appalled that he was forced to choose between his dearest friend and his wife. But marriage required it. 'If I were free I were yours,' he told Hogg, '. . . But I *am* Harriet's.' And Harriet wished only to be his. The birth of Ianthe, in June 1813, gave him another reason, 'so eloquently weak', to stay. 'Duty's hard and cold control' led him to marry Harriet again, in a brief religious ceremony in Holborn in March 1814, in case the Scottish civil rite had not been strict enough.

But Love was languishing. Even his affection for Ianthe, Shelley told Harriet, was merely the result of 'habit & self-persuasion'. As he remarried his wife, his thoughts were already straying. By June, they had come to settle on the small, fair girl he had noticed in William Godwin's house in Islington, hovering quietly among the shelves of ancient books. This was Godwin's daughter Mary, then sixteen. Shelley had been frequenting the house to talk with his mentor of justice, equality, truth, sincerity, reform; but the pale, solemn girl in her strange tartan dress called his name, and he darted after her.

Mary — imbued with the feminist free-thinking of her mother, Mary Wollstonecraft, who had died just after she was born — believed in the essential liberty of love. She gave herself to Shelley, to his amazement, without the least nod to custom or conventional morality:

> How beautiful and calm and free thou wert
>   In thy young wisdom, when the mortal chain
>   Of Custom thou didst burst and rend in twain
> And walked as free as light the clouds among . . .

They seem to have first made love in St Pancras churchyard, by her mother's grave, on the night of 26 June 1814. That was their wedding, their altar 'the grassy earth outspread', under the open sky. There were no registers or witnesses, save the stars. This love was free. The Godwins tried to keep Mary from Shelley for a time, in the prison of the school-room at their house in Skinner Street, but she defied their 'tyranny' and, a month later, fled away with him to France.

Harriet, four months pregnant, was left alone. After Shelley had abandoned her (she neither understanding nor accepting his rejection), he wrote her teacher's letters, acidly virtuous and full of self-righteous pain, lamenting that he had shown her the way to freedom and she had failed to follow it. Since she did not understand his liberated way of love, since 'It is no reproach to me that you have never filled my heart with an all-sufficing passion', she did not deserve to monopolise him. He had hoped she might come and live with Mary and himself ('I as his sister, she as his wife', as Harriet explained, appalled, to a friend), but he had clearly been 'an idiot' to expect such greatness or generosity from her. In curt postscripts, he asked her to send him 'hanks' and stockings and to lend him money.

In December 1816 Harriet, unable to live without him, committed suicide. Her death persuaded him all the more that indissoluble bonds were unbearable. But marriage lay in wait for him all the same, like Dante's soaring prison gates at the mouth of Hell. *Lasciate ogni speranza voi ch'intrate!* he cried out to himself. After two years of illicit love, he was forced by custom and the Godwins – their scorn of monopoly and property quickly stifled by the prospect of a moneyed, titled son-in-law – to marry Mary too. 'The ceremony' took place on 30 December 1816 at a church in the City: commerce, superstition and fetters all combined.

For a time it did not seem to trouble him. Mary had always been a kindred soul, reading and writing alongside him, learning Greek, embracing his sympathies and interests, with a lively intellectual curiosity poor Harriet had never acquired. She remained, if rather tentatively, free in love, even seeming to indulge Shelley's eagerness that Hogg should share her as 'our common treasure'. William was born in 1816, Clara in 1817, to fill their homes with life and babble. That year Shelley dedicated to her his *Revolt of Islam*, in which he re-staged the French Revolution with an idealised young lover at his side. She was his 'heart's home' and 'sweet friend' and his delight.

It could not last. Eventually even Mary, the bright rebel spirit, became a fretting and domesticated wife. She worried increasingly about what was 'proper', and what 'Everybody' said or did; and she was hamstrung by jealousy, especially of Claire Clairmont, her step-half-sister. Claire (originally Jane) had been brought up with her, educated in that same schoolroom into which Shelley had once rushed, frantic with desire, to try to take Mary away. She was the same age, sixteen, in 1814; when Shelley and Mary eloped, she went with them. From then on, intermittently, she was a third member of their household. Claire was noisy, emotional, attractive; for much of the time, her more sober 'sister' could barely stand her.

Though she kept herself busy with reading and writing, Mary was often despondent and mistrustful. In relatively happy Marlow in 1817 she worried about her milk flow, Shelley's absences and the darkness of the north-facing garden. The next year she was in anxious exile, with Shelley and two small children, in Italy. In a little over a year, by June 1819, the Italian climate – and, to her mind, Shelley's impetuous plans – had killed first Clara, then William. Their deaths shattered both parents; but where Shelley's grief was quickly distracted and sublimated in writing, Mary's lasted. She and Shelley still read and, sometimes, wrote together; in November 1819 another son, Percy Florence, was born to them. They acquired a social circle. Yet, to her, there often seemed little left but sorrow.

Shelley could not reach her and, weltering in his own unhappiness, did not much try. Instead, he sought others to comfort him. One sadly expressive little note from him to her, in Pisa in 1820 – addressed to 'Signora Shelley in Casa Galetti', as though he did not live there too – was written across her neat, long list of groceries and linen: 1 table-cloth, 9 do. napkins, 4 pr stock[ing]s 2 shirts.

> Such hope as is the sick despair of good—
> Such fear, as is the certainty of ill—
> Such doubt, as is pale Expectations food
> Turned while she tastes, to poison—

Throughout his Italian exile, 'Duty's chains' grew tighter and harder. He wrote poems, small scraps of longing, in which he could neither kiss nor touch a succession of lovely, flirting women. Shackled and mute, he merely watched them. When he could he escaped with Claire, who would love him – perhaps physically, perhaps not – but would not, in any case, possess him. In March 1820 he told their friends the Gisbornes that 'Mary considers me as a portion of herself, and feels no more remorse in torturing me than in torturing her own mind.' He drew her with her mouth full of needles, her work and her words. This figure of Misery had to be instructed again even in the liberating arts of love, which turned to ice as she touched them:

> Kiss me; —oh thy lips are cold—
> Round my neck thine arms enfold: —
> They are soft, but chill & dead
> And thy tears upon my head
> Burn like points of frozen lead

'The quick coupled with the dead' he remarked, in 1822, of their

44

marriage. So it had been by the end in his union with Harriet: 'a dead & living body . . . linked together in loathsome & horrible communion'. In Mary's case, however, their mutual love had not altogether gone. Nor was it Mary, as he acknowledged, in whom the pulses of the heart had long since fallen quiet.

At one of the lowest points in his marriage, in 1820, Shelley found a new prisoner and planned her rescue with even more passion than he had done before. Teresa Emilia Viviani, aged nineteen, had been sent to board in a convent in Pisa while her marriage was arranged. For an Italian girl of the nobility, the circumstance was not unusual. But for Shelley, introduced to her that winter by a mutual acquaintance and visiting the dreary convent more and more often, it was immurement of the worst kind, by custom, parental tyranny, cold chastity and brute religion. Emilia had two small rooms, looking out on a bare kitchen garden; in chill December she warmed her hands on a tiny crock of ashes. In the parlour hung a caged lark to which she sadly spoke and sang. Her dark hair was dressed simply, in the Grecian style, and her skin was pale from confinement.

Emilia had written, in her childish, flowery hand, of 'this dark and miserable abyss', the world, out of which love could transport her. In response Shelley gave her his most recent celebrations of physical and spiritual freedom, put into Italian for her, from *Prometheus Unbound* and *Hellas*. Together, using the same pen, they revised 'Una Favola', the story he had written in Italian of his adolescent encounters with Love and Death. One day he drafted, then cancelled with wildly spiralling scribbles, a letter describing how at night he saw her form surrounding him, her face close to his, their lips meeting . . . until day came, and found them back in their respective prisons.

He also made a poem of this. It was written in violent pencil that broke halfway through but he scrawled on, digging with the bare splintered stub, as if he had no alternative.

> Thy gentle ~~voice~~ face, Emilia dear
> ~~No dream~~
> At night seems hanging over mine
> I feel thy ~~quivering~~ trembling lips—I hear
> The murmurs of thy voice divine
>
> O God why comes the morning blank
> To quench in day this dream of grace

45

From which the joys my being drank
Yet quiver thro my burning face

Yet Emilia too was only human. The marriage contract made, she left the convent to live contentedly and soberly with her 'clod of earth' as Harriet Grove, Shelley's first love, had done ten years before. Shuddering, Shelley professed that he could no longer look at the poems of abandonment he had dedicated to her. She had joined him, but only in a different prison, from which it was far harder to escape.

★   ★   ★

Once married, Emilia asked him for money. She was neither the first nor the last to weigh down love with greed. For most of his life Shelley had enough, either in anticipation or reality, to be 'the purse of his friends', including Hunt, Peacock and Claire. But he felt gold sullied affection, as it did life in general. Though he gave readily enough, in accordance with all that Godwin had taught him about equality and justice, he hated to be asked and, even more, not to be thanked for it.

Godwin's own importunings for his debts and rent arrears were especially painful and protracted. Shelley began to help him, partly out of guilt, partly out of sympathy with Mary, as soon as he returned from running away with her in the summer of 1814. By 1817, when he had married into the Godwin family, his impoverished father-in-law made it clear that it was Shelley's duty to bail him out. The needy man was bound to demand, the rich man to give. This obligation, though Shelley readily accepted it, brought out his coldest and most businesslike side, page after page of precise accounting of his financial condition and expectations. By August 1819 he reckoned he had given Godwin £4,700, and had 'bought bitter knowledge' with it. That begging was to continue, and worsen, for the remaining three years of Shelley's life.

He needed money, but it sickened him. It made tyranny possible, and crushed out the life of the poor. ('Blood and Gold' went naturally together, a glittering mulch of horror.) Most unbearably, in his view, prodigious government borrowing to finance wars with France had produced a national debt that hung grotesquely over Britain. In 1816 £45million a year was payable in interest alone, much of it drawn from taxes on the necessities of the poor. But by Shelley's calculations, 'no combination of the heaviest tyranny can raise the taxes for its payment'.

Abolition was the only answer. He scratched 'Of the National Debt' in his blackest ink across the first draft of his most detailed political manifesto, *A Philosophical View of Reform*, as if it was all that mattered, and once startled Hunt by asking, after long and silent gazing into the fire, how much the debt was. In 1819, he tried to work it out himself:

$$44\ 000,\ 000$$

a thousand millions

$$300,\ 000,\ 000$$

$$300,\ 000,\ 000$$

$$300\ 0\ x\ 0$$

He gave up; his zeros became eggs, the eggs became sun-discs, the discs caught fire and flew.

Often he was desperate for money, especially in the first months of his marriage to Harriet, when his father temporarily stopped his allowance, and in late 1814 to early 1815, when he was heavily in debt to his carriage-maker. He left for Italy, in March 1818, still owing substantial sums to at least seven creditors in England. But he handled cash with almost physical disgust. Coins brought home from the bank in Italy were tipped out on the rug, trodden flat underfoot and divided up with a shovel, or were flung down in front of Mary, with the cry that she should pick them up. Money was a burden to him, far better out of his pockets and in the hands of beggars, or squirrelled away, as in Dublin in 1812, in some 'hole or corner' of someone else's clothes. 'S return[s] staggering under the weight of a large canvass bag full of silver,' he wrote in Neufchâtel in 1814, collecting the cash for the French travels of himself, Mary and Claire:

S alone looks grave on the occasion, for he alone clearly apprehends that francs & ecus & louis d'or are like the white & flying cloud of noon that is gone before one can say Jack Robinson.

Yet if coins were bad, he loathed paper money more. This was 'fairy-money', 'fabrications' and 'trash', tied not to the only commodity that had real value, the labour of man, but to inflated, fantastical expectations of what the issuer was worth. Paper currency had so little basis in reality that the soldiers of Horsham barracks, for a 'freak' on pay day, would eat pound notes pressed between brown bread and butter or smoke them in their pipes. Shelley himself, by several accounts,

47

twisted notes or bank-post bills into paper boats or used them as tiny sails.

In this 'Fool's Paradise', as Godwin had noted in *Political Justice*, a poor man was obliged to work 16 hours to earn the shillings that would buy his bread. Before the advent of paper money, he had perhaps worked eight. He became enslaved, along with his children, by financial promises that were worth little or nothing. And as a slave he would never know that precious leisure (his *right*, Shelley insisted, because it was his *duty* to attain knowledge) in which he could start to ease his fetters by reading and thinking.

> How many a rustic Milton has passed by,
> Stifling the speechless longings of his heart,
> In unremitting drudgery and care!

Yet Shelley himself left a trail of cheques, promissory notes and, most notional of all, post-obit bonds by which he promised to pay when he arrived at his inheritance. These carried such colossal rates of interest that by March 1822, four months before his death, he reckoned his debts might amount to £25,000.

His gouty grandfather, whom he thought 'a bad man', ignored bankers; instead, he sewed banknotes into his dressing gown or hid them in the folds of the sofa. Shelley's father had therefore tried to train his son young in handling cash and doing accounts. In his last year at Eton Shelley was meant to record his expenses in Baxter's Sussex Pocket Book, ready-ruled and set up in columns for his incomings and outgoings. He made a few desultory entries, pretending they balanced, but otherwise used the pages for matter more attractive:

> I looked, & behold a pale horse & his name that sat on him was death & Hell followed with him—

To his friends, he claimed to be no good at figures. 'You know I am an infernal arithmetician,' he told Peacock, proudly. He hated sums, but often seemed bogged down in them. Calculations filled his notebooks, edging their way into poems and sketches (though verses marched over some, and trees grew up round others). Many were line-counts, some tottings-up of bills or rough estimates of quarterly expenses; most were simple additions and subtractions that could have been done in his head.

1200
070
―――
1270

Even so, he sometimes got them wrong.

4400
1300
―――
6700

For some weeks he tried to work out Plato's contention, in the *Republic*, that the just man lived 729 times more pleasantly than the tyrant and the tyrant 729 times more miserably. In one notebook, after flirting with a few unsolvable equations ('729 x $x = y$'), he squared 729 to produce 535, 941. In another notebook he made it 531,441, exactly.

Byron called him a goose on such subjects, 'the *least* worldly-minded person' he had ever known. Shelley agreed, happily calling himself an 'anti worldling' and taking as his motto a passage from Plato's *Symposium* on the unimportance of rich friends. His private income – eventually settled as an annuity of £1,000 when, in 1815, his grandfather's death freed up his funds – removed him from the sordidness of earning a living. Yet appearances could be deceptive. On money matters, he was perfectly and precisely informed on whatever he felt he should know. He shocked Harriet by announcing that the birth of a son to them, in November 1814 after the collapse of their marriage, would 'make money cheaper' – in other words, make credit easier. He arranged cleverly, in 1815, to get a loan of £1,000 for Godwin and £200 for himself accounted for as debt repayment, and advised Hunt on how best to exploit the exchange rate between Italy and England. Mary's payments for her books were elaborately and carefully organised. In 1819, when he foresaw (and hoped for) imminent revolution in England, he worried that his friend John Gisborne had invested too much in British Funds.

What did not vary was his contempt for the business: 'my habitual my constitutional inability', as he put it to Godwin, 'to deal with monied men'. Mary, convinced he did not care, had to nag him to visit his banker and check the state of his accounts. He did so reluctantly. As need compelled him he used moneylenders and pawnbrokers who kept him waiting, in their dingy shops, while poor women haggled over the value of armfuls of filthy sheets. Philanthropy could have drawn him to these 'wretches' even more recklessly, borrowing on his future

49

prospects, had not his father and Longdill, his own solicitor, connived (as he stressed to Godwin) 'to tie me up from all . . . irregular applications of my fortune'.

The sheriff's officers and agents sent by his creditors he referred to as 'the People' or 'men dressed in black'. They loitered distantly on his walks, sometimes invisible to others but always clear to him, pursuing or spying on him, set on his arrest. They appeared too as shadows, mimicking his own, in notebook entries for money owing that no one else saw:

~~That man~~   ~~60~~

      . . .

The other   6
Myself   60

In London in the autumn of 1814, in his worst spell of debt and penury, he moved frantically from lodging-house to lodging-house to avoid their visitations: the imperious knock, the quick slamming of the door to trap him, the cry: 'You are Mr Percy Bysshe Shelley!' before they thrust a copy of the writ on him. Yes, he was Shelley: the cornered, indebted self, whose only recourse once from a black-clad pursuer was to charge through a hedge, flee across a hayfield and dive into the nearest ditch, deeper into the dirt.

★   ★   ★

If his past could not fix him, he could perhaps be pinned to some piece of ground. But there, too, Shelley resisted. To tie him to any particular landscape, as Wordsworth was tethered to his lakes and fells, was hopeless. On crowded streets and open hills alike, his nose was usually in a book that took him far away. Even when he paused, stuffed the volume in a pocket and gazed about him, he did not see the scene as it appeared to others. The cedars of Windsor Great Park became pyramids of fire, the woods an enchanted forest laced with creepers of all colours. At Marlow the river bank, overhung with simple willow and hawthorn, acquired glowing whirlpools and waterfalls and rocks cascading with 'strange and star-bright' flowers; a wooden jetty became a stair of fretted ivory, and temples rose among the trees. From his lodgings at Lynmouth in 1812 he saw not the smooth grey Bristol Channel, the distant hills of Wales and the last evening light on the cliff-woods, but wonders:

                    that faery Hall!
        As Heaven, low resting on the wave, it spread
                Its floors of flashing light,
                Its vast and azure dome,
                Its fertile golden islands
                Floating on a silver sea . . .

He drew these visions in his notebooks: an ordinary lake, reeds, trees, then temples, then mountains, then stars.

Besides, he moved incessantly. From Oxford in 1811 he decamped to London, York, Edinburgh, Keswick and Dublin, all within a year, his crates of books tumbling after him. From Ireland he shifted to Nantgwillt in Wales, Lynmouth in north Devon, Wales again, Ireland, London again, Bracknell in Berkshire (by July 1813), London, Bishopsgate and Marlow. Six weeks were spent wandering in France and Germany in the summer of 1814 with Mary and Claire; in July 1816 he was with Mary, Claire and Byron in Switzerland; in March 1818 he left England for definitive exile in Italy. Yet there too he moved constantly, from Milan to Pisa, to Leghorn, to Bagni di Lucca, to Venice, to Rome (by 1819), to Naples, to Pisa, to Villa Magni at San Terenzo, near Lerici. That house, too, he had taken only for the summer of 1822, a seasonal perch before he packed trunks again. He dreamed of Greece, Egypt, the Levant, India, America, their fascination often less important than their sheer distance away.

In his own mind he seldom left gently, but was pushed. 'A prejudice [that] does not permit me to live on equal terms with my fellow beings' – in other words, general disapproval of his liaison with Mary – inspired his brief trip to Switzerland, an intended exile. Government repression and bad health induced him to go to Italy. Bad air or bad water, hastening the deaths of little Clara and William, propelled him in 1818–19 to abandon Venice and Rome. Many wanderings were blamed on government spies, creditors, his father's agents (his father, he was sure, ever seeking a pretext to imprison him), and men of vague but broad menace against him, some real, some imaginary.

In August 1812 government informers forced him to leave north Devon, where he had been spreading pamphlets urging men to form associations for liberty and parliamentary reform. Lord Sidmouth, the new Home Secretary, had begun to take a malign interest in his activities. Shelley imagined an informer on the boat as he left, watching him, then suddenly abducting him, taking him to a remote island, knocking him down and trying to kill him by heaving a great rock

51

over his faintly beating heart. The fight went on as he fled Devon, 'Just, dauntless, rational', and hounded.

Some characters, Shelley was sure, hunted him with grim determination. Most persistent was Robert Leeson, an aristocratic quarry-owner whom Shelley outraged in north Wales in the winter of 1812. Shelley had gone there to help with a Utopian project to reclaim land from the sea at Tremadoc; as the embankment was built he fraternised with Leeson's workers, who were starving and ready to be politicised. Leeson had also procured some of Shelley's seditious pamphlets and meant, very possibly, to betray him to the government. In the end he apparently drove him from Wales and then haunted him for the next six years. Shelley would not walk alone at night for fear of Leeson shadowing his footsteps, meaning to stab him. Even in Italy – in Rome or in Pisa, at the post office – he allegedly ran into him again, and almost bolted from the city.

No one else saw this personage, or several more: the spies who stole his letters, or the 'emissaries' sent by Eliza Westbrook, his carping, watchful sister-in-law, to persecute him. Shelley's closest friends suspected that the stories and 'imaginary beings' were covers for flight that was largely instinctive. As soon as he felt the earth closing round him, roots growing, he had to go. Long before Italy, his natural state was exile and the world a 'wilderness' in which he could only wander, never at peace.

His family home at Field Place, once he had married Harriet, became as distant as the rest of his past. By September 1811 he had been physically barred from 'F.P.', kept out by his father's rage and his own intransigence. Tentatively visiting in mind or memory, he might see only the mellow roof and chimneys from the top of the drive, blind angles of brick walls, the summerhouse. On the lawns that sloped gently away in the sun, his little brother John ran in his petticoats. He, a shadow, stalked among the trees.

On his last visit home, in January 1815 for the reading of his grandfather's will, his father again gave him no admittance. Shelley sat by the door and read Milton's *Comus*, unable to enter but refusing to leave. Later, he seems to have tried (then changed his mind, deleting the thought) to sum up what home was:

> Dear Home thou scene of earliest hopes & joys
> The least of whom wronged Memory ever makes
> Bitterer than all thine unremembered tears—
>
> ~~I visit thee~~

On other pages of the same notebook, perhaps even in another year, the idea was carried on, overlaid in his mind now by other buildings and scenes and echoes of other, bitter words. The lines fell untidily in pencil down the side of a page. He was probably in a coach, cramped and hunched on a hard seat to write on his knees, returning.

> I visit thee but Thou art sadly changed
> Thy former home is now made desolate
> It has become the path of homeless winds . . .

Here the words tumbled down the margin even more steeply to avoid a sketch of a boat sailing towards mountains, past rocks, away.

> And I am changed, & many things are changed
> The Earth the Forests & the sky remain
> These things remain
> And unforgiving memories linger there
> Which heap forth sorrow

The words 'And I am changed' were written with special emphasis, pressing harder. If he had changed, it was futile to wish to stay, among the unwanted memories of his past.

Yet very quickly, quicker than he wanted, he became attached to places. He wished then to stay 'for ever', never moving again. In London in 1811, just expelled from Oxford, he was so transfixed by the wall-paper in the dim back sitting-room of a lodging-house in Poland Street – green vines, bright purple grapes, a dizzying trellis effect – that he took the place immediately, stroking the walls with delight. Four or five years later, walking in the Thames Valley with Peacock – that sharp-witted writer of comic novels now his neighbour, as well as his friend – he fell into a dream at the prospect of a vicarage wall overgrown with corchorus flowers. To Peacock's astonishment he remarked, suddenly, 'I feel strongly inclined to enter the church.' Such an admission, from the sworn enemy of all churches and churchmen, seemed to have nothing to do with logic and everything to do with the mellow, red-brick quiet of an English village in the sunshine of afternoon.

In March 1814, as he fell out of love with Harriet, a house at Bracknell belonging to the radical Boinville circle became 'home' to him. There he found debate, new female beauty, readings from Petrarch, tea, rest: 'The trees, the bridge, the minutest objects,' he told Hogg, 'have already a place in my affections.' By the same token, he knew homesickness. Letters from both Italy and Switzerland talked occasionally and sadly of English lanes, hills and woods; English houses, with chimneys and lattice windows, decorated his Italian notebooks. He acknowledged that England was 'my country dear to me forever', and that he felt 'a regret almost like remorse' at leaving. He kept in his mind an ideal of home, the enclosing nest of a crane or a swan where he might rest his tired, white wings. Even clouds and 'lightest winds' returned to such havens, drowsing and quiet.

From Bath in September 1816 (where he stayed for less than six months) he painted for the exiled Byron an idyllic picture of his own nest, a family fireside, with baby William asleep and a cat and kitten under the sofa. From Switzerland that July he had passed on to Peacock his dreams of a 'fixed, settled, eternal home', somewhere in the Thames Valley, where he would take a lease for 14 or 21 years. He worried about furniture and draperies, and wanted shrubs 'elegantly disposed' on the lawn. 'The shrines of the Penates', he told Peacock,

> are good wood fires, or window frames intertwined with creeping plants; their hymns are the purring of kittens, the hissing of kettles, & long talks over the past & dead, the laugh of children, the warm wind of summer filling the quiet house, & the pelting storm of winter struggling in vain for entrance.

The house Peacock found for him at Marlow, a long stuccoed building on West Street with a dark garden shaded by cypresses and firs, was a place of repose for a time. When Shelley moved there in March 1817, the lease was indeed for 21 years. He decked the huge library with classical statues and the rooms with co-ordinated papers and curtains – purple, yellow, black for a guest room intended for Byron – like any gentleman of property determined to acquire and impress. It seemed a home, yet he spent most of his time away from it. His Marlow memories from Italy were of woods and the river. When he thought of the house, wondering idly who was living there after him, he berated himself for his 'very absurd' interest in such a thing:

> The curse of this life is that whatever is once known can never be unknown. You inhabit a spot which before you inhabit it is as indifferent to you as any other spot upon the earth, & when . . . you think to leave it, you leave it not, —it clings to you . . .

If his roots began to strike at Marlow, he thought they went deepest at Pisa, where he and Mary lived for many months from 1820 in a 'lofty palace' on the Lung'Arno. Their friends Jane and Edward Williams moved there in January 1821, taking the floor below; Edward, an ex-dragoon, became Shelley's sporting companion, while placid, pretty Jane gradually drew his attention and his love. Their dwelling was one in a long row of shuttered houses, painted umber and ochre, overlooking the yellowish river. Shelley wrote happily of their 'neat' furniture – the first they had bought in Italy – the pot plants on the windowsills and the books he had ranged round him, and asked Peacock to send his whole library from Marlow, since 'I have . . . established myself for some indefinite time'.

Yet there was danger here, beyond the risk of memories accumulating. To settle was to be 'tamed', 'benumbed' or 'tranquillized', a word he used often of a quiet domestic state which, like a deep drug, induced a deadness of thought. 'Tranquil uniformity' crept, like a shadow, over the Marlow garden; Pisa was 'humdrum' and 'a city of the dead'. The hearth there, like that at Bracknell, was eventually cold.

> O why do we rest
> On the world's cold breast
> After the warmth has gone which made me blest

He spoke of lovelessness, but his homes were prey to a more insidious and creeping sickness: contentment with the earth. His condition of exile, painful though it seemed, was also vital to him. If he were to settle anywhere he would sink into time, and the hours would close round him. Too dull and comfortable to struggle, he would not escape.

Locke taught, and Shelley agreed, that time was determined by the steady train of ideas and sensations passing; but where he thought quickly and felt instantly, time dragged. In one notebook a typical image, creeping towards *Prometheus Unbound*, clung to the bottom of a page:

How like death-worms the wingless moments crawl!

In another, he welcomed in the year:

Jan 1. 1821
~~Hours hours~~
~~Pale cold~~ Orphan hours

Time inhabited his poems as a figure wrapped in shroud-like wings, driving a chariot slowly forward. Shelley could neither push the chariot faster (though he sometimes longed to whip it till the wheels burned), nor get out of its way. Time weighed him down and tormented him. He longed to be suspended, unthinking and therefore unaware of the slow hours passing, in some spell of inspiration, or in the unknowable state that followed death;

But I am chained to Time, and cannot thence depart!

In a desperately sad lyric of that year he linked time, life and the world together. Trembling, he was climbing their 'last steps', to the very edge of existence. He had stood there before, but was now terrified to be in that high, lonely place. Though days and nights and seasons went on, 'a joy' had fled out of the scene that would not return. With a thin wavering pen, in strangely weak writing, he began an invocation:

O world, o life, o time

And in the top right-hand corner, in the same pen, barely pressing,

I am despair

Since nothing on earth lasted or resisted change, it was a kind of sickness to wish to stay for ever anywhere. If Shelley were to say, with Faust, to the passing moment, *Verweile doch, du bist zu schön!* 'Remain thou, thou art so beautiful!', he was consigning himself to death in life, as surely as if he were to live for ever within the same four walls. He was accepting his chains.

From day to day, he tried not to. He ignored time, disdained it, forgot it if he could. Merely social time, such as lunch-time, tea-time, bed-time, an appointment at half-past eleven o'clock, meant nothing particular to him. ('I dare say I'm very provoking. I ought not to make appointments & not keep them.') The dates on his letters might be wrong as to the day or the year, or might not appear at all. 'Friday 1810' could do well enough. The hour, if he was asked, was notional. He had a gold watch with an appropriate length of chain, but did not necessarily consult it. When he and Mary eloped to France he sold his watch for cash, filling his pockets instead with three small volumes of Shakespeare.

His sailor-friend Edward Trelawny went to drag him downstairs once to dinner, away from *Faust* and the German dictionary. Shelley could not remember eating, nor the servant bringing his plate of meat and bread (which he stowed on a shelf), nor anything he had done in the lapse between morning and evening, save stand at the marble mantelpiece and read, and read more, and run his fingers through his hair, while time slipped fruitlessly away. He told Trelawny, 'I have lost a day'. They were often lost, sifting away like the blotting sand he strewed across his words.

Those words too burdened him, the visible form of his slow unprofitable thoughts. In 1820, in a game with himself or others, he dug as many words as he could out of 'starches': *star, hat, chart, arch*. He began to wriggle and cheat: *crasht, stacth, ah, ha*. At last, he acknowledged both victory and defeat:

~~Headache~~
Ache

If such chains could not be seen he was sure they could be heard in the heavier spondees and trochees of his verse. Line followed line, as the red-overalled convicts under armed guard swept the streets in Pisa, or the galley slaves in shackled pairs hoed weeds in the piazzas of Rome. He too dragged his fetters after him.

> Perhaps the only comfort that remains
> Is the unheeded clanking of my chains
> The which I make & call it melody

★   ★   ★

On the heights of Bisham Wood, outside Marlow, he sat and wrote. Before him the ground fell away to meadows, the Thames, the town and the far hills, mistily blue. Grey-white dust caked his boots. He was among great beech trees, rooted on thin clay over chalk; with each sudden movement, a fine brown scree would fall down through the woods. He could crumble it into powder and discover, as he dug further, whole nuggets of white chalk and the thin grey shells of snails.

In Italy, too, he read and wrote among earth and rocks. He sought out other high promontories, inspiration places: the Euganean Hills that held the tomb of Petrarch, or the hills above San Giuliano di Terme, looking over Pisa to the sea. There he perched among outcrops of ochre-stained white limestone, in a jumble of wild olive and thick thyme where snakes sunned themselves among the stones. Here, in effect – though still walled in by the Earth – he was in Lucretius's 'high calm sanctuaries', from which 'you can look down on others and see them everywhere astray'.

He drew rocks in his notebooks, frequently and squarely, sometimes emphatically crowning them with towers that looked like prisons. Hogg thought he was remembering the limestone tors of north Devon, the stratified stacks that stood like ghosts in the woods and along the coasts, and supposed that his chief inspiration was the Valley of the Rocks at Lynmouth; but they seemed to be any rocks, piled and jumbled to make up the tomb of the Earth. A favourite image from Calderón, whose dramas Shelley read in Italy, was of the soul as a rock overhanging an abyss, longing to detach itself from the dead mass of the mountain yet dreading the fall and the unknown. Mortal life was to teeter like this, on the brink of the dark. In one notebook sketch a Shelley-figure leaned exhausted against a chaos of boulders from which, it seemed, he had just escaped, like an Alpine peasant from an avalanche.

Mere stones he found dull. Mineralogy lectures at Oxford left him sighing and frustrated: 'Stones, stones, stones! nothing but stones! . . . And stones are not interesting things in themselves!' Yet the new science of geology enthralled him, and the thought of secret layers underneath the earth. In 1821 he asked Charles Ollier, his publisher, to find 'the most copious and correct history of the discoveries of Geology', two or three if necessary. Meanwhile he dug down, or forced his way, among marvels:

> anchors, beaks of ships;
> Planks turned to marble; quivers, helms, and spears,
> And gorgon-headed targes, and the wheels
> Of scythèd chariots . . .
> . . . prodigious shapes
> Huddled in grey annihilation, split,
> Jammed in the hard, black deep; and over these,
> The anatomies of unknown wingèd things . . .

In sand and loam beds near Brentford in 1813 tusks had been discovered, the remains of elephants and hippopotami. The clay of Horsham produced ammonites, belemnites and freshwater shells, proof that it had once been covered by sweet water. In Germany, according to new studies, fossils had been found of plants that now thrived in the climate of

Hindustan. The ground had not only swallowed up slavering monsters, but carried inside it proofs of a golden age, Saturn's age, when the Earth had flowed freely with milk and wheat in temperateness and peace.

Shelley did not hanker for that Golden Age. He thought it 'philosophically false', and uncivilised man 'the most pernicious & miserable of beings'. Instead, he mourned above all the disappearance of the Athenian democracy. He never saw Greece but observed, in 1818 in Pompeii, the ruins of what he stressed had been a Greek city. Even that exquisite harmony of urban life with Nature and the divine had been buried, deep under ash, by cycles of history and Necessity that could not be resisted.

Everything on the Earth became the Earth. The dust under his exploring, scratching fingernails had once been men like himself, towns, civilisations. All this dissolved and made up other things, the *primordia* alone unchanging. As the Fairy Queen explained in *Queen Mab*, showing to the human soul the workings of the world,

> 'There's not one atom of yon earth
> But once was living man;
> Nor the minutest drop of rain
> That hangeth in its thinnest cloud,
> But flowed in human veins . . .'

Crowds of men and their cities had passed thus. He would pass thus. The statue of Ozymandias, tyrant of tyrants, had crumbled to two giant legs and a shattered, sneering face, somewhere in the Egyptian desert. Shelley dismissed him in a sonnet written in an hour or so in 1817; and he could dismiss as fast the 'old, mad, blind, despised, and dying king', George III, under whom he and England suffered. All kings became nothing.

> And on the pedestal these words appear:
> 'My name is Ozymandias, king of kings:
> Look on my works, ye Mighty, and despair!'
> Nothing beside remains. Round the decay
> Of that colossal wreck, boundless and bare,
> The lone and level sands stretch far away.

Those high promontories made natural places from which to survey the decay of civilisations. There Shelley could sit, like the thoughtful oriental sage in the frontispiece of Volney's *Ruins of Empire*, gazing on or imagining a desolated city in which only the jackals roamed and howled. In Volney the Genius of Equality, appearing among the tombs, asked the sad dreamer to consider whether *une nécessité funeste, un dieu mystérieux*, or man himself, had brought about this destruction. The answer, of course, was man, and the remedy, said the Genius gently, was to 'raise yourself from the dust you crawl in'.

Shelley had seen such desolation at close hand, the 'more visible ravages' of the tyranny he detested. In August 1814, walking the 120 miles from Paris to Troyes with Mary and Claire – a very young man and two teenage girls, their luggage carried on a pack-mule – he had crossed a theatre of war. The fighting had stopped, but the scene remained 'frightful': 'village after village entirely ruined & burned; the white ruins towering in innumerable forms of destruction among the beautiful trees'. The famished inhabitants were sitting on the blackened thresholds of their houses, begging for bread; Shelley, hungry too, could get only a little milk from them. 'No provisions, no accommodation; filth, misery & famine everywhere.'

Much of this damage had been done by Britain's Cossack allies, an extension of the 'liberticide' war – Shelley's frequent, favourite word for it – unleashed against the French to reverse their revolution. England's own soldiers, once brought home and their numbers swelled with Hanoverians, had then been employed to stifle popular protests against high taxes, exorbitant corn prices and lack of work. After the Pentridge Rising in Derbyshire in 1817 three men had been hanged, drawn and quartered for inciting rebellion at the urging of a government agent; at 'Peterloo', two years later, eleven people had been killed and dozens injured when mounted troops, slashing with sabres, had charged into a peaceful crowd of 60,000 in St Peter's Fields in Manchester as they demanded parliamentary reform. (Shelley, in Italy, seemed to have heard worse: women's breasts cut off, infants' heads dashed against the cobblestones.) The government had also joined forces in 1815 with 'the seven blood-hounds', as Shelley called them – Austria, Bourbon France, Portugal, Prussia, Russia, Spain and Sweden – to suppress reform in Europe and to preserve the slave trade. This was the cycle of history in which he was trapped.

Earth, in his mind, was not indifferent to these things. It breathed and lived and cried out at injustice. At the birth of Prometheus, the fire-stealer, Shelley made Earth's 'stony veins' run with joy, as eager as his own. At Peterloo he made the Earth flinch and her heart cry, like a mother's, as each drop of blood fell upon her. In Shelley's view, great traumas – none greater than the French Revolution, descending to the Terror, then to Napoleon's *imperium*, then in 1815 to the Bourbon restoration – had their birth in physical upheaval as much as in the minds of men. Whichever tyranny crushed or convulsed the Earth ruled also in him, as long as he allowed it to.

This horror seemed unavoidable. Since the Age of Gold, as Laplace described it in his *Exposition du système du monde* (written in 1796, read by Shelley in 1813), Earth's revolutions had become eccentric. In the present brutal reign of Jupiter her axis pointed disastrously to the north polar star; perpetual spring had given way to fleeting seasons, and darkness and vice and the freezing zones had spread together. This Earth breathed out not delight, but contagion. Shelley could smell this death both in the London fogs and in the heavy, malarial climate of Naples and Rome, where its damp hand smothered little William. Noxious exhalations crept through the marshy Maremma of the Tuscan coast, hanging over the 'muddy weeds' and the 'shallow sullen sea'. Shelley fled before them, a man pursued by a miasma.

As the obliquity of Earth's axis was corrected, however (Herschel, England's great astronomer, reported it happening already), conditions would gradually change. The ice would thaw, despotism ease, and flowers would jewel the return of an everlasting spring. And 'There is no great extravagance in presuming', Shelley added in his notes to *Queen Mab*, '. . . that there should be a perfect identity between the moral and physical improvement of the human species.' As Earth was restored and enlightened, so man could be.

Yet that new dawn would not come soon. Earthly existence meant continual frustration. Centuries and generations might pass while the cycles of human progress edged forward, then regressed, as they had done in France. The year 1820, in particular, brought uprisings in both Spain and Naples that seemed likely to cast down two kings or, at the least, force them to grant greater freedoms to their subjects. But neither lasted. Growth and decay, spring and winter, good and evil followed in continuous alternation. Dark gave way to light, and to dark again.

Trelawny recalled Shelley looking 'a good deal' at autumn leaves falling and drifting, in pensive silence. The turning vine leaves in Italy, so beautiful to others, to him were 'stamped with the redness of their decay'. At Bisham, even in summer, a thick mulch of beech leaves deadened his steps through the woods. Some were deeply veined, others pale and open, coal black or yellow or 'hectic red', as though they shadowed the humours of the body or carried the flush of a consumptive. Shelley's own body was among them, diseased and decaying. His death, like theirs, stained the soil and fed into its substance, nourishing the seedlings that would spring and die in turn. Thus, as in Book VI of Homer's *Iliad*, the generations passed.

> Now green in youth, now withering on the ground;
> Another race the following spring supplies;
> They fall successive, and successive rise . . .

Each generation, Paine had written, was equal in rights to those that had died and gone before it; each should have the power to remake its laws, and the world, all over again. Yet it was necessary to free men first, and this, Shelley knew, was unutterably hard. Time itself, it seemed to him, 'was measured and created by the vices and the miseries of men'.

From his perches high above Pisa or Marlow he could watch men minutely toiling in the distant fields, turning the stubborn soil with its poor, thin yields to sustain the tyrant-rulers of Italy or the royal parasites of his own country. In England wartime enclosures had forced small farmers off their own land, depriving them even of common-rights and leaving them destitute. Or he could view the exhausted crowds of the new labouring classes like some master manufacturer, in industrial terms,

> Hardened to hope, insensible to fear,
> Scarce living pulleys of a dead machine,
> Mere wheels of work and articles of trade . . .

In 1820 he wrote a crude, fierce 'ballad' of England's rural poor living on raw turnips, potato parings and boiled leather, fighting with dogs for scraps of bread and begging for beer, which was denied, at the parson's gate. The rich feasted, the poor slaved and starved,

> And . . . this is the bond of God & nation
> And the law of social life—

The law also dictated that only 'one in several hundreds', by his estimate, had the right to vote, and with it the chance to change their condition from subjection to something better. Specifically, to quote Paine again, 'The town of Old Sarum, which contains not three houses, sends two members [to Parliament]; and the town of Manchester, which contains upwards of sixty thousand souls, is not admitted to send any.' Instead, the disenfranchised were cut down.

Shelley hesitated, though, to give these poor masses power. He was not a child of the French Revolution so much as of its awful after-math, when the rule of the people had descended to an orgy of reprisals and blood. He was deeply disappointed by this 'sanguine eagerness', but not surprised: men suddenly released from the slavery that had made them 'brutal and torpid and ferocious' could not immediately be 'liberal-minded' and 'forbearing'. He refused to despair, as so many did; the pessimistic weariness of the revolutionary generation, Wordsworth, Coleridge, Southey and the rest, angered and disgusted him. Shelley insisted on hope as a matter of principle. Yet it was qualified by the fear that the people, once given power, would take revenge, bringing more horrors.

His fundamental opinions on reform of the suffrage therefore kept within the bounds of the feasible, and recommended patience. Once all men were good and wise, he believed, government would decay of itself. In tranquil, earth-bound moods he could contemplate a revolu-tion that was organic and gradual, citizen by citizen turning to virtue, and his time-scale was long. After a night in a filthy cottage in war-ravaged France in 1814 (a 'regular den', in his words, in which he and Mary and Claire had eschewed the beds and slept on kitchen chairs), he reassured them that society was 'progressive' and that 'there would come a time when no where on the Earth, would there be a dirty cottage to be found'. This would happen, however, 'perhaps in a thou-sand years'.

Of course, men's stoicism might not last so long. Between misery at the lower levels and repression at the top, the only release might well be an explosion of violence. Shelley did not always want it, but he expected it. The tension in the land could not be contained for ever. He longed to make it shudder and change, as if with some giant Archimedean lever he could prise up whole cities and hills. ('Give me a place to stand on,' cried one epigraph to *Queen Mab*, 'and I will move the earth!') Tyranny once removed, the very caves and deserts would shout and howl as Liberty burst in on them.

But the working men of England toiled on, mostly silent. Impatiently, Shelley asked them why they ploughed and wove and laboured for 'those ungrateful drones who would/Drain your sweat—nay, drink your blood?' Better to dig their own graves:

> Shrink to your cellars, holes, and cells; . . .
>
> With plough and spade, and hoe and loom,
> Trace your grave, and build your tomb,
> And weave your winding-sheet, till fair
> England be your sepulchre.

Elsewhere, he remarked sadly that 'all, more or less, subdue themselves to the element that surrounds them', the dense and filthy earth.

He had once observed brickmakers closely, with his usual fixed and excited attention, as they spent the summer evening pushing lumps of wet mud through simple wooden frames. Their purpose seemed only to do that, exactly and continually, as though they themselves were 'masses of senseless clay—'

> They are trodden, and move not away—

At times Shelley found himself no better, an earthworm – though one filled somehow with 'spirit, thought, and love' – making his tiny impressions in the immensity of earth and time. He was crushed underfoot, writhing in the mud or the dust, but surprisingly did not die. He endured.

> 'As the slow shadows of the pointed grass
> Mark the eternal periods, his pangs pass
> Slow, ever-moving, —making moments be
> As mine seem—each an immortality!'

Prostrated, almost obliterated, he was at least hidden from his enemies, and might know peace. As he jotted down in 1821, quoting the Book of Job, 'thou shalt be in league with the stones of the field'.

In this state of mind, he could recommend passive resistance as the first step to transforming the political landscape. His *Mask of Anarchy*, a call to moral and political action written in the autumn of 1819 just after Peterloo, imagined his crowds mutely falling to the tyrant's men, their blood and bodies the 'fertilizing gore' for the world's regeneration. The first lesson to be taught was the sempiternal earthly one, patient endurance.

Let them ride among you there,
Slash and stab, and maim, and hew, —
What they like, that let them do.

As a creature of clay, an aggregation of atoms, Shelley could possibly do little else to change the way of the world. Necessity controlled him, even to his moral behaviour; he could not raise himself from the dust he crawled in. Perhaps change, when it came, would mean only a deeper integration with imprisoning soil and stones. Like Job (whose story he loved, and thought of dramatising), he cried out from the depths of his afflicted self, mystified by the purpose of his 'appointed time' and wondering what, if anything, lay beyond it.

Blind, or hardly seeing, he crept towards his burial. The veins within the earth pulsed in unison with his own, pushing round the sap or blood that kept the mechanisms in motion. Eventually he would lie still, a worm or leaf, and rot there. His memorials would be left, on mouldering paper, in ink crushed corrosively from iron sulphate, gum and galls. But from the best of those decaying thoughts something might yet spring and live.

★   ★   ★

At intervals in 1816 and 1817, Shelley covered a sheet of paper with drawings of plants. They were fleshy-leaved and spiky, with pendulous large stamens and drooping heads: flowers not seen on the earth. Unusually, they were set in regular order around a fresh-raked grave. Jumbled in among them were odd, heartfelt remarks:

It is not my fault—this is not to be attributed to me
when said I so?
Breaking thine indissoluble sleep
Miserable
These cannot be forgotten—years
      May flow
I drew this flower pot in October 1816 and now it is 1817

On the other side of the paper he wrote two laments for the dead. Both were probably addressed to Fanny Godwin, Mary's half-sister, who had committed suicide in October 1816 at the age of twenty-two. One was a record of their last, careless conversation, the other an imagining of her, a child, by the sea.

65

> Thy little foot steps on the sands
>   Of a ~~some~~ remote & lonely ~~sea~~ shore; —
> The twinkling of thine infant hands
>   ~~Upon thy~~ Where now ~~even after~~ the worm will feed
>   no more
>
>   . . .
>
> ~~And she~~ these footsteps on the sands are fled
> Thine eyes are dark—thy hands are still
>   cold
> And she is dead—& thou art dead—

The page thus became a sort of *memento mori*: a scrapbook of death, death's pain, and the guilt and questioning it left among the living. At some stage he tore it out and screwed it up, but other hands painstakingly smoothed it out again.

That autumn had also seen a second suicide. In December his wife Harriet, abandoned by him for more than two years but possibly nonetheless pregnant with his child, had drowned herself in the Serpentine. Again, a death 'not to be attributed to me': 'every one does *me* full justice, —bears testimony to the uprightness & liberality of my conduct to her: —There is but one voice in condemnation of the detestable Westbrooks.' This death seemed sometimes to touch him no more than those he had imagined in his Gothic boyhood writings: Louisa sinking on the desert sand, Adolphus sprawled on the black tomb, 'poor Laura' on the mountain in the moonlight. Beyond the mere shock of it, he told Mary, 'so hideous a catastrophe having fallen on a human being once so nearly connected with me', there was 'little to regret'. A silly song dinned in his head, in various versions:

> The death knell is ringing
> The raven is singing
> The earthworm is creeping
> The mourners are weeping
> Heighho!

In truth, however, though he buried it deep, Harriet's death appalled him. Leigh Hunt, who with typically straightforward kindness helped him through the immediate aftermath, thought it 'tore his being to pieces' and was never forgotten. 'Learn to make others happy,' Queen Mab had commanded in the poem Shelley had dedicated in 1813 to his lovely, lively young wife. He had done the reverse. Peacock, noting Shelley's sadness on a walk in Bisham Wood some months after her death, drew from him the admission that he was thinking of her. He was wondering whether, if he took to beer-drinking, he could drive the thought away.

In 1815 or 1816 (he said 1815, but may have been careless, or engaged in mystification) he had written another poem of a young woman dying.

> The moon made thy lips pale, beloved—
> The wind made thy bosom chill—

Some presumed he was meaning Harriet, though this was not her end in any detail. He drew a winter landscape of frost, hedges and thorns in which a girl had lain down on the earth to die, the wind stirring her hair. If this was Harriet he had removed her, tenderly, from the water to the bitter air.

That 'dark dreadful death' had been bad enough. Yet Fanny's end, Shelley told Byron, had caused him 'far severer anguish'. She had been, it seemed, in love with him, though held back by shyness and plainness, and he had registered her hopelessness only in retrospect. He wrote his feelings on the back of the sketch of flowers:

> ~~Friend had I known thy secret grief~~
>
> Her voice did quiver as we parted—
> Yet, knew I not that heart was broken
> From which it came—& I departed
> Heeding not the words then spoken—
> Misery—oh misery
> This world is all too wide for thee!

Fanny had died in a lodging-house in Bath with no dramatics, so properly and quietly in her blue striped skirt and brown fur-trimmed pelisse, a necklace folded in her reticule and in her purse eight shillings and sixpence, a sensible sum for a journey. A small gold watch, Shelley's and Mary's gift from France, had stopped in her pocket. She had taken laudanum. Shelley had raced to Bath on the intimation that she was in danger, scrumpling her last desperate note into his pocket, but he had come too late.

From what did he wish to save her? If earthly life was prison, then death was release, the dissolving of the bonds of the body. In Shelley's 'younger' poems, as he called them, death was already 'a calm habitation' and a friend. The virtuous man, dying in the regenerated world of *Queen Mab*, was full of calm wonder and hope. On her first appearance in Shelley's life, too, the shadow of the Spirit of Beauty 'lured me towards sweet Death', as though they worked together.

At times, being human, he could not repulse a shudder of horror. He lingered over the gluey putrefaction of the flesh, the clinging, choking air of his own decay, his eaten eyes. And yet it was ridiculous to think this way. In the words of Cythna, Laon's young revolutionist-lover in *The Revolt of Islam*,

> 'These are blind fancies—reason cannot know
> What sense can neither feel nor thought conceive;
> There is delusion in the world—and woe,
> And fear, and pain—we know not whence we live,
> Or why, or how, or what mute Power may give
> Their being to each plant, and star, and beast,
> Or even these thoughts. —

Besides, Death's worm-ridden winding-sheets were also mysteriously seductive. In his Italian fable of his youth, 'Una Favola,' the story he had corrected in 1821 with Emilia Viviani in her convent-prison, Death appeared as a beautiful veiled maiden encountered by a young man in a forest. She sewed a shroud on which his name was already half embroidered. And though he had previously been in love with Life, it was now fair Death, 'caressing him and showing him every courtesy both in deed and word', to whom he gave his heart.

Death being so lovely, so inviting, why should he not seek it? Suicide was then the height of fashion. Young men, in imitation of Goethe's despairing Werther, would end their lives impetuously with a draught of wine and a pistol. Why should he not do the same? Debarred from seeing Harriet Grove in January 1811, he took a loaded pistol and 'some poison' to bed with him, but did not die. 'Is suicide wrong?' he asked Hogg afterwards. It had not felt so, but had seemed a natural end to his agitation.

Bold talk often seemed to run ahead of him. In 1817, the mad dreamer Scythrop–Shelley in Peacock's *Nightmare Abbey* proposed leaving the world with 'a pint of port and a pistol' at twenty-five minutes past seven on a Thursday, but avoided the moment of truth by ordering the butler, Raven, to put his watch back. Excuses of some sort or another could usually be found. Shelley and Hunt were once overheard by the local surgeon at Egham 'talking big' about suicide; the surgeon offered his case of instruments for the purpose, but neither young man took him up on it. Shelley himself often stressed that he wanted to live, claiming to Claire that he took 'all sorts of care of myself'. Certainly in 1818, when he was detained by the Italian police for wandering near Lake Como with a loaded pistol, both he and Mary emphatically denied that his purpose had been self-slaughter.

Yet Death drew him. He stood on the brink of precipices, his inspiration-places, coolly considering it. His attitude to his burden of existence, Trelawny said, was 'careless, not to say impatient'. And if death by leaping or pistol shot was perhaps too violent and distressing, there were gentler ways to slip his hand in hers.

The poison that lay by his pillow in 1811 was probably laudanum. At Eton, its pain-soothing power had already delighted him. He took it intermittently at first, then more regularly for agonies of various kinds, until by 1821 he could not be parted from it. Claire claimed he took 'quantities', and that this was the reason he could not distinguish what was false from what was true. The small brown bottle went in his pocket everywhere, though shame made him uncork and gulp it only when he thought no one saw. At least twice, however, he sought death by it. In June 1814, convulsed by his passion for Mary but unable yet to break with Harriet, he showed all the symptoms of addiction. 'Life's sweetest bane', he told Peacock – quoting Sophocles, plugging from the brown bottle, his hair falling into his bloodshot eyes,

is not to be . . .
And when we tread life's thorny steep
Most blest are they, who earliest free
Descend to earth's eternal sleep.

That July – by the wild account of Mrs Godwin, Mary's stepmother – unable to love Mary or even to see her without restriction, he thrust his way into the Godwins' house. He tried violently to force poison on Mary, threatened to shoot himself with a pistol ('this . . . shall reunite me to you'), and then ran away to take laudanum in such quantity that he collapsed and could answer only 'yes' or 'no' to questions. In Naples in 1818, prey to a misery that was always in part mysterious, he seems again to have overdosed deliberately. On both occasions, companions walked him forcibly up and down until the effects were past. On the night of 4 August 1821, his 29th birthday and his last, he took – or implied he took – a double dose of opium quite casually, boasting to Claire afterwards of how well he had slept.

Other poisons fascinated him, though probably as cures for imagined infections rather than doorways to death. He told friends he took arsenic 'inadvertently' at Oxford, ruining his health, in a glass used for mixing lemonade; college teacups he filled with aqua fortis (nitric acid) and aqua regia, possibly sipping these as carelessly as he inhaled the gases he concocted. In his early poems he imagined that yew trees would kill him, exhaling their numbing 'death-drops' in the churchyards where he prowled. For two days in 1811 he made himself ill with 'the poison of laurel leaves', chewed or infused, perhaps imagining they could make him prophesy and sing; some years later he suggested that the wreath of 'false laurel' he wore as a Poet might also, with its chill dark dew, slowly poison him.

In a letter of June 1822 he asked the practical Trelawny if he knew anyone skilled at preparing prussic acid, 'that golden key to the chamber of perpetual rest'. He had no intention, he assured him, of using it there and then, but wanted it in his pocket for the moment when life became unbearable. Plainly fascinated, he underlined every mention of it ('the *Prussic Acid* or *essential oil of bitter almonds*') and began, it seemed, to describe the 'perpetual rest' it would bring him, before smearing out his words with a quick, damp finger. But he had keenly studied its efficacy: 'A single drop, even less, is a dose & it acts by paralysis—'

Dead by his own hand, or worn out by life, he would be buried in an outcast's grave. At sixteen or seventeen he had already foreseen his bones mouldering and his tomb beset by night winds, and had begged Harriet Grove to bestow 'one poor thought on me'. A little later he saw a single tear, shed by an angel, frozen on the icy grass that covered a low-built grave. Purity and virtue received no other notice in the world. In several poems the Poet, passing through to die, left only hearsay that he had leaned against this rock, or wept on this lawn. 'The wild-woods' gloomiest shade' obscured the spot in Cwm Elan where, like a 'wounded echo', he had longed to die. A slight mound of leaves, fast-decaying as the body, marked the grave of the Poet in *Alastor*. In his valetudinarian moods, the only mark Shelley wished to leave on earth was a faint stirring of dust.

Three of his children by Mary went under the earth before him, without memorial. The first, a tiny premature daughter born in February

1815, lived only two weeks, apparently dying of convulsions; her burial was unnoticed, by him at least. The second to die was Clara, aged eighteen months, of typhoid fever in September 1818. She was buried under the wide bare sands of the Venetian Lido, in an unmarked grave. Last came William, three and a half, who on 7 June 1819 succumbed to worms and malaria. For 60 hours Shelley had watched as if his own wakefulness could save him, but Death paid no attention. The little boy was buried in the Protestant cemetery in Rome, under the crumbling red-grey Aurelian walls, on a slope of long grass strewn with daisies. There was to be a monument – an obelisk, or something of plain white marble, like the gleaming pyramid of Cestius that stood close by – but Shelley and Mary, in their grief, could not fix on one.

> The babe is at peace within the womb
> The corpse is at rest within the tomb
> We begin in what we end—

Mary was devastated by the deaths of her children. Shelley's far quicker recovery deepened the estrangement between them. Yet the horror, for him, was not death. True horror was to be condemned, like the Wandering Jew, to eternal earthly life, forever dragging round that worthless body, never able to rest.

In Shelley's youthful version of that story the Jew, a favourite character of his, had been cursed for mocking Christ; he sought death by every means he could, but Death avoided, ignored or rejected him. ('Ha! not to be able to die—not to be able to die—not to be permitted to rest after the toils of life! Awful Avenger in heaven!') In *Queen Mab* Shelley made the Jew a symbol of resignation, a 'scathed' oak blasted by storms who could still spread his weary arms to the sunlight. But this was not yet death.

Death was peace. Shelley imagined that state in the churchyard at Lechlade in Gloucestershire in 1815, in the quiet of a summer evening. He was in the middle of a boating trip on the Thames; now he sat in the dry grass, his arms perhaps still aching from rowing, watching stars and night clouds gather above the faint church spire, and listening to death around him.

> The dead are sleeping in their sepulchres:
> And, mouldering as they sleep, a thrilling sound
> Half sense, half thought, among the darkness stirs,

Breathed from their wormy beds all living things around,
And mingling with the still night and mute sky
Its awful hush is felt inaudibly.

There was no knowing how long that sleep lasted or, if waking came, how it occurred. John Keats's friend Joseph Severn, arguing the night away with Shelley in 1817 (offended, horrified, but clinging on) recalled him quoting Claudio's speech in *Measure for Measure* to prove that Shakespeare, too, saw nothing in death but dissolution. To others, furiously batting away their certainty about the life to come, Shelley quoted the Gaoler's remark from *Cymbeline*. ('Your death has eyes in's head, then; I have not seen him so.')

He longed to die young, swiftly solving the mystery for himself. Failing that, he dreamed of entering an open grave, like a ghost enamoured of a lover's bones. His favourite scene in the Gothic novels of Charles Brockden Brown was the one in *Edgar Huntly* where the villain dug a grave under an elm tree and sat in it, weeping. At some point after the deaths of his children, Shelley dreamed of a marriage bed for him and Mary 'underneath the grave', with Oblivion's stone laid heavily across it. If he, too, were to sit in the fresh-dug earth or to lie in it like a hard, raked bed, perhaps the secrets of the dead would be communicated to him. Yet this was also a dare to be buried in the 'devouring tomb' or 'the obscure, cold, rotting, wormy ground' from which, perhaps, he would not emerge.

A year after the suicides of Fanny and Harriet he pictured himself like a vagrant, loitering, whispering.

> They die—the dead return not—Misery
> Sits near an open grave & calls them over
> A youth with hoary hair & haggard eye—
> They are the names of kindred friend & lover
> Which he so feebly calls—they are all gone
> Fond wretch—all dead—

He got closer, to the edge, leaning over. Discarded lines for *Epipsychidion* preserved the dark flirtation:

> I leapt in
> I leapt out . . .
> ~~How then, over a~~ yawning grave I fell

72

                . . .
          How sadly, words may hide but cannot
                                                    ~~tell~~

          ~~What form what sound what hope~~
                                        ~~did I seek?~~

                ~~what hope~~
          What ~~hope what~~
              Angels lifted me: & kept at bay
              Obl~~ivion~~ sexton   who
          These ~~swarming~~ hours ~~that heap the heavy clay~~
              Upon Upon the shrouded spirits

Reason and experience agreed with the Book of Ecclesiastes, in words
he often repeated, that 'There is no work, nor device, nor knowledge,
nor wisdom, in the grave, whither thou goest.' Hope and imagination
made it less self-evident. From a certain angle, his own sketch of a grave
also looked like a flight of steps down which he might consciously
descend. But Shelley, while a prisoner on earth, could not begin to tell.

3
Masks

Emilia, from her convent-prison, sent him flowers she had grown: mignonette and sweet basil, woven in a wreath together. Dew or rain still dampened them. As Shelley kissed them he imagined her tears on them and on him, nursed and cradled in her arms. Love and health was the message they conveyed to him: his love, his health, which he forlornly told her could not be.

In poem after poem, he hid himself among flowers. The convention was one he delighted in, beauty and mortality combined. In 1810, lamenting his first blighted love for Harriet Grove, he was already a frail anemone under the dark trees. As Lionel, the young, doomed idealist of *Rosalind and Helen*, he gave himself a flower's loveliness, his cheeks 'not pale, but fair,/As rose-o'ershadowed lilies are', but with hair as sparse as the long grass overgrowing graves, hinting at death to come.

Some observers humoured this fancy, describing Shelley (with his shoulders stooped from reading) as a plant deprived of its natural light, or a flower surcharged with rain. Hogg saw him as 'a climber, a creeper, an elegant, beautiful, odoriferous parasitical plant' that needed tying to a firm stick, such as himself. In Shelley's rough drafts the words often sank at the ends of the lines, wilting stems, as in his first version of 'The Indian Serenade':

> I faint   I fail   I die away

Young Thornton Hunt, sitting on his lap once, felt him fall back as though a cruel remark had cut him like a scythe. Friends knew he was not like this; he was vigorous, 'manly' and 'commanding'. But Shelley dwelt on weakness, even indulged it, as if he wished to feel more keenly how tenuous earth-life was.

He knew his flowers, loved them and drew them, especially those of the Sussex woods where he had wandered as a child. The lily of the valley in particular he described with the delicacy of long observation, 'the light of its tremulous bells' seen through 'pavilions of tender green'. But he did not lovingly address flowers, like Wordsworth, or 'herborize' scientifically among them, as Rousseau did. He plucked them as he walked absent-mindedly, barely breaking off from reading. When Hogg in 1821 sent him 'a little flower' from Marlow Shelley knew it at once as milkwort, and pressed it between the leaves of his folio Plato; but he told Hogg once that 'the yellow and blue flowers' were out in the English hedges, and did not trouble to discover the name of the 'radiant' blue specimens whose scent intoxicated him at the Baths of Caracalla in Rome.

His poems were strewn instead with flowers that were oddly sketchy and exotic. In 'The Question', walking in vision by a Sussex turf bank among bluebells, oxlips, green cowbine and wild cherry, he found petals that were azure, black and streaked with gold, and a 'tall flower' that splashed the earth and him with 'Heaven's collected tears'. Over most of them he threw a veil of twilight, moonlight or dreams, confusing their colours further. In a lonely temple on a wooded promontory, more strange arrangements decked an altar:

> crowns of sea-buds white,
> Whose odour is so sweet and faint,
> And weeds, like branching chrysolite . . .

Often his scenes glowed with flowers that were both unearthly and undying. Nepenthe, twined with myrtle or laurel to bring forgetfulness, made wreaths for his heroes; asphodel, the immortal lily, shone on shattered crags and in the meadows; amaranth lay in bright drifts as it had lain that day in Heaven, thick on the celestial pavements, when Milton's golden angels had doffed their crowns to God.

By contrast, earthly flowers withered. When Shelley walked home from writing in Bisham Wood, his head fantastically wreathed with pink-gold honeysuckle and wild clematis, he was draped in beauty that was dying. He thought of his shorter poems as wilting garlands, picked and twisted capriciously as he wandered and living just long enough to be offered to a lover or to Pan, the god of the wild groves. He might, of course, find no takers for them. Dead flowers, dead thoughts; in 1820 he sent Ollier, his publisher, 'all my saddest verses raked up into one heap'.

In this guise, he waited for women to rescue and revive him. Any of those he loved might have been commemorated in one hectic pencilled poem, undated and undatable:

> Upon my heart your accents sweet
>   Of ~~love~~ peace & pity fell like dew
> On flowers half dead, thy lips did meet
>   Mine tremblingly . . .

A dead violet – in a poem 'discovered' for Sophia Stacey, a pretty ward of his uncle's, who visited him in Florence in 1819 – began as a token of lost love but, by the end, was himself in its muteness and sadness. As that violet, he could lie between Sophia's breasts: the nearest he could get to the imagined 'sweet-briar dingle' where they would sink, embracing and entwining, on the secret grass.

For him the act of love was aptly described in the language of plants and flowers. Trees interlaced, tendrils wound about each other, petals opened to the touch of the sun and their perfume fled away. Shelley's senses began to swim then, 'sick with excess of sweetness': the heavy, cloying scent of crimson musk roses in July, or of the meadow of dying jonquils he rode through once in the high Apennines, half fainting in the heat of the day. As their perfume and colour faded his body, too, lost consciousness; after that brief spell of physical splendour came weariness and weakness again.

Sexual love could also deceive him. He pictured it in his poems as bitter-sweet nightshade, bright-berried but deadly, or poisonous white bryony garlanding a cave for erotic and tormented dreams. Love, 'Freedom's own soul', became an unclean passion that clasped and clung to him. From lusts of this sort he shrank in horror. 'No man', he wrote, 'can rise pure from the poisonous embraces of a prostitute.' Even before he touched their bodies he felt their killing contagion, condensing like aphids' glue on the 'green leaves' of his heart. A fragment in Latin in a notebook, later given to Claire, read: 'Why do I drink filthy poison in the cup of life-giving desire?'

Trelawny thought he never dabbled in 'gross amours' of that sort. To love-prone Claire, almost certainly his sometime mistress, Shelley explained that what he felt for Emilia contained no mixture 'of that which you call *love*'. Claire, confused, denied later that 'S was ever in love exactly'. He had hinted rather boastfully to Byron, however, that something more had gone on in Emilia's case, and that 'Mary might be very much annoyed at it': a sign that his sexual virtue was sometimes no more than a pose. To Mary herself, when they were first together, he had admitted that if he could not make love to her more often he would be driven to 'impurity & vice'. ('If I were absent from you long I should shudder with horror at myself.') In his *Discourse on the Manners of the Ancient Greeks* he confessed, delicately and offhandedly, to routine masturbation; and on a spare page among some calculations he drew, carefully, curiously and completely, his own erect penis.

His attitude was often confused in his writings. The physical mechanics of the 'act' itself were sometimes made so disgusting to him by the dead ties of law, custom and propriety that he seemed to wish, like his madman-self in *Julian and Maddalo*,

> That, like some maniac monk, I had torn out
> The nerves of manhood by their bleeding root
> With mine own quivering fingers, so that ne'er
> Our hearts had for a moment mingled there
> To disunite in horror—

His body became as disgusting to him then as flaccid-skinned dead lilies, or 'blistering' death-plants, or the tall, pale fungi whose flesh hung away from them in rags. But this was earthly life, whose chains had already rubbed a 'canker' on his soul like an open wound on a stem.

Two flowers in particular he made his own. Withered pansies, together with faded violets 'white and pied and blue', wreathed his head in *Adonais*, the elegy he wrote for Keats in 1821. The choice seemed strange, for pansies symbolised memory and thoughts, from which he spent his days escaping. Yet by the same token they made a fitting garland for his earthly self, 'eyed flowers' with faces like masks. '*Pansies let my flowers be*,' he wrote in his last months, inserting it in dark, emphatic ink in a poem that was redolent of loneliness and lost hope.

His second flower was more obscure. In December 1821, a time of apparent merry socialising, shooting and billiards with Byron and other friends in Pisa, he played on Claire's nickname for him, 'the Exotic'. This flower, he told her, 'unfortunately [belongs] to the order of mimosa', unable to bear society and drooping in 'a frost both moral & physical— a solitude of the heart—'

He drew himself thus in 'The Sensitive Plant', a symbol of all human beings, struggling to survive in an Eden-garden from which all Beauty had fled. That plant, *Mimosa pudica*, was hermaphrodite, with male and female flowers sharing a stem and feathery leaves that folded at a shadow, or a touch. Shelley-like, it grew alone. It was almost constantly aroused, quivering with desire 'from the leaf to the root', yet could never find love to match the love it felt. Out of all the flowers in the garden, dusk or Death – whatever Death was – would undoubtedly claim it first.

> A sweet child weary of its delight,
> The feeblest and yet the favourite,
> Cradled within the embrace of Night.

★   ★   ★

He wanted pansies on his grave, but no tears and no stone. It was better to remove, if possible, all names and labels from himself. He was 'Bysshe' at home, 'Percy' to the two Harriets he loved when young, 'Shelley' to Mary, and seemed to take no pride in any of them. At school his name, howled by dozens of boys, had been used to torment him. On a shout of 'Shelley! Shelley! Shelley!' they would run after him, claw him with their hands and make the slipping books cascade from his arms.

He affixed that name to only eight of his 14 poetical publications, cutting out the title page from *Queen Mab*, which he had published and distributed himself. *Julian and Maddalo* was not to have his name 'annexed' to the first edition, and for *The Cenci*, the only history play he finished, he wanted 'a complete incognito'. On works that were attributed, he hardly minded whether 'Shelley' appeared or not. 'I do not care,' he told his friend Hunt, as Hunt prepared in 1816 to publish the 'Hymn to Intellectual Beauty', Shelley's account of his boyhood conversion, in the *Examiner*. 'As you like. And yet the poem was composed under the influence of feelings which agitated me even to tears, so that I think it deserves a better fate than the being linked with so stigmatised & unpopular a name ... as mine.' In 1821 the same conviction held him back from being more than 'a sort of link' between Hunt and Byron in a new literary periodical, the *Liberal*. 'I am, and I desire to be, nothing.'

Prosecutions for blasphemous libel, a constant threat in those nervy years, did not bother him. In principle he claimed to think anonymity

81

was wrong; yet, almost compulsively, he disguised himself. His novel *Zastrozzi*, published when he was eighteen, carried only his initials on the title page. The 'Hymn to Intellectual Beauty' eventually appeared over 'E.K.', the Elfin Knight: Spenser's bold Redcrosse from *The Faerie Queene*, whose virtue and boldness for truth lit up the darkness before him. *Peter Bell the Third*, a satire on Wordsworth, was written by 'Miching Mallecho', a tag from *Hamlet* ('it means mischief'). Two political pamphlets of 1817, *A Proposal for Putting Reform to the Vote Throughout the Kingdom* and *An Address to the People on the Death of the Princess Charlotte*, were the work of 'The Hermit of Marlow'. As for *Epipsychidion*, published in 1821, Shelley's metaphysical retelling of his progress through earthly love in search of his 'soul's soul' and of Beauty, this was 'found amongst other papers in the Portfolio of a young Englishman'

> with whom the Editor had contracted . . . an intimacy at Florence . . . He was an accomplished & amiable person but his error was, θυητος ὠυ μη θυητά φρουειν—[though mortal, not to think of mortal things] . . .

He tried again.

> ~~The following Poem was found in the P.F. of a young Englishman, who died in his passage from Leghorn to the Levant. He had bought one of the Sporades~~ He was accompanied by a lady ~~who might have been~~ appeared to be his wife, & an effeminate looking youth, to whom he showed . . . so ~~singular~~ excessive an attachment as to give rise to the suspicion, that she was a woman . . .

And again; this version especially smudged and blotted, and closer to the track of his life.

> The writer of these lines died at Florence ~~in January 1820~~, while he was preparing to leave Italy for one of the wildest of the Sporades, which he had bought & fitted up the ruins of some old building— His life was singular, less on account of the romantic vicissitudes which diversified it, than the ideal tinge, which they received from his own character & feelings . . .

Readers might smile, he supposed, 'at the expense of my unfortunate friend'. He hoped it would be a smile 'not of contempt, but pity.'

The drafts of these advertisements were almost illegible, the letters barely formed in his haste to scrawl them down. He signed the final version 'S.', the editor of his own life. Elsewhere, he enjoined strict secrecy on others. 'If you tell no one *whose* they are, you are welcome to them,' he told Sophia Stacey of the erotic verses he sent her. Old and dull as they were, or as he claimed they were, he thought them almost worthless, but because '[they] look as if they were dictated by the heart', he gave them to her. In 1813 he had approached his boyhood poems with the same professed indifference. 'Being unwilling to offer any outrage to the living portraiture of my own mind', or 'as it appears to shew what I then thought of eternal life' they were worth preserving, like artefacts in a museum. Otherwise they were mostly 'trash', as he later claimed to think *Queen Mab* was.

To blur the trail further, he obscured when poems were written. In June 1811, from Field Place, he sent Hogg poems many months old on the pretence that they had been composed that night, in the rush of maddened love and the chill fear of pacing Warnham churchyard in the dark. In Pisa eleven years later he gave his new love Jane Williams a 'melancholy old song', glistening with fresh despair, which he claimed to have redacted from the torn leaf of a book long out of date. He laid false trails, perhaps unwittingly, rewriting old material in new note-books or hiding his 'scraps' in the middle of blank pages, where later verses would grow in a thicket round them.

Most habitually, he filled his poems with scenes and figures which begged to be decoded, but which were likelier to be symbols or idealisms than actual fragments of his past. In *Epipsychidion*

> One, whose voice was venomed melody
> Sate by a well, under blue nightshade bowers;
> The breath of her false mouth was like faint flowers,
> Her touch was as electric poison,—

This was perhaps his wife Harriet; perhaps an Oxford prostitute who had infected him with venereal disease; perhaps some chemical substance he had imbibed rashly and experimentally; perhaps disappointing Love, or slyly beckoning Death. In cancelled lines, he tried to be more cryptic still:

> ~~She was not there . . . and she~~
> ~~And she was not~~
> ~~That O then ye dumb words hide what ye cannot paint~~ tell

Two lines further on came a single word, written plain and stark:

chaos

His chaos, his life.

The 'young Englishman' and exile who had written this poem had had no intention of disclosing its secrets. In any case, drowned or buried by Shelley's own offices, he was now beyond the reach of questions. As for the poem itself, it was 'a production of a portion of me already dead; and in this sense the advertisement is no fiction'. If anyone was curious, it could tell them something of 'what I am and have been', but Shelley scarcely wanted that. With this as with other poems he severed his connection, almost brutally. In place of him, as he slid away, he invited his readers to put themselves.

★   ★   ★

His letters, too, were sometimes deliberately mystifying. They might go out under different names or with instructions to reply to some invention. From Oxford 'innocent' atheistical arguments were begun, by post, with perfect strangers; to these at various times he was Mr Peyton, Jeremiah Stukeley, the Revd. Charles Meyton, Mr Jones. He would then, in Hogg's words, 'fall upon the unwary disputant, and break his bones'.

The Revd. Meyton was said to be ancient and much-beneficed; indeed, his health had been broken by trips to foreign parts, including Palestine, which 'resembled a stone-quarry more than any thing else'. Philippe Sydney, though perhaps a boy, wrote letters as silly and gushing as a girl's. But these were really just *noms de guerre* or hiding names to flummox the clergy, or his father, or the Post Office, or whatever enemies and government agents Shelley thought were spying on his movements. 'I shall come & live near you as Mr Peyton,' he told Hogg in August 1811, contriving to re-establish the physical contact forbidden by his father since their expulsion five months before,

> and as
>   Your most faithful friend
>   P.B.S—

Some names hid deeper mysteries. 'Joe James' and 'Mr Jones' were aliases to keep from Mary his correspondence with Claire, of which she was justifiably jealous and suspicious, and details of a baby, Elena Adelaide Shelley. Elena was possibly his own; gossiping tongues supposed the mother to be Claire or Elise, the Shelleys' Swiss maid. Whatever the answer, Shelley took charge of her in 1820, paying for some months from Pisa for her care in Naples. His letters shed almost no light on her, except to record her death that June from teething and fever. A little before, the shadow regretted the shadow: 'I suppose she will die, and leave another memory to those which already torture me.'

Even as 'Shelley', he hid himself in his letters. One side only was on display at any time. To his publishers and his banker he was abrupt, precise and businesslike. To those who disappointed him he was preachy and sanctimonious. His letters to Peacock, intended for publication, disguised him as a literary gazeteer. Those to Byron were the respectful missives of a lesser poet to a greater – the greatest of the age, as he thought him – or a suppliant to a patron, or sometimes the proper, pursed-lipped productions of a pure man addressing a libertine.

In all of these he professed the utmost candour. Godwin's *Political Justice* had taught him that frankness and sincerity, to the point of fearlessness, were the core virtues of the good man. Yet beyond a fervent, gripping handshake, often with both hands, little more of himself was laid open to inspection. In June 1811 he began a correspondence with Elizabeth Hitchener, a thin, spinsterish, gushing schoolmistress he had met at his uncle's in Cuckfield; in six months his letters flew from 'My dear Madam' to 'My beloved friend', confiding 'everything that passes in my soul, even the secret thoughts sacred alone to sympathy'. But the fit passed, and he never showed his mind so completely to any correspondent again. 'We all act a false part in the world,' he scrawled in a notebook at the top of a page. At the bottom, other way up, came a sketch of a youth with straggling hair in a revolutionary Phrygian cap.

Just occasionally he managed the 'complete incognito' he was after. On a surreptitious visit home in 1814 at his mother's instigation, he hitched a lift for the last few miles with a farmer driving a cart. Perched beside him, his long hair almost giving him away, he asked questions about Percy Bysshe Shelley and received, very pleasingly, the answer that some people thought him deranged and that 'young Master Shelley never went to church'. Once at Field Place, his father safely away, he swapped clothes with a visiting army officer and called himself Captain Jones. A scarlet jacket was put on him; his hair was cut and the peaked cap stuffed with paper to sit properly on his small, round head. He thus became one of those 'mechanized automatons', killers for hire, who had been billeted up and down England ostensibly to save it from the French. As such, his father might have welcomed him.

He acquired nicknames, and seemed fond of them. (He also loved to assign them to other people: 'Albé', from 'LB', for Byron, 'Leontius', a Latinate pun, for Hunt.) He may not have known that Byron called him Shiloh, after the seraph-man a crazed prophetess, Joanna Southcott, believed she would give birth to. But he knew he was 'the Conchoid' to Hunt and Peacock in 1817, a shy but spiky-limbed creature disappearing into his shell. He became 'Don Quixote' and *el ingenioso hidalgo* for his tendency, as at school, to catapult himself into fights. And from Italy he imagined himself on the English stage as a shadow Harlequin, the sad masked lover in his patchwork clothes, pelted with popular abuse.

Still better was the smiling question of Emilia, thinking in Italian, when she first heard he was Percy: '*Persi*? Lost?'

Yes, lost. Percy, *Persi, orfana anima*, as he wrote to her: 'that orphan one' without father, or mother, or a past that he was willing to recognise as his.

★   ★   ★

Intruders came to his house to find him. Sometimes they knocked him down with sticks, or tried to shoot him through the curtains. More often they cooled their heels on the doorstep, hats and canes under their arms, ready to squeeze their faces into an ingratiating smile.

From upstairs he could smell them. From the very way a visitor rang the doorbell, he could tell it was a bore arriving. He would hide, therefore, leaving by the back door or crouching in the shade of the lane; he would be out, and make the servant fake his apologies. At Marlow he sprang once from the library window and raced across to Peacock's house, where he lay low for the rest of the day. In Pisa the shutters could be barred from the inside, keeping the world away. At Oxford too he had exclaimed often – clasping his hands, shrilling with delight – what a blessing it was to signal, by closing the oak outer door of his room, that he wanted no one in his secret place.

The bore, gaining admittance, would look for signs of him. He might imagine he found them in the books piled everywhere, in tangled knots of discarded stockings, in the faint mark of Shelley's lips on a cup of congealing tea. A night-table by the bed held notebooks, a pen and ink; the bore could find scribbles there, and fragments of his dreams. But the Poet was out and gone.

In 1822 he imagined leaving a general note of rebuff on his door:

> Reflexion, you may come tomorrow,
> Sit by the fireside with Sorrow—
> You, with the unpaid bill, Despair,
> You, tiresome verse-reciter Care,
> I will pay you in the grave . . .

Hogg said he could be tracked by breadcrumbs. Following these, the determined pursuer would eventually come to a pool, or rock, or tree where the Poet, stripped of appurtenances sometimes as far as naked-ness, would look up and sigh at the sight of him.

Trelawny, wishing for an Indian's skills, tracked him once to such a place near Pisa. Through acres of pines and hummocky, sandy wilder-ness he followed rumours of *l'Inglese malincolico* until his spoor appeared. He found papers, books, a hat, dropped here and there on the grass. Spotting the Poet among the trees, he slowed his pace and pretended he was not there. At last he spoke. Shelley said, faintly, 'Hullo'.

From morning until dark he had probably sat there, alone. Trelawny said his life was 'utterly solitary, almost without a parallel'. Yet this soli-tude was not completely natural to him. Already in 1810, at eighteen, he had upbraided himself for daring to live alone, uncaring, 'an isolated thing'. Five years later the Poet of *Alastor* was haunted and plagued by the Spirit of Solitude; even the touch of a human hand, or the appel-lation 'brother' or 'friend' ('false names') drove him like a wraith away. He had chosen a life of companionless searching after idealised desire; yet he longed, at one level, for earthly society and love. 'Among those who attempt to exist without human sympathy,' Shelley wrote,

> the pure and tender-hearted perish through the intensity and passion of their search after its communities, when the vacancy of their spirit suddenly makes itself felt.

He too lived with men and women and yet apart from them, consciously uncomfortable in the press of the world, striving to be 'himself alone'. That last, frequent phrase carried melancholy and difficulty, as well as the sense that this was the only thing he should aim for.

He did not, therefore, hate company. He thought it, as he told Peacock, 'almost' a necessity of life. But the society of two or three was all he needed. A jotting of October 1814 showed him, in his own mind, the still and disciplined centre of the new-formed tiny household of himself, Mary and Claire, into which no other person was to introduce disturbance. The presence of Claire introduced disturbance enough, for in 1816 she became Byron's lover, bore his child, was rejected by him and found comfort in Shelley, to Mary's intense irritation. But Shelley both welcomed her company, and needed it, for most of the time that he and Mary were together. Two women and himself, loosening the monopoly of 'the society of one' (no matter what the cost in jealousy and unhappiness) was his ideal all through his life. Most other would-be familiars he rebuffed. Only one visitor at a time, he wrote, should be allowed 'even to approach the hallowed circle'. 'We see no one' was a frequent remark in his letters from abroad. He did not seem sorry.

Unnecessary socialising was almost offensive to him. At Marlow he gave out that the family in Albion House (The Hermitage, as it was known locally) would associate with no one in the town and would never go to church. In Pisa once, poor party-loving Mary proposed a musical soirée; Shelley was so appalled that he could not sit or read until the plan was abandoned. If Shelley came to dinner, he sometimes left without speaking a word; if he appeared at a ball, he often fled while the introductions were still warm. When escape was impossible, he would abstract himself. He wanted no part of the strutting and social preening of the 'apes asses geese' who attended such functions, or of 'that common, false, cold, hollow talk/ Which makes the heart deny the *yes* it breathes.'

He was aware, for it was obvious, that political reformers belonged in the world. In practical terms, he could do it. In Ireland in 1812 he canvassed in the streets and addressed a packed assembly hall in the cause of Catholic Emancipation, with some success. Proudly, he sent Godwin a clipping of his speech from the *Weekly Messenger*, recommending 'the account of ME'. The emphasis was probably deliberate, for this was a *me* he could acknowledge: 'bold', 'intrepid', a '*missionary of truth*', as the Irish reporter painted him. Shelley drew himself on a page from another Dublin newspaper, a sinewy youth in a shirt collar but otherwise naked, clearing out bad demons with a stick and a broom.

At odd moments he toyed with politics, 'the best career', or with colonial administration. He seemed almost to envy Peacock his job at the India House, and talked of working at the court of an Indian prince. But in the end, as he told Horace Smith in 1822, 'I am glad that my good genius said *refrain*.' Like Socrates, whose daemon had given him the same advice, his path was solitary. It led not only away from society's wearying contamination, but away from the earthly aspects of himself. It led, somehow, to truth.

Alone, then, he waited – longed – for Shelley to disappear.

★   ★   ★

In 1822 two words appeared, faintly and sideways, at the top of a page of his notebook, hovering above a drawing of a tree:

Killing
Self

He may not have meant suicide. Most probably, for it obsessed him far more, he meant the suppression of the selfish instinct. 'I am sick to Death at the name of *self*,' he wrote to Hogg in 1811. And again, to Hunt in 1819, disdaining to put his name to a poem, 'So much for self—*self*, that burr that will stick to one.' He gave self-love its Greek name, *philautia*, like some scabby condition of the skin: the disease of fame, lands, titles, honours, exclusive happiness. All that he owned and experienced in the craving shell of the body was not *me*, his true self, but *mine*, the burden of possession. 'Thou makest me to *possess* the iniquities of my youth,' he cried out, like Job, in a notebook of 1821, desperately trying again to shed the burden of his past.

Self-interest was the essence of the world he moved in. Shelley traced to it every child crying with hunger, every wasted labourer, the pollution of cities, the filthy opulence of monarchs, war and desolation. He traced God, for at the beginning of man's history

> Some moon-struck sophist stood
> Watching the shade from his own soul upthrown
> Fill Heaven and darken Earth, and in such mood
> The Form he saw and worshipped was his own . . .

Self-interest made men acquiesce in tyranny, bringing their evils wilfully upon themselves, enthroning both 'the oppression and the oppressor'. All moral and social wrong and all false gods sprang from self-love and therefore, also, from himself, sitting in the chaos of his own self-centred thoughts. This was 'the horror the *evil* that comes to self in solitude'.

Between self-love and self-esteem there was a vital difference. He

89

tried to define it. The worst part of poverty, he wrote, was not fear, homelessness, cold or pain, though all were dreadful, but

> that inward stain
> Foul Self-contempt, which drowns in sneers
> Youth's starlight smile . . .

To know the true self, to base all upon it, though with no hint of self-ishness, was Shelley's ideal. His three cardinal virtues were Love, Hope and Self-Esteem, that confident sense of equality with the stars.

The pure Godwinian system was meant to turn men outwards, towards the other. The virtuous man practised both philanthropy and *aphilautia*, lack of self-love (Shelley's own word, half-borrowed from Aristotle), for an action could only be generous and good in so far as it was disinterested. In the tiny complacent empire of himself he needed to rule like an ascetic despot – wanting nothing, dreading nothing – and then smash down the walls.

> Man who man would be,
> Must rule the empire of himself; in it
> Must be supreme, establishing his throne
> On vanquished will,—quelling the anarchy
> Of hopes and fears,—being himself alone—

In his endlessly improving world, the shift towards *aphilautia* would supposedly be easy. Once labour, money and possessions were made equal, once men in their hours of leisure and tranquillity turned towards Truth and Good, the circumference of their pity would expand to embrace the whole of man. It would include revolutionists in Spain, loom-breakers in distant counties, imprisoned pamphleteers in Ireland, press-ganged sailors on the high seas, until philanthropy rolled like a tide over 'this wrong world', and there were no more press-gangs or prisons. 'A man,' Shelley wrote,

> to be greatly good, must imagine intensely and comprehensively; he must put himself in the place of another and of many others; the pains and pleasures of his species must become his own.

'The only perfect and genuine republic', he wrote elsewhere, 'is that which comprehends every living being.'

Shelley's own Poet's life put him deeply, or so it seemed, in the selves and the miseries of others. He ached with the aged, crippled woman gathering firewood to supplement parish charity; he throbbed with the pride of a freedom fighter, wrapped in his gore-soaked flag, dying on the field in Mexico. Without entering the lead pencil factory or the woollen mill at Keswick (though in the autumn of 1811 he lived not far away), he could feel the despair of the women workers who drowned their infants in the river. From Italy in 1819 ('indignation . . . boiling in my veins') he could stand on the trampled grass at Peterloo, seeing the 'red mist' of 'this bloody murderous oppression', hearing the screams. He could walk, too, in a London street at night, slowly discerning the shapes and the horrors:

> —a shabby stand
> Of Hackney coaches—a brick house or wall
> Fencing some lonely court, white with the scrawl
> Of our unhappy politics;—or worse—
> A wretched woman reeling by . . .

Before his eyes as he wrote were fireflies, far cornfields and vineyards, 'a chaos of green leaves and fruit' under a moonlit Italian sky. At the circumference of his thought was that London street, darkness, the public coach stand, and one of those 'miserable beings', racked with disease and victimised by Chastity, whose fate he longed to change. In sympathy and love he stood beside her and stretched out a ghostly, rescuing hand.

He desired the same himself. If he extended his human sympathy to others he desperately and urgently wanted it returned, especially by the women with whom he had chosen to live. Yet too often, as it seemed to him, he found only a world 'in which I moved alone'. He was not, after all, the inevitable centre of anyone else's affections; whether or not he loved them, their own love did not unswervingly come to rest in him. He was resisted, argued with, silently left alone. Hunt saw him at parties suddenly sink 'into an expression of misgiving and even of destitution' as he realised that his sympathy was not returned by those around him. With Harriet, her baby and her whispering sister Eliza were preferred to him. With Mary, mourning for her children and sad resentment gradually froze him out. He sympathised with himself, naturally, rather than with them. Self, 'that burr', expostulated, moped, grew self-pitying and quiet.

So he struggled. He had leisure, he had money enough, he was ardent for Beauty and Truth, yet Self would not leave him alone. It took restless, irritating forms: '*Vanity* ... vanity perhaps unconfessed yet self centred self-possessing'. The cynicism and worldliness he regretted in Byron some-times rose to the surface in himself, mocking his idealism and disputing with him like his limping, dashing friend. By moments he too in argu-ment got vicious, personal and hurtful. He embraced 'the indolence of scepticism', though it 'gives us no additional insight into our hidden nature', because Hume and Locke were better for waging verbal warfare. He blamed the French materialists (once he had stopped reading them himself) for binding him so tightly to the realm of Earth and senses.

As a poet, 'the author to others of the highest wisdom, pleasure, virtue, and glory', he should have been above all this. But he could not will or control the poetic power, and when it lapsed he was merely a man again. As such, stupidly, his own feelings fascinated him: whether he loved or how much he was loved, the precise depth of the well of his own unhappiness. He seemed, to himself, nothing but 'an assem-blage of inconsistent & discordant portions', without focus or concen-tration. Out of this 'stormy mist of sensations' came poetry of a sort, in short lyric bursts or with the deadly rhythm of chains moving. He seldom thought it was any good. Writing to Hogg, he dismissed his lines about the frozen tear on the grave:

> As to the stuff wch. I sent you, I write all my poetry of that kind from the feelings of the moment ... it is another proof of that egotizing variability whilst I shudder when I reflect how much I am in it's power.

He was glad, he told a friend in 1821, that he had not known the details of Keats's death when he composed *Adonais* for him, or 'the enthusiasm of the imagination would have been overpowered by senti-ment'. As it was, the dead poet, pale and beautiful as a 'broken lily', tears trembling 'on the silken fringe of his faint eyes', was also Shelley in death, heartbreakingly sentimentalised.

Inevitably, his senses made an egoist of him. 'I *will* feel no more! it is selfish—' he cried to Hogg, but then went on as usual. ('What strange being I am, how inconsistent'.) Though he knew his own heart lay open to every tremor, and spoke of himself as 'a nerve o'er which do creep/ The else unfelt oppressions of this earth', he wrote less often of others' woes than of the reed-like nerve itself. He lay on the sofa, sensing the sinews of his feelings palpitate and tighten; he took tea in others' parlours, 'where small talk dies in agonies', wondering if the rattle of the cup in the saucer portended his decline and death. In his notebooks again and again appeared profiles and fragments of his own face: a sharp nose, a weak chin, wispy hair, wild eyes. They poked into his poems, inquisitive and lean.

In the mirror as he shaved with the open blade stood Self, staring. He could try out smiles, as in his poems: quiet smiles of magnanimity, bitter smiles of scorn, smiles that hid despair. He was not like the other 'apes of humanity', he once told Hunt, 'who make mouths in the glass of the time'. Indeed, his reasons for writing were 'totally different'. Yet the mirror sent back the image of an ordinary, haunted man.

> Sick to death of the name of *self*
> Killing
> Self

* * *

In December 1812 Shelley addressed Fanny, Godwin's shy stepdaughter, who had been wondering whether it was 'proper' to write to him: .

> . . . who & what am I? I am one of those formidable & long clawed animals called a *Man*, & it is not until I have assured you that I am one of the most inoffensive of my species, that I live on vegetable food, & never bit since I was born that I venture to obtrude myself on your attention.

He might be no carnivore, but Shelley could crook his fingers into talons, scratching the air, or screw his long curls grimly into a devilish horn. He could caper and scream at night on Hampstead Heath, now from mounds, now from behind trees, leaping through the prickling, writhing gorse. Claw-branches, claw-hands, fantastic contortions of terror.

Monster-Shelley, looking in the mirror, saw his face split by a shining scar between blind left eye and cheek. He looked again and saw a wide, gaping, Cheshire-cat smile, with no face. A scrawl in a notebook, in pencil:

> I fear that I am hardly human

At Eton once, some boys blacked his face while he was asleep. When he woke he was wild with horror.

Monster-Shelley, out in the garden at Field Place, played games of tipping his little brother out of the baby-carriage into the cabbages, or knocking him down on the lawn. He taught him to lisp 'devil'. His sisters were enjoined to hold hands and be electrified by his galvanic machine. If the Great Old Snake in the garden did not get them, Shelley could scare them as badly with a piece of folded brown packing-paper, a bottle, a wire and a promise that their chilblains would instantly be cured.

At Field Place in May 1811, back in disgrace from Oxford, he kept his own company. Silence surrounded him. He wandered the halls, scorning the lot of them. If his mother or sisters came past he could 'rack my phiz into a smile' most obligingly, the smile of the cruel beaked griffin that crouched on the Shelley coat of arms. In October, suddenly returning to confront his father and scream for his allowance, he frightened the girls so much that, in his father's words, 'now if they hear a Dog Bark they run up stairs'.

Mary once began, in the joint journal, a recipe for medicine for a baby's convulsions:

> a table spoonful of the spirit of aniseed with a small quantity of sper-maceti

Shelley finished it.

> 9 drops of human blood—7 grains of gunpowder
> ½ an oz of putrefied brain   13 mashed grave worms—

Supping on a favourite dish of panada, bread soaked with hot water and strewn with red-brown nutmeg, he shouted: 'I lap up the blood of the slain!' Or, better yet, 'the gore of murdered kings!'

94

Reviewing Mary's *Frankenstein* in 1817 (her first production, which he had eagerly encouraged, corrected, promoted), he found brotherhood with the gruesome monster Frankenstein had created, the would-be benefactor of mankind who was reviled and driven away. He wept with him in his friendless innocence, the tears running down his yellow cheeks and over his thin black lips. Convulsively, his hands worked through his matted, flowing hair. He was thrust down and beaten with sticks.

He hated, though he knew this was also tyrant behaviour. The world would not be changed without a good cathartic dose of it. Critics were 'venal villains' or screaming carrion kites; his friends the Gisbornes, in one moment of sharp disappointment, were 'altogether the most filthy & odious animals with which I ever came in contact'. Eliza Westbrook was a 'beastly viper' and a 'perfect Ghoul' for whom his hate was so deep as to be unknowable. He watched in desperate disgust as she held and rocked his baby Ianthe, transmitting like a plague her obsessions with propriety and nerves. Forced to take dinner with Mrs Godwin, Mary's stepmother, he would 'lean back in his chair and languish into hate'. Not the least of Mary's attributes, he told Hogg, was that she could hate when needed.

If there were *love* songs, he asked Hunt, why should there not be *hate* songs? He meant to write one, and did:

> A Hater he came and sat by a ditch,
> And he took an old cracked lute;
> And he sang a song which was more of a screech
> 'Gainst a woman that was a brute.

Others followed against Castlereagh, the Foreign Secretary, and Sidmouth, the Home Secretary who had spied on him. They were 'gibbering night-birds', 'bloodless wolves', or a shark and a dogfish 'wrinkling their red gills the while' as they prepared to feast on the corpses of slaves flung over-board. Especial, fulminating hate was called down in curses on Lord Eldon, the Chancellor who in 1817, citing Shelley's immorality, had removed his children by Harriet and placed them with sober church-going folk:

> By all the hate which checks a father's love—
> By all the scorn which kills a father's care—
> By those most impious hands which dared remove
> Nature's high bounds—by thee—and by despair—

Shelley's first draft – though he was crying, howling at the thought of his own blood in his children's veins and their souls' 'pollution' by Eldon and their guardians – was almost as calm and focused as if he were writing to his banker. Hate disciplined him.

He fixed his eyes on people: the eyes of his poems, yellow, vacant, stiff, like orbs of ivory in which nothing was reflected. He stared without seeming to see. 'Take your eyes off!' Claire begged him once. (It was two in the morning; they had been talking, low over the fire, about cutting squares of skin from soldiers' backs.) His expression of 'deep & melancholy awe' was terrifying to her; though he covered his face she still felt, and he wished her to feel, the horror of his shining eyes. He could not – would not – take them off, nor repress the 'unutterable' look in them. But he could extract them, as in his sketches, turn them into globes, put them on boats, set them afloat. He could find them in his waistcoat pockets, into which they had slowly slithered as he read too much and too late.

They could also disappear, gouged out and withered in the blinded face of any citizen of the world. Ginotti, the self-destroying seeker of his boyhood novel *St Irvyne*, had eyeless sockets in which 'two pale and ghastly flames' flickered into view. The shade of Rousseau, encountered as a dried-out root in *The Triumph of Life*, had holes where his eyes should have been. It was Shelley's special pleasure to dwell, in his translation of the *Cyclops* of Euripides, on the efforts of Ulysses's men to 'drag & scoop & pull' the single huge eye of the giant Polyphemus.

Eyes also appeared in place of women's nipples, a persistent Shelley nightmare. He imagined them in 1816 as Byron recited Coleridge's 'Christabel' and rushed from the room, screaming. His friends found him leaning on a mantelpiece, bathed in cold sweat and terror. Gazing at Mary, he said, he had suddenly thought of eyes in breasts and of a woman who was said to have them. Eliza Westbrook, he told friends, also had eyes there. She had showed them to him as part of a ghoulish seduction, together with knives which she had brandished like a cannibal in his face.

Horror was the fashion, and he revelled in it. Fear heightened sensibility, offering an entry into the mystery of himself or the selves of others, and terror outlined the places where he dreaded, or desired, to go. Monster-Shelley therefore peopled his poems with night-hags and hell-hounds, with 'such shapes as haunt/ Wet clefts,—and lumps neither alive nor dead, /Dog-headed, bosom-eyed'. The tongues of dying soldiers 'lolled into the air,/Flaccid and foamy, like a mad dog's hanging'. The Furies, as he imagined them, were huge insect forms 'hollow underneath, like death'. He recited horror tales aloud, his own and other people's, in his thrilling, shrieking voice:

> O Mother, Mother!
> Gone is gone!
> Lost is lost!

During musical evenings in London with gentle vegetarian friends, he would take the children into a corner of the dining-room and there, in a 'low and sepulchral' voice, terrify them with ghosts. The word 'ghastly' he used often, dropping his jaw and widening his eyes; 'How rare and grim!', mouthing the words with shuddering delight. Harriet under his influence grew 'truly petrified' of goblins, the Devil and the possibility that her husband would be murdered by the men in black. Byron once begged him, or so he claimed, not to talk of Hell or ghosts after dark. It made him uneasy.

And Shelley knew all about Hell. It was a city much like London, 'a populous and a smoky city', in which, as he surveyed it in 1819 in *Peter Bell the Third*,

> There is great talk of revolution—
>   And a great chance of despotism—
> German soldiers—camps—confusion—
>   Tumults—lotteries—rage—delusion—
>   Gin—suicide—and methodism . . .

The Devil roamed there. 'Who the Devil is the Devil?' Shelley cried out once (deep in Luke's gospel, noting down the revolution-talk). But he had already answered his question. Satan was 'what we are'. In 1812 Shelley had drawn him with hooves and claws (though gloves hid them) and with a snout like Castlereagh's; seven years later, he was merely a 'toad-like lump', 'with smug face, and eye severe'. He could travel in thunderstorms, leaving behind him a litter of scorched bibles and smashed glass; but he was also a man about town, driving smart carriages and, by assiduous circulation of punch and madeira, drawing his followers to the most genteel damnation. In Earth-Hell poets suppressed their most sublime inspirations, as Shelley believed Wordsworth had in middle age, in order to curry favour with the power-brokers of the day. But Shelley was at Satan's parties too, preening, self-interested, sipping tea, like any other sycophantic guest.

> And this is Hell—and in this smother
>   All are damnable and damned;
> Each one damning, damns the other;
> They are damned by one another,
>   By none other are they damned.

Everyone in Shelley's Hell-city had forgotten their true selves long ago. Processing blindly in the thick infected air, lawyers and jobbers and bishops thrown together, none knew why he was there or where he was going. Many wore masks, hiding their better natures behind Murder, Robbery, Fraud or the dry mutual dislike that followed love in marriage. In *The Mask of Anarchy*, Shelley's fulminating cry against repression in England, leering government ministers led them:

> Clothed with the Bible, as with light,
> And the shadows of the night,
> Like Sidmouth, next, Hypocrisy
> On a crocodile rode by.

'Thrusting, toiling, wailing, moiling', the crowd surged on, oblivious to the dark fiend who 'with his iron pen/ Dipped in scorn's fiery poison' made his den in their hearts.

Carnival, which he witnessed in Pisa, was especially appalling to Shelley. The joyous crowds wore masks on top of masks, scarcely able to see at all in the gaudy, raucous parade. His cousin Tom Medwin saw him come in once from the festive streets and throw himself into a chair, 'overpowered by the atmosphere of evil passions, as he used to say, in that sensual and unintellectual crowd'. He tried to keep away, but was haunted by it. The crowd profiles ranged in his notebooks were often expressionless and eyeless. At Ferrara he saw a type of all these men and women, a Penitent in a drapery of white flannel with a network visor over his face. The man passed him, blind, 'rattling his wooden box for charity'.

Shelley too prowled among these figures, disguised as he chose, in the smoke and dark of his own alienation from Truth, from Beauty and from himself. In his occasional bouts of ophthalmia he too was blind, his eyes clogged with 'frozen glue', unable to write or read and conscious only of his struggling body, which revolted him. Alone in London in 1811, he told Hogg he often found himself starting from his own company, 'as it were that of a fiend'. Friends were sometimes begged to come with him on night strolls, for dread of the pursuers he might see. In words of Coleridge he loved declaiming, he was

> Like one, that on a lonesome road
> Doth walk in fear and dread,
> And having once turned round walks on,
> And turns no more his head;
> Because he knows, a frightful fiend
> Doth close behind him tread.

The fiend who was Shelley could not be chased away and, he concluded, should not be. 'Be as thou art,' he coldly admonished himself.

Meanwhile, the men in black kept him in view — across the field, down the street. Leeson and his crony Williams, the devil-forms of government suspicion and his father's 'plots', ran after him, as real as he was. 'If I do not know that I saw Williams,' he asked Peacock once, 'how do I know that I see you?' His tormentor was just as close, inside the house, and with a warrant in his hand to lock him up for good.

As a devil-figure he was interesting, but not uncommon. He could do much worse, scaring the custom-bound much more thoroughly. Monster-Shelley therefore took the title 'Atheist' and blazoned it on his forehead like the cross of the Wandering Jew.

He had broken with God at Eton, but quietly. His furious, public break with Christianity came at seventeen, when the religious squeamishness of Harriet Grove's parents put an end to his 'engagement' to her. The hypocrisy of Christian love was thereby joined to the absurdity of a vengeful anthropomorphic God, 'the most remorseless capricious

& inflexible of tyrants', who 'made man such as he is and then damned him for being so'. Shelley bitterly rejected him, hate bolstered with pain, in what he called 'delirious egotism'.

In January 1811, back at Field Place from Oxford for the holidays, he tried to persuade his father that Christ had never existed, satisfactorily shocking him. Sitting in his room there later that year, Christ gazing mildly at him from the wall, he poured out his hatred for 'J.C.', longing to hurl him into Hell or lance him deep in the heart. If he succeeded, 'may God (if there be a God), blast me!' If he failed, 'let this horrid Galilean rule the Canaille then'.

'The Atheist', he wrote in 1814, revelling in his own horror,

is a monster among men ... He dreads no judge but his own conscience, he fears no hell but the loss of his self-esteem. He is not to be restrained by punishments, for death is divested of its terror, and whatever enters into his heart to conceive, that will he not scruple to execute ...

This dark and terrible doctrine was surely the abortion of some blind speculator's brain, some strange and hideous perversion of intellect, some portentous distortion of reason.

And it was a title he embraced. Its overtones of Jacobinism and depravity pleased him all the more. The pamphlet that got him expelled from Oxford in March 1811, a slim production politely and reasonably asking for better proofs of God's existence than had been provided so far, was given a title of brimstone, *The Necessity of Atheism*. Copies were sent to all bishops and heads of houses; in one swift distribution, they were scattered over the counter of Munday & Slatter's Printing Office and left in the window. The 'advertisement' was signed 'Thro' deficiency of proof, AN ATHEIST'. The last sentence proclaimed, without compromise, 'Every reflecting mind must allow that there is no proof of the existence of a Deity.' Three capitals ended the tract, an appalling challenge: 'Q.E.D.'

Shelley especially liked that conclusion, as potent and rhythmic as a curse. It expressed mathematical and scientific certainty, with not a quiver of doubt. Yet the case was not thereby made obvious, only outrageous; his pamphlet was spotted by a worthy within 20 minutes, and was burned in the back of the shop. The Atheist needed to shout louder. *ECRASEZ L'INFAME!* yelled the epigraph to *Queen Mab* the next year. These were Voltaire's words, as well as the motto of the Jacobin

Illuminists who would abolish private property and marriage, and guillotine kings. The poem's notes contained, twice, another emphasised appeal, this time from the Baron d'Holbach, a French arch-materialist: *S'IL A PARLÉ, POURQUOI L'UNIVERS N'EST IL PAS CONVAINCU?* (IF [GOD] HAS SPOKEN, WHY IS THE UNIVERSE NOT CONVINCED?)

Shelley sent a copy of *The Necessity of Atheism* home; his father wrote 'Impious' on the flyleaf. He was called to answer for it before the 'tribunal' of the master of the college, but refused and was sent down. Shortly afterwards, he was barred from Field Place as though he were infected. He was kept out for fear that 'I want to make a deistical coterie of all my little sisters', and with some reason; twelve-year-old Hellen, Shelley admitted, would be 'a divine little scion of infidelity if I could get hold of her'. Like a leper—or like the Devil, as he eagerly suggested to her – he had to send her a letter by proxy, asking the family huntsman to leave it in the summerhouse. He pretended he was there, in the chill December dusk, diabolically tempting her. ('Where you are now you cannot do as you please. —you are obliged to submit to other people . . . But if you were with me you would be with some one who loved you, you might run & skip read write think just as you liked—') The letter was intercepted and destroyed. 'Father, are you a Christian?' he cried to Timothy Shelley in a letter of September 1811,

> it is perhaps too late to appeal to your love for me. I appeal to your duty to the God whose worship you profess, I appeal to the terrors of that day which you believe to seal the doom of mortals . . . What! will you not forgive?

Instinctively he coupled him with God the Father, tyrants together, both deaf to him. His father had shown kindness in the only way he knew how, by reading him passages from Paley's *Natural Theology* while Shelley, leaning forward, pretended to give the hateful words his full and undivided attention.

As an Atheist-monster, he expected to incur the full wrath of the authorities. He had done so with immediate effect at Oxford, by trashing the 39 Articles and the belief in the 'one living and true God' that he had professed when he matriculated. He described with a sort of proud, cheerful delirium his attempts in the Court of Chancery in 1817 to keep custody of his children by Harriet despite his atheism: 'dragged before the tribunals of tyranny & superstition, to answer with my children my property my liberty and my fame for having exposed their frauds'. This was exactly what the Tyrant-God, or tyrant-father, would do: fix a spurious sin on him, and then destroy him for it. 'I am careless', he told Byron loftily,

> of the consequences [of atheism] as they regard myself. I only feel persecution bitterly, because I bitterly lament the depravity & mistake of those who persecute. As to me, I can but die; I can but be torn to pieces . . .

He was, he explained to Peacock two years later – still with a bitter, self-pitying cheerfulness – 'a rare prodigy of crime & pollution whose look even might infect'.

On a spare leaf of paper, around 1819, he began to sketch out what he meant by atheism. The Greek word *atheos* meant impious, and was a term of reproach. Yet he himself did not deny 'whatever power, and mystery, and might may lie behind the universe'. He simply disagreed 'that this great system of things was arranged by one intellectual being'; to rebuke him for that, or for impiety, was 'insolence', and 'intolerable'. Lightly, he told friends that he could not be an Atheist because he was such a *Théist*, a lover of tea. Yet he never recanted, and had told his father he would never do so. He was in proud, ancient company, of which he pencilled a list in an 1817 notebook from Cicero's *De natura deorum*:

Diogoras,	Melius	Theodorus	Cyrenaicus
Democritus		Atheists	Protagoras

The Atheist's power to shock, thrill and offend continually delighted him. In the visitors' books of at least one Swiss tourist spot he signed himself 'P. B. Shelley, Atheist, Democrat, Philanthropist', written in demotic Greek. In *Julian and Maddalo* Julian–Shelley was 'a complete infidel, and a scoffer at all things reputed holy'; Shelley loved the word 'infidel', especially when applied to himself. With deliberate coarseness, he mocked the idea that 'the Spirit that pervades this infinite machine begat a son upon the body of a Jewish woman', and compared God's damnation of the hapless sinner to 'a troop of idle dirty boys baiting a cat'. Benjamin Haydon met him at a dinner at Hunt's in 1816, a weakly, hectic youth as he thought him, who scarcely raised his soft voice to say 'As to that detestable religion, the Christian . . . !' before bending again to carve his stalk of broccoli, 'as if it had been the substantial wing of a chicken'. His blade was sharp. Claire once devised a caricature of him, 'looking very sweet & smiling', about to murder the child Jesus with a small, silent knife.

Trelawny, not believing Shelley an atheist truly, once asked him why he called himself one. He replied: 'I took up the word, as a knight took up a gauntlet, in defiance of injustice The delusions of Christianity are fatal to genius and originality; they limit thought.' He was a wolf, he told him later, 'and not in sheep's clothing'. This was in 1822; to the end of his life, he preserved the fangs and the claws.

He also kept a more sinuous persona. With his willowy, low-stooping walk and his glittering eyes, he made a natural serpent: the more so, Byron thought, because he was forever whispering atheism into his ear. Byron called him 'the Snake' after Eve's tempter; Shelley, liking it, adopted the tag himself. Serpent-Shelley was insidious, conspiratorial and a corrupter of devoted young ladies foolish enough to stay up with him and to mop the eagerly spilt tea from his shirt-front and his shoes. He was a perfect gentleman, yet 'very wicked', in Coleridge's view; 'the blackest of villains', as he believed Southey thought him, yet mouthing the most delicate thoughts of impropriety and heresy. When critics riled him he reared up to meet them, shaking his crest and flourishing his sting, though he confessed he had no venom to match theirs.

The serpent's own place in the scheme of things was difficult to define. In the draft of his *Essay on Christianity* Shelley twice began to write 'The serpent is avoided because its bite is mortal . . .' but failed to finish the thought, and then deleted it. He knew the serpent as Satan, as Ahriman, the god of evil in the religion of Zoroaster, and as the Python of darkness slain by Apollo, the sun; but most fundamentally, perhaps, he knew him as the monster of his childhood. In St Leonard's Forest a 'Great Serpent' had lived in the reign of James I, nine feet long, equipped with squat legs or primitive wings and slithering sometimes, in his childhood imagination, to the very edges of the lakes and lawns of Field Place. A 'Great Old Snake', perhaps a descendant, lived in the gardens. Shelley was full of stories of him, terror tales he repeated for years, although the monster had been killed by a gardener carelessly scything the grass.

The most monstrous of his snake-selves was the half-human sea snake from Southey's *The Curse of Kehama*, doomed to keep awake or die;

Shelley said he felt like this when staying at Byron's, knotted and half delirious with lack of sleep. The prettiest were the gold serpents, 'like unimprisoned flames', waking and uncoiling in the regenerated world he dreamed would come. What he most admired in snakes was their lack of trace, their silent gliding, their sudden appearances and the beautifully reticulated armour of their scales. His most carefully drawn human head wore a helmet much like a serpent's skin, delicately shaded in pencil.

The most constant Shelley-serpent, however, was the pitiable outcast – the *Pariah*, as he called himself – whose hatefulness could be transformed by love. When he had battled against life for long enough, a woman or a girl would catch him as he wearied and press him, softly, to her breasts. He wished thus to be admitted to Paradise. He had no sting; he meant no harm.

In Pisa in 1822, as he sought refuge and love with Jane and Edward Williams, his friends and neighbours on the floor below, rather than with Mary, he was the serpent outside the gates of their Eden: silent, bright-eyed, sad, waiting. Snake-like, he slid them poems: 'For Jane & Williams alone to see.' 'I commit them to your secresy & your mercy'. 'Looking over the portfolio in which my friend used to keep his verses . . . I have lit upon these.' Whether he was good or evil, you could not say. Like the Amphisbaena of Lucan, with a head at each end of his body, he might go either way, to redemption or damnation; like the wise many-coloured snake of time-clasping Eternity, the *drakon ouroborus* endlessly devouring its own tail, he lay quiet and tranquillised sometimes within the coils of himself. Even to tread on him might not rouse him, merely stir him to seek some deeper hiding-place.

> Wake the serpent not—lest he
> Should not know the way to go—
> Let him crawl which yet lies sleeping
> Through the deep grass . . .

Where would the serpent go? You could barely follow his track: so faint in the dust that the moving grains covered it again, so subtle in the grass that the thin blades closed their ranks behind him. But if you could follow, it was almost certain where he would take you: to the water.

Water

I
Immersion

In July 1803 young Percy Shelley, aged ten, composed a letter:

Dear Kate—
   We have proposed a day at the pond next Wednesday, and, if you will come tomorrow morning I would be much obliged to you, and, if you could any how bring Tom to stay all the night, I would thank you. We are to have a cold dinner over at the pond, and come home to eat a bit of roast chicken and peas at about nine o'clock. Mama depends upon your bringing Tom over to-morrow, and if you don't we shall be very much disap-pointed. Tell the bearer not to forget to bring me a fairing, which is some ginger-bread, sweetmeat, hunting-nuts, and a pocket-book. Now I end.
                                      I am not
                                            Your obedient servant,
                                            P.B. Shelley

'The pond' was the millpond outside Warnham, 100 acres of water ringed by meadows, shrubs and woods. Some years later his father dug out small lakes at Field Place, linking them by a bridge and ornamenting them with a summerhouse; but 'the pond' remained Warnham, with its muddy, reedy edges and wide vistas of reflected trees. Timothy Shelley kept a boat there. In cold winters Shelley, slipping and stumbling on the margins, saw fish suspended stiff and dead underneath the ice. In summer, moorhens fussed in the shallows; there were yellow flag-iris, dragonflies and, to a small boy lying on the bank with dreams of ginger-bread, a whole horizon of shining water.

Shelley sought water always. Trelawny called it a mania with him, and Hogg attributed all his restlessness to the need to see streams and green banks, or hear waterfalls. At Eton, according to Mary, his favourite spot was a little spring that rose in the fields outside the town. He would sit on the rough-hewn steps that led down to it, musing on metaphysics. Schoolmates were certain that he had discovered young his love of boats and of moving water. A truant excursion from Syon House took him to Richmond, rowing fast. A small, swift wherry was his delight at Eton. In the autumn of 1811 he was boating on Buttermere and Windermere; the next year he fled Dublin for the lakes of Killarney, dotted with fuschia and arbutus trees. This water landscape, he wrote later, was the most beautiful he had ever encountered until he saw Lake Como, where groves of chestnut, bay and laurel came down steeply to the wide, still blue.

In house after house, water lay outside his door. His Lynmouth lodg-ings in 1812 commanded a north-western sweep of the Bristol Channel looking towards Wales. In Switzerland in 1816 Lake Geneva filled his windows and shone at the bottom of the garden. At Naples he lived by the Mediterranean, at Pisa by the broad green Arno or the sprightly Serchio, flowing down from Lucca over scatterings of stones. At San Giuliano his back windows opened on the tiny canal that linked those rivers, placid and overhung with trees. His last summer, from May to July of 1822, was spent with Mary and the Williamses in a former boat-house, Villa Magni at San Terenzo on the Bay of Lerici, where the southerly blue sea with its islands and promontories was all he saw, or wished to see. Most of his 'homes', but especially this one, were points of departure where high hills barred his retreat or water beckoned, places from which to leave.

He drew water in his notebooks, often from memory: pools fringed by grass and reeds, rivers meandering past willows, smooth sheets over-hung by trees and backed by sharp-edged mountains. The mountains were sketchy, the water careful, its undulations and reflections inked in painstakingly with his darting, pressing pen. Boats sailed on it, natu-rally, and in the boats himself, with jacket and tall hat, mirrored in the stillness.

His writings showed that he had looked at water for long absorbing hours. Both Mary and Claire were surprised, on the elopement trip to France, to discover how patiently Shelley could sit on jetties, watching the wind whip the surface of a lake. The Welsh waterfalls filled him with such excitement that he paced the room, gesticulating, as he described them later in the dullness of St James's Street. In a letter of November 1818 he took Peacock to the cataract of the Velino at Terni, near Spoleto, leading him eagerly over the slick rocks:

> Stand upon the brink of the platform of cliff which is directly oppo-site. You see the evermoving water stream down. It comes in thick & tawny folds flaking off like solid snow gliding down a mountain. It does not seem hollow within, but without it is unequal like the folding of linen thrown carelessly down. Your eye follows it & it is lost below, not in the black rocks which gird it around but in its own foam & spray, in the cloudlike vapours boiling up from below, which is not like rain nor mist nor spray nor foam, but water in a shape wholly unlike any thing I ever saw before. It is as white as snow, but thick & impenetrable to the eye. The very imagination is bewildered in it.

He stayed for half an hour on the cliff edge, gazing; it seemed that only minutes had gone by. Each water-scene was 'forever changing yet forever the same', the mutable and eternal in constant tension, as seemed to be the case within himself.

Calmer moments were precious, too. He would let his boat carry him, drifting, under the trees by the Thames near Marlow, where he lay with the river rocking beneath him, its waves 'pranked' with the green and golden dazzle of the sun. Under his prow the light weeds moved as one in the rippling flow of the current. He noticed the behav-iour of water in the shallows, dimpled and clear, or running in almost invisible threads across the meadows. By such a stream – 'dark, dark, yet clear' – Dante, lost in the deepest forest, had glimpsed 'with charmed sight' Matilda gathering flowers, the maiden and the water alike suddenly soothing and delighting him. Shelley, translating that passage from the *Purgatorio*, had followed, brushing through the tangled branches and the thick may blossom until his feet caught in longer grass, slowing and stilling him, and the stream-light gleamed:

> water of purest dew
> On Earth, would appear turbid & impure
> Compared with this . . .

From that passage, his favourite of the whole *Divine Comedy* for 'exquisite tenderness and sensibility and ideal beauty', he borrowed for his
own *Triumph of Life*

> a gentle rivulet
> Whose water like clear air in its calm sweep
>
> Bent the soft grass & kept for ever wet
> The stems of the sweet flowers, and filled the grove
> With sound which all who hear must needs forget
>
> All pleasure & all pain, all hate & love . . .

'Very little brooks', trickling over the dark clay, losing themselves in
brambles, drew him too in his Hampstead walks with Hunt. Like Dante,
he pursued clear running water as the distillation of wisdom, slaking a
thirst that was spiritual as much as physical in the desert of the world.

As for the sea, he spent all possible hours either on it or beside it,
watching with passion each move and every change. He recorded it
creeping with 'little lapping waves' over grey stones at dawn, or sighing
at evening with the wind's inflection. The wide main stretched before
him, 'Chequered with sunbeams and with shade,/Alternate to infinity'.
In *The Revolt of Islam* he swam, as a serpent, through the 'foam-wreaths
which the faint tide wove below' to seek refuge in white breasts dappled
by 'the green/ And glancing shadows of the sea'. A poetic thought, he
wrote, was 'as evanescent as the wrinkled sand over which the waves
pass'. The first tumbling breaker half erased it (or washed, blotted,
covered it, as he tried the words) and, with the second, it was gone.

At Villa Magni on the Bay of Lerici, sitting at night on the sand near
the white, arcaded house of his last summer, he watched the moon
climbing over the sea and the vessels that glided past. In draft, he noticed
more: how

> Like silver
> ~~Only~~ a thread of moonlight ~~lay~~
> ~~Upon~~ ~~On the disentangled spray~~
> ~~murmuring~~

To the sight of water was added the sound of it. At Cwm Elan in
1811 the Elan roared incessantly in its deep valley, swirling and frothing

over rocks in the steep shade of the woods. The woods too 'tongued', echoing the torrent. Past his lodgings in Lynmouth the west Lyn sang, splashing in waterfalls, to the harbour and the sea; near his cottage in Keswick the Greta flowed, unseen, over pebbles that made musical notes and were collected as curiosities. When he and Harriet lived near Tremadoc in North Wales in the winter of 1812–13, involved in fund-raising to reclaim land by embanking the estuary, the half-tamed sea burst through its enclosure with 'tumultuous melody', like a beast. At Bagni di Lucca, in 1818, the white-foaming Lima sounded day and night as it ran down through the chestnut woods. And at Villa Magni the sea, racing into the lower floor that was open to the tides, thumped like a beating heart and crashed like artillery.

Inevitably the water's music echoed in his verses. 'Mont Blanc', written partly on a bridge above the pelting Arve, carried that 'unresting' force pouring from line to line. In *Prometheus Unbound* the song of the heroine Asia, the embodiment of Love, flowed like a rapturous rippling river on which her soul seemed 'to float ever, for ever', rocking like a sleeping swan,

> Till, like one in slumber bound,
> Borne to the ocean, I float down, around,
> Into a sea profound, of ever-spreading sound . . .

Yet Shelley could also catch the more humdrum rhythms of water and the waves. His 'Stanzas written in Dejection, near Naples' – composed in the sad December of 1818, when Italy had claimed both little Clara and Mary's affection – could follow in octosyllabics the steady music of the sea until, spreading out like a long alexandrine, a wave would reach his feet and break there in soft and tired confusion.

> I see the Deep's untrampled floor
> With green and purple seaweeds strown,
> I see the waves upon the shore
> Like light dissolved in star-showers, thrown;
> I sit upon the sands alone;
> The lightning of the noontide Ocean
> Is flashing round me, and a tone
> Arises from its measured motion,
> How sweet! did any heart now share in my emotion.

His own music-making had the same hypnotic quality: a simple tune of a few notes taught to him by Harriet Grove, picked out time after time with one hand on the piano at Field Place, or the strange made-up chant he sang to baby Ianthe as he carried her and soothed her crying, 'Yáhmani, yáhmani, yáhmani, yáhmani'. Peacock described this as 'three notes, not very true in their intervals' but uniformly repeated, over and over again.

Shelley gave such a song to his heroine Beatrice Cenci just before she went to her death for the murder of her father. As in other death-ditties in his notebooks, its burden was two wistful notes repeating, 'Farewell! Heigho!':

> Come, I will sing you some low, sleepy tune,
> Not cheerful, nor yet sad; some dull old thing . . .

The diffidence concealed Shelley's love for such creations. At Villa Magni in the summer of 1822, on the first-floor terrace by the evening sea, he listened with 'excessive delight' to the simple melodies played by Jane Williams on her guitar, the sound − as it seemed to him − of pattering rain and murmuring waves, as well as his growing infatuation. He joined in, singing with her. Such tender music, he wrote once, could produce 'the most overwhelming emotions'. In the ideal, tranquil cave in which his hero Prometheus was to dwell at last, embraced by Asia and attended by nymphs of Ocean, it was 'fragments of sea-music' that the Titan wished to hear.

More than a poet's interest bred Shelley's affinity with water. Scientifically, its suppleness delighted him: its molecules spreading out, as old Dr Walker had described it in lectures at Eton, and its parts sliding smoothly over each other as its purity increased. Water marked the first escape from densest matter, slippery and quick and translucent. When he translated Plato's *Symposium* Shelley made Love in its operations a 'moist and liquid' god. 'Tender' and 'pliant' were closer to the Greek, but perhaps too material; and 'if [Love] were otherwise' (Plato speaking, Shelley translating), 'he could not, as he does, fold himself round every thing and secretly flow out and into every soul.'

Dr Walker had touched, too, on this, describing how water adhered to any substance, mixing its particles with whatever it ran over: 'If water has come over an *alkaline stratum* the *syrup of violets* turns it *green*; if over an *acid stratum* the *syrup* turns it *red*; if over *iron stone* . . . a solution of *galls* turns it *black*.' Love did as water, water as Love, with a sinuous empathy Shelley longed for in himself.

But whatever he watched, he could also be. 'It is a faculty of the human mind', Paine said – in a phrase Shelley took and repeated and adopted – 'to become what it contemplates, and to act in unison with its object.' In the ceaseless braiding and unfurling of mountain torrents Shelley was both the falling force, *forever changing yet forever the same,* and the bubbles that were battered and broken in the surf, constantly remade. Or he could follow the river nymph Arethusa leaping down the rocks, 'gliding and springing', his wet green feet leaving trails of moss and his hair streaming in rainbows. 'Hues from the green leaves and the daylight wood' dappled the current of his ideas, cheering him,

> Even if blank darkness must descend and brood
> Upon its waves . . .

The fountains of St Peter's Square, rising 'in spirelike columns' from vases of red porphyry, also held his thoughts. He leapt and fell with them, in misted lines of light.

Whenever the impulse seized him he himself appeared as a water creature, beginning to rinse away the impurity of the earth. Several times a day he plunged his head in a brimming basin of cold water, running his hands madly through his hair until it stood up like reeds round the pale pool of his face. In France in August 1814 he tried to bathe by the road, begging the post-chaise to stop so that he, 'as if he were Adam in Paradise before his fall', in Claire's words, might slip into a stream and dry himself with leaves. (Mary, urged to do the same, protested that it would be 'most indecent'; the coachman, shaking his head, drove on.) At Bagni di Lucca in the heat of summer he found a forest pool and spent his noons beside it, sunning himself naked on the rocks 'until the perspiration has subsided' and then jumping in, splashing tremendously. It was 'exceedingly cold', he told Peacock, still shivering with delight, but also 'exceedingly refreshing'. Afterwards, climbing up the slippery, shining rocks beside the waterfall that fed it, he received the spray 'over all my body'.

At Villa Magni, of necessity, he both washed and relieved himself in the sea, and lived from day to day with his locks as oozy as those of Milton's Lycidas. He let the salt water dry on him, disdaining combs and towels. At *festas* the local people sang, danced and sported for hours in the waves at night, mostly half naked. Mary hated the racket, but Shelley loved it and joined them, as wildly improper – as he defiantly remarked to her – as a seal, a sea bird or a water rat. Even on the nauseous grey deck of a heaving cross-Channel packet, he loved to feel the sea break over him.

His Maniac-self in *Julian and Maddalo* was also a creature of the water. The madhouse where he lived by the Venetian Lido was approached by gondola 'through the fast-falling rain and high-wrought sea', up green-slimed steps, and appeared as a wrecked palace festooned with seaweed, the tangled and trailing hair of the lunatics confined there. The Maniac himself, a piteous piece of human flotsam, sat near a piano (as Shelley might sit, idly repeating notes):

> his pale fingers twined
> One with the other, and the ooze and wind
> Rushed through an open casement, and did sway
> His hair, and starred it with the brackish spray . . .

His apartment kept mostly a smell of shipwreck and salt water, the same gusting brine that had intoxicated Julian, his other self, as he had galloped on the Lido sands the day before:

> —for the winds drove
> The living spray along the sunny air
> Into our faces; the blue heavens were bare,
> Stripped to their depths by the awakening north,
> And from the waves, sound like delight broke forth . . .

Salt drops also blotted the Maniac's notebooks, 'dizzying, scalding tears', obscuring whatever love-disappointment he had tried to commit to paper. Shelley may have been thinking of Mary, at least in part, and her coldness since the death of little Clara some months earlier, but he tried to blur her as much as he was able. Tears blurred her for him. To be 'wild with weeping' was a common state with him, and not always bound up with sadness. He once called it 'inexplicably pleasing', and sometimes laughed until he cried. Water as delight, water as tears, tears as 'sweet medicine and relief' all swelled and trembled in Shelley's head, and at any time you might find his face wet with any of them, trickling saltily into his mouth or brushed hectically away from his eyes. To swim, with him, was a mental state, perilously close to the dissolving of his senses in outright madness or in ecstasy.

His most celebrated appearance as a merman occurred at Villa Magni in 1822. There was a party to dinner; and as they sat in elegant conversation (in so far as anything could be elegant in that spartan, sea-battered house), Shelley came in from a ducking, naked. Sea water trickled down his nose, and there was seaweed in his hair. He smelt of brine. For a creature of the sea, wetness was normal, nakedness normal; what was abnormal was the clothed creatures sitting at the table, eating from plates and holding up their horrified hands. Disturbed from his careful, quiet circumnavigation of the room, screened by the Italian maid, he drew himself up beside a lady's chair. There he launched his own defence, explaining loudly that he had to go to his room to fetch his clothes. Water running down him formed a puddle on the floor; the lady averted her eyes. But Shelley's body was as innocent as the foam he had tumbled from.

For all that, he could not swim. He had never learned, though occasionally he tried. 'Why can't I swim?' he asked Trelawny once. 'It seems so very easy.' Trelawny, an old salt, made it look so, diving and turning arabesques in a pool of the Arno like the boys he had watched in the South Seas; but when Shelley copied him, kicking off enthusiastically his jacket, trousers, shoes and socks, he went straight to the bottom. There, in Trelawny's words, he lay 'stretched out . . . like a conger eel', unmoving. Not for the last time, Trelawny fished him out. He spluttered and jerked on the bank, where in the water he had been still, calm, as if asleep.

Trelawny thought his spine was curved the wrong way; if he could only unbend it, and turn on his back as he rose to the air, he could swim perfectly well. He failed to bear in mind that Shelley might have no wish to keep his body floating.

★   ★   ★

Water could not be counted his friend. It had waylaid him from the first. The loathed baptismal fluid had been splashed on his infant head at the font in Warnham church, under the small west window. He must have wept; the crass aspersion mingled with his tears.

In Switzerland in 1814 a sudden downpour caught him, drenching his only set of clothes. Gazing on the last glowing strip of the sunset, he hardly cared. In the morning he rolled on damp stockings and forced his feet into tight, wet shoes. Rain made his sprained ankle worse, and soaked the books in his pockets.

117

Damp crept through his library at Marlow, covering the volumes with a spotted film of mildew. It nestled too in his lungs, a slippery green bacillus that made him cough and ache.

The English rain, whenever it fell, turned him aguish, bilious and weak. 'In . . . the chilling fogs & rain of our own country', he told Peacock, 'I can hardly be said to live.' Mary warned him not to go out in wet weather, because the effect was too debilitating. In London the rain hunted him, spitting on his hatless hair.

In his poems, rain fell bleakly over cities ruled by tyrants: sullen, rotting, poisoned rain. The wind, heavy and pained with it, could hardly move through the grey air. Very rarely was Shelley's rain vernal, or soft, or sweet. On the unreformed Earth, as in England in the dead, dull summer of 1816, it was the destroyer of harvests, blackening the sodden fields and raising by several times the price of bread. Rain reinforced the burden of government, as well as the misery it caused.

> The vast roof is torn asunder
> And pours down a rain of ruin
> To the dust & the *slime* of annihilation;
> We are beaten down & we rise no more.

He sketched it on his pages in hard, dark lines, pelting from the unseen side of clouds.

In his unfinished play *Charles the First* Archy, the court fool, was punished by being made to stand for ten minutes in the rain. Rain punished Shelley, too. He stood in it, his heart naked to its freezing, battering drops. Or he lived in it,

> Walking beneath the night of life
> Whose hours extinguished, like slow rain
> Falling for ever, pain by pain
> The very hope of death's dear rest

On too many days he would 'wake to weep', pressing the cold wet pillow to his face, without knowing or remembering why.

Even in Italy, dampness laid a finger in his collar. He wrote in a note-book

Rain—Maremma rain   cold

Other notebooks fell into the water with him. He smeared the wet away and went on writing, gouging the soft paper, making the letters run. Sea water gnawed at his drafts of *A Defence of Poetry* and *Adonais*; it corroded the pages and stuck them together with its silty, animal glue. Salt saturated his thoughts.

The April swell in the Pisa canal caught him unawares, pulling him under. (Edward Williams, like a landlubber, had tipped their little boat over by standing up and grabbing the mast.) Chillingly, the water coated his drowsy limbs; he did not resist. 'Never more comfortable in my life,' he told Henry Reveley, the boat's best swimmer; 'do what you will with me.' Feeling Shelley cold, slowing the blood in him, the water gave him up. He fainted on the bank. His pockets were full of coffee and arrowroot released from their sodden bags and now in solution, running down his legs. Water daubed him like an incontinent clown.

At Villa Magni the sea capsized his tiny coracle, throwing him into the surf. It battered him, knocked him sideways, rolled him over, tossed his Aeschylus away. It forced itself into his mouth, choking him like a maniac lover. He shrieked with happiness.

Perhaps water could never truly hurt him. In Southey's *Curse of Kehama* the hero, Ladurlad, was placed under a curse by which the elements would not touch him. Water would neither soothe him, nor bring him death; he was both invulnerable and inconsolable. So perhaps Shelley, too, could plunge his arms in the sea and watch it retreat, stung and astonished after one soft lick of his skin; or he could wade into rivers that curled from his feet like silver slow-worms, burying themselves in the sand. He knew the Curse by heart, screaming it out sometimes as fiercely as Kehama himself:

119

> And Water shall hear me,
> And know thee and fly thee!

A wave would rise up, hover and turn, 'the green and jagged moun-tain-wave/ . . . With lightnings tinging all its fleeting form'. It would curl; but it would not fall.

> And the Curse shall be on thee
> For ever and ever!

Water could not kill the Wandering Jew; he leapt off a cliff into the sea, and the sea spewed him up again. Nor did it kill the Ancient Mariner in the end, though it tried every horror that Coleridge could imagine and Shelley could recite, thundering it out with 'wild energy' as the supper plates were cleared and the curtains drawn:

> The very deep did rot: O Christ!
> That ever this should be!
> Yea, slimy things did crawl with legs
> Upon the slimy sea.

At Villa Magni near the end of his life, on a night of rain and inces-sant roaring waves, he dreamed that Jane and Edward Williams came in to him as he lay in bed, their bodies lacerated and their faces stained with blood. 'Get up, Shelley,' Williams told him; 'the sea is flooding the house, and it is all coming down.' Shelley, shocked, jumped up and went to his window, which looked out over the bay. The sea was rushing in, but before it could reach him or touch him his vision changed, and he was safe.

Perhaps his affinity would preserve him; for, from long looking and musing, he was already part of the sea. 'A breaking billow' was how he described himself in *Adonais*: not noisily crashing on the beach but rising and subsiding, with a slight trail of foam, on the vast surface of the ocean. As the young idealist Lionel he was the noonday sea, changing colour as the least wind passed. A little light would glint from him, his own contribution to the shining, glittering plain that stretched from horizon to horizon. And the western breeze would ruffle him, lifting him, keeping him awake.

In his water guise, he could be tugged or seduced as the moon compelled the tides. The moon was mutability, 'ever changing, like a joyless eye/That finds no object worth its constancy'. It was also reason, luring him to argument and analysis with its 'cold & uncertain & borrowed light'. Hogg said Shelley found unbearable the thought of the man in the moon, eternally caught in that cool, magnetic, ever-shifting glare. 'Poor fellow!' he cried once, staring piteously up at him. But he was to find that enchantment, or paralysis, in his own life. Mary was always the moon to him, Homer's white-armed divinity, with her broad pale forehead and her eventual 'dead despondence', despite their love.

> The cold chaste Moon, the Queen of Heaven's bright isles,
> Who makes all beautiful on which she smiles,
> That wandering shrine of soft yet icy flame ...

She held him, as Lionel, in her pallid spell, hanging over him and watching him as he slept, until 'like an image in the lake/ Which rains disturb', her tears woke him.

In the early summer of 1814, when his passion for Mary had first erupted and he was threatening suicide if he could not have her, it was she – so he claimed – who was exerting influence on him, her passive lover. His mind without her, he told her later, was 'dead & cold as the dark midnight river when the moon is down'. Love was often a woman hovering above him, her hands caressing his brow or his body, yet often with dimness and detachment compared with the image he desired. Quiescent, as he wrote in *Epipsychidion* in 1821, he would receive the moonlight like the touch of fingers on his face:

> And I was laid asleep, spirit and limb,
> And all my being became bright or dim
> As the Moon's image in a summer sea,
> According as she smiled or frowned on me;
> And there I lay, within a chaste cold bed:
> Alas, I then was nor alive nor dead:—

Gradually, in his poems, the Mary-moon grew colder. Shrinking and white, her lips withdrew from his; 'like a sick matron wan', swathed in grey veils, she tottered slowly from the east. As the months passed, disappointed in his hopes both of her and of other, more shadowy *amours*, haunted by Harriet and his lost children, he found himself encased in ice under her blank, still gaze:

121

                                        what frost
Crept o'er those waters, till from coast to coast
The moving billows of my being fell
Into a death of ice, immovable;—
And then—what earthquakes made it gape and split,
The white Moon smiling all the while on it,
These words conceal:—

By the spring of 1822 it was not Mary, but Jane Williams, who 'bade the frozen streams be free'. For more than a year, often under the same roof and in her husband's company, Shelley had been slowly falling for her. Jane too was the alluring moon in loveliness, though 'far more true', refusing the inconstancy that might bring comfort to him. But she could be his friend.

In their house in Pisa she had used Mesmerism, a new technique, to try to soothe his nervous spasms. She would place her hand gently on his forehead and calm him until, in the soft words he imagined her speaking, 'By mine thy being is to its deep/ Possest—'

        And from my fingers flow
    The powers of life, and like a sign,
    Seal thee from thine hour of woe;
    And brood on thee, but may not blend
                With thine.

Her 'Patient' was too turbulent to hold her image steady. He loved and trembled silently, letting her magnetism move him as long as the moment lasted. Tranquillity, he knew, would never follow, for she was firmly Edward's and not his: 'Less oft is peace in S——'s mind/ Than calm in water seen.' But he had laid himself open to her influence and her pity.

Ecstasy, for him, was a condition of dissolution. 'To sink and die' was a favourite phrase, commingling death and love as consummations to be longed for. He would expire in the deep like a lover subsiding with the spasms of the sexual act, 'the quick dying gasps/ Of the life meeting',

                        when the faint eyes swim
    Through tears of a wide mist boundless and dim,
        In one caress . . .

Love would fill every pore of him until he was as malleable, soft and impulsive as water. He would be

> The wave that died the death which lovers love,
> Living in what it sought.

Already in 1810 he saw himself, responding as he supposed to 'death's accents cold', lying down by the sea. Eight years later, touched by the same loneliness, he stretched himself on the beach at Naples:

> Yet now despair itself is mild,
> Even as the winds and waters are;
> I could lie down like a tired child,
> And weep away the life of care
> Which I have borne and yet must bear,
> Till Death like Sleep might steal on me
> And I might feel in the warm air
> My cheek grow cold, and hear the sea
> Breathe o'er my dying brain its last monotony.

Yet to sleep like a child, he wrote elsewhere, was to be reconciled to all things and to oneself, a harmony of being. Even on that lonely beach the 'wave-worn sand' of his heart, as he thought of it, shone as the tide fell; even the hard, dull stones, which were also his heart, trembled and sparkled at the water's touch. And surely under those 'quick, faint kisses of the sea' he could not die, but would love and live.

★ ★ ★

The world beneath those caressing waves was both beautiful and alive. Under the sea at Baiae, near Naples, Shelley (hanging from the boat, almost diving, into the azure calm) saw the ruins of great palaces and gardens of flowing weed. The waves, he told Peacock, were 'so translucent that you could see the hollow caverns clothed with the glaucous sea-moss, & the leaves & branches of those delicate weeds that pave the unequal bottom of the water'.

In the depths of ocean grew flowers and woods; not merely the 'starry green' and purple moss, pulled up slimy in his fingers, but tall trees stirring in the current and sea buds bursting and unfolding. Naturalists knew, he wrote, that plants on the beds of seas and lakes changed with the land-seasons and were influenced by the winds. He pictured dead boughs waking and flowering there, 'under the wave'. Yet their growth was slow, their opening gradual, moulded and weighted by the water. Change under the sea was towards a more permanent beauty, as Ariel had sung in *The Tempest*:

> Full fathom five thy father lies.
> Of his bones are coral made;
> Those are pearls that were his eyes . . .

When Shelley first toyed with the name *Ariel* for his yacht in Italy, it was in honour of the lasting 'sea-change' he expected her to effect on him.

The bottom of the sea he pictured as a mine of treasure: coral, pearls, gold-grained sand, purple shells engraved with mystical words. In Virgil's fourth *Georgic* Aristeus, wandering there half bewildered in the sway and wash of the wave-air, had found lakes, woods and rivers. Shelley, translating this scene, imbued it with greater mysteries: for *amnem*, river, 'the deep's untrampled fountains', for *lyci*, groves, 'groves profaned not by the step of mortal'; rivers paved with stars, glimmering marble caves and water not merely glowing, but flowing with light.

The underwater world was silent. His footsteps made no sound, and no voice called. Yet the light was bright there, sometimes more so than on the surface. The wave's 'intenser day' knew no clouding or changing. Sunbeams fell in emerald nets through the blue quivering deep, 'like sunlight through acacia woods at even'; the profoundest dark still kept gleams of the forest, green and ever-moving. Nereids lay on thrones of crystal, attending old Ocean in his cavern floored with dark blue sand,

> Their wavering limbs borne on the wind-like stream,
> Their white arms lifted o'er their streaming hair
> With garlands pied and starry sea-flower crowns . . .

Shelley's Asia, or Love, was born there in the sea foam, a child of Ocean stepping from a 'veinèd shell'. In her train another nymph of Ocean brought a mystic conch, 'pale azure fading into silver', which, when sounded, began the political and moral renewal of the world:

> Soon as the sound had ceased whose thunder filled
> The abysses of the sky and the wide earth,
> There was a change: the impalpable thin air

And the all-circling sunlight were transformed,
As if the sense of love dissolved in them
Had folded itself round the spherèd world.
My vision then grew clear, and I could see
Into the mysteries of the universe . . .

Shelley too could be that many-folded sounding shell, carrying within
him 'a voice to be accomplished'. At various times, playing on the name
he often wished to forget, he could be shells sacred, shells profane: oysters
shucked, sucked and thrown in the road from a coffee-house, or ceramic
spirals of secret sounds that surged in his ear like his own whispering
blood. He could be a 'shell of ocean' – Trelawny told him the proverb,
from Hafiz, and it delighted him – that quietly filled with pearls the hand
of the enemy, or the critic, who had wounded him. And as that luminous
trumpet-shell he could be fished from the blue deep, among the sea
flowers, to sound forth mysteries the world had not yet begun to grasp.

★   ★   ★

Under the water was also the realm of dreams. Shelley painted it in
softest words, an ocean 'without a sound',

Whose waves never mark, though they ever impress
The light sand which paves it, consciousness; . . .

All animals, birds and noises of the day were gently drowned there as
night fell. Mutability was submerged in silence. Distinctions blurred,
and human forms lay lapped by thought, 'mingled in love and sleep'.

His Witch of Atlas, having moored her boat on the banks of the
Nile, slipped beneath the surface of the river. There she visited palaces
and huts and dormitories, whole sleeping worlds, with infants, priests
and lovers arranged in their cell-like beds. She saw the slumbering
bodies as diaphanous, their souls laid bare; subtly mingling their spirits
with her own, she changed their dreams. They now acted out what
their deeper, purer selves had truly longed to do.

Shelley's own sleeping self lay there too. The Witch ('my Witch'),
passing swiftly in a coruscation of underwater light, would see him on
his bed in Florence, tossed among the sheets, or on the hard beech-
wood sofa in his library at Pisa, or curled in the bottom of his boat
on the Serchio, with the shadows of poplar trees moving on his face.

He slept randomly always, with no pattern and little preparation. Wherever he found himself when 'liquid sleep' began to wash across him, there he stayed, sliding from his chair to the hearthrug or the carpet, stretching himself on the hard ground or the grass. If no one else's arm would pillow his head, his own would do. He was discovered asleep under trees, on cold marble floors and by the railings in Leicester Square. Soft ripples of unconsciousness smudged his words as he wrote, 'Between sleep & awake' to Byron once; drowsiness slurred his pencil as he tried to write poetry in 1817, perhaps sitting up in the dark:

~~heavily oh heavily~~
~~weight not on me now~~

Yet it seemed that he resented and resisted sleep. He would rather talk till dawn, no matter how fidgety and heavy-eyed the company became. He boasted at Oxford that he could do without 'that *morbid suspension of every energy*', and could thrive on as little as three hours a night. Hogg said Shelley never went to bed of his own accord and voluntarily; he was put there, sent there or taken there, like a recalcitrant child. He evidently scrutinised the easy sleep of his own children, their milk-fed bliss, and seemed to envy it. Yet when he woke he was fierce, energetic, instantly arguing, as though Morpheus had waylaid him without his permission and had wasted precious time.

Sleep brought a disconnect between body and mind, and mind and spirit, that ceaselessly interested him. On at least three occasions he walked in his sleep, heading for open doors and windows. After one such event, on a moonlit night at Syon House, his cousin Tom Medwin led him back to bed, soothing an intense agitation. After another, at Villa Magni in the summer of 1822, Mary found him standing over her unmoving, holding a lighted candle at arm's length. His eyes were wide open, but 'with no speculation in them'; Mary said he resembled a statue. He followed her across the saloon, strode to the veranda door, listened for a while to the waves crashing, then stretched himself on his bed again, having carefully placed his candle on the table. He had never been asleep, he said afterwards. He had been awake, dreaming.

His experiments with animal magnetism began in 1820, when Medwin, visiting him in Pisa, persuaded him to try it for his spasms. At the touch of Medwin's hand on his brow, he fell into a deep trance with his eyes open. Placidly, he allowed himself to be walked to the sofa, where he slept. He woke convinced of the separation of mind and body, the mind talkative and active, the body inert. On a second occasion, he improvised verses in Italian and begged his friends, as Claire recalled, 'not to ask him more questions because he shall say what he ought not'. He had answered some already in a voice pitched like that of his questioner, as if the fluid energies of their bodies had somehow mingled and made them alike. When Jane assumed the therapy it became an act of love in all but name, at least as he perceived it. Softly, she urged him to enter 'the slumber of / The dead and the unborn', and to forget all that earth-life had imposed on him.

The body could also be stilled in repose while the spirit left it, like a conjurer's trick. In *Queen Mab* the Fairy Queen worked such magic on the sleeping heroine Ianthe, summoning her to travel among the stars in the light, translucent chariot of her ethereal form. In a draft of *The Revolt of Islam*, too, Laon seemed 'to feel that I was dead/ To leave my own ~~corpse~~ self moveless lax & sere/ . . . Upon the mountain' when visions came. As the body lay asleep, all appetites and pains forgotten, mind perceived some intelligible world and spirit voyaged there, in a vehicle subtler than flesh.

In London in April 1811, in the lonely vine-trellised bower of his rooms in Poland Street, Shelley tried for a while to record his own dreams. He apparently covered many pages, until that world filled most of his existence, but it was not a habit with him. A few years later he took notes again. He recorded a recurrent image in sleep of a boy he had known at school, always the same dream, though at intervals of two or three years. He dreamed of scenes observed long before, unremarkable and forgotten, which then returned to haunt him. Conversely, a waking landscape would suddenly and irresistibly impress him, as if it had already established some 'intimate and unaccountable connexion . . . with the obscure parts of my own nature'. His dreams, he found, could be divided into 'Phrenic' and 'Psychic', the second deeper than the first and shockingly disrupting it, a 'dream of the soul' for which the mind was unprepared.

Around 1821 he wrote down, in fragments and in ink and pencil, what seemed to be the landscape of a dream. He was on a broad green way that wound across a plain. Wild mountains and deserts surrounded it but, typically of dreams, he was also in a crowd in a city:

> Some imperial metropolis
> Whose misty shapes, pyramid, dome & tower

Gleamed, like a pile of crags,
~~Over the forests of some weird~~

Noise seemed suspended. No voices came from the 'dispeopled city';
it was an ocean 'at once . . . deaf and loud', stunning itself, roaring in
silence. Shelley stood – 'I a man' – by the broad green road, with the
clouds rushing overhead.

More disturbingly he once found himself, awake and in the body,
in a landscape he had dreamed of. He was at Oxford in the winter
of 1810–11, walking in the nearby fields. The scene pleased him, quiet
and rural in an old-fashioned way; it held no threats. Intent on
'earnest' conversation, probably with Hogg, he turned the corner of
a lane,

> and the view, which its high banks and hedges had concealed,
> presented itself. The view consisted of a windmill, standing in one
> among many plashy meadows, inclosed with stone walls; the irreg-
> ular and broken ground between the wall and the road on which
> we stood; a long low hill behind the windmill, and a grey covering
> of uniform cloud spread over the evening sky. It was the season when
> the last leaf had just fallen from the scant and stunted ash. The scene
> surely was a common scene . . .

Yet it terrified him. He had been there before.

> I suddenly remembered to have seen that exact scene in some dream
> of long—

The sentence broke off, as if the pen had dropped from his fingers. It
seemed he had been in that place in a state of separation from the body,
in a different, fainter vehicle in which he was still sensually aware. Nothing
else could account for the 'thrilling horror' of seeing once more the
wall, the windmill and the grey unbroken sky. Even to think of them
five years later filled him with fear again. He sought the parlour and
Mary; he talked suddenly and urgently of warmth, the evening fireside,
sober conversation, winter fruits, shoring up solid things against his
ghosts.

'Pure anticipated cognition' – the sense 'that makes us seem/ To patch
up fragments of a dream' – constantly intrigued him, especially when
he peopled his poems with women he had not yet met, or mused on

the finished forms that lay within seeds and unsculpted stone. But to enter physically on a dream-scene was evidently quite different. It raised questions of consciousness and being he could not answer. It threw doubt on what he was.

Mary implied that there were many such episodes. 'Intense meditations on his own nature . . . thrilled him with pain,' she wrote, then with terror and awe, until Shelley could no longer bear to be alone in the unplumbed depths of himself. Like poor mad Tasso, whose cramped, frightened writing he pored over in the museum at Ferrara, he could feel his mind 'exceeding at times its own depth, and admonished to return by the chillness of the waters of oblivion striking upon its adventurous feet'. And the water through which he fell, full of 'glimmerings' of a different state of being, was often that of dreams.

To be awake on earth, on the other hand, was a form of dreaming to him. Emerging from sleep he would rub his eyes violently, as though he could not see properly in the 'garish', 'vacant' light that seemed, 'like a harsh voice', to slap him in the face; and he knew he could not. Whatever his practical ambitions for a world of wars, repression and inequality, his Poet's life informed him that it was all illusion. Mortal existence was no more than a reverie in passing,

> Where nothing is, but all things seem,
> And we the shadows of the dream . . .

He seemed to write those particular words, in 1820, under the spell of *La vida es sueño* by Calderón. There the hero, Segismundo, was dragged for a brief spell from his dark prison to his real birthright, the royal court. He was told, lest he get too ambitious, that the glittering show was merely a dream. Back in prison, he drew the obvious moral: that all life was fiction and deception.

> *Que es la vida? Una ilusión,*
> *una sombra, una ficción,*
> *y el mayor bien es pequeño;*
> *que toda la vida es sueño,*
> *y los sueños, sueños son.*

'All life and being are but dreams,' Shelley translated, aloud, straight from the book, as Edward Williams wrote it down early in 1822,

                                and dreams
        Themselves are but the dreams of other dreams.

This thought was nothing new to him. He had written of 'life's unquiet
dream' three years before reading Calderón, and of the world's 'phan-
tasmal scene' five years before that, in 1812. He could cite Plato and
Shakespeare, even at Eton, to back him up, as well as the conventions
of whole schools of poets. And he could play unendingly with *sueños*,
sueños son, delightedly layering and dimming the levels of material reality:

        Absorbed like one within a dream who dreams
        That he is dreaming . . .

With a Platonic gloss, Segismundo's dark prison was worldly life and
the glittering court was Reality, glimpsed for a moment only. It did
not matter that the prison–world was false; all the more reason to change
it, reform it, flood it with light, so that all men's minds could see things
as they should be. Segismundo, having established the illusion of life,
had nonetheless decided to act on the earth as if it could be saved.
    Shelley could do the same. To float away from the phantasmal scene
of earth, in sleep or in deep thought, was perhaps to reverse that false
waking into the realm of the senses that had begun at birth. To dream
might be to uncover truths from his subconscious mind, like those he
dared not utter under Mesmerism; to act out the true self, as the Witch
of Atlas had allowed; and to begin to understand, possibly, what death
was.
    That question had been with him since his first attempts at poetry.
It formed the last stanza of a poem written in 1810, when he was
seventeen. He had been wandering by moonlight with his first love,
Harriet Grove, through the Gothic shades of Hill Place near Horsham.
The overgrown gardens had become 'ivied bowers', the fountains
'cascades' and the chimneys, now gleaming white, tall towers against
the moon from which long, rank grass blew like tangled hair. The scene
made him think of 'mysteries' and, inevitably, death.

        Ah! Why do darkling shades conceal
        The hour, when man must cease to be?
        Why may not human minds unveil
        The dark shade of futurity?

Some years later he found a formulation, though it was not a
He had merely moved his dark curtain from 'the other side'

> Death is the veil which those who live call life:
> They sleep, and it is lifted: . . .

According to Trelawny, Shelley slid these words into conversations as
well as into poems. He meant to voice the questions that drummed in
his head, to debate them. Was sleep a form of death, or a deeper form
of waking life? Was life death, at least of the spirit? Was death a form
of sleep in which, in Hamlet's words, 'what dreams may come . . . Must
give us pause'? Or was it like the slumber of a baby, which 'in the dim
newness of its being feels/ The impulses of sublunary things'? In *Queen
Mab* Shelley called Death Sleep's brother, and described the quiescent
body of Ianthe as though either Sleep or Death had embraced her,
leaving her state indeterminate. His own sudden, random sleeps seemed
to take him to a brink from which, one day, he might not be pulled
back, and would not wish to be.

> Some say that gleams of a remoter world
> Visit the soul in sleep—that death is slumber,
> And that its shapes the busy thoughts outnumber
> Of those who wake and live.—

This intermediate state was naturally described by Shelley in terms
of water. The realm of mind, waking or sleeping, lay between flesh and
spirit, softer and more fluid than the body but heavier and darker than
the soul. He already knew, from those Phrenic and Psychic dreams, the
feel of different levels of his being, and was not inclined to confuse
them. Mind absorbed, and was passive. He encountered, as he entered
dreams, wide circles of the world of sleep spreading round him. The
Earth, seen through a 'dusk aery veil', had lost its solidity and spurious
clarity; its atoms grew slippery and diffuse, and the ghostly colour blue
began to steal across the scene. The shapes that swarmed there, thick
as fish in the ceaseless flow of the current, were neither confined nor
weighted down by words. Some, it seemed, might be shadows of idealisms
existing far beyond the Earth. And they could reach him in his dreams.
    This world was full of phantoms, many of them of the dead. In
Homer and Virgil the psyche left the body with the breath, a grey shade
fleeing as each warrior slumped to the earth. Some could not bear to

131

go far. In Plato's *Phaedo* and Milton's *Comus* ghosts clung to their graves, loving the sensual body and dreading separation. As a boy Shelley had waited, filled with 'fluttering fears', to see such apparitions round Warnham church, flitting among the headstones or approaching him under the heavy trees. He told stories of them, in his strange shrilling whisper, to frightened friends, and his boyhood writings – coloured vividly by Gothic penny dreadfuls – were crowded with spectral forms huddling and howling in the night air. Some were skeletons, others wispy rags of flesh, their eyeballs wide with longing and regret. In one early poem a phantom clung to him, his erstwhile love, sitting on his bed and stroking her long, cold fingers down his face:

> '[For] thou art mine and I am thine
> Till the sinking of the world . . .'

As an enlightened man he could laugh at these forms, classing them with witchcraft and the miracles of the Romish saints. But in 1820 he was still drawing them, haggard and wavy-lined as if they moved in water-light, with sagging mouths that seemed about to tell him 'what we are'. Across some he wrote the word 'Intelligences', suggesting they were bearers of information from another state of being. From that existence too seemed to come his own strange, wavering pseudo-writing, parallel undulating lines and quivering repeated letters that were the ghosts of what he might say, or might have said.

Dear Sir
    I am natu
    rally at a
    loss how to
    〰〰〰〰
    〰〰〰〰
    interpret your
    silence
    〰〰〰〰

Lucretius held that thoughts, dreams and apparitions were films thrown off from the surface of things, like the light skin of a snake. Shelley went much further, seeing all tyrannised notions of government, religion and God as clouds of phantoms, or bats, or Spenser's swarming flies, continually forming and fluttering round men's heads. Often they were images of the men who dreamed them, masks of their own faces, much as he had seen them in the streets of London or Pisa. In his regenerated world such disguises would fall and dissolve like leaves; but in the world as it was they grew ever more numerous and distorted until the bodies that produced them were drained of strength and grace, and the phantoms lived.

Shelley also saw and felt his own ideas around him, forms, scenes and phantasms as solid as any delusion of material life. 'Excess of passion' seemed to make them so, as well as 'the confusion of thought with the objects of thought'. It happened often, 'a sort of natural magic' as it seemed to him, or perhaps 'a waking dream'. (Laudanum, used heavily, could have much the same effect on him.) Those who observed him in such states found his eyes dull and insensible, as though he did not see the world about him or viewed it, in his cousin Medwin's words, in a sort of inner *camera obscura* where the image, projected through lenses or through gems, flashed with unearthly brightness.

Sitting once on a grassy slope behind Villa Magni, under the shadows of a chestnut tree and within the sound of the sea, he felt this state creep over him again. He was in trance

Which was not slumber, for the shade it spread

Was so transparent that the scene came through
As clear as when a veil of light is drawn
O'er evening hills they glimmer; and I knew

That I had felt the freshness of that dawn,
Bathed in the same cold dew my brow & hair
And sate as thus upon that slope of lawn

Under the self same bough . . .

Again he was dreaming, yet awake, in a light that gradually grew harder and colder around him. He was beside a dusty road; a procession, led by blind Life driving a chariot, was approaching. As it rolled towards him, he 'arose aghast/Or seemed to rise, so mighty was the trance'. He was in a body, and could ask questions which he apparently spoke aloud. But he could feel neither the proper weight nor the pain of flesh and blood.

He could easily live like this, at a distance from himself, immersed in his ideas rather than in the world. Thinking in early 1814 of an imaginary young woman he might love, rather than Harriet, he began to believe that he knew her, had declared himself to her, and that 'already were the difficulties surmounted that opposed an entire union'. As he mused he was tramping, in his old black coat with the metal buttons, along 40 miles of muddy roads between Bracknell and Field Place; he barely noticed the woods and hills, green with the budding spring, and was unconscious of his physical fatigue. That same 'veil of light' lay across his life, bathing the scene with the love he had invented in the world of his mind. The unknown young woman also lay there, a ghost sleeping in the lie of the landscape, as the peaceful dead might sleep, stretch and stir under the graveyard grass.

Sometimes, too, he seemed to make a phantasm of himself that could be seen by others. He appeared thus in misty pencil lines written for *Adonais*, then scribbled out—

Another yet ~~he is alone~~ ~~himself alone~~
~~He walks~~ a weak & wandering Form
                    ~~wanders as~~
~~A dis~~ As little like the rest as ghosts are men
The last, the weakest as behind the storm
it is ~~the last~~ a Form
~~Most like a ghost's~~

There was no horror in this apparition, no clutching hand or rictus of a scream. He had painted two of his hero-selves as ghosts in early novels, their hideous eyes glaring like meteors and their flesh suddenly crumbling from the bone. But here he was a silent shadow in his ordinary body and clothes. Jane Williams glimpsed him thus in Italy, crossing and then recrossing the terrace of Villa Magni; he could not have done so without leaping 20 feet to the ground at either side, but he strode by the window unconcerned, hatless and jacketless, off sailing. Friends saw him walking in the woods at Lerici, when he was nowhere near. 'He wanders, like a day-appearing dream,' he wrote,

~~Over the desarts of~~
~~Thro~~ the dim wildernesses of the mind
~~Over Thro~~ desert ~~heaths~~ woods, & tracts which seem
    ~~Like Ocean, homeless~~ . . .

Like Ocean, homeless, boundless, unconfined
~~Him have I met in savage woods as one~~

In that same state of mind, the concept becoming the image, he saw others as ghosts. Returning to Wales in 1812 after a year away, he found his old sad thoughts of friends there, now 'in appearance' dim and strange, 'since I felt that they were alive'. And in the late spring of 1822 he caught sight of five-year-old Allegra, Byron's daughter by Claire, dead a fortnight or so before. She appeared to him as a naked child rising from the sea foam in the moonlight, joyfully clapping her hands (the hands that had slipped into his when he had last seen her, pulling him across the lawns of the convent where she was kept). Edward Williams remembered Shelley grabbing his arm violently, in terror, crying 'There it is again—there!' For his part, though he tried, Williams could make out nothing. 'This', he reported, 'was a trance that it required some reasoning and philosophy entirely to awaken him from, so forcibly had the vision operated on his mind.'

More often, however, Shelley saw himself. At times of illness or distress his own double walked beside him or came silently to meet him. In June 1822, that haunted summer of his own death, he met his double at Villa Magni. A cloaked phantasm drew him from bed to the saloon, thence to the terrace where the sea shone to the horizon, and raised its hood to reveal his own face. It asked him '*Shelley, siete soddisfato?*' 'Shelley, are you satisfied?' or, as he also translated it, 'How long do you mean to be content?' – that Faustian challenge to him, to slip the bonds of Earth. Immediately afterwards his friends found him leaning against the wall, his eyes open but 'evidently unconscious', repeating the words.

This, he insisted, was another waking vision. He had not been asleep. The figure he had seen was not fiend-Shelley, but his ordinary idea of himself made tangible. In *Prometheus Unbound* his hero had been instructed by the Earth in the science and meaning of such sightings, as though, at a certain level of enlightenment, they were almost ordinary:

> . . . Ere Babylon was dust,
> The Magus Zoroaster, my dead child,
> Met his own image walking in the garden.
> That apparition, sole of men, he saw.
> For know there are two worlds of life and death:
> One that which thou beholdest; but the other

Is underneath the grave, where do inhabit
The shadows of all forms that think and live
Till death unite them and they part no more;
Dreams and the light imaginings of men,
And all that faith creates or love desires,
Terrible, strange, sublime and beauteous shapes.
There thou art, and dost hang, a writhing shade . . .

There was also, sometimes, something vaguer beside him. It was difficult to see, for the harsh daylight obscured it; but it kept pace with his footsteps, glimmering like the shade of 'a forgotten form of sleep', familiarly attentive and 'silent as a ghost'. It was not 'pale Pain/ My shadow', though Pain too crouched often at his shoulder, determined not to leave. This particular shape and shadow was neither to be dreaded nor repulsed. On the contrary, though apparently a dream or 'light imagining' like the rest, it was to be desperately longed for.

2
Reflection

Two anglers saw Shelley on the river at Marlow in 1817, as they punted slowly past. The poet was crouching in the bow of his boat, alone, and transfixed by something in the water. His look was so piteous and horror-struck that one fisherman supposed he wished to drown himself. His friend thought he had probably dropped his brandy flask in the river.

What Shelley was gazing at was his own reflection – 'the thing in the water', as he mildly told them. In *The Revolt of Islam*, which he had broken off from writing, he described, as it seemed, what he had seen that day.

> I saw my countenance reflected there;—
>> And then my youth fell on me like a wind
> Descending on still waters—my thin hair
>> Was prematurely gray, my face was lined
>> With channels, such as suffering leaves behind,
> Not age . . .

In *Alastor*, too, the Poet came to a well among the trees and lingered, looking.

>> His eyes beheld
> Their own wan light through the reflected lines
> Of his thin hair, distinct in the dark depth
> Of that still fountain; as the human heart,

Gazing in dreams over the gloomy grave,
Sees its own treacherous likeness there.

In truth he would have seen little of this: only his own obscure form
leaning down, as the leaves threw their shadows on the surface. Near
Marlow the Thames, flowing over chalk, showed a clear bed and translucent water in which all images faded. But Shelley was gazing into his
own mind, as well as into water. Invariably that glass was dark, still and
quiet, wind rarely stirring it. And there, naturally, he saw perfect pictures.
Across the first rough draft of 'Ozymandias', skewing his notebook sideways, he tried the mirror-effect himself, sketching a range of peaks and
foothills and then, below, attempting their exact reflections. Things seen
in water were unmoved by surface turbulence. What sense obscured his
mind held fast, and dreamed or brooded on.

Of all the flowers whose characters Shelley borrowed, the 'fairest'
were the narcissi that grew at the water's edge. He became the golden
plant of the Greek meadows and the Sussex forest-fields, a young man
resting languidly by the stream, or the fountains, or the abyss, in which
he lovingly observed himself. The garland of the Poet of *Alastor*, appro-
priately, was to have been of narcissi,

                              whose yellow flowers
          For ever gaze on their own drooping eyes,
          Reflected in the crystal calm.

In a furious, much-deleted fragment Shelley told a critic he was only
this flower, lost in abstractions, so self-absorbed (if that was how his
enemy chose to see him) that nothing he could do could possibly hurt
him:

          ~~since~~ I am the Narcissus, ~~thou~~ art free
          To pine into a sound with hating me.

Still water had an almost hypnotic attraction for him. Hogg recalled
him, in Oxford days, loitering until dusk at the edge of a quarry-pond
at Shotover Hill, 'gazing in silence on the water, repeating verses aloud'
or sometimes earnestly debating, as if the water argued back. When
Trelawny and Mary lost him on the Pisan shore he was naturally traced
to the side of a gloomy, secluded pool, a 'cauldron' as he told them,
where witches made their incantations. In *Rosalind and Helen* a pale

snake crept, like him, to a pool deep in the woods, becoming as it sipped a creature of rainbow beauty 'bathed in the light of his own loveliness'. Pools and springs, he knew, were sacred to the Camenae who imparted prophecy and inspiration, and he told Maria Gisborne that his poems came from 'Helicon or Himeros', the love-lit haunt of the water nymphs.

Reflection was almost always more beautiful than life. Sunset on the Jura snowfields looked far lovelier to Shelley in the lake that lay below; at noon, 'a more heavenly and serener light' than daylight was reflected from the 'icy mirrors' of the mountain peaks. The small pools in the forest of the Pisan shore, suddenly encountered in the long grass or among the pines, held perfect fragments of the trees, the blue sky and the clouds. Indeed they were brighter and more perfect, 'sweet views' within a firmament

> More boundless than the depth of night
> And purer than the day . . .

It might even seem, if he looked long enough, that the trees above were in underwater dimness, 'As still as in the silent deep/ The Ocean woods may be', while those below were real.

Hogg also saw Shelley transfixed by the least puddle on his path. He would loiter near it, abstracted, 'and it was no easy task to get him to quit it' – as if, like Lucretius, he believed that in puddles 'you seem to look down upon the clouds and heaven, and see the heavenly bodies after a wonderful fashion buried in a heaven below the earth'. Such an image reappeared in the climactic third act of *Prometheus Unbound*, two kingfishers seen in water in a world inverted and transformed:

> And thinning one bright bunch of amber berries
> With quick long beaks, and in the deep there lay
> Those lovely forms imaged as in a sky . . .

One evening at Pisa in 1821, watching the sunset over the Arno–Serchio canal, Shelley asked himself the obvious question.

Why is the reflexion in that canal far more beautiful than the objects it reflects. The colours are more vivid, & yet blended with more harmony & the openings from within into the soft & tender colours of the distant wood & the intersection of the mountain line surpass & misrepresent truth.

A little later, he returned to the problem.

It is by no means indisputable that what is true, or rather that which the disciples of a certain mechanistic and superficial philosophy call true, is more excellent than the beautiful.

There were deeper, lovelier things, in short, than those his senses took to be the right way round and real.

On the Ponte al Mare that spanned the Arno, leaning over the parapet in another soft dusk that summer, he mused again on the city's reflection. Night was drawing in, and a light wind blew dust and straws around the streets; the evening star hung to the east, above the mountains. Within the 'fleeting river' of his thoughts lay the image of the city, ochre houses and stone towers, 'Immovably unquiet',

> . . . and forever
> It trembles, but it never fades away . . .

That line, picked up from Wordsworth, had become a favourite with him. His Witch of Atlas dispensed her magic, changing sleepers' dreams,

> where within the surface of the river
> The shadows of the massy temples lie
> And never are erased—but tremble ever
> Like things which every cloud can doom to die . . .

In his 'Ode to Liberty', too, written to urge on the popular uprisings of 1820 in Naples and Spain, the shining, wavering columns of ancient Greece underpinned the bold, brash structures of the present day. On the surface frothed the stories which Shelley, like any onlooker, pieced together from rumour and the newspapers. But silently beneath lay the 'divine work' of Greece, 'her harmonies and forms'. Plato in the *Republic* had taught: that beyond the world's illusions, those shadows men saw on the walls of their prison-cave, lay the unchanging realm of what was real and what was true.

The ripples of the surface current could not change this scene. It became for Shelley an image of timelessness and purity, the reverse of human life. His identity as a man, he knew, was dependent on ever-changing time and space: the constant repositioning of objects seen ('*we move, they move*') and the sense of moments lived ('*it has been, it is, it shall be*'). 'Mind', he sighed, thinking also of his own, 'cannot be considered pure.' Yet under this obsessive chopping and dividing lay unchanging perfect forms: Beauty, Justice, Truth, Equality, preserved in thought as deep and still as 'the clear hyaline', sheer glass. By considering such ideals the mind moved closer to them, again becoming what it contemplated, spotless, unmoving and calm. They existed where 'time and place and number are not' and as a poet he walked among them, as he had walked beneath the sea.

If he copied the Greeks he might be pure like this, even as a man. For him they were 'those divine people who, in their very errors, are the mirrors, as it were, in which all that is delicate and graceful contemplates itself'. They were, he told Peacock, 'the Gods whom we should worship—pardon me'. He confessed Plato his god especially, and seemed to think of his own octavo copy of the *Dialogues* as a pocket mirror, holding the light and his own best reflection. The dramas of Aeschylus, Sophocles and Euripides were also a glass in which he saw himself, 'under a thin disguise of circumstance, stript of all but that ideal perfection and energy which every one feels to be the internal type of all that he loves, admires and would become'. His Poet-selves, in childhood, had been taught in Greece or by Greeks; as a man, reading Greek works incessantly in translation and in the original, he hoped to approach the ideal they reflected.

His longing was given added force when, in March 1821, the Greeks rose up against their Turkish occupiers. For Shelley, no matter how degraded the modern Greeks had become, this was the new dawn of an Athenian Republic in the style of Plato and Homer. He never thought of fighting there – his health did not seem to allow it – but in his verse drama *Hellas*, written in conscious imitation of the *Persae* of Aeschylus, he urged the revolution on. 'I try to be what I might have been,' he told his friend John Gisborne. In his preface he declared that 'We are all Greeks', and wished it might be true.

He could make himself yet more Greek by gazing at the statues they had made. In the library at Marlow he kept his own life-size casts of Apollo and Venus Urania, their plaster carefully scraped to perfect smoothness and whiteness. He imagined how, when Greece first came to be, the forms of its statues already lay there,

And, like unfolded flowers beneath the sea,
  Like the man's thought dark in the infant's brain,
  Like aught that is which wraps what is to be,
  Art's deathless dreams lay veiled by many a vein
Of Parian stone . . .

In the first draft, he played with the image:

~~Those forms of marble shapes~~
~~shadows of a shadows of eternal grace~~
living shapes

He visited the galleries of Rome and Florence in 1819 especially to observe how far 'that ideal Beauty of which we have so intense yet so obscure an apprehension, is realised in external forms'. Day after day he returned there, with notebook in hand and his whole frame aching from the effort of standing and viewing. In the dim interior light the statues stood, crowding, white and still, like ghosts, or the bodies of naked bathers seen under water. He circled them, getting as close as he could, chin to smooth stone, to drink in 'the spirit of their forms'.

The association of living body and graven image had long fascinated him. In *Queen Mab* the heroine Ianthe, her spirit lulled in sleep or translated in death, was 'fair/ As breathing marble', her blue veins showing faintly through white skin; in *The Revolt of Islam* the bodies of young women, wound in their own fair hair, lay piled

As if not dead, but slumbering quietly
Like forms which sculptors carve, then love to agony.

Emilia Viviani entranced him, Medwin thought, because her Grecian hair and pale skin, and the faultless lines of her profile, were those of a marble image of loveliness come alive.

Shelley in the galleries was searching explicitly for unity, harmony and simplicity, for light and life. He found them in unexpected places. The breast and belly of a Bacchus, for example, 'whose lines fading into each other, are continued with a gentle motion as it were to the utmost extremity of his limbs', suggested to Shelley 'divine and supernatural beauty':

like some fine strain of harmony which flows round the soul and enfolds it and leaves it in the soft astonishment of a satisfaction, like the pleasure of love with one whom we most love, which having taken away desire, leaves pleasure, sweet pleasure.

The exact modelling of the human body was not important to him. Far better, he noted more than once, if the sculptor had known nothing of modern discoveries in anatomy, or the 'lying forms' of earth. Shelley revelled instead in shapes made vaguer and more abstract, even effaced, as if fluid Love enfolded them, and as if a deeper, higher Beauty informed or defined them. Thus a Ganymede enthralled him because its fingers, half lifted by 'the spirit of pleasure, of light, life and beauty', seemed deprived of 'the natural weight of human flesh'. And the limbs of Venus Anadyomene, rising from the sea, 'flow into each other with never-ending continuity of sweetness', less like an earthly woman than like the element from which she had come.

Shelley dwelt on nakedness, wishing also ('Curse these fig leaves') that the male anatomy had been left uncensored. Yet some forms, he noted, seemed too beautiful to show so explicitly. Many female subjects in the galleries wore a film of silk that blurred the body's contours much as water would do, or the last unchiselled layer of the stone. 'Few poets of the highest class', he wrote later, 'have chosen to exhibit the beauty of their conceptions in its naked truth and splendour.' For these lovely forms reflected others even lovelier, unimaginable by him and, perhaps, by any mortal man. 'If the reflection is so beautiful,' he jotted in Italian in his notebook in 1820, 'only think how they must be the right way round!'

Yet there was a darker side to this, also noted as he strolled through the churches and galleries of Italy. Works of art could hold terrors, reflecting aspects of himself he did not want to see and stamping him with evil and despair. Shelley looked all the same, staring hard, as he had gazed on the grey hair and pain lines of his own young, shadowy face. The Moses of Michelangelo horrified him, 'distorted from all that is natural & majestic . . . no temperance no modesty no feeling . . . no sense of beauty'. Disgusting too was a painting by Guercino at Bologna of a Carthusian in the desert, his face 'wrinkled like a dried snakes skin' and in a robe of 'death-coloured flannel'. This death robe shed a 'yellow putrified ghastly hue' on everything around it, including Shelley, jaundiced too with grave-shadows as he stood and gazed.

In Florence he paused for some time before Leonardo's *Medusa*, which showed the monster lying dead in the 'hideous light' of the night mountains. Her snake-hair was still writhing. Bats flew in a sky that seemed to flare with dread, while a venomous lizard crept across the rocks. He gazed until he felt himself under the picture's spell, his life too draining out of him, and was tempted to turn away in revulsion from what he was absorbing and becoming. Yet he also saw loveliness in that terror and beauty in that face, even 'radiance' in the tangling, viperous locks, because Medusa in death was looking on Heaven and reflecting, like a mirror, Heaven to him.

> Yet it is less the horror than the grace
>   Which turns the gazer's spirit into stone,
> Whereon the lineaments of that dead face
>   Are graven, till the characters be grown
> Into itself, and thought no more can trace . . .

Perhaps great art, by its nature, could not wreak evil on him. Sculpture especially, he wrote in his notebook in Florence, could not express 'coarser and more violent effects'. On the other hand,

> Tenderness, sensibility, enthusiasm, terror, poetic inspiration, the profound, the beautiful, Yes.

His poems were also meant to do this. As 'idealisms of moral excellence', 'dreams of what ought to be, or may be' as he explained them once to Hunt, he placed them before the public mind. His own ideal character was also set down there, a challenge to himself: the Shelley he could be.

Yet he did not underestimate the difficulty. Time and again he made idealisms of his friends, only to be disappointed. Elizabeth Hitchener, the Sussex schoolmistress who became in 1811–12 his chief confidante and correspondent, was given 'a tongue of energy and an eye of fire', and imagined as 'the embryon of a mighty intellect which may one day enlighten thousands.' She could not possibly live up to it. Hogg too, his best friend, Shelley turned into 'a character moulded as I imagine in all the symmetry of virtue', excellence and strength incarnate, surely fitted for 'friendship . . . celestial & intellectual', capable of being divine. The Hogg who walked the streets was laughably unlike this: a worldly, mocking, sarcastic young man, well fitted for his life in the law. Hogg liked to dream of being buried under a milliner's step, where pretty feet and ankles

would tread over him all day. He also showed an unhealthil
interest in Shelley's women, and, left alone with the newly marrie
for some days in October 1811, did his best to seduce her. The
this traumatised Shelley. 'How I have loved you!' he cried out in a letter
of that November. 'I was even ashamed to tell you how!' Once he was
obliged to see his friend as a fallen man, one of those 'votaries of selfishness', Shelley for a time could not write to him or bear to think of
him, as if a shape of perfection had been shattered.

As Goethe put it, something foreign, some dullness and dirt, always
clung to the noblest conception the mind could form. Shelley quoted
his lines with feeling in a letter, 'though I dare say I shall quote it wrong':

> Den herrlichsten, den sich der Geist empängt
> Drängt immer fremd und fremder stoff sich an.

★   ★   ★

What he also sought in water or in mirrors were forms too dazzling,
or too profound, to be seen by ordinary earthly sight. When men were
brought blinking out of Plato's cave, facing Reality rather than the
shadows of things, they were advised to look at 'the divine reflections'
first in water or through dark glass, lest the truth should blind them.
The mind, Plato said, should be treated like an eye, guided gently from
obscurity to light. In the third book of the *Republic* the forms of letters
of the alphabet were pictured floating in mirrors; in the sixth, reflections of diagonals and squares in water were described as closer to their
realities than when they were drawn on paper. Only in reflections could
Dante view the spirits of Paradise or the light divine; when he tried
to see the realities that cast them, his weak Earth-sight could make out
nothing there. Such 'shadows', in fact still bright, made a paradox Shelley
loved and pursued. To glimpse them was not only dazzling but left,
before his eyes, a ghost-shape of darkness shot through with the remains
of the light: a dream of a shadow, as he also was.

In search of each 'shadow which was light' he looked longingly at
night water under the moon and the stars. Almost always, he described
the reflection rather than the actuality of the lights of Heaven. Like his
Witch of Atlas in her hollow gourd, he could play 'quips and cranks'
with them that way, sailing on pavements of the constellations or, like
a skater, 'circling the image of a shooting star'.

Yet he also loved these reflections for their own sake. On the morning of man's deliverance in *Prometheus Unbound* he watched one white point, the Morning Star, quivering in a lake at dawn: now growing fainter, now gleaming again as the waves faded, then lost in the mirrored splendour of the rising sun. The ocean in *Queen Mab*, typically, reflected 'The pale and waning stars',

. . .

> And vesper's image on the western main
> Is beautifully still.

His clouds, drifting in the night sky, deliberately dispersed to let the stars shine through on the waters of the world.

Shelley never tired of this. In one of his *Prometheus* notebooks, an image of stars that 'gaze upon themselves within the sea' seemed to please him so much that he wrote nothing after it, but swooped a double diagonal line to the bottom of the page. And the noonday well to which the Poet came in *Alastor* reflected, as well as 'all the woven boughs above,/ And each depending leaf, and every speck/ Of azure sky,' a strange but irresistible visitor, 'some inconstant star'.

This long still gaze was very like love. He saw it in Nature, in the quiet reflected scenes of the Pisan shore, with Jane beside him. Each pool embraced the green forest; in return,

> Like one beloved the scene had lent
> To the dark water's breast,
> Its every leaf and lineament
> With more than truth exprest . . .

He had seen it, too, as Harriet soothed the newborn Ianthe, the child's 'faintly dimpled' face reflecting the mother's and the mother's the child's as she hugged it to her breast. Each gazed on the other, one lovingly active, one passive; each seeking, as in a constantly tested line from the making of *Epipsychidion*,

> The ~~image~~ shadow reflex of my heart

In Mary's grey-brown eyes he saw the same. He sometimes seemed to draw them, or his own, in his notebooks, the web of the iris carefully cross-hatched and detailed. Eyes, he believed, became intricate from 'the acquisition of knowledge and the cultivation of sentiment'. Dreams, too, could be read there. In their 'mazy depth of colour behind colour' he could lose himself with looking, as Narcissus did, at his own idealised image reflected in the mind of another. Shelley wrote of this and then, later, covered the facing page with a swarm of eyes.

> Yet look on me—take not thine eyes away
>   Which feed upon the love within mine own
> Although it be but the reflected ray
>   Of thy sweet beauty from my spirit thrown . . .
>   Yet speak to me! Thy voice is as the tone
> Of my heart's echo, and I think I hear
>   That thou yet lovest me—yet thou alone
> Like one before a mirror, ~~take no~~ care
> Of aught but thine own ~~form~~ imaged too truly there.

At such moments Shelley saw himself graced by 'mind's shadow', calmer and more pure. This was what his Poet-self looked for, leaning over lakes and pools; this was what he was seeking, crouching in his boat, in the Thames that day.

> How many a one though none be near to love
>
> Loves then the shade of his own soul half seen
> In any mirror

In deepest thought, using the inner eye of his mind, he could sometimes begin to observe within himself the bright form of which Shelley, with his lined cheeks and greying hair, was only the mortal shadow. 'We see dimly see,' he wrote – and then broke off, struggling.

These words ineffectual & metaphorical—Most words so. No help—

But he resumed:

within our intellectual nature a miniature as it were of our entire self, yet deprived of all that we condemn or despise, the ideal proto-type of ~~all that of~~ every thing excellent or lovely that we are capable of conceiving as belonging to the nature of man. Not only the portrait of our external being but an assemblage of the minutest particulars of which our nature is composed: a mirror whose surface reflects only the forms of purity & brightness . . . To this we eagerly refer all sensations, thirsting that they should resemble or correspond with it. The discovery of its antitype . . . is the invisible & unattainable point to which Love tends.

This form, though apparently so distant from him, was to himself as the die to the impression, the perfect mirror-image in which he could sink and settle, line for line, form to form, in the purest union of being. This, indeed, was the ambition of those stars

That gaze upon themselves within the sea.

Hence the hours spent musing by ponds and pools and, in female company, the uncomfortable intensity of his longing, blue-eyed stare.

★   ★   ★

Shelley's visit to Southey in Keswick in 1811 had not been an unqualified success. He fell asleep and slid under the table while Southey was reading his *Kehama* to him ('my most favourite poem', or not). He pronounced Mrs Southey's teacakes nasty because they oozed too deliciously with currants and butter, starting an argument and unnecessarily upsetting her. He shocked Southey by remarking to Harriet (Southey remembered it a decade later) that he would go on living with her only as long as he liked her. The elder poet humoured him as a younger version of himself, still with his revolutionary ardour: an errant spirit who, once loose in the parlour, should be kept well clear of the best china.

They agreed on man's perfectibility, disagreed on parliamentary reform and talked God, naturally. Shelley, then full of Godwin, Holbach and the French encyclopaedists, called himself an atheist. Southey picked that apart: since his young shadow seemed to see the universe as God, he was surely more of a pantheist, like Coleridge. Shelley objected; in the language of reason, 'God' was just 'another signification of the Universe', but he confessed he saw Deity as 'the mass of infinite *intelligence*'. Southey, sensing an opening, recommended him to read Berkeley, and expected him to be a Berkeleian in a week.

Being a Berkeleian meant seeing the world not as a random coalescence of atoms, but as a construct of mind. Things existed as they were perceived by the percipient, and varied with the point of view. A proper Berkeleian would have gone further, arguing that objects did not exist *unless* they were perceived, but Shelley never did so. 'All things exist as they are perceived—at least in relation to the percipient' was his own, more flexible, formulation.

In other words, he himself made the world appear the way it was. '[Man's] own mind is his law,' as he put it; 'his own mind is all things to him'. The supposedly solid universe around him, he concluded then, slightly misquoting Prospero in *The Tempest*, 'is "such stuff as dreams are made of".' Being so, his waking dreams were as valid as ordinary sight; being so, they could extend as far as, even beyond, the universe itself.

Yet mind was passive. That 'particularly acute' opinion, 'a doctrine of which even then I had long been persuaded', had already been noted down in his borrowed copy of Berkeley by Charles Lloyd, the owner. Shelley took the thought further:

> that the basis of all things cannot be, as the popular philosophy alleges, mind, is sufficiently evident. Mind, as far as we have any experience of its properties, and beyond that experience how vain is argument! cannot create, it can only perceive.

Like a sheet of calm water, his mind was 'the mirror upon which all forms are reflected, and in which they compose one form'. And if all minds made One Mind, a universe of congregating thoughts, then some power behind Mind acted on it constantly, though dwelling itself apart from all that moved and changed. Shelley had no idea, no experience, that could suggest what that power might be. But as he wrote in his *Essay on Life* in 1819, 'it is infinitely improbable that the cause of mind, that is, of existence, is similar to mind'.

He had professed, to Southey and others, that he believed in a vast intelligence ('the Soul of the Universe, the intelligent & *necessarily* beneficent actuating principle'). The notion that some intellectual force should animate mind, and thus existence, seemed true within the ambit of himself; therefore it might be true beyond him. 'I may not be able to adduce proofs,' he told Hogg in January 1811,

> but I think that the leaf of a tree, the meanest insect on wh. we trample are in themselves more conclusive than any which can be adduced that some vast intellect animates Infinity—

Shelley knew how dangerous this was. 'Intelligence' could drift perilously close to creation or design, and thus to God, as the Jews and Christians imaged him. Hume's works had disabused him of such notions long ago, rendering them as absurd as the Hottentot's worship of an insect or the Negro's of a bunch of feathers. Yet there had to remain, if his perceptions were to have any meaning, a source from which his thoughts drew energy and to which his ideas were referred. Lying in the grass, drifting on water – observing the leaf-light or the tiny fly crushed on the page of his book – he felt this to be true.

His first sight of the Alps in 1814 found his thoughts in turmoil. ('Their immensity staggers the imagination, & so far surpasses all conception that it requires an effort of understanding to believe that they are indeed mountains.') The high peaks were always to produce in him both awe and, inevitably, defiance. Claire remembered how he sang as they crossed the Mount Cenis pass in 1818, going to Italy: a strange Shakespearean ditty repeated over and over as the coach conveyed them upwards.

> Now Heaven neglected is by Men
> And Gods are hung upon every tree
> But not the more for loss of them
> Shall this fair world unhappy be.

Yet Shelley sensed a presence in the mountains. In *The Assassins*, a fragment started when the Alps first loomed above him, he described Nature in her 'omnipotence' creating a paradise there of crystalline fountains, sighing pines, rainbow vapours and meteors that mingled with the falling snow. 'The fluctuating elements', he wrote,

> seemed to have been rendered everlastingly permanent in forms of wonder and delight . . . No spectator could have refused to believe that some spirit of great intelligence and power had hallowed these wild and beautiful solitudes to a deep and solemn mystery.

In the summer of 1816, on a second visit to the Alps with Mary and Claire, he scrawled his defiance of God in the visitors' books but wondered, as his mule slithered and stumbled over the Mer de Glace at Chamonix, exactly what power lay behind the petrified waves and pinnacles of ice, the deep blue ravines and the peaks. The first name he gave it – writing to Peacock, a lively aficionado of obscure cults

and sects – was Ahriman, the evil principle of the Zoroastrians. '[...]
you . . . imagine him', he wrote,

> throned among these desolating snows, among these palaces of death
> & frost, sculptured in this their terrible magnificence by the unsparing
> hand of necessity . . .

Ahriman's realm was one in which thought was frozen and man's will
held prisoner. It was 'as if frost had suddenly bound up the waves &
whirlpools of a mighty torrent', Shelley's mind too caught fast and
breathless in the huge ice sea. The streams were 'voiceless', their springs
'changed to mines of sunless crystal'. Yet these thoughts might be freed.
The great glacier was not still. On the contrary, he told Peacock, 'It
breaks & rises for ever; its undulations sink whilst others rise. In these
regions every thing changes & is in motion.' As he picnicked with Mary
and Claire at the glacier's edge they could hear it creak and crack; they
once saw, not far off, the thunderclap smoke and rubble of an avalanche
it caused, bearing down into the valley 'all the ruins of the mountains'.

The more Shelley gazed in his astonishment, the more the landscape
shifted. Far away, he could hear

> the roar
> Of the rent ice-cliff which the sunbeams call
> Plunging into the vale—. . . the blast
> Descending on the pines—the torrents pour

Three years later, in *Prometheus Unbound*, he made this the echo of all
men's thoughts suddenly released from the ice. What, then, was the
cause? Behind the turmoil he could sense an immense strength bearing
down on things, moulding and shaping them. It seemed to preside
among the peaks, far above the jumble of the landscape, like Mont
Blanc – the highest mountain he could see – in its unmoving realms
of ice. No man could reach such altitudes by climbing. But Shelley
could walk there among snowflakes hushed in thick white drifts, meteors
in repose, storm vapours stilled in the blue air, silent winds; and he
imagined that, if he were buried there, he might share something of
'their own eternity' among the deep, pure fields of snow.

In his notebook, in quick pencil, he began to speculate and sketch.
The great mountain represented the secret law that governed thought:
solemn, inaccessible, transcendent. Mutability and chance could not

come near it. Only mind could ponder it. In its remoteness it marked the last of the visible and natural causes men could see before, as Holbach wrote, they lost the thread of their understanding of the world and reached, clumsily and blindly, for the notion 'God'. Shelley saw the peak far off, floating above the clouds; he drew the range, a series of squarish castellated shapes, and pencilled in the distant air one faint word, 'Power'.

Meanwhile, closer, on the little wooden bridge that spanned the ravine of the Arve, he watched the river far beneath him. This too was 'Power', driving furiously through mind 'the everlasting universe' of things and thoughts, never stopping. From where he stood he gazed deep into the narrow vale: the image of his mind and all others, 'many-coloured, many voiced', losing itself in darkness, shrouded by pines and overhung by rainbows. He had kept company with the 'terrible' Arve, swollen with rains, as it ran in its savage chasm alongside the road from Geneva to Chamonix. The river copied his own thoughts, 'now dark—now glittering', and ceaselessly bursting and raving among the rocks. Within the tumult of the falling water lay images, as yet 'unsculptured', like the goddess-figure of black rock he had begun to see in the waterfall near Maglans under veil after veil of foam. Mind received all this, constantly battered by impressions, yet hoarding them also in its caverns and its silence. Overwhelmingly, too, his mind framed the scene as if the landscape's very existence – Arve, forests, mountain, Power – flowed from his.

Not only Berkeley had prepared him for this thought. Shelley had wandered through Clarens some days earlier with Rousseau's *Julie* in his hand, aware that another and 'mighty' mind had carved out the landscape before him. The characters of Rousseau's novel, Julie and St Preux, fated to love but doomed to part, seemed to walk with Shelley on the narrow road or among the hanging vines, 'looking towards those mountains which I now behold.—nay treading on the ground where now I tread'. In 'Julie's' wood, where St Preux had first embraced her, the sweet smell of haymaking at evening breathed both Rousseau's spirit, and hers. On the castle terrace 'her' roses grew, the posterity of others she had touched. Shelley fought back tears as he pressed the withered petals between the pages of her story. These were not mortal things but 'imperishable creations' that he would fold away in his heart.

St Preux himself explained that at the height of his love for Julie every part of the scene was beautified by the thought of her. Each tree sheltered her, each grassy bank invited her, the streams delightfully obstructed her way across the rocks. Conversely, when he had lost her,

One sees nothing green any more, the grass is yellow and withered, the trees are bare, the dry and cold north-east wind heaps up snow and ice, and all nature is dead in my eyes, like the hope in the bottom of my heart.

Back at his hotel in Chamonix Shelley inked over, on pages still smudged with spray, the lines he had written about Mont Blanc. But the second draft of his poem was as wild as the first. He had viewed the mountain, he told Peacock, with 'a sentiment of extatic wonder, not unallied to madness'. The madness, this time, stemmed not from his sense of dislocation in the world, but from the realisation that his existence and the mountain's were one in his mind. He had made the whole landscape his idea, his thought, and part of him. Mind became what it contemplated, and what he saw became himself. Indeed, as he explained to Peacock, 'All was as much our own, as if we had been the creators of such impressions in the minds of others, as now occupied our own.' He could do this; he could shape, colour, fill with meaning, invest with light and life. Hence his ecstasy, which he told Byron he could not relate in a letter; hence the 'undisciplined overflowing of the soul' in his poem, which he did not try to hide.

The river he had watched, of course, would not stay pure for long. Though it fell foaming and white from its source among the snows, it would soon choke itself with the flotsam of human scheming. Before long it would become the 'dark stream' of history, 'tainted with death' and floating with sceptres and swords, just as the glacier at Chamonix had carried the ruins of rocks and sand and stones. Blood, mixed with hard rain, would pollute the melting snow. His own thoughts could not escape this stain, much as he might try. He had brought to the River Arve his own 'tribute of waters' from 'secret springs':

> —with a sound but half its own,
> Such as a feeble brook will oft assume
> In the wild woods, among the mountains lone,
> Where waterfalls around it leap forever . . .

But this was one rivulet only, one faint voice, in the flood of all men's thoughts. It was changed and coloured by all that it encountered, as by 'every word and suggestion' which he ever admitted to act upon his consciousness. And it was surely so soon lost, as he had watched from a boat the muddy waters of the Rhône swirling and spreading in the blue of Lake Geneva, or the dark green Reuss dissolving instantly in the strong yellow swell of the Rhine.

Yet perhaps his thoughts did not so swiftly disappear. Even in calm, the wide surfaces of lakes and oceans were a vast amalgamation of tiny waves. The sea of mind was a composite of movement and tone, suggestion and perception, as mirrored by the minds of men. All existence lay there; his existence lay there, in the serene reflecting ocean.

> One mind, the type of all, the moveless wave
> Whose calm reflects all moving things that are,
> Necessity, and love, and life, the grave,
> And sympathy, fountains of hope and fear;
> Justice, and truth, and time, and the world's natural sphere.

He too, the breaking billow, added the slight ferment of his thoughts to the long, regular swell. But he was part of the sea, not separate from it. 'The words *I, you, they,*' he wrote in 1819, 'are not signs of any actual difference subsisting between the assemblage of thoughts thus indicated, but are merely marks employed to denote the different modifications of the one mind ... I am but a portion of it.' The notion of 'distinct individual minds, similar to that which is employed in now questioning its own nature', was a delusion. He was simply an infinitesimal ripple in a Mind infinitely extensive. Mary confirmed it: the 'restless sympathies' and 'eager desire' of Shelley's own mind made him long to be united, 'hereafter, as now' with the vast mind of which he was a part.

That vast mind he addressed tentatively, in fragments in his notebooks. He was, he knew, 'on that verge where words abandon us, and what wonder if we grow dizzy to look down the dark abyss of how little we know!' He would begin, stray close to Deity, then retract; he would try to picture unlimited power and extent and then trace them, as he knew he had to, to the unexplored centre of himself.

> Great Spirit, whom the ~~Ocean~~ sea of boundless ~~human~~ thought
> Nurtures within its unimagined caves;   ~~mind~~
> In which thou sittest solemnly reclined
> Giving a voice to its mysterious waves
> Thou must a   portion be

Around the same time, 1821, in another notebook, he began again:

> O thou Immortal Deity
> Whose throne is in the ~~Heaven~~ depth of Human thought,
> ~~O thou From~~
>   I do adjure thy power & thee
> By all that man may be, by all that he is not
>   By all that he has been, & yet must be!

Certain ideas, almost too extraordinary to entertain for long, flickered behind these scraps. To suppose that 'I, the person who now write and think' was the One Mind was, of course, a 'monstrous presumption'. But as 'a portion' of the One Mind he might share the Great Spirit's perceptions, and on as grand a scale. In Dante's *Convito*, God dreamed man and the divine Intelligences made him, according to God's idea. But in Shelley's *Queen Mab*, man dreamed God. *Y los sueños, sueños son.*

At times, when his thoughts contracted to the compass of himself, he could not manage the scale of this conception. Mind's Ocean became only 'the wide sea of misery' of his own life. Boats launched on this sea made no wake or phosphorescence, and the thick clouds overhanging ensured unbroken darkness on the water. So it seemed at Este in 1818, during one of his saddest summers, with little Clara dead and his marriage cold, as he tried to write in the hills at dawn:

> Day and night, and night and day,
> Drifting on his dreary way . . .
> And the dim low line before
> Of a dark and distant shore
> Still recedes . . .

Yet he had some purpose even as a chronicler of unhappiness. Not only the phantoms and shadows that beset him, but the scene they moved in, drew life and meaning from his own breast. (Between 'heart' and 'mind' he often did not distinguish, using them interchangeably, feeling the deep charge of his truer self in either place.) By being born and living, seeing and thinking – as he had written in 1815 in *The Daemon of the World* – he contributed his own experience to the One Mind:

> For birth but wakes the universal mind
> Whose mighty streams might else in silence flow
> Thro' the vast world, to individual sense
> Of outward shows, whose unexperienced shape

New modes of passion to its frame may lend;
Life is its state of action . . .

At the end of 'Mont Blanc' he returned to himself, the lone figure on the wooden bridge whose mind was nonetheless identical with the mighty landscape before him. The thought was overwhelming, yet he could hold it. In his first draft, he began daringly to frame a question.

~~What~~ And what were thou & Earth & stars & sea
~~Pause, Poet   in~~
~~Start no~~t

He gathered courage. Equal to equal, he threw out his challenge to the mountain that contained the 'secret strength of things':

And what were thou, and earth, and stars, and sea,
If to the human mind's imaginings
Silence and solitude were vacancy?

★   ★   ★

Others, standing in awe under the same Swiss sky, had bowed before the God who made the mountain. Shelley had been made aware of, and had tested, his own power. 'The mind of man & the universe' was 'the great whole' on which he meant to focus his speculations and his hopes. If mind could not create, it was nonetheless 'the creature of education'. Perceptions, opinions and dispositions could be changed, not least by his own writing and incessant, urgent arguing.

He had always believed this. Impatiently, even bullyingly, he had tried to improve those closest to him, encouraging his sisters to write poems, urging Harriet to learn Latin and Mary to write tragedies, keeping Claire committed to her German exercises, while feeding them all with his atheism and his longing for moral revolution. 'Occupy, amuse, instruct, multiply yourself,' he told Claire. 'Have confidence in yourself,' he exhorted Miss Hitchener; 'dare to believe "I am great".' And to Hogg, pushing farther and higher, 'Assert yourself be what you were love Adore! It will exalt your nature, bid you a man be a God.'

Good, he was sure, would spread this way. Evil would 'become annihilate'. Mind would triumph over matter, and the world could be transformed. He went further: *only* by changed minds, flooded with virtue, courage and selflessness, could the world be transformed. Mind was 'that faculty of human nature on which every gradation of its progress, nay, every, the minutest, change depends'.

Others, he knew, would mock that notion. 'It is our will/ That thus enchains us to permitted ill,' he told Byron in *Julian and Maddalo*:

> We might be otherwise—we might be all
> We dream of, happy, high, majestical.
> Where is the love, beauty and truth we seek
> But in our mind?

They were standing in the billiard room in Byron's Venetian *palazzo*; the light of a dim, grey day came through the windows. 'Salutations past', they had fallen immediately to debating again. Godlike as Byron was in Shelley's eyes, he too was ever to be urged towards 'some greater enterprise of thought': less cynical, purged of bad habits and indiscipline. 'We know', Shelley insisted,

> That we have power over ourselves to do
> And suffer—what, we know not till we try;
> But something nobler than to live and die—

'You talk Utopia,' said Byron shortly. Perhaps Shelley did; he knew that men did not dare this, that they did not even know their lack of daring, that 'the good want power, but to weep barren tears', and that the revolution in France had failed precisely because its promoters had persisted in seeing the world in terms of oppression and revenge. But he talked Utopia because 'some few, like we know who' saw it, believed it, and knew it had to be shown forth to other minds. It could be built that way.

'A story of particular facts', he wrote, 'is as a mirror which distorts and obscures that which should be beautiful.' A story of the earthbound self, confessional and biographical, could do the same. But idealising poetry, like the idealised Greek forms he so admired, was a mirror that could make those dark, twisted facts beautiful again. Men's minds could be renewed by it, slowly but steadily, into 'a sea reflecting love', glassily calm. Looked at long enough, bright sunlight on water could begin to tint crimson, like gems or fire.

With utmost delicacy, Shelley described the process:

And lovely apparitions—dim at first,
Then radiant, as the mind, arising bright
From the embrace of beauty, whence the forms
Of which these are the phantoms, casts on them
The gathered rays which are reality—
Shall visit us . . .

In the hope of that embrace, his own mind waited. Shelley imagined it prismatic, many-sided, even infinitely sided, a truth-shield with every reflection multiplied. And if not that wondrous mirror, then at least the tiny, glinting surface of a wave, at the edge of the sunlit sea.

★   ★   ★

To leave Shelley beside any pool was not a guarantee of quiet. Having watched for a while he might spring up, grab a stone and hurl it into the sleeping water. Where there were thinner, friable stones – as at the quarry pond at Shotover Hill – he would split and trim them, then fling them out as ducks and drakes, watching them skim and bounce across the surface with tiny detonations of spray. He counted the bounds, shouting with glee. Larger stones he reserved, staggering sometimes with the largest he could lift, throwing it to the very limit of his strength, to make as much noise and disturbance as he could possibly manage.

He would then be calm again. Quietly, he would watch the decreasing agitation, Hogg reported, 'until the last faint ring and almost imperceptible ripple had disappeared on the still surface'. Such, Shelley would say, was the effect of sound on silence.

He complained to Hogg that not enough was known about sound: how mysterious it was, how contradictory its phenomena, how obscure the science of acoustics. It should be studied, he told him, and experiments performed. But he was already well aware of how it worked on his own body, stirring the more fluid particles to the point of agony or of deep, intense pleasure. Lodging-house cacophonies – a Scottish maid squalling for the 'kittle', the chink of glasses rinsed in a stone sink, a sleepless child crying – sharpened and grew as they rippled outwards, until in screaming pain he had to clap his hands over his ears. But then might come a quivering balm of sweet and melting tones, Claire singing, or drops of music from a harp that fell as water to water, plangent 'circles of life-dissolving sound' spreading to the edges of the room. The gentle repeated notes made his head swim, though happily, as if with the convulsions of crying.

The ripple effect could be extended further, to the whole sleeping community of mankind. For Paine insisted that they did sleep, as calm as any pond under the noonday trees. 'There is existing in man', he wrote, 'a mass of sense lying in a dormant state which, unless something excites to action, will descend with him, in that condition, to the grave.' This was why government feared 'to awaken a single reflection'. And this was why men and women needed rousing. The sullen quietness, in England, had been deepened by the passing of Libel and Sedition Acts to silence dissenting voices, such as Hunt's and Eaton's and Finnerty's and the voice of Paine himself. But minds, Shelley insisted, needed only one impulse to begin to reform themselves. As the 'peerless' Lafayette had told the National Assembly of France at the dawn of revolution, in July 1789, 'For a Nation to love Liberty it is sufficient that she knows it; to be free, it is sufficient that she wills it.'

The question, as ever, was how much force to apply and how much commotion to cause. 'No man', Shelley had written in 1812, in his own *Declaration of Rights*,

> has the right to disturb the public peace, by personally resisting the execution of a law however bad. He ought to acquiesce, using at the same time the utmost powers of his reason, to promote its repeal.

Godwin had persuaded him to take this line. He advised him to engage in 'a quiet, but incessant activity, like a rill of water, to irrigate and fertilise the intellectual soil'. But Shelley preferred a different water metaphor. Truth, Godwin also wrote, was 'the pebble in the lake'. That pebble, small though it might be, would send ripples right to the rim, from still, pure centre to circumference, like the steady turning outwards of the self to the other. 'However slowly', Godwin continued,

> in the present case the circles succeed each other, they will infallibly go on till they overspread the surface. No order of mankind will for ever remain ignorant of the principles of justice, equality and public good. No sooner will they understand them, than they will perceive the coincidence of virtue and public good with private interest; nor will any erroneous establishment be able effectually to support itself against general opinion.

The man of virtue had only to lay out his argument, and the effects would start to reverberate. His listeners would begin to question the teaching of schools and universities, the creeds of priests and the assumed authority of rulers. Thoughts never entertained before, dreams scorned as impossible, would begin to move minds as the pebble moved the water. The tiny waves, now here, now there, would catch light and coalesce. The crowd would stir, and their growing force would reach to the edge of the world.

The Necessity of Atheism had been one such pebble, in Shelley's view. When he had lived long enough with self-satisfied dons and bishops and the creed of a God revenging himself on the beings he had supposedly created, he had hurled his little pamphlet into the Oxford pond. No atheist pamphlet had ever before been published in England. Yet it made no ripples, beyond his expulsion and eventual exclusion from home. The sharp spray, it seemed, had been dashed in his own face.

More stones had followed. He had chosen them, trimming and shaping them as he did his little missiles on the edge of Shotover Pond, for their capacity to make the waves he hoped for. In November 1817 his *Address to the People on the Death of the Princess Charlotte* was written to point the glaring difference between grief for a young princess and indifference to the death of Liberty in England, epitomised by the fate of the three rebels hanged that year in Derbyshire. Passionately, Shelley exhorted Englishmen to shroud themselves in black, to mourn, to toll the bells, for the death of that true 'beautiful Princess'. He asked Ollier to send the *Address* instantly to press, feeling confident that he would not have objections. But Ollier, though he printed some, seemed unable or unwilling to find a distributor. The little pamphlet sank almost without a trace.

Earlier the same year, Shelley had sought to seize a moment when a popular party seemed almost strong enough to force change on Parliament. If it succeeded, the general male population might be represented there for the first time. His *Proposal for Putting Reform to the Vote* suggested a referendum to see whether Englishmen wished 'to be slaves or freemen', and laid out a programme of reform: annual parliaments, new parliamentary boundaries to enfranchise the industrial towns, a return to the gold standard and, naturally, the abolition of the national debt. Universal suffrage Shelley did not recommend; it was still 'fraught with peril'. But he volunteered to get things moving, calling on the Friends of Reform to meet at the Crown and Anchor Tavern in the Strand, the central hive of dissent, to set priorities and to get the referendum organised. He also offered £100, a tenth of his annual income, to push the cause forward, 'and I will not deem so proudly of myself, as to believe that I shall stand alone in this respect'.

He waited for the effect. There was no effect. Fifty or sixty prominent figures, including MPs and aristocrats and members of the reformist Hampden Clubs in Birmingham and London, were sent copies in the hope that his reasonings would stir them. But again the pool settled, quietly, under the trees. In such calm it might be possible to imagine, in the depths, the true shape of republicanism and democracy:

> Beside the windless and crystàlline pool,
> Where ever lies, on unerasing waves,
> The image of a temple, built above,
> Distinct with column, arch and architrave,
> And palm-like capital, and over-wrought,
> And populous with most living imagery,
> Praxitelean shapes, whose marble smiles
> Fill the hushed air with everlasting love.

Yet this water was murky and empty, and the impact of truth caused no ripples of imitation. Sometimes the quietude of the English people impressed him, a steadiness that might bring – as he had told Byron hopefully, some months before – 'reform . . . without revolution'. This time, however, they seemed deaf to his ideas, as did the virtuous few he had hoped might actively copy him.

Two years later, in 1819 in Italy, he began work on a full plan of action. *A Philosophical View of Reform* was given edge by the Peterloo massacre and the government's repression of free speech and fair trials at home. Most people in England, Shelley wrote, were destitute and miserable; the cause was unequal distribution of property and wealth, because of 'a defect in the government'; in consequence, 'every enlightened and honourable person . . . ought to excite them to the discovery of the true state of the case and to the temperate but irresistible vindication of their rights'. The people should defy the government, provoking it to prosecute them for libel and refusing to pay their taxes. They should petition Parliament and organise mass meetings until they obtained 'by whatever means, the victory over their oppressors' – the rich and those in authority, who were anyway hand in glove. Then, having taken their seats in Parliament, they should 'assume the control of public affairs according to constitutional rules'.

This was strong, compelling stuff, yet still softened by Shelley's wish to be incremental. He did not advocate an instant republic, much as his own heart longed for one. Rather than try too fast and fail, he was prepared to 'temporize'. Parliaments should be elected not every year, but every three; that might, after all, be enough to accustom ordinary men to the thrill of exercising power. He had refined his views, too, on the national debt: it should not be abolished, but paid off by those who had profited from it and the money given to the poor.

Possibly, the first bettering impulse would not come from him. 'If Reform shall be begun by the existing Government,' he wrote,

> let us be contented with a limited *beginning*, with any whatsoever opening . . . it is no matter how slow, gradual and cautious be the change; we shall demand more and more with firmness and moderation, never anticipating, but never deferring the moment of successful opposition . . .

This might have been Godwin talking, with his recommendation of 'zealous and constant' reasonings with authority. But Paine, in words after Shelley's own heart, encouraged him to think that change might happen faster than he supposed: that the progress of time and circumstances 'is too mechanical to measure the force of the mind, and the rapidity of reflection, by which Revolutions are generated'. They were perhaps better measured by Shelley's spreading ripples and bounding, unpredictable stones.

Yet *A Philosophical View* was never finished or published in his lifetime, or indeed for a century afterwards. It stayed in draft in a notebook, or in Shelley's dreams as 'a commonplace kind of book' in octavo, reason in pocket form. His central principle of reform, the equality of man in possessions as well as rights, was 'an object which is, because we will it, and may be because we hope and desire it', nothing less and nothing more. 'For this season', however, he put his ideas of changing minds aside. The time did not seem right to him.

England, meanwhile, was stirred only by diffuse and disorganised unrest. George IV and his ministers continued to rule in extravagance and corruption; reformers attacked entrenched representatives on behalf of the disenfranchised citizens of coal and mill towns; the desperate poor sought work and bread. 'The great struggle', unsurprisingly, was postponed by party politics for another year. An appeal to the thoughtful, no matter how well argued, was lost both in indifference and in constant surface noise.

Shelley waited on the bank with his stones in his hands. The last ripples he had caused died out among the reeds. He was too far away, and the day was fading, to his frustration. A fish rising to feed, snapping at the evening flies, made stronger rings than he had done. There was no doubt, as Paine had written, that once the mind had discovered truth 'it is impossible to put [it] back to the same condition it was in before it saw it'. It had to be hoped that, in the depths, some noiseless change was occurring. Shelley crouched by the water with his mind full of spreading circles of light. But the pond, and England, slept again.

3
Escape

Water in all its guises, then, was thought in all its modes of expression. Thought refreshed and shaped the desert of unformed opinion, or fell soothingly on withered hearts. It became a torrent that could carve out chasms and topple palace walls. The 'overflowing of the mind' made Shelley's poems, sweeping everything else aside. Even dreams pelted past, 'like some dark stream/ Thro shattered mines & caverns underground', when they might have soothed and calmed him.

His life seemed compounded of eddying ideas that begged to be heeded and followed. Sudden notions drove him to grab friends by the arm and tug them eastwards, westwards, sideways, into bread-shops and pawn-shops, in the London streets. ('I always go on until I am stopped,' he told Trelawny, 'and I never am stopped.') Imperious, desperate plans drove his elopement with Mary: the 4 a.m. chaise from London clattering down the sleeping road, the change to four horses at Dartford 'that we might outstrip pursuit', the small boat engaged because, in Mary's weary words, 'we would not wait for the packet of the following day', the boxes left behind. The same impetuosity, in Italy, forced Mary to travel from Lucca to Venice with little Clara, who did not survive. Soldiers at Venice demanding Shelley's passport soon thought better of it, and retreated. 'His flashing eyes and vehement eager manner', wrote Trelawny, 'determined on the instant execution of any project that took his fancy, however perilous. He overbore all opposition in those less self-willed than he was.'

Tumultuous thought also burst through in his letters, spraying out ink and forcing the writing almost horizontal with impatience. ('My

soul is bursting, ideas millions of ideas are crowding into it.') At school
he wrote Latin verses 'as fast as his pen could move', though his tutor
as rapidly ripped them up again. Thought blotted his notebooks with
deletions, smeared erasures (a licked finger, a quill dragged sideways)
and pages of defiant, barely legible scrawl in which dashes were the
only punctuation. At times, it knocked his rhythms flying:

> those millions swept
> Like waves before the tempest—these alarms
> Came to me, as to know their case I lept
> On the gate's turret, and in rage and grief and scorn I wept!

– but in this instance he disdained revision, fearing to lose 'the newness
and energy of imagery and language as it flowed fresh from my mind'.
Thought demanded fresh pages in new notebooks, used pages in old
ones (turned upside down, thrown sideways, one poem burying another),
or any spare piece of paper, or letter-back, or bill, which he was sometimes reduced to begging from visitors or friends.

Thought also swept him up physically, with his bags and chattels
and boxes of books, depositing him in carriages and post-chaises going
off in all directions. If he drove himself it was at breakneck speed,
smashing main plates, springs and lamps; if carried he would take an
outside seat, reading, with the clatter of the passing world incessant
in his ears. On such a seat, he told Miss Hitchener, three nights and
two days sleepless between York and Sussex, he had mused on what
human minds could be, constantly strengthening, progressing and
perfecting, 'tracing general history to the point where now we stand;
the series is *infinite*, can never end!' Each jolt, each connection of
thought, brought perfection closer. The cry most often heard from
him was 'Come along!'

He claimed that he wanted to pause and reflect, but admitted it was
scarcely possible. 'Thought', he wrote, in a fragment he never finished,

> can with difficulty visit the intricate & winding chambers which it
> *inhabits* . . . It is like a river whose rapid & perpetual stream flows
> outwards;—like one in dread who speeds thro the recesses of some
> haunted pile & dares not look behind.

As Hogg saw it, Shelley never fled towards, but escaped from, whatever it was that moved him. Shelley put it better: 'He pants to reach

what yet he seems to fly', death or life. He loved, and applied to himself, a snatch from Byron's *Childe Harold's Pilgrimage*:

> But there are wanderers o'er Eternity
> Whose bark drives on and on, and anchor'd ne'er shall be.

At Syon House Academy, and again with Mary, he had read with huge delight Robert Paltock's *The Adventures of Peter Wilkins*. Peter, shipwrecked on a great unscalable rock, took a little boat exploring round it. Suddenly he was caught in a current, sucked beneath an arch, hurled 'as I thought' down a precipice and tossed round and round with incredible violence, 'the Water roaring on all Sides, and dashing against the Rock with a most amazing Noise'. For five weeks he sailed through darkness before emerging, dazed, into a wide lake of calm. As the Poet of *Alastor*, questing for the ideal Beauty he had glimpsed and lost, Shelley did the same. He skirted the craggy base of Caucasus, then rode the enormous, roaring flood into an eddying whirlpool that bore his boat up, step by step, stair above stair, ridge by ridge, 'circling immeasurably fast' until it paused at last 'on the verge of the extremest curve':

> Shall it sink
> Down the abyss? Shall the reverting stress
> Of that resistless gulf embosom it?
> Now shall it fall?—

None of these happened. With the suddenness of dream – for this was dream- or mind-wandering – the scene switched to a placid river, and the boat sailed gently on. For the moment, the Poet's turmoil was over. He was in what seemed to be daylight, and was safe; he might dare, now, to look behind.

It was not clear, in Peter's story or in Shelley's, quite where the sailor was. He might be beyond the Earth, or deep in the caverns of his mind; the dome above him was possibly the wide vault of the universe, or a skull of rock imprisoning the unrelenting flood of his thoughts. In *Alastor*, in any case, the Poet continued to follow water. From the haven where he had abandoned his boat a river ran through glades and woods; he walked beside it, rapidly, feeling the moss tremble, the torrent once more the image of his wandering ideas.

> 'O stream!
> Whose source is inaccessibly profound,
> Whither do thy mysterious waters tend?
> Thou imagest my life. Thy darksome stillness,
> Thy dazzling waves, thy loud and hollow gulfs,
> Thy searchless fountain, and invisible course
> Have each their type in me . . .'

The windings of the river were inevitable and natural. Thought mean-dered ever onwards, shaping and colouring the landscape as it went. As the Poet grew sadder the scene became 'blasted' and 'ghastly', the stream running between black towers of rock until it emerged, suddenly, in a vast prospect of a barren world, fringed with volcanoes spitting fire. He had followed the water to its natural end, 'an immeasurable void', into which it plunged with its foam scattering to the winds. And this was apparently his end, too, the point of death.

The Poet paused. Shelley did not, but laughed, and jumped.

★ ★ ★

> To the Deep, to the Deep,
> Down, down!

He loved those words. On another blank leaf of his notebook he wrote them again, leaving them to float or sink on the whiteness of the page:

> Thro the void of the Abyss
> Down, down

He was writing the 'Song of Spirits' in the second act of *Prometheus Unbound*. His heroines – Asia and Panthea, Love and Hope – were plunging to the deepest recesses of the Earth, to confront the power that determined man's subjection to cycles of life, death, history and change. But Shelley was also delighting in free fall through nothing-ness, or water, or the illusory solidity of the body and the self:

> Through the shade of sleep,
> Through the cloudy strife
> Of Death and of Life;
> Through the veil and the bar

172

> Of things which seem and are
> Even to the steps of the remotest throne,
> Down, down!

Virgil put Elysium under the Earth, Hesiod placed it on the edge of the Ocean. Either route lay through profundities of water or perhaps, as in *Prometheus*, through Earth made as light and translucent as the sea.

~~Down down down down dizzily, far & deep~~

As a child, Shelley repeated word for word – having read it once – Thomas Gray's elegy to a cat drowned in a tub of goldfish. In his small, piping voice he described the lure of the underwater world:

> Still had she gazed; but 'midst the tide
> Two angel forms were seen to glide,
> The Genii of the stream:
> Their scaly armour's Tyrian hue
> Thro' richest purple to the view
> Betray'd a golden gleam.

The cat, enchanted, tumbled in, longing for the loveliness in the water. 'The pensive Selima' had seen first herself, with emerald eyes and tortoise-shell fur, and then the beauty of the fish. When Shelley had finished, his mother was astonished at him.

Boys, too, could be snared and drowned. Auburn-haired Hylas, filling his urn from the spring in a lyric by Theocritus, felt a nymph's hand closing round his wrist. Sheer into the water he fell, 'as when a fiery star falls from the sky into the sea'. He slid under among the blue flowers.

The body of Henry, 'The Drowned Lover', floated on the stormy lake in Shelley's novel *St Irvyne*, written when he was seventeen. His boat had been wrecked there. Dark waves laved him, like mourners; the tempest tossed him in the swell. His lover Eloise ran down to the lake, through the myrtle grove, not knowing she would not find him.

High on the rocks at Cwm Elan Shelley watched the torrent descending. Moonlight silvered the rushing water. He too, with a step, could be part of the 'unremitting roar' and the 'ideal flow'. His body and his miseries would be dissolved together. Nothing would be left of them.

In 1820 the 'Young Englishman' who had written *Epipsychidion* leapt into the Arno from the Ponte della Trinità in Florence. The river, swollen by spring rain, swept through the city 'with the swiftness of a tempest' –

~~Nor were~~
~~melancholy consummation of his fate,~~
~~his remains ever found.~~

But it would not do. Shelley scored it through heavily with vertical lines, saving himself.

Harriet had not been saved. On a rainy night in December 1816, she threw herself into the grey Serpentine. The date was never known exactly. She had not been observed leaving her lodgings or approaching the water. The landlady's servant told the coroner that the deceased had dined early on the day she had last seen her, at around four o'clock. Before this she had chiefly spent her time in bed, afflicted with 'a continual lowness of Spirits'. Her body, bloated with death and pregnancy, was found on 10 December. It was pulled out with hooks. 'The circumstances which attended this event', Shelley told Byron, 'are of a nature of such awful and appalling horror, that I dare hardly avert to them in thought.'

In November the next year he gazed on the past, a dark stream in which his hopes had been submerged. He mentioned no names, but stood on the bank as still and sad as a tomb.

That time is dead for ever, child!
Drowned, frozen, dead for ever!

He too would fall into that water, or be swept on it like a bubble until it broke him.

To the deep, to the deep
Down, down

174

A reviewer for the *Quarterly* in April 1819 portrayed Shelley as Pharaoh crossing the Red Sea in his chariot. Arrogant, blind, spouting drivel, he was overwhelmed by God's vengeance in the form of a wall of waves:

> . . . for a short time are seen his impotent struggles against a resist-less power, his blasphemous execrations are heard, his despair but poorly assumes the tone of triumph and defiance and he calls inef-fectually on others to follow him in the same ruin—finally he sinks 'like lead' to the bottom to be forgotten. So it is now in part, so shortly will it be entirely with Mr Shelley.

Shelley saw this review in a reading room in Florence, letting out a whoop of joy among the silent books. 'It is like the end of the first act of an opera,' he told his publisher Ollier, embroidering freely:

> It describes the result of my battle with their Omnipotent God his pulling me under the sea by the hair of my head, like Pharoah my calling out like the Devil who was *game* to the last; swearing & cursing in all comic & horrid oaths like a French postillion on Mount Cenis, entreating everybody to drown themselves pretending not to be drowned myself when I *am* drowned, & lastly *being* drowned.

As he raced out of the reading room, his shrieks of hysterical laughter echoed down the stairs.

He would drown differently. Amid a sea of scattered wreckage and white water, as he glimpsed it in *Prometheus Unbound*, he would offer his plank to an enemy, then '[plunge] aside to die'. Or he would drift like Milton's virtuous, gentle Lycidas, borne away, perhaps beyond the Hebrides, by the sea in which he had drowned:

> So sinks the day-star in the Ocean bed,
> And yet anon repairs his drooping head,
> And tricks his beams, and with new-spangl'd Ore
> Flames in the forehead of the morning sky . . .

He would not shout or struggle. He had been close enough to tell. As he sailed with Byron on Lake Geneva in June 1816, their new friend-ship cemented by a tour together, a violent wind suddenly whipped

175

up the waves to terrifying heights. Their boatman, 'a dreadfully stupid fellow', mismanaged the sail. The boat veered wildly towards the rocks at Meillerie, slewed round, and fell towards capsizing. 'It seemed at any moment we would be overset,' Shelley told Peacock later. He wrote his will that evening, as if sobered by this brush with death.

Byron, as the boat plunged, took his coat off. Shelley, under persuasion, stripped off his. The high, sharp rocks were almost above them, echoing the crash of the waves. Byron told him to sit with his arms crossed; he did so, and then, a better idea, sat down quietly on a locker and grasped the iron rings at either end. He was one with the boat then, bound to go down 'with the rest of the pigs', as he put it on a later occasion. Pigs could not swim.

'If you can't swim/ Beware of Providence,' Byron told him in *Julian and Maddalo*, the 'gay smile' fading from his face. But Shelley dared Providence all the time, insulting and haranguing God, mocking the works of revealed religion, while the water gathered round him. He sat now serenely in his shirt, gripping the cold locker-handles as the bucking boat conveyed him to death. Byron assured him he could save him, as long as he did not struggle. Shelley replied that he had no notion of being saved.

He probably had Rousseau's *Julie*, his constant reading on this trip, stuffed in the pocket of his wet discarded coat. St Preux had watched Julie at this very spot on the lake, pale and sick but still beautiful as the boat pitched in the waves. He imagined how she would slip under, her chestnut hair spreading on the water and 'the pallor of death dulling the roses in her cheeks'. Shelley supposed St Preux had longed to plunge in beside her, but that was his own extension of Rousseau's story. Love demanded immolation and immersion. To love was to drown, and to drown was to be wrapped around, longingly and jealously, by 'the amorous Deep' that had no wish to restore him to life or to the air.

> To the deep, to the deep
> Down, down!

So simple a death, without fuss. In the second Canto of *Don Juan* Byron painted shipwreck as a screaming, drawn-out farce of broken pumps, shattered beam-ends, rum, religion and cannibalism, the jaunty rhythms and bitter closing couplets never relenting for an instant. Shelley found this 'strange'. His drownings were quiet, almost by the way. He would not be missed. Out on Lake Geneva, a white sail would disappear. The cargo would go to the bottom with his body flung lightly across it, pulled straight down. It happened almost daily. A boatman on the Rhine in 1814 had shrugged when Shelley and Mary saw an upturned vessel floating past: 'It was only a boat, which was only capsized, and all the people only drowned.' *C'est seulement un bateau, qui etoit seulement renversée, et tous les peuples sont seulement noyés.*

★   ★   ★

When Trelawny hauled him up from the bottom of the Arno, having failed to teach him to swim, Shelley was sorely disappointed that he had not left him there. 'I always find the bottom of the well,' he cried, 'and they say Truth lies there. In another minute I should have found it, and you would have found an empty shell. It is an easy way of getting rid of the body.'

He tried to find the bottom again. One sultry evening in the spring of 1822, showing off his seamanship, he took Jane Williams and her two babies out in the coracle that he used to come ashore from his yacht. In this fragile shell of reeds he paddled far across the Bay of Lerici, rested on his oar and fell silent.

'Life', he had written in 1819,

> and the world, or whatever we call that which we are and feel, is an astonishing thing ... We are struck with admiration at some of its transient modifications, but it is itself the great miracle. What are changes of empires, the wreck of dynasties, with the opinions which supported them; what is the birth and the extinction of religions and of political systems, to life? ... What is the universe of stars, and suns ... and their motions, and their destiny, compared with life?

Jane watched him as he sat, head bowed, motionless and wordless. His melancholy was terrifying. The little craft, heavily overladen, floated only inches above the sea; the water was blue and deep, and no other vessel was within a mile of them. Jane, knowing Shelley well by now, said she saw death in his eyes. Suddenly he revived, 'as with a bright thought', raised his head, and cried: 'Now let us together solve the great mystery!'

It may have been 'Shall we now try the Great Unknown?' Jane was not sure, and was aware only of the necessity of distracting him and, with careful prattle, bringing him back to the world.

'How vain is it', Shelley had written,

to think that words can penetrate the mystery of our being! Rightly used they may make evident our ignorance to ourselves, and this is much. For what are we? Whence do we come? And whither do we go? Is birth the commencement, is death the conclusion of our being? What is birth and death?

He asked the question, too, in *Adonais* in 1821.

> Whence are we, and why are we? of what scene
> The actors or spectators?

At times he said he was happy not to know the answer. But he longed to know it. He could find out then and there, so easily, just by rocking the coracle over.

With astonishing presence of mind, Jane checked him. 'No, thank you, not now; I should like my dinner first, and so would the children.'

They got back somehow. Jane swore she would never go out in a boat with Shelley again, and could not face her fish supper. Shelley seemed unaware that he had said, or done, anything remotely strange. In beaching the coracle, unbalanced by Jane's rush to leave it, he tipped himself into the sea again, as usual.

★   ★   ★

Drowning, he had persuaded himself, was a state much like sleeping. Death was a 'gulf-dream', a startling fall in a sleep otherwise undisturbed: 'With whirlwind swiftness—a fall far and deep,—/ A gulf, a void, a sense of senselessness—'. After that first shock the body in suspension did not panic and thrash, but calmly drank its fate from 'the o'erbrimming deep',

> And sinks down, down, like that sleep
> When the dreamer seems to be
> Weltering through eternity . . .

To overdose on laudanum, as Fanny Godwin had done and as he had tried to, brought much the same result: pain ceasing, sleep increasing, the breath suppressed.

The dead were conducted quite naturally through water, drifting to Hades like somnambulists. Lake Avernus led to the Underworld, and that world itself was watered by three rivers, Cocytus, Acheron and Styx. Souls were gathered there in an intermediate place between Earth and enlightenment, like the pale sleeping forms suspended under the Nile. In 1818 Shelley visited the real Avernus near Naples, finding 'a calm & lovely basin of water surrounded by dark woody hills, & profoundly solitary'. Rowing out across this 'windless mirror' he would see, under water that was peculiarly deep and opaque, his own boat and his own face, denizens of Hades. Self seemed to persist there, free of the heavy craving body but not free of form and thought. And was this death?

As early as June 1811 – barely three months after his expulsion from Oxford, before his flight with Harriet – he had already refined the question and posed it to Miss Hitchener, the schoolmistress who, on the briefest acquaintance at Cuckfield, was now his epistolary sounding-board on matters of dreams and love and death:

> *This* brings me again to the point which I aim at: the eternal exis-tence of intellect. You have read Locke—you are convinced that there are no innate ideas, & that you do not always think when asleep. Yet, let me enquire in these moments of intellectual suspension, do you suppose that the soul is annihilated. You cannot suppose it, knowing the infallibility of the rule, '*From nothing, nothing can come, to nothing nothing can return*' . . .
>
> You have witnessed *one* suspension of intellect in dreamless sleep— you witness another in Death. From the first you well know that you cannot infer any diminution of intellectual force. How contrary then to all analogy to infer *annihilation* from Death, which you cannot prove suspends for a moment the force of mind.

Day by day flowers, too, slept and woke again. Carried to the dung heap they seemed putrefying and dead, yet was this the end? Their beauty, Shelley mused, might lie not in the body but in separate 'properties' that persisted. ('Yet where does [that beauty] exist, in what state of being?') Perhaps something in them, as in him, was at constant odds with tran-sience and decay. Perhaps, as he suggested to Hogg in the same year,

> the flowers think like this, perhaps they moralize upon their state, have their attachments, their pursuits of virtue, adore despond, hope, despise—Alas! then do we like they perish, or do they like us live for ever!

In flowers or in him, mind seemed to survive beyond the grave. The apparitions and spectres he saw were figments of thought, especially memories, fears, regrets and base desires that could not quit the earth. Mind held them, like sleepers 'folded within their own eternity'. His thoughts and Miss Hitchener's, in particular, would live on, for their passionate communion of minds would surely 'bear our identity to Heaven' – an identity that would not be mixed up, he assured her, with 'Jews, aristocrats, and commercialists'. At the very least their souls, 'embodied on paper', would survive as long as their letters were preserved.

Those letters, on his side, were dominated by eager questionings as to whether mind and soul persisted, and if so how. Reason told him 'that death is the boundary of the life of man', but 'I feel, I believe, the direct contrary.' 'Yet are we, are these souls,' he wrote again, almost stammering with excitement,

> which measure in their circumscribed domain the distance of yon orbs, are we but bubbles which arise from the filth of a stagnant pool, merely to be again reabsorbed into the mass of its corruption? I think not. I feel not—can *you* PROVE it.

In 1822, days from his own death, he made the same point: 'The destiny of man can scarcely be so degraded that he was born only to die, and if such *should* be the case, delusions, especially the gross & preposterous ones of the existing religion, can scarcely be supposed to exalt it.'

Faint hope sometimes reached the point of defiance. 'You have said no more of the immortality of the Soul?' he asked Miss Hitchener in January 1812. 'Do you not believe it. I do . . .' His letters were signed off accordingly:

> Yours most sincerely inviolably eternally
> Ever ever yours unalterably
> Yours most *imperishably* & eternally
> Yours beyond this being *most imperishably*

In August that year Miss Hitchener at last stood beside him on the slippery grey rocks at Lynmouth, at the edge of the Bristol Channel. At his urgent insistence, she had left her teaching position to come and live with him and Harriet and Eliza in 'my little circle': a radical commune of supposed like minds, shared property and, it was rumoured, bodies. She was helping him, on those long summer evenings, to stuff pamphlets listing the Rights of Man into bottles and little waxed boxes that might float across, silently and illegally, to stir up rebellion in Ireland. The 'dearest friend' of his mind's eye, the partner of his highest thoughts, had been revealed as mannish, voluble, dark-skinned, and keen to lure Shelley away. He now hated her, called her the Brown Demon, and was preparing to pack her off home. But somewhere above the sea there still drifted, perhaps, the bright idealism he had made of her in their months of correspondence.

The question he had ceaselessly raised then remained as pressing as ever. As he crossed the English Channel on his elopement with Mary two years later, the waves swelling and surging into the boat, he was not so sick (though he was very sick) as to forgo philosophising; cradling Mary's head on his trembling knees, he fell to wondering 'what will befall this inestimable spirit when we appear to die'. They would not, he was sure, be separated, 'but in death we might not know & feel our union as now. I hope—but my hopes are not unmixed with fear'.

He was confident, at least, that thought itself did not die. It might even become more influential once the thinker had gone. Books, paintings, sculptures, products of mind, survived, with immortality in them as long as men lived to admire them. He too could go on communing with Bacon and Shakespeare; he too might be able to die, like Plato (Medwin remembered him opening his copy and declaiming it), 'secure of the Inheritance of glory' that stemmed from what he had written. Yet the question for Shelley was whether minds themselves persisted, and whether his own mind, with all its pulsings of thought, would dissolve as a billow in the ocean or go on.

His reasoning self insisted that things beyond the grave could not be known. Men could believe, if they cared to, in eternal life; but in belief of that sort, the sort that priests demanded, the will was passive and the intellect suspended. He had written as much at Oxford, in *The Necessity of Atheism*, and never varied in that opinion. Nothing beyond visible phenomena could be subjected to rational analysis. It was a realm of phantoms and faith. The first he had outgrown, the second he rejected as poison. But looking into water – water running deep and quiet, his own face looking back at him – he sometimes felt he was on the edge of understanding, and leaned down towards an embrace.

★   ★   ★

Many of his Poet-journeys were inward, towards that 'searchless fountain' of his being and his thoughts. In mirrors, in eyes, in statues, in the very depths of himself he had sensed, with a start, something finer and purer, perhaps divine. Captivated, he dived or ran towards it.

In ordinary life, too, Shelley made for the source, in expeditions notable for their happiness. In July 1815 he ventured with Mary, Peacock and Charles Clairmont, Claire's brother, to find the 'very spring' of the Thames by boat. The journey, a merry one, found him feasting on mutton chops and beer, putting on weight, catching the sun. Before they reached the end their wherry ran into thick weed above Lechlade, where cattle stood idly in the water and a broken sluice-gate creaked mournfully in the breeze. Clearly there was no way through. But Shelley proposed going on and on, to the source of the Severn, even to the Falls of the Clyde; only a fee of £20 for the Severn Canal dissuaded him.

From Pisa his most famous expedition by boat, complete with schoolboy provisions, was not west to the sea but east to Lake Bientina, against the flow of both the Serchio and the canals. Shelley reported the skiff battling the torrent, hanging on the wave and traversing the sparkling, boiling eddies as it forced its way upstream. The same boat was sailed up the Arno, against a violent current and often in scything wind and rain. His idle hours in mountains were spent 'hunting waterfalls', climbing an ever-narrowing valley to where they flashed and shone among the sunbows and the soaking leaves. He journeyed that way, too, up the River Arve, through forests ever darker and mountains ever more crowding and precipitous, up to the dazzling realms of snow.

In these 'adventurings' Shelley sought the beginnning, the very point of inspiration. Like his Witch of Atlas, he meant to ascend

> The labyrinths of some many-winding vale,
> Which to the inmost mountain upward tend—

Further up – deeper in – the water would run more vividly, more fiercely resisting him, faster and purer, brilliant with both contained and reflected light. To go that way, as Asia sang in *Prometheus Unbound*, was to run life in swift reverse, back to the time when it was least corrupted:

> We have passed Age's icy caves,
> And Manhood's dark and tossing waves,
> And Youth's smooth ocean, smiling to betray:

182

Beyond the glassy gulfs we flee
Of shadow-peopled Infancy,
Through Death and Birth, to a diviner day . . .

But Shelley's own destination was less certain. Perhaps, again, it might be the immeasurable void, the grey nothingness through which Asia too had fallen on her way to the deep. That dimness had been lit by one point of light, a diamond out of the dark that was caught by the dark again.

He longed to get to the fountainhead of other minds: Godwin's, Byron's, Hunt's, Dr Lind's. But most of all he wished to make that journey to the depths of himself. At some point thought, like water, disappeared underground, enticing him into the dark. The roaming bee, and the noon heat, were left outside; he proceeded to the faint sound of music and the fainter scent of night flowers. He speculated on what he would see and hear there, in passages and caves as intricate as the bones inside the ear. 'The caverns of the mind', Shelley wrote, tentatively entering,

> are obscure & shadowy, or pervaded with a lustre, beautifully bright indeed, but *shining* not beyond their portals. If it were possible to be where we have been, vitally & indeed—if at the moment of our presence there we could ~~describe~~ define the results of our experience—if the passage from sensation to reflexion—from a state of ~~passivene~~ to voluntary contemplation were not so dizzying & so tumultuous—this attempt would be less difficult.

He pictured his fancies struggling to climb there like weak insects in the half-light, or appearing on the damp cave walls as phantoms and ghosts. Sometimes he would return 'quite subdued' by his adventure, sobered and quiet. But deep within other chambers, if he was fearless enough to go on, lay mysteries and wonders. His heroine Cythna, confined, in *The Revolt of Islam,* to a prison under the sea, found her mind a store-room of wisdom and secrets, 'like a mine I rifled through and through'. The Poet of *Alastor* discovered 'numberless and immeasurable halls' filled with crystal columns, shrines and thrones, and domed with stars. The 'casket' of Shelley's unknown mind was perhaps much like this, in the moments when he could rest there. Or it could be, in itself, a world reflecting Heaven, an ante-chamber to the presence chamber of the One Mind he was a part of, like the smallest piece of mirrored glass.

Somewhere in these depths lay the wellspring of his thoughts: the miniature, the antitype, or Bacon's 'Idol of the Cave', the locus of the 'peculiar images' that made up Shelley, and to which his every act and word and observation of the world referred. He imagined it shining, lighting the caverns around it. A secret fountain rose in the cave of the Witch of Atlas, flinging to the roof 'inconstant spheres/And intertangled lines' of brightness, at which all living creatures congregated to pay homage and to drink. In 'Mont Blanc' the Witch Poesy lived in 'a still cave' on the mountain's flank, visited by images and shadows, where Shelley's thoughts floated lovingly as if in a forbidden place. If thought could only pause, it could be cupped in these sweet haunts, rocked in them – as he too rocked in the light-and-shade of the caves round Lerici, cradling his notebook on his knees – and receive soft echoes from their shining walls, like the sound inside a shell.

But his thoughts could not stop. They kept going, an endless surge of responses that barely considered the meaning of what he felt or saw. At times they raced towards light and truth where those shone, however faintly, in mind's depths; more often they poured away from them in babbling, chaotic error, bent on their own path.

Or they flowed towards the dark. The profundities of Shelley's mind were not necessarily luminous, but shadowy and steadily more terrifying. Asia and Panthea, falling into the abyss, found Demogorgon there, a shape-less 'mighty darkness' on his black throne. Implacable fate and Necessity were lodged with him; he was both imprisoner and emancipator, the master of chaos and progenitor of gods. Shelley's thoughts could keep returning to such a place, wandering deeper and deeper as he had done in the subter-ranean prison-chambers of the Cenci palace, to gaze on the fearful mirror of himself and the monsters he had made. In his preface to *The Cenci* he described, as if he knew it well, 'a gloomy passion for penetrating the impenetrable mysteries of our being, which terrifies its possessor at the darkness of the abyss to the brink of which it has conducted him'.

One of his favourite Gothic novels, Brockden Brown's *Edgar Huntly*, featured page after page of dark and frightening cave-wandering. At length the hero emerged in a wilderness of rocks and trails, somewhere in unmapped America. The thread that had guided Huntly – his hands in horror grazing the clammy walls, his feet inches from the precipice, his eyes blind – was the sound of water. It led, he knew, to daylight. Theseus had made a similar journey, following Ariadne's thread through the labyrinth of the Minotaur to the light of truth. But Shelley in his searchings found only a maze of tracks 'wide as the universe . . . a world within a world', in which he wandered as a lost man.

In one notebook entry, two reviewers trailed him. They were looking for the monster of his thought, hoping to kill it, but instead found themselves being drawn ever deeper into Shelley's 'winding sophistries'. Puzzled, even scared, hearing his mad laugh ahead of them, they decided not to go on:

> I fear lest we should find no thread ~~or words~~ to guide us back thro the labyrinths . . . We should have arrived at a conclusion & have forgotten the premises which led to them. We should have scaled the ~~inaccessible~~ a tower without ~~stairs~~ whose stairs are ~~ruined~~ with a ladder which is immediately withdrawn—

Shelley needed no mazes outside the universe of himself, yet he sought them. The Baths of Caracalla in Rome, where he wrote much of *Prometheus Unbound*, offered him the thrill of 'ever-winding labyrinths' in massive red-brick ruins sprawling in untended fields. Treading the little paths, like sheep tracks, that led through them he found twisting stairs opening on passages, arches leading to platforms, ledges crumbling to sudden, dizzying drops. He clambered in search of hidden lawns where he could scribble among ivy and myrtle, white-flowering laurustinus and the blue flowers whose names he never knew.

With intent, or so it seemed, he also lost himself in woods and streets. Both Hogg and little Thornton Hunt reported ramblings in Kentish Town fields and on Hampstead Heath with no limit and, it seemed, without design. Mary confirmed the tendency in the joint journal in November 1816: 'Shelley . . . in the evening goes out to take a little walk and loses—himself—' Above him in those night wanderings stretched 'the unquiet republic of the maze/ Of planets', struggling towards the 'free wilderness' of Heaven.

In several notebooks he drew mazes, sometimes constructed around grids of numbers and full of curving dead-end paths. Their shape was vaguely that of a cranium in section, the paths dug deep. Shelley had no guide to lead him on or out, nor the instinct of Orpheus to find his love Eurydice through the mazes of the mental world. Instead he roamed through uncharted deserts or, more often, stumbled out of the unrewarding caverns to the edge of Homer's 'trackless' sea.

Yet he also loved such places, where argument seemed infinite and possibility endless. Mary recalled going with him once to the shore where the Arno met the sea, 'a waste and dreary scene' where the empty sands stretched out into the idly breaking waves. She found it deadly.

He, however, was eager to share this wide barrenness with her. The swelling and failing sea stirred a surge of sympathy in him. As he watched it he felt 'his life beyond his limbs dilated', out across the 'immeasurable world', until he too was immeasurable; until he tasted

> The pleasure of believing what we see
> Is boundless, as we wish our souls to be.

★   ★   ★

In the grounds of Field Place, newly improved in the picturesque style with a little set of lakes, his mother and sisters strolled on a late spring afternoon. The year was 1814, the occasion the last when Shelley was allowed at home. Captain Kennedy, an officer friend on furlough, was with them, his scarlet jacket resplendent against the green of the lawns. In the summerhouse they sat and chatted as Shelley's sisters sewed, or sketched, or read. The Poet himself knelt at the edge of the water.

He took an old copy-book from his pocket, ripped out pages, dropped them on the grass. Each page was folded swiftly, dextrously, first in half, then on the diagonal. Two more diagonal folds, a pinch for the bow, and it was done. The little craft were launched, softly jostling each other. He jumped in ecstasy as the fleet bobbed away.

His mother watched him. He was twenty-one, almost twenty-two. How singular it was, she remarked, that a person of his age should enjoy such a childish amusement!

'Why should you be surprised?' he asked her. 'Kennedy takes pleasure in shooting . . . I deprive no dam of its mate—I spill no blood—yet I receive pleasure.'

He made other boats, all improvised, some dangerous. Tiny card boxes, waterproofed and resined, weighted with lead and fitted with sails, carried his seditious pamplets from Devon to Ireland in 1812. In Wales a foot-long plank of wood became a raft on which a cat could cling and squall like Odysseus, borne headlong down a stream. At Bracknell a washtub, possibly one of several, was paddled in a stream until the bottom fell out. At Lerici Shelley helped to make his tiny coracle, woven from reeds, covered with tarred canvas and painted red and black: a toy to float in, slapped here and there by the huge commanding sea.

About bigger boats he was unfussy, as long as he could voyage in them. In 1814 he went with Mary and Claire down part of the Rhine in a 'slight canoe', tacked together with nails, which shipped water with every bump as it whirled through the rapids near Mumpf. He was in raptures as he described the journey afterwards. The yacht he shared with Byron at Geneva two years later was dismissed by others as narrow, rickety and easily swamped, but Shelley thought it wonderful, 'exceedingly manageable & convenient', and lived in it night and day. The skiff he sailed on the Serchio was 10 feet long, flat-bottomed and with a detachable mast and sail: no more than a college punt, painted green and white, but still 'a very nice little shell' for him.

In 1822 he designed and ordered his own sailing boat, his 'perfect plaything' for the summer. Shelley saw her not as a 24-foot two-masted yacht, open and undecked, but as a beautiful 'witch', outsailing the other small craft in the Bay of Spezia 'as a comet might pass the dullest planets of the Heavens'. Her two tons of iron ballast, built into the keel, held her lightly in the swell of the sea; her stirring forest of canvas caught every whim of the breeze; her hull, with less than a foot of clearance, let waves wash over it constantly in a shining slick of foam. Out in the bay, 'my little schooner' made the flimsiest barrier between the water and himself. She was rather an extension of his body experiencing the sea.

And she was therefore pure, or had to be rendered so. She had arrived with the name *Don Juan* painted in large black letters on the mainsail – Byron's joke, since his own bigger and better yacht was being built in the same yard. Mary complained that this made 'a coal-barge of our boat'. The sail was scrubbed with turpentine and spirits of wine in 'a thousand processes', as Shelley sighed, to remove the name; it remained dappled and stained. Days were spent wondering what to do. At last it was patched, and new reefs put in, so that nothing should sully its anonymous white beauty unfurling to the breeze.

A later refit made the *Don Juan* yet swifter, slimmer and less stable. She now had reconfigured fore and aft sections, new topmast rigging to take three spinnakers and a storm jib, and even less ballast to keep her keel in the sea. Most remarkable and foolish was a gaff topsail, providing more surface to the wind than unskilled sailors could possibly manage. But that was the point of her.

In contemplation Shelley made these vessels more tenuous and his experience deeper. Lying full-length, the damp planks under him and a book held up to his face, he let the current move him on Lake Geneva as it had carried Rousseau in his *Rêveries*, man and craft as a single being. He was a floating leaf, casting his own shadow on the sands of the shallows, or a *picciol legno* in the style of Petrarch, a wood-chip tossed on the storm. His various illnesses assailed him

> Like some frail bark which cannot bear
> The impulse of an altered wind,
> Though prosperous . . .

Writing to Claire, he called himself 'the Nautilus your friend', spreading on the water his blue unfolding shawl, like those that covered the sea at Lerici in the wake of storms.

The most delicate craft that could be devised were astral or ethereal forms that could also be his own, the natural, light containers in which his spirit could float free from the body, as it seemed to do in sleep. He sketched them in soft pencil, moon-crescents adrift in his words. He also delighted to describe them: a 'curved shell of hollow pearl,/ Almost translucent with the light divine', or a boat 'like the moon's shade',

> which had no sail
> But its own curved brow of thin moonstone,
> Wrought like a web . . .

Most delicate of all was the boat of the Witch of Atlas, sprung ('some say') from a 'strange seed' stolen and sown in the morning star by the God of Love. The seed grew into a plant, then a snowy flower, then a gourd-like fruit which Love hollowed out, leaving a paper-thin husk veined with light. Such a form, if Shelley could make it his, had no need to struggle and swim, and imposed no burden to drag him too far under; it was buoyant as mind was, merely chafing and straining at the rope that bound him to the shore.

In this shell of a body, he could cross from the known to the unknown.

★   ★   ★

'I should have liked', he told Edward Williams, 'to be a sailor—Tre says I cannot.'

'Why?' asked Williams.

'Because he cannot smoke, or drink, or swear,' cut in Trelawny; 'and those are essential qualifications for a sailor.'

Trelawny watched Shelley one day in the Bay of Spezia, trying to sail the *Don Juan* with Williams. His pocket Plato was in his hand, and his hair fell over his eyes; he was in his sailing clothes of old black jacket and trousers, both too small for him. 'Intent on catching images from the ever-changing sea and sky', he paid no heed to the boat. When Williams cried 'Luff!' he put the helm the wrong way, and nearly overset her. Trelawny, highly amused and refusing to lend a hand, settled in the stern to observe them:

> 'Luff!' said Williams, as the boat was yawing about. 'Shelley, you can't steer, you have got her in the wind's eye; give me the tiller, and you attend the main-sheet. Ready about!' said Williams. 'Helms down—let go the fore-sheet—see how she spins round on her heel—is she not a beauty? Now, Shelley, let go the main-sheet, and boy, haul aft the jib-sheet!'
>
> The main-sheet was jammed, and the boat unmanageable, or as sailors express it, in irons; when the two had cleared it, Shelley's hat was knocked overboard, and he would probably have followed, if I had not held him. He was so uncommonly awkward, that when they had things ship-shape, Williams, somewhat scandalised at the lubberly manoeuvre, blew up the Poet for his neglect and inattention to orders. Shelley was, however, so happy and in such high glee, and the nautical terms so tickled his fancy, that he even put his beloved 'Plato' in his pocket, and gave his mind up to fun and frolic.

'You will do no good with Shelley', Trelawny concluded, 'until you heave his books and papers overboard; shear the wisps of hair that hang over his eyes; and plunge his arms up to the elbows in a tar bucket.'

Yet the longing to handle boats was an old one, and not untouched by practice. At Eton Shelley had twice played the sailor, in a midshipman's blue jacket and silk stockings, to lead the regatta of Oppidans along the river. He learned to scull there, Medwin said, and lent a hand with rowing for the rest of his life. At Marlow he progressed to a craft with a simple lateen sail, but no mishaps were reported. It was not he who upset the little skiff on the Serchio–Arno canal (though it had been his idea to sail it, the minute he had it, back to Pisa by moonlight). Byron remembered him alone in it, on the Arno in flood, typically but not unskilfully trying to force his way upstream. In the *Don Juan*, 'crank' as it was, rigid with ballast and fantastically over-rigged, he nonetheless managed several voyages in bad weather and perilous approaches to shorelines in lee winds.

The technicalities of sailing intrigued him. His notebooks were filled not only with boats sailing but with diagrams of tacking, compasses and wind direction, fierce straight converging lines in which his boat was transfixed like an insect. Some sketches were made over drafts of his poems, as if for that moment they were more important. He drew yachts with the usual rigging, then rigged both fore and aft and squarely, then with two mainsails on the same mast, then with mainsails set as spritsails on big diagonal spars. The crazy complement of canvas on the *Don Juan* was probably his idea, to make her go fast. A few days after his little boat had foundered in the canal ('Our ducking last night has added fire instead of quenching the nautical ardour which produced it'), a technical letter with a diagram went to Henry Reveley, who had procured and fitted her, to change the position of the rowlock and put on a false keel ('it may be as thin as you please.—') With Trelawny and Williams, proper sailors, he squatted on the shores of the Arno, designing cabins and hulls with a finger in the sand, invoking Drake and Diaz and Captain Bligh and talking fervently, endlessly, of the voyages they would make on proper oceans.

He loved the company of seafarers. In 1812 'The Voyage' pictured sailors as the best of men, free, generous and brave. He had noticed 'that few are more experimentally convinced of the doctrine of necessity than old sailors, who have seen much and various service'. They were fatalists, yet they whistled for a wind, as though they controlled the elements and not vice versa. In sailor company he tried to act the part, rushing downstairs to meet Trelawny 'prompt as a seaman in a squall', lounging and storytelling with them on the dock at Leghorn, chattering of sheets, reefs and halyards, even knocking back a wineglass of weak grog on board an American clipper, which made him loud for Washington and liberty. Talk of sailing itself made Shelley drunk, Trelawny noticed: howling with laughter at his own Greek puns and intoxicated with happiness. 'I dreamed of nothing [last night]', he told Jane once, 'but sailing, and fishing up coral.'

Nonetheless, he accepted that on boats he was subordinate. The Irish Sea made him sick, and the English Channel reduced him to a state of prostrate weakness (though not so weak that, once landed, he could not yell out Kehama's curse again, *And water shall see thee/ And fear thee and fly thee!*). He called himself a 'landsman', and ruefully thought that his sailing skills were the best such a creature could manage. On the *Don Juan*, 'Williams is captain'. Shelley obeyed his commands and seemed to think of nothing for himself, as if in his joyous abstraction he was hardly on a craft that needed handling. Yet it was on the little skiff that his role showed up most clearly. There, as Lionel, he knew his place as Melchior–Williams gave the orders:

> 'Dominic, bring the oars and sails and mast;
> You see that those fore halliards are made fast;
> You hoist the sails . . . Does this stone ballast cock her
> Too much? Aye . . . heave the ballast overboard
> And stow the eatables in the aft locker.—'

Lionel, though he boldly jotted 'God damns' into his draft, kept out of the way. Melchior told him to 'Sit at the helm—fasten this sheet', and he obeyed. Melchior whistled for a wind and cried 'All ready!'; Lionel wondered aloud how the boat thought, what it felt and whether, like him – white wings folded – it was dreaming. He stowed the sweet warm tea in straw, and sat quietly.

Shelley always found such boats when he needed them, just as, venturing or despairing, he reached the edge of earthbound thought. Running down the beach, he would see a little craft 'upon the sea-mark', waiting: single-sailed, scarcely seaworthy, but ready. In *Alastor* he jumped into a shallop whose frail joints already gave with the tide, hoisting his cloak on the bare mast. Alternatively, looking up, he would spot a vessel as a white speck on the horizon, or a strange shadow crossing the sun as it set. His favourite reading was full of such things: Dante's spirit ship in the *Purgatorio*, 'coming over the sea . . . like Mars rising from the vapours of the horizon'; the Pilot's skiff in *The Rime of the Ancient Mariner*, cheerily dashing its oars towards the lights of a seraphic vision; or the 'crazy vessel' in *The Curse of Kehama*, its sides broken, that carried its trembling passengers to the end of the world.

> Aboard! aboard!
> An awful voice, that left no choice,
> Sent forth its stern command,
> Aboard! aboard!

For Shelley a painting by Guido Reni, a horror-compilation of slaughtered Philistines after battle, was relieved by a distant view of the sea and, yet more distant, 'one white and tranquil sail'.

From boyhood, boats took him away. At Eton, when the six o'clock bell rang in summer, he could find one fast. Lock-up was at eight, allowing two hours of freedom; with speed he could get along the High Street, down Brocas Lane, through the boat-builder's yard, down the wooden stair-step, out on a springing plank, into a boat. 'Chance boats' were tied up there, to be seized by the first who came. The pockets of Shelley's greatcoat held iron rations of rolls and bottled tea; these he would devour later, when the little wherry – swift, shallow, pointed at stem and stern – had reached its secret 'arbour', lined with stolen hay, under the trees.

At Marlow, as he turned out of West Street into the top of the High Street, the bridge already marked out the river, with the woods of Bisham blue beyond it. His boat the *Vaga*, shared with Peacock, lay waiting. Shelley would drift in it for whole days, sometimes for a night, taking it to Henley or Cookham or Medmenham, sleeping in it in his 'lone retreat/ Of moss-grown trees and weeds', like a swan under the banks. The locals thought he lived for nothing else: 'always boating, boating—never easy but when he was in that boat'. When one of them, with a piece of chalk, turned *Vaga* to *Vagabond*, Shelley laughed as delightedly as if it was his own invention. He and the boat were made the same.

At the end of his gardens, ideally, a boat lay. The yacht he shared with Byron on Lake Geneva he viewed as 'his', rocking among the bushes at the end of his lawn. His back gate at San Giuliano opened on a stone jetty and, again, his little boat, moored under vine-clad walls. It was the action of a few minutes – the boatman helping – to fit the mast and sail, loosen the chain, seize the oar, and be gone. He took exercise in boats, he told Claire, 'to dissipate thought', or in other words to stop time weighing on him.

Through his childhood he knew small boats as refugee craft, beaching on the Sussex shingle with cargoes of seasick French aristocrats. Missing the ferry to France with Mary in 1814, he commandeered a fishing boat that was tossed like a cockle in the storm that followed. From Ireland in 1812 he took a slate-galliot, again almost overwhelmed by heavy seas. In 1821 he imagined fleeing with Emilia, their flight physical as well as spiritual: the little single-sailed vessel waiting, ready, with one worn sea blanket under which they would embrace 'with proud pleasure' as the white hail pitted the sea. 'Away!' he cried, 'come away!', that constant, swooping Shelley-cry.

In 1817, terrified that his son William would be taken from him by the Lord Chancellor as his children by Harriet had been, he imagined their flight in a sailing boat. 'Willmouse' had been out with him several times that spring in the *Vaga*, baby though he was. Now Shelley, scrawling madly in his agony, proposed to take him on and on, not stopping, never going back.

> Come with me, thou delightful child!
> Come with me, though the wave is wild,
> And the winds are loose, we must not stay . . .

In their dream-haven in the Greek islands, he once told Mary, he would build another boat, ready to flee farther and faster with his son held tight in his arms. This was the sole memory his son Percy, who was two when he died, preserved of him: strong, cradling arms lifting him on board.

In Shelley's mind, such vessels could move themselves. If they had no sail they proceeded by eagerness and instinct, knowing where they were going, like Homer's Phaeacian ships, 'as swift as a bird or as thought itself', or like Phaedria's painted gondola in *The Faerie Queene*:

> More swift, then swallow sheres the liquid skie,
> Withouten oare or Pilot it to guide,
> Or wingèd canuas with the wind to flie.

The sail-less spirit-boat in *The Revolt of Islam* made its own wind by the sheer speed with which the prow, though frail as moonlight, cut through the sea. Among his very last drafts of poetry Shelley drew a page of sleek prows, giving them wings.

The chain loosed, he sat at the helm serenely as the craft made its track of phosphorescence through the deep. Sometimes he ensouled the boat: standing in a trance in the Serchio skiff, a tea-bottle in one hand, he moved 'when Melchior brought him steady', like the vessel itself. Sometimes he was both boat and pilot, voyaging under a spell, as when Claire sang to him at Marlow (the fragment confided to a notebook, secret, like his astonished tears):

> My spirit like a charmèd bark doth swim
> Upon the liquid waves of thy sweet singing
> Far far away into the regions dim

Of rapture, as a boat with swift sails winging
Its way adown some many-winding river
Speeds thro dark forests oer the waters swinging

He imagined, too, that he might flee with Emilia in Dante's 'magic ship' – his phrase, not Dante's – whose sails would be blown wherever his thoughts, and hers, desired them to go.

Yet often he was passive, as if unconscious. He was laid asleep, or too weary to move, in the bottom of a boat controlled by powers he could not see. In *The Assassins* his serpent-self, having 'unwreathed its shining circles', crept into a boat of bark and woven feathers and let itself be taken by the current. The crucial words were those from *Adonais*: 'I am borne darkly, fearfully afar'. Or those from 'Lines written among the Euganean Hills', curiously describing himself alone on the sea: 'He is ever drifted on'.

Bright daemons sometimes helped him: a spirit-woman, a spirit-child, impulsive hopes billowing out the sails. Some used their 'silver-shining wings', like Dante's angel conducting, with ever-growing and gleaming plumes of light, the ship of souls across the sea. 'A star/Shining beside a sail', as Laon saw it, was sometimes the only guidance visible. But these boats were essentially steered by the force of Love, both inwardly and outwardly.

Without a course, without a star,
But, by the instinct of sweet music driven . . .

Thus guided, he began his escape from the world of dreams and shadows. His destination was unknown to him. In *Alastor* the Poet's journey was to death, and he knew it was – but not what death meant, or where it might lead. Other voyages were still less certain. In Southey's *Thalaba the Destroyer* – which Shelley loved, and knew almost by heart – Thalaba took the little unsailed boat that lay by the Well because it seemed to wait for him, and because 'a Damsel bright and bold of eye' asked him, then pressed him, to embark with her. She took the helm; he sat on the single seat; the boat ran rapidly down streams, rivers, broader and broader waters, to the sea. Several times she asked him, with a melancholy smile, 'Wilt thou go on with me?'

'Sail on!' he told her.

He had no idea of her direction, or whether they would ever see land again. But this, Shelley wrote, was as it should be.

We know not where we go, or what sweet dream
    May pilot us through caverns strange and fair
Of far and pathless passion, while the stream
    Of life, our bark doth on its whirlpools bear,
    Spreading swift wings as sails to the dim air;
Nor should we seek to know . . .

The sailor entrusted himself to his craft. He glided out, usually alone, on the wide and empty sea, picking up speed as he went. At the beginning of the *Paradiso* Dante warned anyone seeking to follow his visions not to commit himself and his *piccioletta barca* to the open ocean, 'for the water which I take was never coursed before', and sailors did not 'return as they set forth'. To Shelley, this was an invitation. The ragged sails blew, the helm lifted, the waves thinned and fretted around him like atoms dispersing in the morning sun. And he was in the air.

Air

I
The shadow

In 1823 a Geneva boatman gave his views on Shelley. He remembered him stretched on the bottom of the boat 'gazing at Heaven, where he would never enter'. Mary had a similar memory of Shelley observing skies and clouds as he drifted on the river at Marlow. He floated in a light cocoon between the water and the air.

Often the two were interchangeable. The sea was 'Heaven's ever-changing shadow', the sky 'the inverse deep', each mirroring the other. The air was eddying and liquid; birds dived in it, as fish in the sea; clouds became sunrise-tinted foam, and waves broke in shiverings of mist and light. Though Shelley could not cope in water, in air he imagined he could move like a swimmer, his 'subtle spirit' gliding and turning in an element that could carry him.

His spirit-boats spread sails as wings, with his soul, as before, impelling and directing them. They could break through the morning sunlight like the prow of a ship through spray, or waft 'like gossamer/ On the swift breath of morn'. With one step they might become air-chariots, taking him still higher, still faster:

> O that a chariot of ~~wind~~ cloud were mine
>   Of cloud which the wild tempest ~~winds~~ weave in air . . .

In a vehicle like this, 'pearly and pellucid', offering no barrier to the moonlight, Queen Mab had come for the sleeping Ianthe,

>   to rend
>   The veil of mortal frailty, that the spirit,

Clothed in its changeless purity, may know
How soonest to accomplish the great end
For which it hath its being . . .

Yet that swift escape was not to be his. The veil still lay over him.
Moving among clouds, he had left the Earth, but not existence; their
dense mutability was that of his own thoughts and his own human life.

We are as clouds that veil the midnight moon;
How restlessly they speed, and gleam, and quiver,
Streaking the darkness radiantly!—yet soon
Night closes round, and they are lost for ever . . .

Clouds, as Shelley noticed, sometimes could not ascend the sky. They
clung like thought itself to the tops of the woods, or trailed on the
flanks of mountains. (On the Devon coast mists rose through thin, lich-
ened oak trees; at Marlow fog settled on the river banks.) When he saw
for the first time the peaks of the Alps, he was astonished to find them
higher and brighter than the clouds. From that moment – a moment
ruined by the crass *voiturier* lauding the local butter until Shelley, desperate,
bolted from the coach and walked alone – his mountain summits were
always 'aery', 'aëreal', 'floating' or 'islanded' in the deep sea of the sky.
He made them 'a second world', 'so pure and heavenly white', like truth,
across which the thick air rolled in slow obscuring layers.

Only once did he join himself in sympathy with a cloud that relished
mutability. With her, an intrepid 'daughter of Earth and Water', he
unleashed the showers and hail and built up the charged water particles until 'lightning, my pilot' flashed loose, and the storm broke. In
Bagni di Lucca in 1818, among the Apennine Alps, Shelley watched
such shapes growing steadily around midday until there was thunder,
lightning 'and hail about the size of a pigeon's egg', which then cleared
away,

leaving only those finely woven webs of vapour which we see in
English skies, and flocks of fleecy and slow-moving clouds, which
all vanish before sunset . . .

In contemplation he joined them, spreading out across the sky, letting
the cloud-body of his mortal thoughts be teased and torn apart. Inevitably
it formed again to become a dove, a tent, a 'fleecelike floor', the turrets

and towers of a city both dazzling and crumbling. His Cloud exulted in this continuous revision of state and shape,

I change, but I cannot die—

Yet Shelley's desires already seemed quite different: to dissipate, to die, never again to change.

Typically, he placed himself at the very edge of materiality. Both Berkeley's philosophy and the latest science suggested that he belonged there. At Eton Dr Walker had described a world of the tiniest jostling particles, interpenetrated (a favourite Shelley-word) with innumerable pores through which motion raced and swirled. The same solid, tiny *primordia* that made his body made the air, but now spread out and rarefied; through the spaces in between came impressions, repulsions and persuasions, all crowding in to make him think and act. Through the 'gentle', 'chrystal', 'soft, liquid, plastic', 'everlasting' air, motion increasingly invaded until almost all that mattered was movement itself, spirit itself.

Humphry Davy, in writings Shelley eagerly followed, pictured transparent atoms in tiny revolutions about their own axes and about each other, copying the motions of the universe. They were mostly empty, letting movement in. In *Prometheus Unbound* Shelley made a mirror-image of the circling, rushing wheels of the material world, 'inter-transpicuous' and interweaving:

A sphere, which is as many thousand spheres,
Solid as crystal, yet through all its mass
Flow, as through empty space, music and light:
Ten thousand orbs involving and involved,
Purple and azure, white, and green, and golden,
Sphere within sphere; and every space between
Peopled with unimaginable shapes . . .

All these wheeling orbs were linked to his own thoughts, his emotions and 'the weak touch/ That moves the finest nerve'. His body was the model of the moving universe; his substance, which seemed so solid, was as porous and open to influence as the wide pulsating air.

He could therefore draw himself as a cloud of the most tenuous kind: wisping smoke, obscuring the stars, or the last rags left in the wake of a storm. His own dissolution he could anticipate and feel.

O that I may
Be melted away
Like a mist in the warmth of the coming day

As a matter of course, he was homeless and wandering. He had, as clouds seemed to have, some radiance and motion and desire of his own; he was not blown heedless over the sky. Yet the wind impelled and shaped him as it wanted, and the evening sun gilded him, hanging alone, with moments of almost unbearable light.

'There late was One', he wrote in 1816,

within whose subtle being,
As light and wind within some delicate cloud
That fades amid the blue noon's burning sky,
Genius and death contended. None may know
The sweetness of the joy which made his breath
Fail, like the trances of the summer air . . .

'Thought-inwoven', he took on the hues of everything around him. Sunlight, refracting through him as through the ambient air, produced both his own colours and those of the sky. He could be purple, golden, crimson, 'cinereous', transfused with pearl and fire. All such hues were 'given,/ And then withdrawn', by what agency he would not – could not? – say. The moment when sunset faded from him and he acquired the blue and silver of the moon was especially important, a step from life-realms to dreams:

How beautiful they were—how firm they stood,
Freckling the starry sky like woven pearl!—

This 'camaeleonic' character, he wrote, was typical of poets, who 'take the colour not only of what they feed on, but of the very leaves under which they pass'. In ordinary men this might be seen as syco-phancy, or as views that changed with the day; indeed, the 'surface' of his own being could not escape the prejudices and usages of his age, even if he detested them. 'Spite of ourselves,' as he told Hogg in 1815, 'the human beings which surround us infect us with their opinions.'

His chameleon nature also sensitised him to the least sign of good or evil in the world. Friends saw that sensitivity in Shelley's own changes of colour, from the pallor of his 'languid' days to the furious blushing when he was forced to be sociable or was caught out in lying. Once the earthly masks had fallen, he was as transparent as he was vulnerable. Like Ianthe's spirit, listening to the words of Queen Mab, the least sound or breath could alter him.

> O'er the thin texture of its frame,
> The varying periods painted changing glows,
> As on a summer even . . .

The poet, he noted proudly, was not like ordinary 'earth-lizards'. He lived on light and air.

*   *   *

As an air-lizard, you could not catch him. His bright eyes watched from the hall, he slid in to perch on a chair, he talked, and then he disappeared, as noiselessly as he had come. He could move through a crowd with perfect delicacy, pausing only to touch the heads of children he admired. Though he could also make, when he wanted, the most tremendous racket of hollering, crashing and thunderously knocking, he had perfected the art of silent shifting. In neighbours' kitchens at Marlow he appeared sometimes from nowhere, talked thrillingly for an hour or so of poetry, politics, love, liberty, the nature of the Deity, the condition of the poor, and then, as suddenly, had gone.

His idealised selves were just as elusive. He was a llama, moving through the grass with a wind's swiftness, or a deer, whose thirsting steps at the edge of the lake were smoothly erased by the water. He was the skylark, 'unbodied', or a serpent, letting the sands of the desert blow across his silent track. 'Light, quick and bold' was how he wished to be, and 'printless' on the earth.

Socrates, his hero, was sometimes a type of him: careless of clothes and shoes, happy on a diet of bread and vegetables and, most of all, suddenly losing himself, so wrapped in thought that he took no stock of where he was. Aristophanes pictured Socrates hovering in a basket to contemplate the sun. Leaning out, he claimed that he could better learn celestial matters by blending his subtle spirit with 'the kindred air'. Hogg treated Shelley with much the same cynicism, finding him 'fugitive, volatile', or like the flying colours of a phantasmagoria flashed on a white sheet, then fading away.

In 1820, Shelley wrote out in a notebook most of the fifth chapter of the Wisdom of Solomon from the Apocrypha:

Or as when a bird hath flown through the air, there is no token of her way to be found, but the light air being beaten with the stroke of her wings, & parted with a violent noise & motion of them, is passed through, & therein afterwards no sign where she went is to be found . . .

. . .

[So] the hope of the ungodly is like dust that is blown away with the wind; like a thin froth that is driven away with the storm; like as the smoke which is dispersed here & there with a tempest, & passeth away as the *remembrance of a guest that tarrieth but a day.*

He was no more dependable. Summoned to appointments, he did not come. Called to dinner, he was out in the woods or by water, writing. He told Trelawny, rather sharply, that the Muses who lived in the air did not dine. Bird-like, he picked at any food he found – wild strawberries, 'milky' pine-nuts shaken in the grass – and winged his way back with the birds as evening fell.

Winter or summer, he kept his body open to the breeze.'Philanthropic nudity' (all men, naked, being brothers) would have suited him, Hogg thought, and he was surprised Shelley had not adopted it. Neckerchiefs and waistcoats were discarded (though there was sometimes, said Hogg, 'an ellipsis of his waistcoat'). His hat was 'a crown of thorns' to him, his cravat 'a halter' round his neck. He refused to be 'muffled' with cloaks or flannel, and in the street in Italy affected a long grey dressing gown trailing at his heels and open to his soft white throat; to his intense annoyance, he was once taken for a *signorina*. At Eton he had been renowned for his slovenliness, and for not wearing laces in his shoes. Everywhere interfering womenfolk tried to cut and comb his hair to 'tidy him up', or, worse, make him 'look like a Christian'. He untidied it again, messing it constantly with his long hands, so that he could feel and hear the wind in it.

No portrait could capture him, though he was forced at times to sit for one. Amelia Curran painted him in lifeless oils, and a Mr Tomkins sketched him in charcoal; Edward Williams made spirited attempts in pencil and watercolour, no face like another. Hunt's wife Marianne snipped his profile in paper and modelled a scowling head in plaster. Peacock saw his features in a drawing of a sharp, gesticulating artist in an Italian book of portraits; Jane Williams had a composite made of a softly inoffensive angel face. Both Medwin and Claire thought that Shelley's expression ('ever flitting and varied', 'a perpetual emanation' transfigured by rare smiles) could never be fixed on paper. Mary supposed that some Italian portraitist might catch the nose and perhaps the mouth, but nothing else. After his death she too drew him in laborious pencil, another different and fleeting face.

All these friends presumed him uncatchable because he was not of the earth. He was 'a bright planetary spirit enshrined in an earthly temple', thought Mary; 'a spirit caged, an elemental being . . . not one of *us*, though like to us'. 'I never looked on him', Claire wrote, 'that he did not present to my imagination the idea of an airy substance. His whole life was a sigh and a pant after a more etherial existence.' To Hunt, the most tender-hearted of his male friends,

> He was like a spirit that had darted out of its orb, and found itself in another world. When I heard of the catastrophe that overtook him it seemed as if this spirit . . . had been found dead on a solitary shore of the earth, its wings stiffened, its warm heart cold; the relics of a misunderstood nature, slain by the ungenial elements.

These friends, only half joking, had long presumed Shelley could fly. He would tumble upstairs like a wind god, strewing penny buns; he would appear on a sudden in Chancery Lane, awestruck and dishevelled, as though he had fallen from the sky. 'I have but just entered on the scene of human operations,' Shelley told Godwin in 1812, as if the world was a new, strange stage to him.

Perhaps it was. Long-suffering Hogg made him the Attendant Spirit in Milton's *Comus*:

> I can fly, or I can run
> Quickly to the green earths end . . .
> And from thence can soar as soon
> To the corners of the Moon.

To others he was Oberon and Puck from *A Midsummer Night's Dream* ('I'll put a girdle round about the earth/In ninety minutes'), or a visitor from Mercury, the wandering planet, complete with magic wand. Hunt saw him flying always ahead of him, touching him briefly, flying on, and was afraid that his wings would scorch in the fierce

sun. William Hazlitt, a radical essayist who met him on occa-
·ornfully dismissed him as 'drawn up by irresistible levity', like
a feather, 'to the regions of mere speculation and fancy, to the sphere
of air and fire'. Keats – who encountered him at Hunt's in Hampstead,
but found him too overbearing – once remarked, with slight jealousy,
that Shelley probably never sat with his wings furled for six months
together.

Sentimentality aside, wings were essential to him. They symbolised
possibility, swiftness, potential and escape. Boats, chariots, spirits and
powers possessed them as a matter of course. His own 'wingèd words',
like Homer's winged thoughts, swarmed in the air; winged seeds blew
in the wind, carrying inside them the leaves of a remade world. In
sketches and poems that world, too, could sail or soar, uplifted on
feathery ash-keys or 'plumes of overshadowing wings'.

Since childhood he had dreamed of flying, and envied whatever
could. Medwin recalled him in class at Syon House, watching longingly through the high windows the free, darting flight of swallows. In
his favourite *Adventures of Peter Wilkins* Peter's wife, discovered in the
land of Graundevolet, was one of a race of flying humanoids, equipped
with a neat wing-case of silk enfolding her soft white limbs. Her wings
bore her through the sky and, on water, became a boat like a supple
shell; in both elements she travelled weightlessly, on woven filaments of
her own flesh. Shelley longed to follow. In 1822 in Pisa he could still
be found discussing with Byron contraptions by which men could fly,
though this time with tensile wires and steam.

As a poet, wings had grown round him in the womb. He had come
to maturity with his powers still 'folded', a spirit asleep and waiting to
spring. With only a touch, he would awake and leap. On the proof title-
page of *A Proposal for Putting Reform to the Vote* he sketched an 'S', for
Shelley, soaring into the air on a stream of dots from a bending, wind-
blown tree.

His own wings could not always take him so far. Like Keats, he did
not doubt he had them, sprouting ticklish and sore from the shoulders
of his soul, as Plato had described them in the *Phaedrus*. Yet he felt
them too often timorously beating, his soul faltering 'on tired pinion'
and dragged down by 'cold control',

> Which the vile slaves of earthly night
> Would twine around its struggling flight.

Sitting once with his wings furled, inverting his quill to make a fallen feather, he dipped the tip in ink. It became black and heavy, unable to fly, as he could not. But he would try to bear existence somehow. Turning his notebook sideways, he wrote along the edge

I am not sad   not to me

Then, several times, heavily blotting, the Greek word ουτι, 'not', or 'not at all':

not not not not not

On the next page he continued, almost smothered by inkings of dark, heavy, overwhelming trees growing from the black Earth,

ουτι ουτι ουτι ουτι
not not not not

The winged spirits brought to earth in his drafts were often deliberately blind, folding their dazzling plumes across their eyes so as not to know and not to see.

At times he pictured the 'gorgeous fly' of his soul springing from the grave-worm of his corporeal senses, but hardly dared to dwell on this. He stayed a chrysalis, dreaming in his papery tomb of a liberty almost beyond imagining, or a newly hatched pupa drowsing on water, 'unconscious of the day' in which he would spread his wings. Most often he was a moth, earthier, duller,

whose flight
Is as a dead leaf's in the owlet light . . .

In a letter to Claire in 1821, describing where he still found pleasure amid his sadness, he listed 'The wind the light the air, the smell of a flower'. All these affected him 'with violent emotions'. There was no need, he added, to catalogue the causes of pain.

Tiny mayflies, too, drew his serious attention. He observed them on the Serchio–Arno canal, darting on the surface as his boat glided past or gathering 'thick as mist' above the marshes. In quantity these were mere 'common souls', emerging and dying in clouds on any summer evening, but individually they could be like him and he, in tender moods, like them. Hunt remembered him 'pitching himself' into the feelings of a filmy-winged insect on the trunk of a tree, becoming through 'the most poetical & philosophical speculations' the creature he scrutinised and touched until, in imagination, the fly became a Spirit

> [which] floats with rainbow pinions o'er the stream
> Of life, which flows, like a   dream
> Into the light of morning, to the grave
>   As to an ocean.

Shelley once drew a mayfly at the corner of a notebook page, with bedraggled wings and feelers and, almost inevitably, a half-human face.

Those tiny wings took on, like a Poet's, every colour they passed over. His mayfly life merely flicked the surface in 'one faint April sungleam', yet it was filled with such dazzle of light on water that it might be considered long. 'The life of a man of virtue and talent, who should die in his thirtieth year,' he wrote – carelessly, as though he knew – 'is, with regard to his own feelings, longer than that of a miserable priest-ridden slave, who dreams out a century of dulness.' The ephemeron outlived the tortoise. And among his crammed, ardent thoughts came 'intoxicating', 'almost supernatural' moments, when he was so involved in the beauty and the light that he was almost released from earthly life, almost divine. Like the fly, he was 'beamlike' then, his path 'the lightning's', though he would fade and fall unnoticed when the twilight came.

Pindar, he thought, put it well.

> Creatures of a day, what is anyone? What is anyone not? Man is but a dream of a shadow; but when a gleam of sunshine comes as a gift from heaven, a radiant light rests on men, and life is sweet.

⋆   ⋆   ⋆

The air Shelley moved through, in whatever guise, was full of other beings. They were vital, elusive and in constant motion round him. Some were genii of the wind, some spirits of growth and decay, some (closely following Darwin and Davy) visualisations of physical forces in and below the atmosphere. All these, like the 'half created images' and 'winged children' of his own brain, tracked briefly in the air and lost

again, were invisible until he had coloured them to 'intellectual sight'
in written or spoken words.

> Oh! there are spirits of the air,
>   And genii of the evening breeze,
> And gentle ghosts, with eyes as fair
> As star-beams among twilight trees . . .

Shelley met these beings, and heard them, in solitude. He chose loneliness for the sake of doing so. There was no horror in this contact.
Rather than clinging to the earth, they glanced across it, stroking sounds
from the valleys and the woods. They touched his face, but with no
sense of possession, or shone a sudden, curious light on him, only to
disappear. It seemed at times − if he could only arrest them, only find
their source − that they carried answers to the mystery of himself. But
whatever understanding he imagined lasted no longer than that touch,
or that light.

> With mountain winds, and babbling springs,
>   And moonlight seas, that are the voice
> Of these inexplicable things
>   Thou didst hold commune, and rejoice
> When they did answer thee; but they
> Cast, like a worthless boon, thy love away.

Walking back from these encounters, he would remind himself not to
be surprised at his disappointment. These earthly beauties were decep-
tions only. The world was an illusion, and the true object of his love
was never to be found there.

He once seemed to sketch himself in such a quest, naked and with
claws for hands but with a mild, querulous face, pursuing a naked
woman from crag to crag. He had almost caught her by her long, fair,
streaming hair. But he was not necessarily bent on hurting or deflow-
ering her. Perhaps he was only trying to catch what those spirits of the
air denied him; or perhaps he was Love in pursuit of Beauty, as described
in Plato's *Symposium*.

He translated the *Symposium*, in ten mornings, in the garden of the
Casa Bertini in Bagni di Lucca in 1818. Two sorts of Love were described
there, both deeply interesting to him. The first was drawn by Agathon,
the winner of the poetry contest in whose honour the Symposium was

held, in language as delicate as Plato ever wrote or Shelley ever shaped in English:

> For Love walks not upon the earth, nor over the heads of men . . . but he dwells within, and treads on the softest of existing things, having established his habitation within the souls and inmost nature of Gods and men . . . Love is the divinity who creates peace among men, and calm upon the sea, the windless silence of storms, repose and sleep in sadness.

Shelley thought this description 'wonderful', a summation of 'all that is admirable & lovely in human Nature'. He covered a page with references to the best passages, among soft pencil sketches of rocks and trees. But this was not often the Love that lived in him. Diotima, a prophetess, explained to Socrates and the company a more subtle personification: a being who, lacking beauty himself, yearned and hunted for the beautiful unendingly. He was neither immortal, like Agathon's Love, nor mortal, but a mediator between those states, a 'great daemon' moving like a messenger between gods and men. What he longed for constantly retreated from him; yet whatever webs were woven by the spirits of the air could be constructed, too, by him, binding the realms of Earth and Heaven together in a ceaseless mesh of desire. This Love-daemon, Shelley translated,

> is for ever poor, and so far from being delicate and beautiful as mankind imagine, he is squalid and withered; he flies low along the ground, and is homeless and unsandalled; he sleeps without covering before the doors, and in the unsheltered streets . . . But . . . he is [also] fearless, vehement and strong; a dreadful hunter, forever weaving some new contrivance . . . a philosopher, a powerful inchanter, a wizard, and a subtle sophist.

Such a Love goaded Shelley. It drove his arguments, his writing, his journeys, his thoughts, reminding him of what he lacked, pestering him to find it, to the point of exhaustion. It pricked his eyes and made his cheek flush and alter, enraged to see the world as it was. Ever since the shadow of the Spirit of Beauty had touched him in the school-yard, he had been filled with a desperate desire 'to love, to be loved'. It had become 'an insatiable famine of his nature, which the wide circle of the universe . . . appeared too narrow and confined to satiate'. This longing was encapsulated in a favourite quotation from St Augustine, chosen as the motto for *Alastor* and written out with care, in 1814, into a little red morocco notebook later given to Claire:

Nondum amabam, et amare amabam, quaerebam quid amarem, amans amare.

I was not yet in love and was in love with the idea of loving; I was looking for something to love, loving to love.

Six years later nothing had changed. Shelley drew himself then in an earthly Eden, a typical mortal in a flower's guise, sighing for the unattainable.

> It loves, even like Love, its deep heart is full,
> It desires what it has not, the Beautiful!

'I think', he wrote more offhandedly to his friend John Gisborne, 'one is always in love with something or other.' Far from never being in love exactly, as Claire thought, he was always hopelessly head-over-heels in it; but not, as he had told her, in the way she understood.

In 1811 he pursued the Beautiful through the pages of Sydney Owenson's Indian tale, *The Missionary*. Her name was Luxima, a priestess of Brahma, dove-eyed, veiled and filled with spiritual grace. The missionary Hilarion, 'neither loving nor beloved in the world', pursued her in order to convert her: longing for love but afraid to confess it, in terror of confusing the desires of Earth and Heaven. Trembling, he would touch and then recoil from her; she would take his hand, then let it fall; and at the climax of each meeting she would vanish lightly among the trees, like an evening mist or 'as vapour lit by a sunbeam', unpossessable. 'Will you read it,' Shelley begged Hogg, 'it is really a divine thing. Luxima the Indian is an Angel . . . she is *perfect* . . . Since I have read this book I have read no other—but I have thought strangely.' On the brink of his elopement with Harriet, who resembled Luxima in nothing but surface beauty, he had been considering the forms and workings of a higher type of Love.

He had read the *Symposium* already, with Dr Lind at school. As he translated it again in 1818 he knew Earth-love better, but his ideal was no nearer. This time he took Diotima for his own instructress, beginning, though not finishing, a story in which he intended to sit at her feet, a pale Greek ghost. The Love she taught, Plato's system, was an arduous climb from the physical, through the intelligible, to the ideal: love of the body increasingly abstracted and sublimated, into love of the mind and love of the soul, in pursuit of the Beautiful and the Good. And Shelley was her disciple and her agent. As Lionel he took this role explicitly, arguing ceaselessly for the betterment of man, stirring up longings for liberty, shaping dreams. Love drove him to prison and almost to madness. Yet he failed in his daemon's task of bringing men's minds closer to the Beauty beyond the world. The notebooks found after his death, like Shelley's, were full of his despair.

In his story of Diotima, 'The Coliseum', Shelley gave himself ivory sandals tipped with wings. He was otherwise just a ghostly night-wanderer, an emaciated, graceful youth in an old cloak of the Greek fashion, with profound and piercing eyes and an expression of 'womanish tenderness and hesitation'. But his shoes were 'delicately sculptured in the likeness of two female figures, whose wings met upon the heel, and whose eager and half-divided lips seemed quivering to meet'. This was his daemon-gear. And indeed he might have come from the divine realms, as far as anyone could tell:

> There was no circumstance connected with him that gave the least intimation of his country, his origin, or his occupation. His dress was strange, but splendid and solemn. He was for ever alone. The literati of Rome thought him a curiosity, but there was something in his manner unintelligible but impressive, which awed their obtrusions into distance and silence.

With winged sandals he could also be a more explicit messenger from the gods: Mercury, the heavenly lyre-player, 'nervous yet light',

> With golden-sandalled feet, that glow
> Under plumes of purple dye,
> Like rose-ensanguined ivory . . .

In Homer's hymn to this 'sly chameleon spirit', which Shelley translated with an impish touch, baby Mercury stole Apollo's oxen away, cutting their flesh into strips and roasting their fat on the fire. The outrage done, he slipped back like a mist through the keyhole of his chamber, into his cradle, lisping sweetly that he was 'but a little newborn thing', incapable of tricks. To hide his tracks he had tied bundles of bone-dry tamarisk round his feet, kicking off his sandals at the edge of the sea and flummoxing the stupid gods. Shelley, following across the sand to where the ocean tumbled in spray, could do the same, clutching his lyre, covering his footsteps, with the deities of Law and Custom raging in his wake.

Spirit-trickery could also take another name. Shelley was called 'Ariel' early, at Oxford or soon after, in honour of his lightness, wildness and strange vanishings, and *The Tempest* was always his favourite of Shakespeare's plays, full of Ariel's mysterious 'sounds, and sweet airs',

That give delight, and hurt not.

He and Edward Williams thought they had heard such sounds once, out in the *Don Juan*, as they approached to windward an island in the Bay of Spezia. 'Magic' murmured and whistled all around them, 'now on the sea, now here, now there' but turned out, on closer listening, to be the wind in the rigging of the boat. The yacht itself Shelley meant to call *Ariel*, more an air-craft than a vessel of the sea. But mostly he kept that name for himself: 'quaint Ariel', 'my bird', as his master Prospero called him, the darting and sulking spirit of the air.

In this guise, perched under the pines of the Pisan shore in the spring of 1822, he began a poem to Jane Williams, the tranquil dark-haired beauty he longed for but could not have.

Ariel to Miranda;—Take
This slave of music

Many blots and deletions followed, until the page was scarcely legible; he threw it in the grass. Within the smearings and overwritings lay the lament of a 'poor sprite', captive on the Earth. The witch Sycorax had once shut Ariel in a pine tree, much like those that surrounded Shelley in the Pisan forest. Ariel in the tree had cried for release, as Shelley did,

Imprisoned for some fault of his
In a body like a grave:—

Since he could not put his longing into spoken words, he was sending Jane a 'silent token'. Because he could never prise her from the husband who was also his friend, he hoped only for a smile and a song. Either would make him shine again with the full intensity of the love, and the pain, that he embodied. Sighing, never quite touching, he grasped the empty air.

★   ★   ★

> Kissing Agathon, together
> With my kiss, my soul beside it
> Came to my lips, and there I kept it—

He tried Plato's epigram several ways, on several pages, trying to catch the very moment of the capture of the beautiful and the good.

> Kissing Agathon   ~~my soul~~
> ~~On to my~~   ~~With the kiss & with~~
>   ~~spirit came~~
> With the kiss   ~~my soul arose~~
>   ~~I held my soul~~

In kissing the soul could be softly sucked away, the soul living in breath. 'Suck' and 'soul' (φυκην) were of similar sounds in Greek, the image reinforced. Shelley wrote the Greek out again and again, in letters increasingly wavering and careless, as if it hypnotised him.

> Την φυκην Αγαθωνα φιλων
> Την φυκην Αγαθωνα

He had first attempted this idea at eighteen, clumsily enough, in a 'Fragment Supposed to be an Epithalamium of Francis Ravaillac and Charlotte Corday':

> Soft, my dearest angel, stay,
> Oh! You suck my soul away . . .
> Suck on, suck on, I glow, I glow!

'There were some verses', Hogg remembered, 'with a good deal about sucking in them; to these I objected, as unsuitable to the gravity of an university, but Shelley declared they would be the most impressive of all.' Shelley claimed a friend's mistress had written them, as though he could not possibly have done so.

The ancients made this a death scene. Venus kissed the gored Adonis as he died, his blood staining her robes and springing from the ground as scarlet anemone flowers. Nature died and lived again as his soul fled, brushing her lips. Shelley began, but did not finish, a translation of her lament for him:

> Wake yet a while, Adonis—oh but once
> That I may kiss thee now for the last time—
> But for as long as one short kiss may live—

As Sophia Stacey kissed him, the violet flower, her lips gave life to him. When she withdrew, life left him.

The message of several of Shelley's poems could be compressed to one imperative: Kiss me. The drafts might weave and wander for a dozen lines round the subject, but then

Kiss me

The word kicked into the line, then softened instantly: he ordered, demanded, pleaded, then withdrew. Having blurted it out, he could not finish; he left the words hanging, or deleted them, or in later versions ignored them.

~~Kiss~~ Clasp me,

They remained in his notebooks like a whisper, over and over again.

Yet kiss me

Out in the Field Place garden, home from school and convalescent from a fever of the brain, Shelley kissed his little sister Margaret through the dining-room window. His pursed lips misted the glass.

Lips moving, in Shelley's view, were the deepest expression of the self and its emotions. The soul, wrote Dante in the *Convito*, 'shows herself in the mouth almost like colour under glass'. In the *Vita Nuova* he waited for the 'little smile' from Beatrice that would become, with a few breaths, a kiss.

In 1821 or 1822 – with Emilia, with Jane – a kiss almost happened. For a moment it was a quivering, aching possibility. The moment passed. Sweet lips, he wrote, still in turmoil, the pen barely obeying him,

> ye dare not yield
> ~~when desire~~
> ~~I stole~~
> The sweetness ~~that cost my pain~~
> ~~not given to me~~

As Shelley wandered through the galleries of the Uffizi in Florence, Pomona, goddess of fruitfulness, stepped lightly in his direction. The wind of her own movement blew back her robes, rippling the white marble. Her lips were parted, showing she was alive. 'A breathless yet passive and innocent voluptuousness' hovered on the lips of Venus Anadyomene rising, half-crouching, from her shell and from the sea:

> Her lips . . . have the tenderness of arch yet pure and affectionate desire, and the mode in which the ends are drawn in yet opened by the smile which forever circles round them, and the tremulous curve into which they are wrought by inextinguishable desire, and the tongue lying against the lip as in the listlessness of passive joy, express love, still love.

So essential to beauty were these things, Shelley told Peacock, 'that 'almost no ideal figure of antiquity . . . is to be found with closed lips'.

The Poet of *Alastor* was watched by an Arab maiden as he breathed and slept. She fell in love with his moving lips. The 'tremulous firmness' of Shelley's mouth, friends said, was the hardest feature to catch. Mary insisted later that his lips should be parted in every portrait that was done of him.

As Prince Athanase died, the dark-haired Muse Urania, 'the Lady who really can reply to his soul', came to him for the first time. Bending over his deathbed, she kissed him on the lips.

On the last scrap-page on which he ever wrote poetry, among the draft lines of *The Triumph of Life*, a phrase appeared from nowhere, out of context, in his tiniest writing:

Alas I kiss you—

★   ★   ★

In Shelley's favourite passage of Rousseau's *Julie* the hero, St Preux, crept into the secret room of his beloved. She was not there, but the whole room exhaled her scent, 'an indefinable perfume, almost imperceptible, sweeter than the rose and more delicate than the iris'. Pieces of her clothing, too, were scattered there. Overcome with desire, he touched and kissed them: the bodice shawl, the gown and especially the whalebone corset, imprinted with the soft form of her hips and her breasts. Beauty had been there and gone, leaving an absence that was tangible and unbearable. 'Gods! Gods!' wrote St Preux, desperately scrawling to calm his fever, 'What will it be when . . . ?'

In January 1822 Shelley saw what he called an 'idealism' of this scene: Moritz Retzsch's 'astonishing' etching of Faust in the summerhouse, embracing Margaret. Faust, like St Preux, had earlier entered his beloved's room, lingering to look at the tumbled sheets that had lightly covered her in bed. Now he held her against him and devoured with mouth and hands the body he had imagined. Retzsch drew with the finest, most tenuous of lines, barely differentiating his subjects from white space. The thin muslin of Margaret's robe still concealed her, her limbs dim and yielding as the gauzy film fell over them.

Shelley dared not look on this picture more than once. His brain swam round, he told John Gisborne, 'only to touch the leaf on the opposite side of which I knew that it was figured'. The white paper too veiled Beauty from him, yet still bore the impression and the memory of her. 'So much', Shelley sighed, 'for the world of shadows.'

That world surrounded him. Nature, even in her lightest guise, was still a series of concealing veils in which he was caught fast. Reality lay behind or beyond them, through the 'woof', or woven texture, of existence. He loved that word almost too much, applying it to branches in a forest or weeds overgrowing stones, the layering of clouds or the netting of gossamers strung on the morning grass. Lightest of all was the action of the hoar-frost on bare, dark spots of lawn,

> [Whose] delicate brief touch in silver weaves
> The likeness of the wood's remembered leaves.

Moment by moment the veil was unravelled and made again, mutable as life itself.

He too was part of the enterprise. At Marlow he wove 'a glorious woof of words' among the green wood-weeds and river foam. In Italy he spun 'rare and subtle' thought-threads into a shroud of silk from which memory might one day disinter him. Or he moved like Diotima's Love, tying together with longing and magic the human and the divine. He played weaving love-games, first entwining fingers, then winding his lover's hair around his neck and hers, sometimes deliberately around his eyes to blind him, until their bodies mingled. ('Mingling' was always his word, even atoms blending.) Stroking Harriet's hair, which he admired especially, he felt it knitting softly around his soul; with Mary's 'gauzy wavings', as Claire described them, 'so fine it looks as if the wind had tangled it together into golden network', his 'speechless caresses' began and ended. In 1820 Sophia Stacey was the recipient of verses urging her, she might imagine, to enlace her body with his:

> The fountains mingle with the river
>   And the rivers with the Ocean,
> The winds of Heaven mix for ever
>   With a sweet emotion;
> Nothing in the world is single;
>   All things, by a law divine,
> In one spirit meet and mingle—
>   Why not I with thine?—

Having drawn his lover to him, Shelley would hide away with her in more natural mazes doubling as veils, under canopies of 'dark-linked' ivy or in tapestries of sweetbrier. In the first chaotic draft of *Epipsychidion* he imagined making love to Emilia:

~~where in some labyrinth of untrodden copse~~
                noonday
~~Where, on the myrtle sprays, bright the waterdrops~~
   ~~through~~
~~Glimmer through the~~
     ~~All things which the twilight~~
          ~~cannot end~~
A ~~curtain curtain our~~ veil for our ~~seclusion~~ close as nights

      . . .

~~Kiss me,~~

This woven world was also daubed with colour, like a painted stage-set for the play of life. In Switzerland Shelley marvelled at the blending tints of woods and crags, or rocks and ice, and the changing shades of blue within the fissures of the Mer de Glace. In Bologna, looking keenly at Correggios and Guidos, he noticed especially how the pale orange overtones of the sky, or the shades of evening, shed their light on human faces and figures and were in turn absorbed. Sometimes, as it seemed to him, the very 'colours of a diviner nature' made the subjects lift, and their limbs writhe, as if with the beginnings of flame. ('How evanescent are paintings & must necessarily be.')

Beyond mere colour, rainbows glinted everywhere he looked. He saw 'rainbow-skirted showers' in the woods, prisms of dew strewn across the morning fields, his own image – staining fragile as the world – on the rainbow film of the bubbles he blew. More prism-triangles appeared in his notebooks, flashing imagined iridescence. In the margin of the first draft of 'To a Skylark' he wrote the word 'rainbow' almost pre-emptively, as if he planned to embellish, with ultramarine and crimson, the plain silver drops of the bird's song. Round a waterfall in Switzerland he saw 'a multitude' of circling sunbows, 'which faded or became unspeakably vivid, as the inconstant sun shone through the clouds'.

Like St Preux then, dizzy with longing, he picked up the silken clothes and pressed them to his cheek. He listed what he loved: new leaves, 'the starry night', autumn evenings, dawn mists, snow, 'all the forms/ Of the radiant frost',

      I love waves, and winds, and storms,
        Everything almost

Which is Nature's, and may be
Untainted by man's misery.

This was still the essence of deception. He scorned himself for believing, like most poets, in 'the false earth's inconstancy' and in the wiles of the spirits of the air who seemed to press its beauties on him. On his best days, he knew better:

Life, like a dome of many-coloured glass
Stains the white radiance of eternity
Until Death tramples it to fragments.—

Yet within those transitory things – shifts of colour, perfume, changes of light – lay intimations of the true essence of the world he observed. The deep red of a rose and its scent, sweetening and fading in almost visible clouds above it, hinted at the rose's soul, just as poetry was the sign of the highest condition of a man:

It is the perfect and consummate surface and bloom of all things; it is as the odour and colour of the rose to the texture of the elements which compose it, as the form and splendour of unfaded beauty to the secrets of anatomy and corruption.

In Shelley's more materialist moods, matter could refine as far as this: atoms of colour, atoms of thought. In his immaterialist thinking, the heaviest matter was so invaded by spirit as to dissolve and fly. He therefore played with these lightest properties and qualities, only half endeavouring to catch them. As the winged dream-coursers of Queen Mab pawed the night air in front of him, he struck out 'filmy pennons', 'gauzy' and 'prismy', settling at last for 'wings of braided air', obedient to reins of light. He touched on them, barely visualised them, let them go before he weighed them down. His Witch of Atlas spun threads of mist, 'long lines of light', starbeams and clouds to cover her. Keats begged him to aim for a more substantial verse, to 'load every rift with ore'. But Shelley's method was deliberate. In earthly existence, webs and veils were necessary both to catch reality and to hide it from weak-sighted mortal eyes.

'Lift not the painted veil which those who live/ Call Life,' he wrote – a sonnet in a notebook, never polished or published –

> though unreal shapes be pictured there,
> And it but mimic all we would believe
> With colours idly spread—behind lurk fear
> And hope, twin Destinies, & forever weave
> Their shadows oer the chasm, sightless and drear

He had written first 'Tear not', then, calmer, 'Lift not', but could not take his own advice. In rough draft, he tried the theme again:

> What hast thou done then . . . Lifted up the ~~veil~~
> Which between that which seems & that which is
> Hangs oer the scene of life? ~~within the~~ with shapes uncertain . . .
> Confusedly oerwrought—tombs palaces
> Battles

He knew someone who had dared do this, or so he said. That risk-taker, with his 'lost heart', had gained nothing by his boldness but discontent with the world. In another draft Shelley wished he had never known 'this mournful man', a shadow 'unfaded' but also unheeded among the careless crowd. To be 'himself alone', like him, was to be as sad as the Poet of *Alastor*, whose love for ideal and vanished Beauty had lured him to his death. In yet another attempt Shelley broke off at the moment of drawing the veil aside, unable or unwilling to say what he had glimpsed, or lost.

His sudden apprehension in boyhood of the shadow of the Spirit of Beauty had been much like this. It had been less a glimpse of Reality than a shivering of the veil of Mutability that obscured it. More than that, for he tried often to describe it, the veil was 'rent' and 'there came a shadow', understood as a shadow of light. He sensed it beside him, something, a stranger-visitant, yet in deep association with himself. At best he saw perhaps a flash of silver, for 'silver vision', 'silver shapes' and 'shadowy silver' shone through his poems when he first described it. But beyond this lay only a desperate sense of absence and abandonment.

> Spirit of BEAUTY, that dost consecrate
> With thine own hues all thou dost shine upon
> Of human thought or form,—where art thou gone?

223

> Why dost thou pass away and leave our state,
> This dim vast vale of tears, vacant and desolate?

Though the effect was sensual, even shockingly so, his perceptions were the faintest imaginable, and the cause still hidden. His aching questions brought back an echo only. The best he could do, having no desire in any case to tie this down, was to reach instinctively for things seen and lost: words of air.

> Like moonbeams that behind some piny mountain shower,
>   It visits with inconstant glance
>   Each human heart and countenance;
> Like hues and harmonies of evening,—
>   Like clouds in starlight widely spread,—
>   Like memory of music fled,—

There were no 'facts' here, no 'mere divisions' or 'arbitrary points', but instead the 'delicate and evanescent hues of mind' that Shelley would seek, somehow, to follow beyond language. Even as he tried, the veil drifted across his words.

In *Alastor* his Poet-self encountered a Spirit in breeze-blown woods, the leaping of water and the slow gathering of dusk. It stood beside him, completing the world, 'as if he and it/ Were all that was'. Not long before his death he listed again the things in which 'I the most/ Adore thee present or lament thee lost': wild flowers appearing, leaves dying, grass springing, 'the soft motions and rare smile' of women and the 'unconscious tone' of men or of the trees. He caught something of the Spirit in his Witch of Atlas, who scattered 'mystic snatches of harmonious sound' around her as she flew, but once more all he could tie down was the silence left behind. Perhaps this was the best he could do; perhaps

> Beauty is like remembrance, cast
> From Time long past.

Inevitably, on the earth, even this fleeting encounter had a version that was sinister and dark. In Wales in 1811, perhaps two years after his experience of Beauty's shadow, the sad and exiled Shelley glimpsed something that again eluded him and could not be described. He sensed it in sunless glades and black water; it brushed past him in the flight of a 'sooty' owl and a hint of red, sullen eyes. At dusk he found himself searching for it, but it was neither dusk nor night, whose cloak soothed him. It seemed to be gloom itself, death and decay, and his own cowed thoughts that dwelt on them. The dark had come from him.

That year, too, he had tried to describe where Beauty's shadow sprang from. A sense and sound of it lay in 'The winds, the pineboughs and the waters'. And yet its temple was in his heart, as if those outward pulses stemmed from a source inside himself, unaltering and pure. Mysteriously, absence became presence there, though still almost indescribable: 'perfection's germ' as he called it in *Queen Mab*, at the centre of his body and his life. Some years later he strove to analyse it further, invoking that 'invisible & unattainable point to which Love tends':

> Hence in solitude, or in that deserted state when we are surrounded by human beings, & yet they sympathize not with us, we love the flowers the grass & the waters & the sky. In the motion of the very leaves of spring in the blue air there is then found a secret correspondence with our heart.

In this silent sympathy, thought stopped and time paused. He was aware only of 'the listening soul in my suspended blood'. It seemed he could slip from his chains and step towards eternity. His first attempt to describe this 'undivided joy' of living, breathing and being came at the age of nineteen, in the sunlight and the spring,

> When unpercipient of all other things
> Than those that press around, the breathing Earth
> The gleaming sky and the fresh season's birth,
> Sensation all its wondrous rapture brings
> And to itself not once the mind recurs—
>   Is it foretaste of Heaven?
> So sweet as this the nerves it stirs . . .

In reverie – 'in lonely glades, amid the roar of rivers', or when the stars shone hushed in the sea – he was sometimes aroused to auto-erotic love, as if the whole of Nature were the entity in which he longed to mingle and die.

In lovemaking too, when love was free, he felt the same timeless, oblivious lightness. 'Faintness' and 'abandonment' were the words he used most often for this state, when he seemed almost to forsake his body in a total union of the higher conscious powers. He once wrote, then crossed out, that the sexual act was or should be 'an imaginary point', a moment when the body's substance was lost in its own ecstasy. Indeed, the body of the beloved was so often an idol-image, embraced in dreams, that even in the tempest of the physical act the lovers sought more: the total merging of their bodies one into the other.

In *The Revolt of Islam*, writing wildly in ink over scratched-out pencil, Shelley described the first lovemaking of his brother-and-sister revolutionaries much this way. The bodies of Laon and Cythna faded into 'one reposing soul' and 'one unutterable power' in which fear and time and the world fell away,

> . . . when we had gone
> Into a wide and wild oblivion
> Of tumult and of tenderness . . .

Sexual ecstasy made their eyes misty and dull, but sight was unnecessary. Mortal things were disappearing. '*There is eternity in these moments*', Shelley wrote to Mary in 1814, when their passion was new and all-involving; '—they contain the true elixir of immortal life.' Each of them had made love, when forced to be alone, to the imagined body of the other before they slept. ('Adieu remember love at vespers—before sleep. I do not omit *my* prayers.') Now their material bodies became imaginary, together with all earthly imprisonments, in the dissolving violence of delight. They were almost free.

Yet in the dream of life nothing lasted. Those moments of eternity had been tasted for two days only, from Sunday, 30 October to Tuesday, in a bedroom at the Cross Keys in St John Street. Shelley, on the run from his creditors, could not stay longer. He found himself living for 'sweet moments' in strange, cold beds, or 'the divine rapture of the few & fleeting kisses' exchanged in the street, at Gray's Inn or St Paul's. Mary was hugged close to him, only to disappear.

> Oh my dearest love why are our pleasures so short & so uninterrupted [*sic*]? How long is this to last? . . . All that is exalted & buoyant in my nature urges me towards you—reproaches me with cold delay —laughs at all fear & spurns to dream of prudence! Why am I not with you?—Alas we must not meet.
>   . . .

Thursday Evening.
... My own beloved Mary do I not love you? is not your image the only consolation to my lonely & benighted condition? ... Tomorrow blest creature I shall clasp you again—*forever.* shall it be so?
Shall it be so? ...

> Best dearest adieu One kiss

Although by January 1815 he and Mary could be together permanently, familiarity and domesticity could not fit with his desire. Whenever passion subsided the ache returned, a yearning for more than the world could supply to him. By 1818 Mary's love, too, was no more than a pale imitation of what he wanted. Shelley hid brief cries in his notebooks, never meant to be seen by others and certainly not by her:

> My dearest M. wherefore hast thou gone
> And left me in this dreary world alone

As always in the world of Mutability, Beauty touched him for a moment and then abandoned him. The memories of the 'lovely' form were left, like clothes thrown lightly and carelessly on a bed. Until he could possess the 'faintest shadow' of what he had encountered, there would be no rest or respite for him. Yet what he sought was itself a glancing shadow, with no firm assurance of anything more lasting.

2

The song

On his best days the curtain of clouds was gone. The blue sky stretched above him unmarked and unobscured and inspiration moved there, almost visible.

He told Trelawny that the Muses lived 'in the blue regions of the air' and that he spent his time there, in pursuit of them. Medwin recalled that on clear frosty days Shelley's spirits would run riot and his talk would become 'electric'. Cooped up in England, writing *The Revolt of Islam* in 1817, he dwelt lovingly on 'the blue serene' of more southern places; arriving in Italy the next spring, he told Peacock that the serenity of the sky had made 'the greatest difference in my sensations'. He depended on it, he said, for life. In 1820 he wanted Keats too, who was dying, to see that sky and live.

In the half-light of mind and dreams blue signified mortality: 'Death's blue vault, with loathliest vapours hung', or the cobweb hair of ghosts. But in the upper regions it meant clarity and hope, the shining life of the spirit. Blue sky would make a sacred witness, in Shelley's new world, to a great Assembly of 'the fearless and the free' who would overturn tyranny in England. Both the West Wind and the spring were blue, and could only be so.

Ideally, blue sky intermingled with the earthly scene. Shelley's temples were almost always open to the air, 'upaithric' in his peculiar borrowing from the Greek, allowing the light and wind to penetrate inside them. This rooflessness, he believed, had been deliberate among the ancients, not merely the result of ruin and decay. They wished to be in a 'perpetual commerce' with 'the flying clouds the stars or the deep sky' and 'the ever changing illumination of the air'. The Greeks, he told Peacock, 'lived in harmony with nature, & the interstices of their incomparable

231

columns, were portals as it were to admit the spirit of beauty which animates this glorious universe'. Their poetry was made this way. Reading, too, he insisted to Claire, was much better done under the wide open heavens; poetry never came so near the soul as then.

After his first visit to the ruined Colosseum, in November 1818, Shelley began a story. In it, an old blind man asked his daughter whether the place where they sat was open to the sky. 'Yes,' she assured him:

> '. . . The blue sky is above—the wide, bright, blue sky—it glows through the great rents on high, and through the bare boughs of the marble rooted fig-tree . . . I see—I feel its clear and piercing beams fill the universe, and impregnate the joy-inspiring wind with life and light, and casting the veil of its splendour over all things—even me.'

Shelley was in this scene. Wandering past, a stranger in his Greek cloak and ivory daemon-shoes, he had mocked the old man for not knowing where he was. The girl explained that he was blind. 'Blind!' Shelley echoed, his eyes filling with tears. He sat now apart from them, on a ruined staircase, listening.

> 'What else see you?' the old man asked.
> 'Nothing.'
> 'Nothing?'

The old man refused to believe her. He could hear the sound of wings and leaves and feel the 'living wind' around him. Suddenly, 'lifting his sightless eyes towards the undazzling sun', he cried out: 'O Power . . . thou which interpenetratest all things, and without which this glorious world were a blind and formless Chaos, Love, Author of Good, God, King, Father.' Shelley, astonished and contrite, recognised then the voice of a kindred soul.

He had tried to address that power many times. He had called it Necessity, the Soul of the Universe, all-sufficing Power, the Spirit of Nature. Or, like the old blind man, he could call it Love. That word was 'too often profaned', he told Jane, 'for me to profane it'. Yet despite his caution or his reverence, Shelley again and again wrote and recited it. It seemed that his true need was to repeat it constantly, leaning on it like a mantra or a spell,

love o love

– to make it as pervading and enwrapping as the air, within him and without him, his own being.

In 1818, in a fragment apparently intended for his 'autobiographical' *Prince Athanase*, Shelley sang explicitly to Love as power, a god of inner brightness diffused into the air.

> Thou art the radiance which where Ocean rolls
>
> Investeth it and when the Heavens are blue
> Thou fillest them, and when the earth is fair
> The shadow of thy moving wings imbue
>
> Its deserts & its mountains, till they wear
> Beauty like some light robe; thou ever soarest
> Among the towers of men, and as soft air
>
> In spring which moves the unawakened forest
> Clothing with leaves its branches bare & bleak
> Thou floatest among men . . .

His early reading had encouraged him in this. Erasmus Darwin in *The Temple of Nature* made Love the controlling force of all things living:

> You! whose wide arms, in soft embraces hurl'd
> Round the vast frame, connect the whirling world!

Lucretius, arch-materialist though he was, had dedicated his great work to Venus, 'without whom nothing comes forth into the shining borders of light'; and he had also allowed for an *exiguum clinamen*, a minute swerving of the primordial atoms, away from Fate and towards desire. In January 1811, writing to Hogg, Shelley pushed the idea further:

> Stay! I have an idea, I think I can prove the existence of a Deity. A first cause—I will ask a materialist how came this universe at first. He will answer by chance. —What chance? I will answer in the words of Spinoza— 'An *infinite* number of atoms had been ~~falling floating~~ from all eternity in space, till at last one of them fortuitously diverged from it's track which dragging with it another formed the principle of Gravitation & in consequence the universe' —What cause produced this change, this chance? surely some . . . Was not this then

233

a *cause*, was it not a *first* cause. —was not this first cause a Deity . . .
Oh! That this Deity were the Soul of the Universe, the spirit of
universal imperishable love. —Indeed I believe it . . .

He was not so far out on a limb as he supposed. Even Holbach and
Davy had endowed matter with sympathy, affinity and antipathy,
properties of spirit. The finer the atoms – progressing from the
weight of earth through water, to air, to fire – the greater the diver-
gence from cause and effect to attraction and repulsion, the law of
Love.

All Nature, as Shelley wrote in *Adonais* ten years later, fulfilled and
proclaimed this law.

> Through wood and stream and field and hill and Ocean
> A quickening life from the Earth's heart has burst
> As it has ever done, with change and motion . . .
> All baser things pant with life's sacred thirst;
> Diffuse themselves; and spend in love's delight,
> The beauty and the joy of their renewèd might.

Only man was an outcast from this scene. Something far more difficult and demanding seemed to live in him. The renewal of the world
in spring, though it stirred his blood, could neither ease his sadness nor lighten his burdens for long. Love did not work in him that
way.

Some time in 1817, desperate about something – Godwin's endless
begging, Wordsworth's sycophantic praises of the Tory government –
Shelley blundered out of doors. It did not help.

> My head is wild with weeping for a grief
> Which is the shadow of a gentle mind
> I walk into the air, yet no relief
> I seek   or ~~haply~~ if I sought should find

The words were jagged with the effort of writing, his pencil digging
and jerking as if in paroxysms of tears. He could not expect comfort,
and should not have expected it.

> It comes uncalled—the woes of human kind
> Their actual miseries   their false belief

234

He broke off, began again. This time he addressed, as it seemed, indifferent Nature and the comfortless air – or rather something far more compelling, and closer to him.

> Fair spirit thou art cold as clean and blind
> As beautiful

Nothing more could be said. Nothing worked. He began to scribble fiercely, messily on the white 'unfeeling' page, striking the words out, stabbing and ripping a long tear in the paper.

The Spirit remained unmoved by him. Whatever Shelley was addressing, it would not help him with the passing miseries of mortal life. Reproaches or tears made no difference. Yet its 'throne of power' was in his heart, the deep place in which he had perceived, distantly and dimly, the antitype of all the absolutes he pursued and served. The 'god of my own heart', he once told Hunt, was Love: 'blind Love', as he described it in *Hellas, as clean and blind/ As beautiful*. And Love demanded everything of him.

The bright shadow of the Spirit of Beauty, when it had first appeared in the school-yard, induced in him a similar chaos of rapture, compulsion and pain. It had touched him on a morning in spring, 'at that sweet time when winds are wooing/ All vital things', yet he stood there trembling, moved by something far greater. Love, light and motion were suddenly intermixed with all he felt and saw. He was transported, yet he wept. He was captured (the shadow fell, he cried out), yet released. Were this power allowed free rein, the world's 'dark slavery' would vanish; were this force admitted in his being, he could do anything.

> Man were immortal, and omnipotent,
> Didst thou, unknown and awful as thou art,
> Keep with thy glorious train firm state within his heart.

Touched thus, transformed – or reminded – he armed himself with secret learning, chose words as his weapons, and walked out on his mission to change men's minds and the world. The god of his own heart seemed to have required it. 'Deep calm' descended over him, silver-cold, and hiding an almost frightening sense of purpose. At the behest of a shadow that had brushed him, for one moment, with the challenge of unlimited liberty and love, he had vowed to do whatever was required of him.

Shortly afterwards, he seems to have tried to explain what had happened. His poem was dated simply '1809', with a design drawn under it.

> Thine, thine is the bond that alone binds the free.
>   Can the free worship bondage? nay, more,
> What they feel not, believe not, adore—
> What if felt, if believed, if existing, must give
> To thee to create, to eternize, to live—

'Control' was how Shelley also described this. In his rhyme patterns 'soul' and 'control' inevitably found each other, their tension palpable, as well as their connection. His prankish Witch of Atlas worked this way, exercising 'some control/Mightier than life' by which soldiers beat their swords into ploughshares, misers gave away their gold and lovers, once shy, indulged their most concealed desires. The startling freedom of Love was forced upon them, as it had been upon him.

As a rule he loathed coercion, displaying, as his father put it, an 'unusual spirit of Resistance to any controul'. But this was quite different, bound up tightly with his own desire. Twice he used 'awful' to explain the power of this Spirit over him and his disposition to worship it: 'awful LOVELINESS', he wrote, gasping out the words. A later discarded 'scrap' seemed to record another episode in the same long, stilling compulsion:

> The ~~living frame which sustains my soul~~
> ~~I sinking beneath the fierce controul~~
> Down through the lampless deep of song
>   I am drawn & driven   along—

In 1819, reading Xenophon's *Memorabilia*, a thought seemed to strike Shelley about the daemon of Socrates. Among the statues in Florence he paused and made a note of it:

[Socrates] said—a supernatural force has sway over the greatest things in all human undertakings . . . and that the uncertainty belonging to them all, is the intervention of that power, or rather, that all events except those which the human will modifies, are modified by the divine will.

Like Necessity – but less focused, more inconstant – Love seemed to control his life wherever his own will did not. Socrates understood (Xenophon continued) that the gods knew all things: 'both the things that are said and the things that are done, and the things that are counselled in the silent chambers of the heart'. Shelley too was apparently filled with this power, compelling him towards everything he most lacked and most hungered for.

At Pompeii in 1819 he sat among the ruins, sucking on sweet figs and chewing bread, as he admired the white colonnades and pediments, 'that ideal type of a sacred forest', rising against the landscape and the sky. The distant deep thunder of Vesuvius entered the scene too, 'interpenetrating' his body along with the light and air. And beyond all this was another song: longed for, transcendent, almost never heard. The source of that, too, seemed to lie inside himself. Between them, like Davy's atoms converging with the circuits of the spheres, they made a harmony that might either transport him or – callously, carelessly – take his breath away.

★   ★   ★

Instinctively, when writing, Shelley turned his gaze upwards. He lay on the grass or in his boat under a canopy of green, in 'the emerald light of leaf-entangled beams'. The trees in his notebooks were sometimes rooted firmly in the earth, sometimes dangerously poised at the edges of cliffs whose stones had begun to give. But most often he drew swags and snatches of foliage adrift in the air.

Long familiarity made him good at trees; sympathy made him draw them everywhere, scratching them eagerly into doorposts and scribbling them on walls. Medwin saw such sketches in his schoolbooks at Syon House, pines and spreading cedars like those on the lawn at Field Place. Hunt recalled him busy with his pencil as they waited at coaching inns, swivelling in his chair to decorate the wainscot: trees, then water, then a boat, then himself. He seemed to sketch most readily the deeply layered backdrop of the river banks at Marlow, hawthorn and willow rising to oak and birch, with gleaming water beside them.

Some trees he drew in detail, beautifully ranged and shaded, begun in pencil and picked out in ink which, on vellum or poor paper, smudged an agreeable softness over the whole. Others he hung in drooping melancholy fronds, cartoons of his own nerves shrinking and freezing like 'sapless leaflets' on a winter branch. He did not, he told

Claire disdainfully, draw daubs for trees as other people did. He knew their character and habits, from the 'floating' acacias to the 'light' beech to the umbrella pines of Pisa with their rounded topiaries, 'like green waves on the sea'. Their order of opening – chestnut, wild brier, oak, the 'tender unrisen cones' of the larches – he could give with precision and delight.

The leaf swags and tree summits in his notebooks, however, had no exactness to them. They were tiny, rough, vestigial things, a few strokes of pencil or pen. They marked pauses, interruptions, considerations. He doodled them in his study as readily as outside, in the margins or between the lines. In many cases it was hard to tell whether tree-tops or clouds were his subjects. Both were removed from Earth, as he wished to be, and both mediated the light and sounds of Heaven, as he tried to. He might have been a devotee of the Oracle at Dodona, where the will of Zeus was declared in the rustling of beeches and oaks.

Wherever he was, he sought woods and arbours where branches interlaced above his head. At Marlow he wrote under long drapes of willow, 'pavilions', as he called them: the trees Orpheus had touched in the grove of Persephone, filling him with mystical songs. At Este he wrote in a summerhouse at the end of a pergola overhung with vines. His friend Horace Smith once walked and talked with him in the Bisham beech-woods, mostly about religion, and noted how the high leafy vaults seemed directly to inspire him. Shelley himself recorded the 'Pythian' power of the laurels near Lake Como and the way the cypresses there, like the cloud-peaks of the Alps, seemed not merely to brush against the sky but pierce through it. Though he might be 'curtained out from Heaven's wide blue' by leaves, these trees were his roofless temples,

> . . . where meeting branches lean
> Even from the Earth, to mingle the delight
> Which lives within the *light*

He sought, too, green lawns among the trees, soft-carpeted with moss and strewn almost too formally with tiny, brightly coloured flowers. As a child he had stumbled on them in St Leonard's Forest, patches of 'breathing calm' bathed suddenly in light. He found such a spot at Meillerie on Lake Geneva, a dell 'inconceivably verdant' in which he lay, his lips still tasting honey, on the 'enchanted ground' of the deep thyme-scented grass. These lawns made natural resting places for his wandering thoughts, recesses for 'voluptuous faintness' as he tried to write. There the shadow of Beauty, or the vapour of Wisdom, presided over lovers coupling or poets dying among the drifting leaves. Life began here, and ended, in the wind's path through the woods.

As it passed, the trees sang. A man might not hear them, but a Poet could, stepping lightly from the ruins of Rome to a vale in the Indian Caucasus:

> A wind arose among the pines; it shook
> The clinging music from their boughs, and then
> Low, sweet, faint sounds, like the farewell of ghosts . . .

The music Shelley heard lived especially in pines and reeds, thin murmurs of joy or sadness, like the reed pipes played by the shepherds of ancient Greece under the shading trees. Streams ran down beside them from the hidden caves of the nymphs, while all things breathed the incense of summer and autumn heat. These were Pan's pipes, too, blown by the god of wood-wandering, whose rivals fell silent to hear him:

> The wind in the reeds and the rushes,
> The bees on the bells of thyme,
> The birds in the myrtle bushes,
> The cicadae above in the lime . . .

Yet in the end these 'sweet pipings' were the sound of corporeal, earthbound longing, the pursuit of lusting Pan for lovely Syrinx who was turned into a reed as all worldly things changed, and of nothing deeper or higher.

There was something else, in Nature yet beyond it, that Shelley heard. The Sussex night made 'a weird sound of its own stillness', thrilling him. In Italy too, after sunset, the dusk falling but the candles not yet brought, a tone of incomparable softness and sadness seemed to rise from the landscape:

> Such as nor voice, nor lute, nor wind, nor bird,
> The soul ever stirred;
> Unlike and far sweeter than them all.

Again and again he heard it. Mary told him it was an owl, the Aziola, hooting gently and plaintively in the woods. Shelley had made of it something quite different, fixed deeper in the scene and in himself, until it might almost have seemed the spare, fluting sound of his own melancholy given back to him.

He also heard sounds more sublime. These were often an intimation, nothing more: a hint of Beauty that had passed, or was about to pass. Or it might be a mysterious sympathy extended, through Nature's softest sounds, to the listening soul:

> There is eloquence in the tongueless wind & a melody in the flowing of brooks, & the rustling of the reeds beside them which by their inconceivable relation to something within the soul awaken the spirits to a dance of breathless rapture, & bring tears of mysterious tenderness to the eyes like . . . the voice of one beloved singing to you alone.

This melody once heard, there was no more peace for the listener. No matter how faintly, he longed to hear it again. Perhaps the only way to do so was to follow it, out of the body, through dreams or rapture or through death. In an unfinished fragment Shelley once begged the Spirit of Silence to spare him and pity him,

> Until the sounds I hear become my soul
> And it has left these faint & weary limbs
> To track, along the lapses of the air
> This wandering melody until it rest
> Among lone mountains in some

The Spirit of Beauty, the constant object of his love and his pursuit, he had compared not to music but to 'memory of music fled': a melody heard as a child but now fading, even as far as silence.

Absence remained. What he thought he had heard might, in the end, be inexpressible. So much was: the fall of a line, the motion of a dress, the varying greens of chestnut woods in August, or the sheer shouting joy he felt when, at Leghorn after years of absence, he rushed into Hunt's arms and was pressed warmly, violently against him: 'You cannot think how *inexpressibly* happy it makes me!' 'I am so *inexpressibly* delighted!' In his writings, too, that word seemed to represent the deepest note of his emotion. 'The deep truth is imageless,' he wrote once, and it was soundless also. His most profound response to what he felt and saw was often no words at all.

And it was vital, if no words would come, to write none. They were so easily misleading, so clumsily suggestive, one thought leading to another until 'our whole life . . . is an education of error'. In Shelley's view the duty of the moral and political reformer, error once removed, was often to leave 'a vacancy'. In that emptiness, mind was free to act; or to wait for what it might begin to hear in its own responding depths.

★   ★   ★

Among the towers of a palace in the ancient East a lyre lay abandoned in the desert wind. The palace was in ruins, its halls strewn with heroes' bones. Air wandered there and woke the strings in passing. Shelley painted this scene in 'A retrospect of Times of Old', when he was nineteen. In its elements it seldom changed: a harp or lyre suspended, the moving air and, more often than not, the boundless ocean, listening.

'External and internal impressions' played ceaselessly over him, drawing notes from the nerve-strings of his body. He might have been a fashionable box-harp in a window, his tense and silent cords already tuned. 'The scented gale of summer can wake [me] to sweet melody,' he told Mary in 1814, 'but rough cold blasts draw forth discordances & jarring sounds.' Since he was mortal he was violently fickle, '[no] mood or modulation like the last'.

In *Alastor*, narrating the Poet's story, he spoke in a lyre's voice. 'Serenely now, and moveless',

> Suspended in the solitary dome
> Of some mysterious and deserted fane,
> I wait thy breath, Great Parent, that my strain
> May modulate with murmurs of the air,
> And motions of the forests and the sea . . .

Harp shapes were sketched this way and that, in lightest pencil, on a draft of the 'Song of Spirits' from *Prometheus Unbound*. Two were empty and unstrung. On one the 'life-strings', as Shelley had long called them, were forming in faint lines, as if they would grow with the poem when the breath came, if it came.

Yet Shelley also had a song of his own, drawn not from Nature's wind but from some deeper and more constant source. 'There is a principle within the human being', he wrote,

> which acts otherwise than in a lyre and produces not melody alone but harmony, by an instinctive adjustment of the sounds and motions thus excited to the impressions which excite them.

He had watched this in children playing alone as he sat quietly nearby on the floor. The child, delighted by something, would respond with a gesture or a sound, consciously trying to prolong the effect so that it might prolong also 'the consciousness of the cause'. Shelley did the same; his strings continued to tremble and sing when the visiting breath had died away.

There was something divine in this. The Poet of *Alastor* was described in death as a lyre laid down without music, his 'harmonious strings' silent:

> No sense, no motion, no divinity—

And indeed it seemed to be the breath of Heaven, not merely Nature, that had wandered over him.

In the Vale of Cashmire, Luxima's place, a veiled maid came to him in dreams. She sang first from the stream-sounds and the breezes, then swept 'from some strange harp/ Strange symphony', pacing the song to her agitated heart. She was strung to his pitch, two lyres together; her voice was 'the voice of his own soul'. Pervaded with longing, he stretched out his whole being to her:

>   . . . she drew back a while,
> Then, yielding to the irresistible joy,
> With frantic gesture and short breathless cry
> Folded his frame in her dissolving arms.

Then, in a moment, she was gone. Night blinded him. Suddenly awake from these visions of 'aëreal joy', Shelley found only despair beside him, as he had so often done. Some 'inexplicable defect of harmony' in him, as in all human nature, confounded highest pleasure with deepest pain.

Sophia Stacey played the harp as Shelley watched her, her bare arms moving delicately over the wires, her thin dress draping

> Those soft limbs of thine, whose motion
> ~~As it~~   ~~thy spirit~~
> ~~As thy spirit~~   shifts & glances—
> Ever falls
>   As their life within them dances

He wrote out the poem and slipped it to her, two small sheets of paper folded over, swiftly into her hand, his song in hers.

> As dew beneath the wind of morning,
>   As the sea which whirlwinds waken,
> As the birds at thunder's warning,
>   As aught mute yet deeply shaken,
> As one who feels an unseen spirit
> Is my heart when thine is near it.

The impact of song on him was often unbearable in its physical intensity. When women played, they played him; when they sang, they stole his own breath from him. He was in love with them, ached with wanting them, whatever his reasonings otherwise. The draft of 'To Constantia', written as Claire sang at the piano in 1817, was among the most desperate and illegible he ever produced. The words *lost, dissolved, consumed, drunk* were tried and deleted again and again, blotted, smudged. Claire's fingers, warm with blood and life, moved over him; a 'power like light' lingered as perfume on her hair and in her touch; her voice was the air surrounding him. He was becoming not merely the instrument but music itself, breath itself, inside her.

> I am ~~eons~~ dissolved in these
> ~~it is my~~ My
>   ~~Thy voice~~
> ~~My soul is lost, dissolved in~~ was

~~Body & soul dissolves in liquid extasies~~
~~Slowly I am drunk up by~~
~~dissolved in~~
I am dissolved in these consuming
~~Now like~~ Constantia now   thee
~~I have no life~~ ~~or rest or~~ but
~~I am not body or soul or ought but thee~~

Somehow he put these thoughts in order, apparently sending them to
the *Oxford Herald*. But he did not own up to them. He was 'Pleyel', a
rationalist from the pages of Brockden Brown, the sort who could watch
and listen calmly; not Shelley, who was still in chaos.

My brain is wild, my breath comes quick,
    The blood is listening in my frame,
And thronging shadows fast and thick
    Fall on my overflowing eyes;
My heart is quivering like a flame;
    As morning dew, that in the sunbeam dies,
I am dissolved in these consuming extasies.
I have no life, Constantia, but in thee;
    Whilst, like the world-surrounding air, thy song
Flows on, and fills all things with melody . . .

The god Mercury had shaped his lyre from a tortoise shell, scooping
out the body and pulling soft guts into strings. For those who mis-
handled or misunderstood this instrument, it would not sing. When
played properly, however, these poor remains of a body made music so
sweet that Apollo himself wished to learn it.

In 1822 Shelley bought Jane a guitar of pine and mahogany, encased
in a box like a coffin. The guitar, he implied, contained his spirit,
imprisoned like Ariel in the tree. Sighing conifers, after all, often made
his own melodies, his voice in their needle-leaves as if they shared
bodies. In *The Assassins* a stranger, a fallen Shelley-spirit, was discovered
impaled in a cedar tree, his voice 'mild and clear as the responses of
Aeolian music', his blood falling from its branches.

With the guitar he enclosed his instructions in the form of a poem.
He could make music, he told Jane, only for those who had the wit
to understand him. For them he could produce all the loveliest, simplest

sounds of Nature: echoes of the hills, stream-notes, birdsong, 'sweet oracles of woods and dells'. He knew also – or his spirit knew, when softly encouraged to sing,

> That seldom heard mysterious sound,
> Which, driven on its diurnal round
> As it floats through boundless day
> Our world enkindles on its way—

This too, in his tortured captivity, he offered to Jane and her gentleness.

That summer he sat at her feet, 'within her presence', on the beach near Villa Magni as night fell. She placed her hand gently on his forehead; it trembled there.

> And feeling ever—O too much—
> The soft vibrations of her touch

He had reserved his 'highest holiest tone' of love for her, plucked from 'the most removed and divine of the strings of that which makes music within my thoughts'. But Jane, who could not hear that particular tone, kept a sensible distance from him: soothing him, then leaving him, as the echoes of her playing died away.

★   ★   ★

In the ordinary way of composition – if there was, with Shelley, any ordinary way – his ear was for rhythm first. He found the metre, then the rhymes, leaving gaps, as was necessary, when words would not come. He beat time before he sang. When a rhythm caught him he would try it in the notebook for a line or two, to see if he liked it and how well it would carry words. Testing a metre, he would often mark it as small lines on the page, | | | | | | |, set out imperiously at the start like the tick of a metronome. He ranged beats in a grid, ringed them round in a circle, shook them down his margins, made them into a hum:

> Ham, Humb um haumb haum, aum

> na na, na na na na / na

or again (playing with the rhythm of 'Ah time, oh night, oh day' and dreaming of Emilia, who was writing in the notebook with him),

> ~~Ni na ni na, na ni~~
> ~~Ni na ni na, ni na~~
> Oh life o death, o time

 Translating Plato, he despaired that his own 'fainting & inefficient periods' could ever catch that 'irresistible stream of musical impressions which hurry the persuasions onward as in a breathless career'. *Breathless, irresistible, musical, persuasions*, were for him the epitome of poetry as something that lived and moved. His preferred word for rhythm and cadences was 'pauses', sometimes 'interstices', as though these were chinks among his hustling ideas through which spirit entered and breathed.

 When he thought he was alone he said his lines to himself – Trelawny heard him – beating and chanting, to make sure they worked. He checked as he walked, still in the open air. Weak rhythms pained him, and he apologised to readers once for 'most inadvertently' leaving a slow-loping alexandrine in the middle of a stanza. (It was not the only one he ever left, but he wished to emphasise his awareness of imperfection.) In early fair copies he underlined syllables, diphthongs, even single letters, to show where the stresses should fall. He felt impelled to explain why Spenserian stanzas, 'inexpressibly beautiful', especially suited *The Revolt of Islam*, and why his metres were mixed in *Rosalind and Helen*, to vary 'with the flow of the feeling'. Both *terza* and *ottava rima* were subtly speeded up, suiting his impetuous temper, by interweaving lines, reducing their stresses and running them on where he could. In his last poem, in *terza rima*, the irresistible rhythm leapt up with the dawn:

> Swift as a spirit hastening to his task
>   Of glory & of good, the Sun sprang forth
> Rejoicing in his splendour, & the mask
>
>   Of darkness fell from the awakened Earth. /

The forward-slash was Shelley's, steadying him for the next step. Sometimes the very cross-strokes and serifs of his letters were neat-footed, fierce or ornamental, matching the beat, like a dancing master. Yet at Syon House the dancing master had despaired of him, saying he was so gauche as to be unteachable.

Rhythm was integral to inspiration. Dance had come into the world, as Lucan said, along with creation and with Love. Shelley saw it everywhere, from the 'implicated orbits' of planets and stars to the interweaving honey-flight of bees. He glimpsed it in the compulsive skipping and rhyming of children, the first signs (as Plato wrote in the *Laws*, and as Shelley copied out in Greek) that men aspired to harmony and order, and that the gods and circling Muses kept company with them. He heard it, with Calderón, in a night garden, standing in the cool air, aware of the enlacing jasmine and the lifting wind in the leaves:

> *Alli, el silencio de la noche fria,*
> *el jazmin que en las redes se enlazava,*
> *el cristal de la fuente que corria*
> *el arroyo que a solas murmurava,*
> *el viento que en las hojas se movia*
> *el Aura que en las flores respirava; —*
> *todo era amor: che mucho, si en tal calma*
> *aves fuentes e flores tienen alma*

With rhythm came harmony – rhythm's spirit, as Shelley termed it – and with harmony, meaning and power. Sound itself carried sense. Its 'uniform and harmonious recurrence', he wrote in *A Defence of Poetry*, 'is scarcely less indispensable to the communication of [poetry's] influence than the words themselves'. He went further:

All the authors of revolutions in opinion are not only necessarily poets as they are inventors, nor even as their words unveil the permanent analogy of things by images which participate in the life of truth; but as their periods are harmonious and rhythmical and contain in themselves the elements of verse; being the echo of the eternal music.

In his drafts he struggled to describe that eternal music. It lay 'beyond the tumult of the world', 'unheard by outward ears', nourishing like an invisible wind Earth's swift course through the heavens. Crossly, at that point, he stopped himself:

this is ~~neither~~ not argument ~~nor illustration~~ & illustration ought not to precede the thing to be illustrated

But he had heard it nonetheless. It was within him, caught as fragments in trance, a faint disjointed echo of the harmony of the spheres. 'Listen to the music,' he had begun to say.

Music, rather than words, made him a Poet. Indeed metrical language, Shelley thought, worked better even than music to express 'the actions and passions of our internal being', and was 'susceptible of more various and delicate combinations than colour, form, or motion.' Poetry had no intermediary, no instrument or canvas or sculptor's marble, but was sheer thought modified only by arrangement 'by that imperial faculty, whose throne is curtained within the invisible nature of man'. Obedient to that power, grammar bowed to melody and rhythm and still worked at some fleeting, flying, symphonic level. His words had to keep up with him.

As he wrote he threw out cascades of them, testing each one for pitch and feeling. He readily gave Medwin a list of those he disliked: 'glib', 'flush', 'whiffling', 'perking up', 'lightsome'. On the other hand he liked 'immedicable', 'inter-texture' and 'capaciously expatiative'. Among his favourites were 'glimmering', 'murmuring' and 'scattering', words of half-seeing, half-hearing and half-apprehension: his human life.

Trelawny said Shelley was acutely aware that there was always some 'best word or phrase of all discoverable' for any case: one that would not distort or weigh down, but lift the line on. Hence the days, some-times weeks, of rewriting and correcting that followed his brief spells of inspiration, the painstaking errata lists sent to Ollier, his publisher, and the anxious steering from afar of his proofs through the press. Though only 'a feeble shadow' of the original conception, such a poem was the best he could produce as he was and where he was, attempting to be free.

From Italy, visualising Ollier's cluttered London print-shop, he dreaded that the 'common rules' of poetry would be applied to him. Callow sub-editors, focused on grammar and structure, would surely murder his poems as their harmonies were ignored. This, after all, was the vanity of translation; 'it were as wise to cast a violet into a crucible that you might discover the formal principles of its colour and odour, as to seek to transfuse from one language into another the creations of a poet.'

He himself, translating from Greek, Latin, Italian, German and Spanish in the intervals when inspiration faltered, proceeded differently. Dictionaries were consulted (open in one hand, the text in the other, as he paced about), but lexicons disdained. Redacting Latin prose at Syon House, he instinctively rearranged the words to turn it into verse.

Writing out Greek, he left out accents and breath-marks (the music was in him, he did not need them) and often ran the words together into one melodic line. 'Every original language near to its source', he explained, 'is in itself the chaos of a cyclic poem.' He sought that first, fresh apprehension almost before words.

In his technique, he knew, he was no common wordsmith. He was letting the living motion of his being dictate to him, as well as the promptings of the air. Those tiny doodles, too, lingering among his lines, had the same meaning: the cloud or the swatch of leaves in stillness, waiting.

★   ★   ★

The song Shelley hoped for he heard on an evening in late June 1820, as he walked with Mary near Leghorn. The dusky meadows were alive with skylarks, less seen than heard; he was among them, singing, flying.

His own lines took shape from the bird's song, simple and light, springing and leaping. Yet the melody itself was beyond exact description: pure 'joyance' and gladness, silver arrows or glass, poured out in an unfailing stream. Two years earlier he had translated Homer's *Hymn to Mercury*, sliding in words of his own to make Mercury's first great lyre–song 'unpremeditated', 'unconquerable', 'joyous and wild and wanton', 'sweet as Love'. He needed those words again. Most thrillingly, the bird had vanished in its singing, mounting so high that it became all music, impossible to see. Shelley too, becoming that music, catching at what notes he could, could lose himself in the song:

> Hail to thee!
> ~~What art~~ ~~thou~~ blithe Spirit
> ~~For~~ bird thou ~~hardly art~~ *never wert!*
>
>   . . .
>
> ~~Ah,~~ what thou art we know not
> ~~But~~ what is like to thee?
>   ~~clou~~   ~~moon~~ *rainbow*
>   ~~clouds that~~
> From the ~~morning star~~ flow not
>   *~~Drops~~*
>   *~~Beams so sweet~~*
> ~~Clear so~~   to see

249

> *Drops, so bright*   to a rain
> As from thy presence showers   ~~quick~~
>   melody

Again Shelley heaped up his images, hinting, moving on, deliberately leaving the beauty and the song for his readers to imagine.

The 'real' skylark, he knew, was more confident in its song than in its flying. It mounted and fell, mounted and fell, struggling to shake off the murky pull of the Earth. Like the Poet-philosopher of Plato's *Phaedrus*, or indeed like Shelley, 'he would like to fly away, but he cannot; he is like a bird fluttering and looking upward and careless of the world below . . . And thus he loves, but he knows not what.' His own flying, though stronger, was still faltering like this, far weaker than his desire. And most especially he was this spirit in its compulsion to sing, and sing, and sing.

> Hail to thee, blithe Spirit!
>   Bird thou never wert,
> That from Heaven, or near it,
>   Pourest thy full heart
> In profuse strains of unpremeditated art.
>
> Higher still and higher
>   From the earth thou springest
> Like a cloud of fire;
>   The blue deep thou wingest,
> And singing still dost soar, and soaring ever singest.

His own hymns came to him like this, in 'joy almost wholly unalloyed', or 'unbounded and sustained enthusiasm'. They had nothing to do with consciousness or will or 'the active powers of the mind'. A man, he insisted,

> cannot say, 'I will compose poetry.' The greatest poet even cannot say it; for the mind in creation is as a fading coal which some invisible influence, like an inconstant wind, awakens to transitory brightness; this power arises from within like the colour of a flower which fades and changes as it is developed, and the conscious portions of our natures are unprophetic either of its approach or its departure.

Elsewhere in the *Phaedrus* Socrates spoke of the madness common to poets, listing several kinds. One was a form of enchantment by water nymphs and dryads that caused him to fall, without thinking, into wild pentameters. (Pentameters, Shelley agreed, were the measure into which his own poetic conceptions 'necessarily' fell.) Another type of insanity stemmed from 'the Muses taking possession of a tender and unoccupied soul, awakening, and bacchically inspiring it towards songs':

> but he who, without this madness from the Muses, approaches the poetical gates . . . will find in the end his own imperfections, and see the poetry of his cold prudence vanish into nothingness before the light of that which has sprung from divine insanity.

Shelley called this passage 'wonderful', thought every aspiring poet should impress himself with it, and knew it to be true. If he were really like the skylark, or only half as happy, 'harmonious madness' would possess him too. He could not write poetry as long as there was reason in him.

In 1820 he compared poem-making to sipping laudanum, and promised Maria Gisborne that he would not do it any more. But his nerves, as he put it, disobeyed him. Nerves, or madness, assailed him too when, under the singing fountains and the azure sky in Rome, he heard the chains of hundreds of prisoners clanking on the stones as they laboured. This 'iron discord' brought a clash of states of being – the height to be flown, the weight to be endured – that was intolerable to him.

Poets naturally knew this burst of feeling, crazily coalescing into words. Fools knew it too, and Shelley instinctively sympathised with them: Calderón's Pasquín, with his disquieting tales of blindness and masks; Shakespeare's Feste from *Twelfth Night*, with his sad song of rain; Edgar's Poor Tom from *Lear*, shadowed like Shelley by the 'foul fiend'; and his own fool, Archy, in his unfinished play *Charles the First*. Archy–Shelley saw a rainbow once, hanging over London and its shops, 'like a bridge of congregated lightnings pierced by the masonry of heaven'. But at the end of the rainbow he found the carcass of a dead ass, rotten rags and broken dishes: earth-rubbish, though his eyes were still full of gold and purple light.

There was danger in such quick shifts from heavenly things to earthly: the same danger friends saw in Shelley's abrupt appearances, in Marlow

251

or Pisa or the London streets, as if he had suddenly fallen there, with terror on his face. Medwin reported that when Shelley emerged from his waking dreams he would be trembling and ecstatic, talking more like 'a spirit or an angel' than a man. In 'Kubla Khan', laced with opium, Coleridge seemed to depict a figure just like this:

> And all should cry, Beware! Beware!
> His flashing eyes, his floating hair!
> Weave a circle round him thrice
> And close your eyes with holy dread,
> For he on honey-dew hath fed,
> And drunk the milk of Paradise.

Such a poet, left in Nature under the trees, would not write of them. Given 'Pens Ink & Paper' to calm him down – as Shelley once was, by his anxious mother at Field Place – he would describe not the scene before him, but the absence it suggested to him and the divinity that lay beyond it. Feeding on the 'aërial kisses' of passing thoughts, or pauses in thought,

> He will watch from dawn to gloom
> The lake-reflected sun illume
> The yellow bees in the ivy-bloom,
> Nor heed nor see, what things they be;
> But from these create he can
> Forms more real than living man,
> Nurslings of immortality!

Of the yellow bees, nuzzling the yellow flowers whose pollen fell on his pages, Shelley made Hours and Poets, sunbeams, pity and sleep. In the ivy leaves he found the toxin of Dionysus, the Liberator-god who, in madness and ecstasy, freed him from himself. On another day, describing the deepening of his trance at the beginning of *The Triumph of Life*, he jotted down the process of poem-making as it occurred:

> Gazing awhile, my ~~weary~~ senses grew
> ~~Into the glow~~ scene which I contemplated
> Part of
> ~~And a soft extasy~~ ~~and madness now~~
>   ~~swift and clear as h~~
> ~~suddenly~~   ~~madly~~

And ~~as Heaven changed methought I~~ knew
 ~~Gazing & absorbed~~

The source of poetry, Shelley insisted, was 'native and involuntary'. But 'agony & bloody sweat' – in the words of the Litany – followed his abandoned flights. In the making of *Adonais* and *Hellas* in 1821 whole pages were covered with false starts. On yawning blank pages he scribbled, very small, stray words: 'Incapable', 'Insuperable'. In the *Revolt of Islam* draft came '*Weary*', followed by trailing dots and leaves.

But he could not be tired. All his energy was needed. His repeated refrain to the skylark was 'Teach me': to forget, to delight, to love without satiety, to scorn the ground. Like Socrates's swan, his dying song would be of hope, not regret; like the skylark, he would sing of the Beyond and the divine.

The skylark was not his only model. From his earliest poems he had sung with the nightingale, letting the sympathetic wind carry his melodies away. That 'heaven-resounding minstrelsy' flowed about him, and from him,

> now loud,
> Climbing in circles the windless sky,
> Now dying music; suddenly
> 'Tis scattered in a thousand notes,
> And now to the hushed ear it floats . . .

Truly it was just the song that mattered. The bird was immaterial. Wordsworth's cuckoo too, in lines he loved to repeat, was

> No bird, but an invisible thing,
> A voice, a mystery.

So he wished to be. As he sat to write in the laurel bower at Bagni di Lucca, or in a grove of yews in Kensington Gardens, or among the clustering pines on the Pisan shore, he became that 'secret bird' and 'poor fond soul', singing like any fool through both the darkness and the light. In *A Defence of Poetry*, he explained further:

A Poet is a nightingale, who sits in darkness, and sings to cheer its own solitude with sweet sounds; his auditors are as men entranced

253

by the melody of an unseen musician, who feel that they are moved and softened, yet know not whence or why.

He did not show himself. He merely sang – sometimes a rippling banner of sound, sometimes two or three sad, repeated notes 'in the accents of an unknown land' – for those who could hear him.

3
The wind

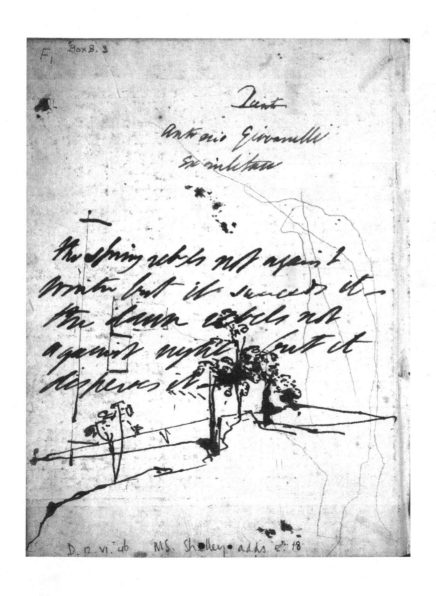

In a fragment for *Adonais* in 1821, Shelley walked the woods as Orpheus. He had not intended to at first. Behind a crowd of famous poets he had tagged on like a ghost, moving diffidently on silent feet. With his ivy-wound wand and his wreath of pansies flopping on his pale forehead, he seemed a bedraggled Nature spirit, little more. Yet as he walked on further he found a lyre of curious power in his hands. From that point, passionately, dangerously, he began to play:

> And ever as he went he swept a lyre
> Of unaccustomed shape & ~~added~~ strings
> Now like the murmurs of impetuous fire
> Which shakes the forest with its murmurings,
> Now like the rush of those aereal wings
> Of the enamoured wind among the tree[s]
> Whispering unimaginable things

His music was so shattering, his lyre so 'holy', that he threw the stanza aside. But this was how he meant to be, convulsing the world with his visions. He could 'shake the Anarch Custom's reign', he had promised in *The Revolt of Islam*, if he lived, 'And charm the minds of men to truth's own sway/ Holier than was Amphion's'. Amphion had moved stones with his poetry. He would do more.

On the back cover of an 1817 notebook he scratched with a knife, lengthways, in inch-high capitals, the words SINCERITY AND ZEAL. The motto had been his at least since 1812, a stout Godwinian tag for a young man who knew he had truth to tell, and meant to tell it. He needed to share, communicate, publish, sell, urge by example, as long as he had strength and breath. This was his duty as a Poet.

Ollier, who published him from 1817 onwards, was constantly pressed to extend the print-runs of poems, to advertise them in *The Times* and the *Morning Chronicle*, and to give him news of sales. ('Keep it well *advertized*, and write for money directly the other is gone'. 'Don't relax in the advertizing'. 'Can't you *make* the Booksellers subscribe more of the Poem?') Everyone in Marlow who took Hunt's literary and political magazine, the *Examiner*, was pestered in December 1816 for a sight of Shelley's first favourable notice; though no copy could be had locally, he told his friend, 'I hear there is one at a village 5 miles off'. When Ollier balked at printing a work called *Laon and Cythna*, with its brother-and-sister lovers and its mockery of God-worship, Shelley retitled it *The Revolt of Islam*, deleted the most blatant offences and proposed a cheap edition rather than forfeit readers. The poem had little to do with Islam, being notionally set in a Constantinople, 'the Golden City', that was really revolutionary Paris, but Shelley had no patience with details. His message was urgent: that the urge for liberty, even if betrayed and crushed, would triumph in the end. Leaves of *Laon and Cythna* ready for the printer had been torn from the notebook, to waste no time.

He sometimes claimed not to know why he was doing this, and hardly to care. His poems were 'effusions', 'jingling food', '*alms* for *oblivion*' – a favourite phrase, as though he scattered his shining coins in the dark. In 1817 he began a poem, or perhaps simply cried out in frustration:

> Why write I in my solitude
> Why

'I wonder why I write verses for nobody reads them,' he sighed to Peacock three years later. 'It is a kind of disorder.'

But he knew very well why. He wrote, first, 'to unburthen my full heart', whether or not it would be disciplined, and second to impress and move others with his 'ardent and unbounded love'. To write for the unborn and unknown was 'a feeble mode of allaying the love within us'. He had to be sure he would find sympathy that was present, listening and alive. And there were always grander schemes in play. As he had explained in 1817, in his preface to *The Revolt of Islam*,

> I have sought to enlist the harmony of metrical language, the ethe-real combinations of the fancy, the rapid and subtle transitions of

human passion, all those elements which essentially compose a Poem, in the cause of a liberal and comprehensive morality; and in the view of kindling within the bosoms of my readers a virtuous enthusiasm for those doctrines of liberty and justice, that faith and hope in something good, which neither violence nor misrepresentation nor prejudice can ever totally extinguish among mankind.

With *The Cenci*, his only completed drama, Shelley's moral purpose was even higher: 'the teaching the human heart, through its sympathies and antipathies, the knowledge of itself.' Such knowledge, after all, was what he most desired in his own life. He wanted to do for his readers what Homer did for him as he read the *Iliad* aloud, crouching in the glow of the fire, letting the word-music race and mount and flow until, 'at the high & solemn close of the whole bloody tale in tenderness & inexpiable sorrow', he would close the book reverently, set it softly down, raise his eyes to the ceiling and exclaim, in adoration, 'Hah!'

His Poet's duty, then, was 'to awaken in all things that are, a community with what we experience within ourselves'. On good days he did not doubt he could do it. His talents, he told Godwin, ranged from catching 'minute & remote distinctions of feeling' to 'considering either the moral or material universe as a whole'. From the centre of himself he moved to the very edge of what could be seen and known or dreamed of, 'peopling with thoughts the boundless universe', drawing 'millions' or 'multitudes' to hear him. In his own 'Orpheus' of 1821 Orpheus played the lyre in the distance, almost beyond hearing; but the wind picked up his waning notes, scattering them far and wide, to shock the unwitting listener into new thoughts and new life.

Poetry, Shelley wrote in the *Defence*, 'is indeed something divine; it is at once the centre and the circumference of thought'. He went further: as a Poet he could touch the reader's mind as Milton or Plato or Bacon touched his, distend it, expand it, make it burst through that circumference 'and [pour] itself forth together with it into the universal element with which it has perpetual sympathy'. This was the effect of those 'unimaginable things' of which he wrote and sang.

That sense of sympathies expanding, almost without limit, was not new to him. He had felt it as a child. And those feelings were not childish or immature, but touched with wisdom. In that fresh and marvelling condition,

> every thing familiar seems to be
> Wonderful, and the immortality
> Of the great world, which all things must inherit
> Is felt as one with the awakening spirit
> Unconscious of itself, & of the strange
> Distinctions, which in its proceeding change
> It feels & knows, and mourns, as if each were
> A desolation

He felt then as if his nature were 'dissolved into the surrounding universe' or the universe absorbed into his being. The whole was centred in himself, and was himself. Nothing existed but his own potential.

One fragment of half-made poetry from 1822, his last year, seemed to preserve that extraordinary childhood understanding. It began with a schoolboy lying near a pond in a copse, drowsing on a summer day. Tiny pieces of his own past littered the scene: his lesson-book, a bowl of milk, gnats whining in the yellow broom flowers, onion plants. Blackberries 'just were out of bloom':

> The pine cones they fell like thunder claps
> When the lazy languid noon breathed so hard in its trance
> That it wakened the sleeping firtree tops.—
> Under a branch all leafless & bare
> He was watching the motes, in their . . .
> Rolling like worlds through the dewy air
> And he closed his eyes at last to see
> The net work of darkness woven inside
> Till the fire tailed stars of the world ~~night~~ of his brain
> Like birds round a pond did flutter & glide
> And then he would open them wide again

In later spells of reverie – stretched on the new-mown grass, surrounded by the sea – he was in the same state of consciousness. The universe was in him, he in the universe, with no differentiation between them. He contained the oceans, the forests, the cities, the stars; to the farthest limit of his thought extended 'this world of love, this *me*'. Such states sometimes went with, or came before, or followed 'an unusually intense and vivid apprehension of life'. Some people, he wrote, in this facility were always children.

Shelley named no one. Yet he kept tucked away, like the dried plums in his pockets and the surreptitious paper boats, the persona of a child. 'Impetuous boy', he imagined others mocking, 'presumptuous boy' – remarks that were also half admiring, because that boy he still resembled in his short, outgrown clothes, fresh-faced and eager, was more open to wonders than the man he was required to be.

There was a moral dimension to this. Men and women were surrounded by mutually repelling circles of self-interest, but their happiness, Shelley insisted, depended on diminishing those circles until the world could be one with them, and they themselves a part of 'all things which feel'. 'It is because we enter into the meditations, designs and destinies of something beyond ourselves', he wrote,

> . . . that the ocean, the glacier, the cataract, the tempest, the volcano, have each a spirit which animates the extremities of our frame with tingling joy. It is therefore that the singing of birds, and the motion of leaves, the sensation of the odorous earth beneath, and the freshness of the living wind around, is sweet. And this is Love. This is the religion of eternity . . .

Under such influences, he added in the *Defence*, 'self appears as what it is, an atom to a universe'.

His friends observed him often in such states, merging into the tragedy or beauty of the world, and knew that he was better not disturbed. Hunt noticed how miserable Shelley became at the sight of worn grey faces in the Strand. The same hopeless sympathy seemed to cry out from a single line in *The Mask of Anarchy*, as he felt the poor of England shivering and starving or emerging, pale as ghosts, from the workhouse, the factory and the prison:

> They are dying whilst I speak.

Medwin remembered standing at an open window of Shelley's house in Pisa, watching the sunset. Shelley appeared to be completely abstracted, one with the golden light that filled the river and the sky. Returning to himself – or from himself – he remarked, 'What a glorious world! There is, after all, something worth living for. This makes me retract the wish that I had never been born.'

That sense of universal sympathy might come upon him suddenly, out of conversation as well as silence. In 1812, at nineteen, he described himself walking at twilight with a friend, weaving 'an impassioned web of talk',

> Till mysteries the spirit press
> In wild yet tender awfulness,
> Then feel within our narrow sphere
> How little yet how great we are!

Not long before his death a similar apprehension stole over him. In the pine woods near Pisa in February 1822, walking with Jane among the blue pools and the drowsing trees, he felt a 'magic circle' round them. It grew from deep calm, Beauty's 'breath of peace' within themselves. A 'thrilling silent life' connected everything they saw, from the far mountain peaks, shining with snow, to the tiny flowers they trod upon. At the centre of the circle was 'one fair form' for whom he was fast falling, the focus of his sense and thought; from her, the whole atmosphere was filled and stilled with love. He could encompass all that existed to make his poem. With her beside him in these wild and empty places,

> the soul need not repress
> Its music lest it should not find
> An echo in another's mind,
> While the touch of Nature's art
> Harmonizes heart to heart.

They would stand on the shore together where, with the sky above them and the sea at their feet,

> all things seem only one
> In the universal Sun.—

His song itself, to follow Plato, was formed in mystic and magnetic circles. In *Ion*, which he translated in or around 1821, inspiration flowed like a series of linked rings from divine power, forceful as a magnetstone, to the Poet and thence to his listeners, each link a human spirit. The best Poet, 'held' and 'possessed' – the skylark again, in his spirals of flight – sang the notes and enthusiasms divinity poured through him, in a chain of harmony falling from Heaven and onward to everyone who heard him. 'The sacred links of that chain', Shelley wrote, have never been entirely disjoined, which descending through the minds of many men, is attached to those great minds, whence as from a magnet the invisible effluence is sent forth, which at once connects, animates and sustains the life of all. It is the faculty which contains within itself the seeds at once of its own and of social renovation.

Those pre-eminent minds included Plato, Dante, Shakespeare, Bacon, Milton, all joining to himself. Together, they worked to produce the great poem that had been forming, Shelley believed, since the beginning of the world. And with this poem would come revolution: 'For the most unfailing herald, or companion, or follower, of an universal employment of the sentiments of a nation to the production of beneficial change is poetry.'

Orpheus had known this, and his listeners had sensed it. In his prime he had sung so sweetly that on board the *Argo*, bound for the Hesperides, his shipmates had been enraptured even by 'the charm of song' that lingered in the silence afterwards. Returning from Hades, where he had rescued his dead love Eurydice and then lost her, he poured out his misery in a new strain. Shelley traced him then not to green woods and grassy banks but to 'a lonely seat of unhewn stone,/Blackened with lichens, on a herbless plain', a place where no one could see him. But his song still rang through the air.

Gradually as Orpheus rhapsodised the trees crept near to listen, spreading their branches to protect him. Nothing so magical happened when Shelley sang. Hunched on his rock, alone, he versified in the wilderness, while the reviewers from *Blackwood's Magazine* and the *Quarterly* wheeled like 'carrion-jays' above him. He sometimes foresaw for himself an Orphean fate, his body torn in pieces by the outraged mob until the Hebrus or the Thames ran scarlet with his blood.

His failure to find public favour was, indeed, almost complete. 'If [Mr Shelley] desired popularity, he should have written in a style intelligible to common understandings,' wrote the *Champion*'s man of *The Revolt of Islam*. His publishers shifted 'scarcely any thing', Shelley thought, of *Alastor* and 20 copies, it was said, of *Prometheus Unbound*. *The Cenci*, though it went into a second edition, was unacceptable on moral grounds to any London theatre. *Julian and Maddalo* remained unpublished in Shelley's lifetime, as did *Peter Bell the Third*, *The Mask of Anarchy* and *A Defence of Poetry*. Quite unconvincingly, Shelley claimed not to care. His poems were for the few and the initiated, the Συνετοί, not the man in the street or the critic in his den. He was 'morbidly indifferent', he told Byron, whose works sold by the cartload, as to whether the reviewers liked him or not.

They did not always attack him. Hunt strove to give him good billings in the *Examiner*, and *Blackwood's* in several unsigned reviews admitted the beauties of his poetry and 'the genius born within him', to his intrigued delight. Sometimes, in that ever-fascinating exercise of standing outside himself, Shelley pretended to be a critic, with the same arch and patronising voice. Across part of his draft of *A Defence of Poetry* ('a poet ... would do ill to embody his own conceptions of right & wrong which are usually those of his place & time in his poetical creations, which participate in neither'), he scrawled in very blunt pencil a critic's gloss:

> This was Mr Shelley's error in the Revolt of Islam. He has attempted to cure himself in subsequent publications but, except in the tragedy of the Cenci, with little effect.

This was an exercise in masochism, the same impulse that made him beg Ollier, more than once, to 'send me all the *abuse*'. He had no need to invent enemies. He was critic-bitten enough, gnawed raw by 'calumniators' who prostituted their souls 'for twenty pounds *per sheet*'. When in 1821 he began work on *Adonais* – his impassioned, elegiac response to the news that Keats had been driven to his death by a review of his *Endymion* in the *Quarterly* – Shelley told, in at least one draft preface, the story of his own suffering at the critics' hands. 'The bigot will say it was the recompense of my errors,' he wrote, before striking it out; 'the man of the world will call it the result of my imprudence but never upon any head was heaped [calumny] in so profuse a measure as upon mine'. He knew the critics were not done with him, and had only one weapon, his poet's lyre, to turn on them.

Shelley considered *Adonais* 'better than any thing that I have yet written'. He had it printed in Pisa in July 1821 in 'the types of Didot', a font of particular beauty. 'I am especially curious to hear the fate of Adonais,' he wrote. 'I confess I should be surprised if *that* Poem were born to an immortality of oblivion.' But Ollier, 'this thief' as Shelley furiously called him, merely sold the Italian copies, never caring to publish it himself.

As for the critics, the *Literary Gazette* gave its opinion in the issue of December 1821:

The poetry of the work is *contemptible*, a mere collection of bloated words heaped on each other without order, harmony or meaning; the refuse of a schoolboy's commonplace book, full of the vulgarisms of pastoral poetry, yellow gems and blue stars, bright Phoebus and rosy-footed Aurora, and of this stuff is Keats's wretched elegy compiled.

Such words hurt Shelley, mock as he might. As his exile voice grew fainter, his incentive to 'inculcate' the public with long, beautiful, instructive visions gradually disappeared. Even in 1814, in the aftermath of *Queen Mab*, he had confided to a friend that all poetry had gone out of him. In 1820, not long after completing *Prometheus Unbound* – his best poem so far, as he thought – he told Medwin that he was disgusted with writing. Perhaps there was truly nothing left to say. 'My faculties are shaken to atoms & torpid,' he confessed to Hunt in January 1822. 'I can write nothing, & if Adonais had no success & excited no interest what incentive can I have to write?' 'Indeed I have written nothing for this last two months,' he added in March. 'What motives have I to write. I *had* motives . . . but what are *those* motives now?'

Orpheus, torn to pieces, still made music. The winds drew funeral harmonies from his floating lyre, while the waves of the river carried his singing head away.

★   ★   ★

And he did not die. Like all such heroes and gods – Osiris, Dionysus, Adonis – he rose again in the cycles of Nature, and could not be kept down. Hence the motto written, in 1821 or 1822, inside the front cover of Shelley's vellum notebook:

> the spring rebels not against
> winter but it succeeds it—
> the dawn rebels not
> against night but it
> disperses it—

The lettering was as large and bold as he could make it, in the darkest brown ink he could find in Italy. Over it he drew trees in sparse leaf, standing on the hills like sentinels to pass his messages between them.

Outside, in an arc that spanned the Mediterranean, change was stirring. Any new-sprung hope of liberty, Mary wrote later, inspired 'intense and wild' exultation in him. In January 1820, a constitutional struggle had erupted in Spain; that July, in Naples, rebellious army officers had forced reform on King Ferdinand, who was backed by the Austrian tyranny. Neither lasted long, but both presaged greater tumults to come. In 1821, when Genoa declared itself free of the Austrian yoke, Shelley was in ecstasy. He devoured the bulletins issued by the Austrian occupiers, searching for signs of their collapse. 'As to the Austrians,' he told Claire in February 1821, 'I doubt not that they are strong men . . . but all these things if the spirit of Regeneration is abroad are chaff before the storm, the very elements & events will fight against them.' The next month, even more joyously, war began in Greece as nationalists rose up to free the country from the Turks. Shelley made a list, country after country, hope after hope, then whooped out triumphantly in the words of Isaiah: '*The Lord* hath broken the staff of the wicked & the sceptre of the rulers.'

He anticipated storms, hanging on the moment when 'Dreadfully, sweetly, swiftly' the 'consummating hour' would come. Yet the motto in his notebook was gentler. Revolution could perhaps be as natural and irreversible as the change from winter to spring. Men had only to realise, in Paine's words, 'that [they] are born, and always continue, free and equal in respect of their rights'. Once a man was alert to this inner seed of Liberty, the status of his true self, he could never be enslaved again, and the world made new in one place would inexorably be renewed in others. Paine had concluded the second part of *The Rights of Man* with an image of a twig budding, the harbinger of the whole forest. 'Such is the irresistible nature of truth', he wrote, 'that all it asks, and all it wants, is the liberty of appearing.'

The first tremors of revolution might indeed be little more than this. In the second act of *Prometheus Unbound* a dream came to Shelley's two heroines, Asia and Panthea, Love and Hope. This 'thing of air' drew them towards the deep, where they were to confront the figure of Demogorgon – Fate, Necessity, the forces of history – with the countervailing power of Love. From that confrontation, the world would be reborn. Yet this dream seemed nothing. Its message – 'Follow!' – appeared in the weakest things: the fallen petals of an almond tree, cloud-shadows driven in the grey dawn by a slow, unwilling wind, blades of grass on which the dew had dried. The word shone and vanished, sounded and died. Only Asia, with Love's wise eyes, noticed that it was stamped on Nature 'as with a withering fire':

And first there comes a gentle sound
To those in talk or slumber bound,
　　And wakes the destined: soft emotion
Attracts, impels them; those who saw
　　Say from the breathing Earth behind
　　There streams a plume-uplifting wind
Which drives them on their path, while they
　　Believe their own swift wings and feet
The sweet desires within obey . . .

Those desires would be pushed by universal longings, as forceful and inevitable as the seasons changing. Love and Liberty would sweep through all hearts, as they had swept through his. The 'plume-uplifting wind' would pour from the Earth itself, preparing convulsions. As Shelley wrote, racing ahead, the message of the dream grew louder and the letters larger, yelling 'FOLLOW!' to the whole world.

He had attempted his own 'reform or revolution, as you will' – the words were the same to him – in the spring of 1812 in Ireland, when he was nineteen. He chose Ireland deliberately as the most oppressed and exploited corner of the kingdom, where French-inspired rebellion had been bloodily put down not long before, where English landlords profited from sempiternal religious wars ('White-boys and Orange-boys', as Shelley characterised them), and where revolution might more easily take hold, if given a chance. Specifically, he advocated the repeal of the Act of Union with Britain and the emancipation of Catholics, then deprived of most political rights. But Hogg thought his ardent friend knew no details of either the Act or the restrictions. The emancipation Shelley imagined was infinitely wider, of Irish minds; and wider again, like a list in a schoolboy's textbook, 'the peace, the harmony, and the happiness of Ireland, England, Europe, the World'.

Words were his means, and his method was political association. Men would simply meet, talk and spread the truths he had printed for them, as if they were not cowed and starving but curious and reasonable. His *Address to the Irish People* advocated not violence but toleration of contrary opinions, as well as 'habits of SOBRIETY, REGULARITY, and THOUGHT'. 'People', he told them,

have learned to think, and the more thought there is in the world, the more happiness and liberty will there be . . . let every street of

267

the city, and field of [the] country, be connected with thoughts, which liberty has made holy.

Chief among those thoughts –though slipped in halfway through, subversively – was the prospect that rich and poor, all ideas harmonised and all wealth shared, might 'live equally like brothers', and that 'no government will be wanted, but that of your neighbour's opinion'.

Shelley had supposed such words were simple, and would appeal to the Dublin crowd. The *Address* cost fivepence, 'the lowest possible price', in small print on poor paper. He advertised it in the *Evening Post*, and hoped to see it pasted up on walls; he also let the wind distribute it for him, throwing copies from the balcony of his lodgings in Sackville Street to anyone 'who *looks likely*'. He hired a man to give them out, free if necessary, gravely handed them out himself, and slipped one undetected into the hood of a woman passing by. In two days, by his estimate, he had disseminated 400 of the 1,500 pamphlets printed and had forced them on 60 public houses. If words were broadcast scatter-shot they must sometimes fall on ground that was ready to receive them, like the New Testament parable of the sower with his seed; or like his own prank the previous year, when he had printed multiple copies of a scabrous poem on the Prince Regent and tossed them into the carriages of guests returning from a royal extravaganza.

If his Irish readers were to meet and 'talk of how things go on' there could, he believed, be nothing wrong with that. Free speech, as Paine said, was the fundamental liberty on which all else depended. From this sprang association, and from that representative government, which existed not by fraud and sophistry but by inspiring 'language that, passing from heart to heart, is felt and understood'. In both France and America political societies had preceded and followed the revolutions, coalescing from the currents of opinion in the air. They could multiply and spread, involving 'multitudes'; they would not of course be secret, but conducted 'in the open face of day, with the utmost possible publicity'. Since the merits of association had been known to men even in a state of brutishness (see Rousseau, see Volney), they ought not to be too hard to impress on the poor ragged souls of Grafton Street. Men who could think and speak freely on politics, Shelley supposed, would not long tolerate other oppressions; the Irish would soon have had enough of their prayer-beads and their priests.

He had proposed associations before. From Oxford in 1811 he had suggested to Hunt – not yet a friend, but already a brother, since he had suffered several prosecutions for seditious libel – the formation of 'a methodical society which should be organized so as to resist the coalition of the enemies of liberty'. Shelley had in mind the anarchist Illuminist sects of revolutionary France; but he also proposed a more moderate mutual association of men like Hunt, 'fearless enlighteners of the public mind', to defend free speech and pay each other's libel fines. Encouraging the Irish the next year, he told them that 'Man has a right to feel, to think, and to speak . . . He will feel, he must think, and he *ought* to give utterance to those thoughts and feelings with the readiest sincerity and the strictest candour.' 'No law', he wrote elsewhere, 'has a right to discourage the practice of truth. A man ought to speak the truth on every occasion.' Truth made men free.

On 28 February 1812, Shelley addressed a packed-out meeting of the Catholics of Ireland in the Fishamble Street theatre. He gave a frank, earnest speech that was well received, though hissed, to his surprise, in the anti-religious parts. The reporters noted especially the 'very young' English gentleman's evocation of the misery and hunger of the poor. With this, and with his pamphlets, 'Thought-wingèd Liberty' would be fanned and spread, mouth to mouth, as if it rode like a spirit on men's breath. (In 1819 he was to write of elections in this vein, preferring men not to cast their ballots secretly but to meet the candidates face to face to 'share some common impulses', to excite the imagination, to awaken generous sentiment.) His second Irish pamphlet, *Proposals for an Association of Philanthropists*, made his aims crystal clear: once men, meeting together, had determined what had to be done, the next stage was 'united or individual exertion' to achieve it. Thought, speech, action. The prevailing winds in Ireland came directly from the west: from America, turning the land the very colour of the emancipating spring.

All this had begun as his mentor Godwin would have recommended, with encouraging virtue and thought in the mass of mankind. But Shelley had gone much further in rousing his listeners and readers: to association, and to action. Godwin, horrified by what he was doing, accused him of 'preparing a scene of blood' and begged him to stop.

Shelley objected. He had confidently told Godwin, in regular letters, that his Irish publications could not 'in the slightest degree tend to violence'. He was more aware that his words had had almost no effect on the human misery around him. He still held out hopes of a share in a newspaper, possibly moving hearts that way. But Godwin's condemnation so deflated him that he promptly ceased campaigning. In a last letter from Ireland on 18 March he explained himself, in pained terms, to his teacher:

> It is possible to festinate or retard the progress of human perfectibility, such associations as I would have recommended would be calculated to produce the former effect . . . My schemes of organizing the ignorant I confess to be ~~dangerous and~~ ill-timed: I cannot conceive that they were dangerous . . . But I submit. I shall address myself no more to the illiterate . . .

He could not resist pointing out that there was a district of Dublin called 'the Liberty' (in fact, the Liberties), which 'exhibits a spectacle of squalidness and misery such as might reasonably excite impatience in a cooler temperament than mine'. Ireland was no nearer true liberty now than when he had begun.

He therefore did not stop for long. He could not bear to. As he left Ireland he had sent to the printer a new folio poster with fresh, disruptive truths, ready for display and debate.

DECLARATION OF RIGHTS

I. Government has no rights; it is a delegation from several individuals for the purpose of securing their own. It is therefore just, in so far as it exists by their consent; useful, only so far as it operates to their well-being.

II. If these individuals think that the form of government which they or their forefathers constituted is ill-adapted to produce their happiness, they have a right to change it . . .

. . .

XXXI. The only use of government is to repress the vices of man. If man were to-day sinless, to-morrow he would have a right to demand that government and all its evils should cease.

Riding in his post-chaise on the outskirts of Dublin, 'lawless . . . for justice' as Hunt described him, Shelley would eagerly instruct his postilion to 'drive at the pike', crashing through any barrier without paying.

Back in England, despite informers and the threat of prosecution, the *Declaration* was spread around north Devon by Daniel Healy, Shelley's Irish manservant, and pasted up on walls near Barnstaple. As many as

16 letters, some no doubt containing it, were sent off with each post. Shelley dispatched parts of it to the *Sussex Weekly Advertiser*, hoping his ideas of association might touch minds there and, indeed, throughout the land. ('Might I not extend them all over England, and *quietly* revolutionize the country?') His 'Heavenly medicine' was committed in potion- and wine bottles to the sea, to Liberty and 'the fairest breezes of her West that blow'. One evening, from the same slope where he occasionally blew bubbles, he tied the *Declaration* to a parachute of silk and watched as it sailed away. He had once imagined 'intrepid aeronauts' up in a balloon above Africa, where the very shadow of their craft, 'would virtually emancipate every slave, and would annihilate slavery for ever'. Now he was seeding minds.

Perhaps most of all, he dreamed that his works would be recited in the public square. He knew the power of reading or singing poetry aloud, often thundering out Coleridge's 'France:An Ode' with 'marvellous energy', Medwin said, and hoping he might 'politicize' Byron with it:

> And Oye Clouds that far above me soared!
> Thou rising Sun! thou blue rejoicing Sky!
> Yea, everything that is and will be free!
> Bear witness for me, where soe'er ye be,
> With what deep worship I have still adored
> The spirit of divinest Liberty.

The wanton killings and slashings of protesters at Peterloo in 1819 made him long, from Italy, to mobilise the English people with ballads of freedom. He envisaged a 'little volume of *popular songs* wholly political' which ordinary men could sing and whistle in the street. He also began an 'Ode' for music, shouting like a clarion rather than singing:

> Arise, Arise, Arise!
> There is blood on the land which denies ye bread;
>   Be your wounds like eyes
> To weep for the dead—the dead—the dead!

But the laws had been tightened, with political meetings and debates now forbidden and the Libel Acts reinforced. Shelley got his songs and ballads ready for the printer, but only the 'Ode' was published in his lifetime. The authorities thought it was about Spain, as it claimed to be, and let it through.

In one of his songs, 'A New National Anthem' (written to replace the 'cant' of the old one), Shelley presented Liberty as a murdered queen whose spirit still lived, and might be worshipped, in men's hearts. He had acknowledged her, after all, in his own heart, coexistent with Love, enthroned over his life.

> She is Thine own pure soul
> Moulding the mighty whole,—
>   God save the Queen!
> She is Thine own deep love
> Rained down from Heaven above,—
> Wherever she rest or move . . .

These words seemed so far removed from politics as to have left the ground completely. There was indeed a meaning in them that few, besides him, could understand. But reciting such lines alone was a beginning. Liberty, like love, became an incantation that drew strength and power from its very repetition:

> Liberty oh liberty!

With such words Virtue would stir to life. He would sow the wind with them,

> Ringing through each heart and brain
> Heard again—again—again—

And in time the world would reap the whirlwind.

★   ★   ★

In the wood of the Cascine, just outside Florence, the wind tore dry leaves from the chestnut trees and threw hard rain in Shelley's face. It was late October in 1819, the time just after sunset. There were houses in view, and the dome of Santa Maria del Carmine marked the near edge of the city; this walk and this wood were familiar, the groves tamed by paths and fountains. Yet that evening he was caught in cosmic forces, violently enmeshed in black clouds, ochre leaves, flailing branches and the lash of hail. He knew this wind for a winter-bringer and also as the herald of spring: his own revolutionary rabble-rouser, blowing from the west.

The winds of Italy had become his familiar spirits. He spoke of them as enemies or friends: Sirocco, warm and wet, that soothed his side, Tramontana that cleared the skies and pierced every crevice, freezing him, 'inconstant' Libeccio mantling the mountains with white electric rain. Their ancient counterparts, Boreas, Notus, Eurus and Zephyrus, had roared in his Latin exercises at Syon House, mixed in with the cries of his red-faced, snuff-breathing teacher and the smack of hard hands on his ears:

Iam, iam tacturas sidera summa putes

That particular pentameter had been cribbed from Ovid, describing the tempests that almost swamped the poet on his sea voyage to exile in Pontus. The master mocked at Shelley for producing it, demanding to know whether waves on the Sussex coast really blew up to the stars. Yes, Shelley could have answered if he had dared, and he flew with them. He had been, he told the West Wind later, 'the comrade of thy wanderings over Heaven', striving to outrace it in the cloud-shadows and the grass. He had watched the wind's path so keenly that he knew it left 'circlets' like ripples or lark-spirals, gradually fading. In his Poet's childhood, bereft of friends, it was the West Wind that boisterously bumped and challenged him.

As a man, too, he made the wind his model. 'Tameless and swift and proud', they ran through the world together. The wind, buffeting him in the woods, could recognise a brother, 'one too like thee' even when withering and dying. The Poet of *Alastor*, bright-eyed and feverish, so ghostlike that his steps made no impression on the snow, was both the Spirit of the Wind and Shelley. And when, contrariwise, he wrote of exaltation, the wind was inevitably in it, buoying him up ('Ha! ha!') in madness and delight.

There were always two West Winds in his life, even in his school-books. One was Ovid's storm-bringer, or Homer's bullying blast that shoved the beaked ships of Odysseus over the darkening sea. The other was Virgil's Zephyrus, the gentle awakener and guardian of the olive groves. Though Shelley, too, usually made Zephyr male, they were brother and 'azure sister' to him – brother and sister being, in his world, ever-linked and complementary souls. One stripped the autumn trees and laid the Earth bare; the other ushered in the spring. The same principle indifferently brought death, or life. Shelley knew the wind in both guises and, through both, he sang of the harrowing and revival of the world.

In Oxford he seems to have written, anonymously for the *Herald*, a poem of Zephyr playing among sea nymphs, sporting with them in the waves and tangling their soft hair into braids. This West Wind, 'false and fair', had something of his daemon-self, touching and weaving into complicity with love. Two years later, disembodied as the wind again, he stole promises from a lovesick girl that she would inhale his 'balmy breath' and catch him to her breasts, allowing him to die there when he blew in from the sea.

Lucretius had called this soft wind *genitabilis*, teeming with new life. Shelley made him a philanderer. (In one agitated fragment of 1819 he and Sophia Stacey, intermingling in the tangled, secret woods, had the same 'work' to do as the gale and the flower.) On the surface of Mind – so dark and still when·untouched by him – this West Wind sighed repeating thoughts of liberty and love.

> Come, thou Awakener of the spirits ocean
> Zephyr, whom to thy cloud or cave
> No thought can trace . . . feed with thy gentle motion

The Genius of Equality in Volney's *Ruins of Empire* heard the cry of 'Liberty!' coming from the west: from the ocean, or from America, where the wind's home might plausibly be found. Shelley in 1812, leaving London westward for Wales and his radical campaign to reclaim land at Tremadoc from the sea, already seemed to feel the 'spirit-breathing gales' bringing hope to the 'unfriended poor'. The West Wind that awakened minds came, he wrote, from islands wrapped in 'starry waters', Homer's Elysium. Yet it moved sometimes through wide tracts of indifference; and in this respect, too, they were like each other, the wind and him.

So the West Wind was whimsical and liberating; yet it could also be terrifying and momentous. The contrast was pointed even in Shelley's notebook, where immediately after the small, neat, almost languid script of the lines to Zephyr came, in fierce dark ink, a shout of rage:

> As I lay asleep in Italy
> There came a voice from over the sea
> And with great power it forth led me
> To walk in the visions of poesy

A quite different force was at work in him now, rough-drafting *The Mask of Anarchy*. Page after page followed of confident, rhythmic, incandescent verse. His invocation of the West Wind had been answered by the bringer of storms. Indeed they had worked together, as he told the Gisbornes. While his body was in the Cascine, watching the leaves and the river, his mind was in England with the scenes he hoped might follow Peterloo: troops mobilising, the people rising, crown lands and chattels seized by the mob, 'bloody struggle' and 'great actions', while the West Wind roared.

This wind from 'over the sea' could rouse not only ships and waves but the whole expanse of waters or of mind, sweeping as forcefully through the underwater forests as through the trees on land. Its very voice, sounding among the sea plants, made them 'tremble and despoil themselves'. There was no gentle motion here, but thrashing and destruction, the necessary revolution of the season as the year died. In Erasmus Darwin's 'Economy of Vegetation' the West Wind's wings were dangerously unbound, and the raindrops wrung out of his tangled hair; in Shelley's 'Ode to the West Wind', begun that October day in the Cascine, the wind's blue aery surge, and its bright streaming locks, changed in an instant to a vault of black rain and fire.

> O wild West Wind, thou breath of Autumn's being,
> Thou, from whose presence the leaves dead
> Are driven, like ghosts from an enchanter fleeing,
>
> Yellow, and black, and pale, and hectic red,
> Pestilence-stricken multitudes: O thou,
> Who chariotest to their dark wintry bed
>
> The wingèd seeds, where they lie cold and low
> Each like a corpse within its grave, until
> Thine azure sister of the Spring shall blow . . .
> . . .
> Wild Spirit, which art moving everywhere;
> Destroyer and Preserver; hear, O, hear!

At times this dualism might almost be his own: philanthropist and monster, bright and evil daemon, good and bad serpent writhing through the world. Shelley too could tear down and build up again, Destroyer and Preserver, with the words he wrote. Yet he addressed the wind more typically as a force far beyond him: a revolutionary agent, a force of history, Necessity itself.

This power controlled him utterly. It pushed him to the boundaries of life, through death, to whatever was beyond, just as the keen frost-wind, 'the imperishable change/ That renovates the world' hurled the dead leaves over the forest floor. Shelley was sometimes lost in that tumbling crowd; at other times he was singled out and alone. The Poet of *Alastor*, having crossed terrifying seas, arrived at a cave in the deep woods where, as he wandered away towards death, he felt the West Wind pressing at his back. At the end of *The Revolt of Islam* Shelley's young revolution-makers were steered for three days and nights by 'thronging winds' that blew them, from death, towards the spreading gold of the sunrise. The same wind, the Ponente, was the gale that howled around Villa Magni; it could be seen drawing up damp vapours from the sea, letting them form as clouds on the mountains and, as the sun declined, unmaking them again.

In the West Wind, therefore, his own fate was bound up, as well as the fate of the world. On that day in the Cascine this wind impelled him – perhaps hatless and coatless as usual, the pages of his notebook dampening and snapping – with such power that he found himself praying to it, his rational thoughts in disarray.

> If I were a dead leaf thou mightest bear;
> If I were a swift cloud to fly with thee;
> A wave to pant beneath thy power, and share
>
> The impulse of thy strength, only less free
> Than thou, O, uncontrollable! . . .
>   I would ne'er have striven
>
> As thus with thee in prayer in my sore need.
> Oh, lift me as a wave, a leaf, a cloud!
> I fall upon the thorns of life! I bleed!

Yet he was not merely passive in this. He was free. His own will was involved, and he was offering himself. That decision made him equal. His weak, hollow body would catch the wind's force and be filled with the coming storm; but he would also give back harmonies unprompted, music that was his own.

Make me thy lyre, even as the forest is:
What if my leaves are falling like its own!
The tumult of thy mighty harmonies

Will take from both a deep, autumnal tone,
Sweet though in sadness.

In his drafts of the poem he exulted in this, and in the dogged defiance born of earthly experience. 'One too like thee, yet mortal, swift and proud,' he boasted to the wind at first. Below the last lines of his first draft came another challenge, snatched from the *Hercules Furens* of Euripides: 'By virtue I, a mortal, vanquish thee, a mighty god.'

He could not vanquish this force. But, in the most thrilling way, they would absorb each other. Moving through his mind, stirring his thoughts, the wind would pick up his own tune and he, surging with power, would sing out with the storm's energy. His own existence gave the wind this chance. They would be one force again, as in his boyhood, uncontrolled and unbounded. He was no longer Shelley but Liberty's prophet, shouting to the world to follow him.

As he wrote his 'Ode' – some on that October day, some later, scattering lines tempestuously through several notebooks – he struggled to describe exactly how the wind would work on him, or in him, or through him, scratching out word after word:

> ~~Be thy~~ Be
> ~~Be thou~~ ~~through~~ ~~in me, to the~~ to the Earth
> ~~And be then~~
> ~~The voice with~~

Then at last, decisively:

> Be thou, Spirit fierce,
> My spirit! Be thou me, impetuous one!
> . . .
> Be through my lips to unawakened Earth
>
> The trumpet of a prophecy!

He would sing out the wind's words, echoing and resounding some colossal call to change. But the wind, too, would sing out his words. They would roar like the hope of revolution in the pines of Greece and Spain, or scatter through the English streets, rousing the crowds to action. The West Wind, his own unchained spirit, shook them from him – dead thoughts or seeds of regeneration, poems made and poems to be – and threw them across the world. *Be thou me!*

And who, or what, was this power he had implored to be him? He had asked to be part of a work of moral and political renewal, and the wind had replied by pushing him towards dissolution. The wind blew, his soul responded, but in ways far more dangerous and involving than he had perhaps supposed.

> O, Wind,
> If Winter comes, can Spring be far behind?

Alone in the Cascine, under the chestnut trees in the rain-soaked dark, he saluted the West Wind as a comrade and invoked him as a god.

★　　★　　★

At Eton, a decade before, Shelley had read and marked the first book of Pliny the Elder's *Natural History*:

> *Quisquis est deus, si modo est alius, et quacumque in parte, totus est sensus, totus visus, totus auditus, totus animae, totus animi, totus sui, per quae declaratur haut dubie naturae potentia idque esse quod deum vocemus.*

> For whatever God be, if there be any other God, and wherever he exists, he is all sense, all sight, all hearing, all soul, all mind, and all within himself . . . by which it is clearly apparent that the powers of Nature are what we call God.

His cousin Medwin thought no other passage so excited him at school. Dr Lind helped him with the translation; it was read often and with attention. Pliny thus proclaimed himself an atheist, fearlessly. And Lucan drove the argument further, as Shelley noted, somewhat misquoting him, in his *Essay on Christianity*:

Estque dei sedes, nisi terra et pontus et aer
Et caelum et virtus? Superos quid quaerimus ultra?
Juppiter est, quodcumque vides, quodcumque moveris.

Has God any dwelling-place save earth and sea, the air, Heaven, and virtuous hearts? Why seek we further for deities? All that you see is God, and God is whatever [impulse] by which you are moved.

These authors made God and Nature coexistent. For a while, that appeared to be Shelley's creed also. Some acquaintances, on the basis of conversations, thought he never deviated from it. At nineteen, 'Imbued with holiest feelings' in the quiet Sunday woods, he had admitted that

> Yes, in my soul's devotedness
> I love to linger in the wilds.
> I have my God, and worship him
> O vulgar souls, more ardently
> Than ye the Almighty fiend . . .

> It is a lovely winter's day.
> Its brightness speaks of Deity . . .

But his worship was not of Nature around him, as Wordsworth's was. He was responding, even then, to 'the god of my own heart', 'that Divinity whose work and self/Is harmony and wisdom, truth and love'. Alone in the bright cold sun, he felt that god within and beside him, the natural companion of 'the soul/ Of him who dares be free'. He had no need to bow in awe to the landscape or its spirits, and especially no need to follow the pealing bells and go to church, there to 'love by the clock'. That conviction never changed. On a hillside near Vico Pisano in 1821, watching the olive woods moving 'green as a sea' and the cloud-shadows driven over the hills, feeling the same force in him, he concluded, simply, 'I am—'.

That year he told Hogg, a keen classicist, that he had climbed the hill one evening behind San Giuliano, hung up a garland and raised, among the wild olive trees, a small turf altar to mountain-walking Pan. Perhaps he had, for despite his shudders at the act of kneeling, his natural instinct to adore required some outlet somewhere. Hogg noted, even at Oxford, that he had never known anyone in whom the principle of veneration was so strong. Instinctively, all his life, Shelley made prayers as experiments or dares or confessions of love to the powers he sensed about him. But the Poet did not pray to Pan.

When he redacted *The Necessity of Atheism* for his notes to *Queen Mab* in 1813, he added a new gloss to the words '*There is no God*': 'This negation must be understood solely to affect a creative Deity. The hypothesis of a pervading Spirit co-eternal with the universe remains unshaken.' The addition was not noticed, and it did not help. But in his *Essay on Christianity* Shelley repeated it, appearing to endorse with some enthusiasm the motivating, animating God of Jesus Christ: 'the interfused and overruling Spirit of all the energy and wisdom included within the circle of existing things . . . something mysteriously and illimitably pervading the frame of things'.

In 1820 he returned to Spinoza's *Tractatus Theologico-politicus*. He had read it first in 1812, declaring it 'capital'; now he went through it again, pen in hand, intending a translation. Over several pages, Spinoza analysed the notion of the Spirit of God; Shelley marked it in the margin. He particularly noted '5 senses of Πνευμα', meaning, in the Greek, breath, wind, air, spirit and inspiration. But Spinoza, in the Hebrew, had found far more. God was *ruagh*, dry violent wind, free of the heavy moisture of the incarnate state; God was courage, temper, soul, the four quarters of the world from which the winds came. God was prophecy. He blew through Daniel, Zachariah and the rest and they, though 'possessed of the mind of God', had no idea of what he made them say.

Spinoza, like Pliny, could give the name 'God' to this Power that swept implacably through life. Shelley always rejected it. In his vocabulary and his firm belief, the word was a curse. He had used it that way almost every time in *Laon and Cythna*, which was why he had been made to clean things up, substituting 'Power' and 'Lord', for his rejigged *Revolt of Islam*. But he could take God out himself, unpushed. When he rewrote parts of *Queen Mab* in 1815 as *The Daemon of the World*, one reference to God was crossed out with three bold Xs and an exclamation mark. In 1818 another notebook reference was deleted as firmly as could be with a thick wavy line and a row of diagonals:

If God is infinite, every atom <& every thought> of the moral & material world must be pervaded by his spirit

To the end – in *The Triumph of Life* – he struck out 'God' from 'O God have mercy on such wretchedness' and inked 'Heaven' blackly above it.

Yet the pervading Spirit persisted. It acquired a capital, and the adjectives 'awful' and 'great'. It was given transcendent power. This was not the breath of Nature, the wind of the hillside at Vico Pisano that wrapped him in the mutable world of the senses, but something infinitely beyond it,

> . . . before whose breath the universe
> Is as a print of dew.

Shelley also described, in imagery never used by Jesus, what he thought Jesus meant by saying 'Blessed are the pure in heart, for they shall see God':

> There is a power by which we are surrounded, like the atmosphere in which some motionless lyre is suspended, which visits with its *breath* our silent chords at will

He underlined 'breath', perhaps meaning to change it, but found nothing better. He went on:

> and those who have seen God, have, in the period of their purer & more perfect nature, been harmonized by their own will, to so exqui- site [a] consentaneity of powers, as to give forth divinest melody when the breath of universal being sweeps over their frame.

These episodes, Shelley wrote elsewhere, were 'visitations of the divinity in man'. The phrase was ambiguous, perhaps deliberately so. Those 'flashes of thought & feeling' through his being were 'as it were the interpenetration of a diviner nature through our own; but its footsteps are like those of a wind over the sea, which the coming calm erases, and whose traces remain only as on the wrinkled sand which paves it'. He had toyed first with the odour of lilies and the motions of music; but in the end he settled for footsteps, Bacon's metaphor, the little signs in everything of similitude, divinity and power. His fragment to Zephyr of 1819 showed again how he had wrestled with this image: evoking it, discarding it, half fearing to name it.

> ~~What~~ sudden &   ~~Gleam~~
> O ~~thou inconstant~~   ~~light which shinest~~
> On ~~us who wander thro the night of light~~
> ~~Whereby we see the past, . . . O Power divinest~~

O Knowledge
As Come thou Awakener of the spirits Ocean

Possibly these visitations were blessings that came from deep within him, from that pure bright antitype within his mind or heart: that 'spirit of good within, which requires before it send that inspiration forth, which impresses its likeness upon all that it creates, devoted and disinterested homage'. His *Essay on Christianity* explored that thought as far as he could go – and stopped.

> Whoever has maintained with his own heart the strictest correspondence of confidence, who dares to examine & to estimate every imagination which suggests itself to his mind, who is that which he designs to become, & only aspires to that which the divinity of his own nature shall consider & approve . . . he, has already seen God.

But these visitations were also compulsions to action on the part of some external and transcendent power. Shelley's invocation of Liberty in his 'Ode to Naples' ('Great Spirit! deepest Love') carried both senses, without and within, yet the force beyond came first. It compelled, then released. Shelley spoke of 'the Power divine' brooding upon his life, weighing on it, then snatching him into the air. This was the 'mighty wind' that shook the minds of Christ's apostles gathered in the upper room, or whirled round the heavenly chariot of Queen Mab plunging down towards the Earth. That same Power ruled and moved 'all things which live and are', dispensing both death and life. And this Being – for evidently where there was breath, there was being – had chosen to act through him.

When churchmen spoke in such terms, Shelley was quick to mock. In 1821 he heard to his delight that Archdeacon Hare had hoped that he would 'in time humble his soul, and receive the spirit into him'. 'If you know him personally,' Shelley wrote to Ollier, 'pray ask him from me what he means by receiving the *spirit into me*, and (if really it is any good) how one is to get at it.' But the spirit of his own experience, rather than 'the H.G.', was neither laughed at nor resisted. On the contrary, he longed for it. Man's 'high hope and unextinct desire' was to be the instrument not of his own will, but the will of Another far greater and more divine. In that voluntary weakness, 'that sweet bondage which is Freedom's self', lay the chance for man – for Shelley – to realise what he was meant to do and who he was meant to be. This could not be obedience, for he would never obey. It was complicity, freely embraced. His sails were 'given' to the tempest: *Do what you will with me.*

> The breath whose might I have invoked in song
> Descends on me; my spirit's bark is driven
> Far from the shore, far from the trembling throng . . .

Agreeing to this, freely opening his will to it, he would perhaps be modelled, like all other elements, into 'the purest and most perfect shape which it belongs to their nature to assume'. For the Spirit

> Sweeps through the dull dense world, compelling there
> All new successions to the forms they wear;
> Torturing th'unwilling dross that checks its flight
> To its own likeness, as each mass may bear . . .

Not only inspiration flowed from this source. So too, he could suppose, did everything that animated him. His own life was a part of the Breath beyond him, 'the eternal breath breathed out in Love', in Dante's phrase. The exulting sweep and speed of his poetry, image chasing image, was the special sign of that spirit, and its sinking or slowing was proof of that power subsiding. When it withdrew, as he had told the West Wind, he fell again upon 'the thorns of life' and bled, like a man.

In 1817, in a draft stanza for *Laon and Cythna*, he described as much as he felt he knew.

> There is a Power whose passive instrument
> Our nature is—a Spirit that with motion
> Invisible & swift, its breath hath sent
> Amongst us,—like the wind on the wide Ocean—
> Around whose path tho' tumult & commotion
> Throng fast—deep calm doth follow, & precedeth
> This Spirit, chained by some remote devotion
> Our choice or will demandeth not nor heedeth
> But for its *hymns* doth touch the human souls it needeth

For a little while, then, the Spirit gave him 'joy, hope, love . . . power & life'. But

                         thou must resign
                         All that is not thine own
                              . . . when that which gave
                  The Shadow & the God, has need of thine
                  Abandoning thee; weep then no mercy crave
                  But bow thyself in dust, take shelter in the grave

If this argument was true – and Shelley rejected the stanzas, as though he
had thought again – life, love and hope belonged to the universe at large.
They merely passed through to 'enshrine' his body for others, as he told
Miss Hitchener, and were then withdrawn again. For a span of years he
could make them his own, cherishing them, before surrendering them
without complaint when the Spirit required them of him. Like Ariel
released by Prospero, he would return to the elements, his magic gone.
    Would anything of him survive when the body died? In times of
despair, or of rational and logical enquiry, he could not think so.

                       When the lamp is shattered
                  The light in the dust lies dead—
                       When the cloud is scattered
                  The rainbow's glory is shed—
                       When the lute is broken
                  Sweet tones are remembered not—

Yet he hoped differently.
    'What think you the dead are?' he asked Byron once. They had
dismounted after galloping across the Venetian sands; servants were
waiting with the gondola. The evening was cold. Both poets had paused
to look at the sunset, the sky heaped up with clouds 'dark purple at
the zenith' and dazzlingly bright where the sun still caught them.
    'Why, dust and clay,' said Byron dismissively. 'What should they be?'
    By way of answer – perhaps in life, perhaps only in his notebook –
Shelley gave a description of beauty.

                  Look on the West how beautiful it is
                  Vaulted with radiant vapours. the deep bliss
                  Of that unutterable light has made
                  The edges of cloud   fade
                  Into a purple hue like some harmonious thought
                  Wasting itself on that which it had wrought

                              284

It seemed to him then that Love, Hope and Beauty survived – not only as absolutes he could not see, but as the love and beauty the dead had drawn from the scene and sounds around them, released now into the endless renewal of the world. As he wrote of Keats, in death

> He is made one with Nature: there is heard
> His voice in all her music, from the moan
> Of thunder, to the song of night's sweet bird;
> . . .
> He is a portion of the loveliness
> Which once he made more lovely . . .

He imagined this also of 'Willmouse', his little son. He could not finish the poem he began in 1819 to 'My lost William', but his final thought – before breaking off, his tears smearing the lines – was that the grass was somehow softer in that sun-filled cemetery in Rome, the daisies brighter, not because of the mouldering body but because of his dead child's spirit, set free there. Love survived.

Trelawny once asked him, with his sailor's bluntness, whether he believed in the immortality of the spirit. Shelley snapped: 'Certainly not; how can I? We know nothing; we have no evidence; we cannot express our inmost thoughts. They are incomprehensible even to ourselves.' Eight years earlier, Captain Kennedy had asked him the same question; Shelley seemed to avoid an answer. As a rational man, he could not believe in a notion he could not prove. As a Poet, he was well aware that he could hardly put it into words.

As far as evidence went, much of it still seemed to lie in the leaves that beat on the windows of his carriage or piled up in the woods. These were the Spirit's instruments and mediators; they had been in the cycle of life, and were now discarded. Death was unbinding and releasing their atoms, and those leaves would be gone for ever. That much he could be sure of.

The air sent a more ambiguous message. Intimations of Beauty seemed to prepare him for some great and vital work. Divine Breath played on him, releasing music he never knew. The West Wind tugged him like a co-conspirator, or a co-creator. And might not creators live for ever?

★   ★   ★

On extraordinary days he could fly again. Amid the turmoil of his thoughts at Marlow, as Claire sang, he was aware of the means of escape. He dissolved into the music and then, rapturously, into the surrounding air. In trance he was lifted up, sweeping over woods and waves, blown by 'the breath of summer's night', until the sky was suddenly torn open:

> And o'er my shoulders wings are woven
> To follow its sublime career,
>   Beyond the mighty moons that wane
> Upon the verge of Nature's utmost sphere,
> Till the world's shadowy walls are past, and disappear.

Sometimes he needed no effort to cleave the air. In his 'Ode to Naples' Liberty itself swept him up through waves of sunlight, so high that the aether made a horizontal line like the surface of the sea. From this height he could look down on struggling Naples, crying out encouragement and prophecy. More often he spoke of wings growing, 'rapid plumes of song' robing him from head to foot and allowing him to slip, like breath itself, out of the chains of the body. *Oh, lift me.*

Poem after poem suggested that Shelley viewed the Earth from the air. Though he claimed to be on hilltops or on 'heaven-cleaving' turrets, his viewpoint changed constantly, from cities to valleys to mountains to the sea. (There, directly over the mast, he glimpsed his boat, a tiny open shell with himself a shadow in the prow.) He saw the Earth itself in space, a 'green & azure wanderer' shining divinely. He was flying, taking rapture for granted. At a glance he could scan every aspect of the human condition, as if he were Ianthe travelling the universe in the chariot of Queen Mab, or Milton's Satan swooping 'through the pure marble Air his oblique way', dizzyingly high.

Time and again, among his cries of 'What?' and 'Whence?' and 'Why?', Shelley demanded to know whether he was an actor or a spectator on the Earth. His visions gave him an answer, for a while. In March 1821, as he urged on the Greek war of independence against the Turks, he had two seals made that carried the image of a dove with outspread wings and an inscription, from Sophocles's *Oedipus at Colonus*, which he had also used as the motto of his lyrical drama *Hellas*:

> Μάντις εἴμ ἐσθλωγ ἀγώνων
> I am the prophet of glorious struggles

In Sophocles the dove flew high above the field of battle to report on winners and losers. This was Shelley, prophesying over the world. He would not fight, and showed no disposition to follow the life of a soldier; the war in Greece was the only one he supported with any enthusiasm. But he would fly and sing.

His wings were no longer those of the ephemeron or even the skylark's, faltering. These were his soul-wings, unfolded. Plato in the *Phaedrus* had described their steady strengthening as a man was affected more and more deeply by memories, stirred by earthly beauty, of the realm of the divine from which the soul had fallen. That stream of beauty 'quickened the passages of the wings, watering them and inclining them to grow', until they could bear him upwards.

At Eton Dr Walker too had taught him to soar, exhorting him to 'launch into the immensity of space, and behold *system* beyond *system*, *above us, below us*, to the *east*, the *west*, the *north*, the *south*! Let us go so far as to see our sun but a *star* among the rest, and our system itself as a point . . . !' Yet his Poet's wings mounted far higher than this. Writing his 'Ode to Liberty' – mixed up in his notebook with earlier snatches of his 'Ode to the West Wind' – Shelley experienced that farther, faster flight, snatched by 'the Spirit's whirlwind',

> and the ray
> Of the remotest sphere of living flame
> Which paves the void was from behind it flung,
> As foam from a ship's swiftness . . .

In his first draft he was rapt beyond 'night & day & time & space', 'Breathless & blind with speed'. Nothing, it seemed, could stop him. His wings were firm now, aspiring, 'night-dividing'. Above him stretched a dim dome or vault to the world, stained with mutability, but he would burst it apart like a bubble. He could dart out of the world of appearances, uncontrollable, like the West Wind 'at the zenith's height'; and from there he could ascend to Truth and Beauty in their original essence, no longer imagined, but real.

In the draft of *Hellas* that moment was almost palpable. At the end of a line the word *flight* leapt away wildly to the horizontal, a fierce dash following–

> ~~unbounded~~
> From every point of the ~~immense~~ ——

287

                        Infinite
        Like a thousand dawns on a single night
        The splendours rise & spread————

Yet his wings were not permanent. Plato taught that they could be lost
overnight, the feathers dropping one by one, if a soul became embroiled
in the dross of the world. They were lost, too, as soon as the flyer began
to fear the dizzy height of his flying and the possibility, ever increasing,
that he could never go back. As Heaven opened and the walls vanished,
Shelley, soaring in Claire's song, begged her to stop and allow him to
return. To go farther was perhaps to risk madness, perhaps to die, perhaps
to achieve a most glorious apotheosis, but he could not tell and dared
not, for the moment, try. Later, in *Epipsychidion*, rapt into the air by the
nearness of his soul's soul and the fragrance of her softly disentangling
hair, he cried out in terror:

                        Ah, woe is me!
        What have I dared? where am I lifted? how
        Shall I descend, and perish not?

He had fallen before. In his 'Ode to Liberty' the 'great voice' that had
sustained him, the breath of his being, was suddenly withdrawn. As it
stopped, he plunged down:

        . . . as a wild swan, when sublimely winging
                Its path athwart the thunder-smoke of dawn
        Sinks headlong through the aerial golden light
                On the heavy-sounding plain
                When the bolt has pierced its brain . . .

Falling, dying, through the air, his thoughts disintegrated around him. His
song faded, and his feathers fell away. The sheer impetus of his flight upwards
was reversed to a rushing drowning dive into the sea. He was a man again.
    To fly was dangerous. To feel that pricking of the shoulders, and the
sudden giddy lifting of the soul from the body, was a foretaste of death,
even if he did not fall. In his dreams once, a spirit cried out a warning
to another:

        O Thou who plumed with strong desire
        Would float above the Earth—beware!

> A shadow tracks thy flight of fire—
> Night is coming!

Yet the other spirit confidently countered him. With 'the lamp of love' in his heart, he had no fear of the storm:

> I see the glare and I hear the sound—
> I'll sail on the flood of the tempest dark
> With the calm within and light around
> Which make night day;
> And thou when the gloom is deep and stark
> Look from thy dull earth slumberbound—
> My moonlike flight thou then mayst mark
> On high, far away.

He would not necessarily be blasted from the sky, or be made by his own dread to sink to earth again. He might live, and soar on, towards the fire.

Fire

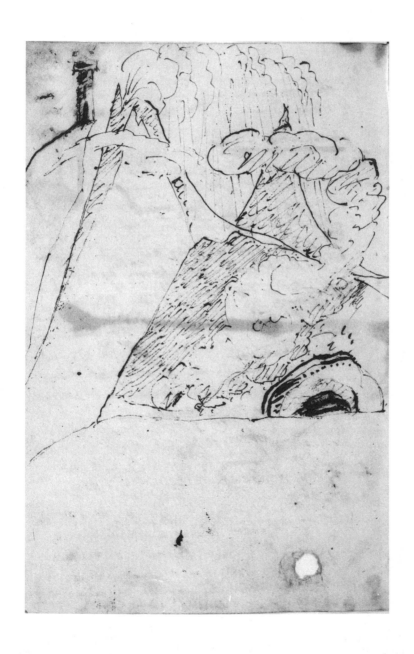

I

Daring

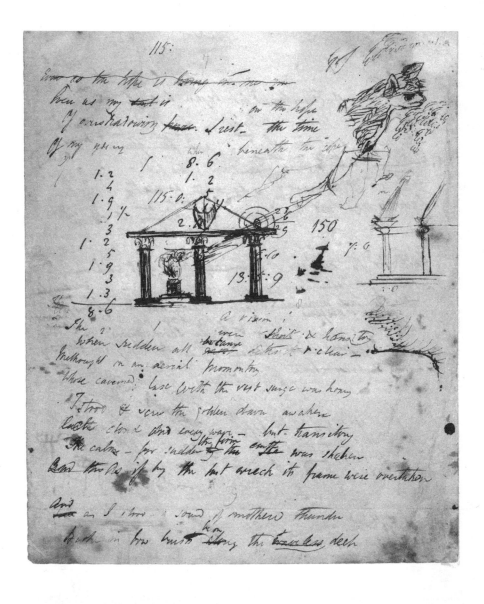

Pulled from a jacket pocket with Plato and his 'hanks', the little box was laid on the table. Inside lay tinder of oiled wool, flint and steel. Shelley struck the spark, ignited the tinder, plunged in a match. It burned with a stink of brimstone and a blue-gold, wavering flame. As it licked towards his fingers he went on holding it, unflinching, entranced.

> Men scarcely know how beautiful fire is—
> Each flame of it is as a precious stone
> Dissolved in ever-moving light, and this
> Belongs to each and all who gaze upon.

Homer's Mercury had first done this. Curiously rubbing two laurel sticks together in his baby palms, he had been startled by the sudden, vaporous, leaping flash. Shelley too imagined how fresh-invented fire sprang from the gods' control, 'most terrible, but lovely'. The Greeks believed that each flame took the shape of a pyramid, the sacred form aspiring to perfectibility or Heaven. Fire, more than any other element (as Dr Walker had taught Shelley), forced fluidity on matter, flung particles apart, and brought release.

Flames of all kinds seethed in his poems: physical, spiritual, metaphorical, good or bad, killing or animating. Meteors were 'wandering', 'green', 'unctuous' or 'uncertain', single or showers of shooting stars. They were messengers that grazed the horizon and snaked into scenes to bring

295

disruption, or selfishness, or flaring sexual desire. Marsh gas flickered when Shelley needed it, licking blue tongues, or rolled in small spheres across floors and in grass; phosphorescence clung round his magic boats and tracked his progress in the water.

In the distance, other fires burned. He saw the chimneys of steel manu-factories, smoking plague pits and funeral pyres, the camp-fires of brave revolutionists, or their cities and houses torched by the armies of despotic European powers. The fire of battlefields was resolutely red, as if Shelley blanked the beauty out: red light, red artillery, red swords, red wrath, canopied by blood-red rainbows. Volcanoes glowed symbol-ically above the revolutions of 1810 in Mexico and of 1820 in Naples while, in *Prometheus Unbound*, the whole pre-revolutionary landscape was gradually charged with purging volcanic fire. Overhead the rare Aurora Borealis shook like a curtain, comets dived past with their presaging of violent change, or the sky showed Lucretian wonders of *nocturnas fasces caeli sublime volantis*, night-flying torches trailing long tails of flame.

In his scenes of revolutionary ruin, the spark of truth was never quenched entirely. Both light and fire had a way of lingering in a landscape, hidden or on the edge. Hence, shortly after his visit to Vesuvius in 1818, his vivid descriptions of golden willow buds 'like points of lambent fire' in the winter woods, and the brightness of oranges and lemons caught by bursts of setting sunlight on the tree, as if subterranean fire was breaking in these forms through the surface of the Earth, or as if mortal fruits and flowers had become, like his favourites, immortal. In Shelley's Aprils, revolution time, 'all the forest-tips began to burn/ With kindling green', under the new blue sky.

Long hours were spent gazing at ordinary fire: the candles he wrote by, the hearths that warmed him. His night-time conversations burned on as the wood or coals did, he and a friend edging ever closer to the glow, feet on the grate and firelight flashing on their faces, as they set the world to rights. For as long as possible he would read by it, crouched by the chimney breast with a poker in one hand, beating up the light.

The red coals, sinking down, filled his head with ghouls and monsters. Gruesome stories and wavering faces were cast out in the shadows. His own eyes grew dry and hot; the conversation became so 'awful' that he hardly dared to breathe. Sitting by the fire very late with Claire, he twenty-two, she sixteen, he was impelled to talk low and conspiratorially of the witching time of night and of how her pillow could have moved, by no human agency, from her bed to a chair. Crowding round the blazing logs at Villa Diodati near Geneva in the rainy summer of 1816, he and Byron and Mary and Monk Lewis told tales to appal each other.

Fire dried his Latin exercises, burned the letters he dared not send and immolated an Oxford supper of tender scalloped oysters. Fire also came after him. It prowled across the floor like a cat, scorching the carpet with its hot, soft tongue. Close to the hearth, too close, Shelley would lie asleep; fire painted his cheeks bright red and decked his hair with sparks. Solicitous friends, wondering how he could bear it, moved him away and put a blanket on him, but he rolled back, throwing it aside. Fire crept to him and boiled his brains.

He claimed to have the temperament of a salamander, a creature generated and nourished by flame. Cold withered and tormented him, sending him to cower by the hearth shivering and chafing his hands; dull weather made him miserable. By contrast, he would go hatless in Italy even in the summer, daring the sun to scorch him. And at Villa Valsovano in 1819 he worked eagerly in a lofty glassed-in terrace baking with sunlight, the forge in which he hammered out *The Cenci* with muscles and with strength he had never used before.

Friends readily saw him as a fire-spirit: a compulsive arguer with his long locks 'streaming like a meteor', a shining seraph. Hogg made him a comet, racing for the sun in a flashing trajectory before swerving away into space. Yet his own fire-image was usually fainter. Earthly existence smothered him until he was an ember barely glowing, or a firebrand dying in its own white ash. In his 'West Wind' notebook he played with the notion of how he might survive as fire, kindled and soon suppressed.

> And this is my distinction, if I fall . . .
> I will not ~~crawl~~ out of the vital ~~air~~
> To common dust, nor wear a common pall
>   decay
> ~~But as my hopes were fire, so my despair~~
> ~~Shall be as ashes   covering them.~~
>   ~~Dear Frien~~
>   ~~If any spark be unextinguished there~~

At the bottom left-hand corner a bleak face with wild hair peered through the words. The outline and features wavered, as in his drawings of ghosts. '*Je suis un homme grave*,' he wrote above it. '*Un homme gravide*.' The bitter bilingual pun perhaps pleased him, a man as a grave. And underneath his ashes, persistent, a point of light.

Walks in the twilight lanes and fields produced another fire-image. By comparison with poets he thought greater, especially Byron, he became a pallid glow-worm creeping among the leaves. He saw the worms go out like a guttering lamp 'which a student forgets to trim', suddenly drowning. After his first meeting with Hogg at Oxford, as he told him his name and left his rooms, he was lit stumblingly downstairs by the stump of a candle that had almost melted, swimming in oil; in bed at night he would read to the extinction of the liquid, quavering flame. There was magic for him in that struggling light, made brighter by the very dark that threatened to devour it:

> Thou small flame,
> Which, as a dying pulse rises and falls,
> Still flickerest up and down, how very soon,
> Did I not feed thee, wouldst thou fail and be
> As thou hadst never been!

For hours in Italy Shelley watched fireflies on the bushes and the river banks: symbols of his own mortality, flashing and vanishing. He noticed that they danced like bees in ever-altering circles, and that each one

Under the dark trees seems a little sun,
A meteor tamed; a fixd star gone astray
From the silver regions of the milky way;—

Yet as often as he was fire he was its hapless, blinded admirer. He was a moth bumping at the night window or fluttering round a candle, drawn helplessly by the light's 'sophistication' towards the most glorious of endings. Calderón's image of this radiant death he lingered over especially, as if hypnotised by the turning, circling grace of the lines:

No has visto enamorada mariposa
dar cercos a la luz, hasta que dexa
en monumento facil abrasadas
las alas de color tornasoladas?

Hast thou not marked the moth's enamoured flight,
About the taper's flame at evening hour,
Till kindle in that monumental fire
His sunflower wings their own funereal pyre?

In *Epipsychidion* he imagined his own moth's flight, unsteadily, towards apotheosis in the evening star. Dreamy overlapping and concentric circles, taking his pencil round and round and round, accompanied the draft lines on the page. To be consumed 'within the purest glow/ Of one serene and unapproachèd star/ As if it were a lamp of earthly light', was so strong a longing in him that he also envied the deluded fish in the sea at Lerici, rising gladly and fatally to the fisherman's flare. Sitting on the night beach, 'disturbed and weak' after Jane had left him, he watched their bright deaths, and thought them happy.

★   ★   ★

This love of fire had surfaced early. His sisters remembered him, as a boy, parading through the kitchen with a blazing stove and setting the butler alight. With terrifying seriousness he would wire the little girls up, stand them round the nursery table and pass electric fluid through them. Their pure white dresses were blackened by his experiments.

At Eton, he was found in his study one day enveloped in blue flame; a deafening shock flashed from the door handle and threw his tutor to the wall. Fireworks bulged in his pockets. He bought, or built with help, a small steam-engine that soon burst, and obtained from somewhere sufficient explosive to blow the lid off his desk. A pollard willow at the edge of South Meadow was half destroyed by gunpowder ignited, some said, with burning-glasses. Shelley himself was sent home once with his face and hands burnt, the result of some trick that had gone wrong.

At Oxford the 'strange and fantastic pranks' continued unabated. By Hogg's description, Shelley's study was dedicated to experiments with fire. The floor was cluttered – among boots, crockery, underwear, ammunition, packets of powdered lemonade – with an electrical machine, an air pump, a galvanic trough, and several large glass jars and receivers. On the table, beside piles of books, a small glass retort was suspended over an oil lamp which, as Hogg watched, brought to ebullition a substance so noxious that Shelley snatched it up and threw it in the grate. The electrical machine had already been tried on a tom-cat (a friend holding the cat down, Shelley applying the wires) and on the dim, terrified son of Shelley's scout. Now, holding the chain that was fastened to the conductor, his feet square-planted on the glass-legged stool that would stop the fire from earthing, Shelley begged Hogg to turn the handle and drive the current through him. Touched then, he would shock and spark; dipping a finger in warm spirits or gunpowder, he could set them alight.

Hogg claimed that analysis of fire especially intrigued his friend. Shelley wished to investigate all its properties, testing whether clay or stones or even water could be made to burn too. He imagined with mounting excitement what a giant galvanic battery, with troughs 'of colossal magnitude' and 'hundreds of metallic plates' could do, and how dazzlingly he could shock the Earth, even to its most secret depths, by using a whole flotilla of kites to pull sheet after sheet of lightning down from Heaven.

By ceaseless, rash experiment he might also make himself more volatile and inflammable. At Oxford he sniffed ether and 'factitious airs' from teacups, and could have brewed up crimson nitrous oxide that made him mad, drunk and oracular. Hanging over pools, he could inhale in imagination the hydrogen that burst from bubbles given off by water-plants until he too could shoot on that thin gas to the electric upper air, riding its trails like meteors,

            and rein their headlong speed,
And bow their burning crests, and glide in fire
Under the waters of the earth again.

His fascination with chemistry long outlasted Oxford. At Keswick in 1811 he carried out experiments that set off explosions in the woods. He also gave Harriet and Eliza a lesson in the garden on 'the nature of the atmosphere', involving such a vivid blaze of hydrogen gas that their landlord asked them to leave. Fire balloons were carefully devised from paper, a stick and a sponge soaked in spirits and were sent up, lit with a taper, from lawns in Devon and Geneva. At night his paper navies were sometimes ornamented with tiny match-helmsmen of flame.

In London in 1814–15 Shelley attended Professor Garnerin's 'Theatre of Grand Philosophical Recreations' to hear lectures on gases, electricity and phantasmagoria, sometimes taking Mary or Claire along with him to witness the shows of shocks and sparks, or to sniff combustible vapours. On Guy Fawkes night, while adults sat in sober conversation, he would creep with their children to let off squibs and rockets underneath the windows. His exile in Italy seemed to put an end to practical experimenting, but not to close encounters with fire. He was delighted when, racing home once from the Gisbornes' at Leghorn, he felt the 'transverse lightning' graze his cheek, but spare him.

He also continued to read Humphry Davy (*Elements of Chemical Philosophy, Elements of Agricultural Chemistry*) and to take notes on him. In consequence his visions kept the shocks and smoke of chemical and physical experiment: electrical charges, green-glowing Leyden jars, gases and combustion. His Earth was singularly subject to, and pervaded by, fire. 'Soil, consists of earths—earths are composed of highly inflammable metals & oxygen,' he jotted down from Davy. Electrical currents might disunite these substances, keeping the solid and fluid parts of Earth in equilibrium. Heat, light and air in leaves modified the sap of plants, and electricity seemed to help them grow: 'Corn sprouted more rapidly in water positively electrified by the Voltaic battery than negatively.' The whole world, indeed, could be understood in terms of electromagnetic force. 'The clouds are usually negative—the Earth therefore positive—.'

Above these particular notes, not for the first time, he had mused about the painted veil of earthly illusion. 'One I have known who lifted it—' he wrote, again. He then changed course, as if, for the moment, Davy's explication of mysteries would be enough for him.

301

Lectures on Agricultural Chemistry.
Chap. 1.

metals 38
36 ~~47~~ Elementary bodies— inflammable Bodies ~~8~~ 6
Acidific—3 .

★ ★ ★

When Hogg had paid Shelley that first visit at Oxford, he had seen him as an alchemist ensconced in his seething equipment. At Eton, too, Shelley had acquired that persona, a mad-eyed boy who ran upstairs singing the witches' incantation from *Macbeth* ('Fire burn and cauldron bubble') and who mocked a colleague as an 'Apurist' because he did not reverence fire. Chemistry books were banned as private reading, so he read them. Experiments were forbidden in the boys' rooms, so he performed them. In *Alastor* he seemed to describe his own boyhood attempts to plumb the deep mysteries and 'inmost sanctuary' of Nature, uniting 'strange tears', 'awful talk' and 'breathless kisses' at dead of night,

Like an inspired and desperate alchymist
Staking his very life on some dark hope . . .

much, in fact, like the Alchemist he had invented to fascinate and scare his sisters, mumbling into his long grey beard in a blocked-up room beneath the garret at Field Place.

Shelley told Godwin that he had read the 'reveries' of both Paracelsus and Albertus Magnus as a boy, filling his head with occult mysteries of fire and gold that he did not necessarily forget. Hogg doubted he had ever tried Albertus Magnus; but 'forbidden mines' of secret lore, purchased with pocket money, had made up much of Shelley's reading at school. Among the objects Hogg remembered in his rooms was a gold seven-shilling piece half submerged in acid in a teacup, perhaps reverting to the celestial fire Paracelsus claimed it was.

Chemistry, Shelley told Hogg, was the key to truth. The crowding batteries and jars were his 'philosophical apparatus'. From chemistry to philosophy was but a small step for him: changing substances, minds, the world, by the agency of fire. Hogg thought Shelley also needed it to verify his ideas and, at times, his state of being, as if he had forgotten.

The first of his alchemist models was Dr Lind, his teacher and friend at Eton. Lind was often suspected of being a magician, partly for oper-

302

ating a private printing press with curious fonts, partly for his interest in 'pneumatic' medicine and hallucinogenic plants. In *The Revolt of Islam*, as Laon's teacher in the virtues necessary for revolution, he became a dispenser of 'arrowy' light, shining 'like the reflex of a thousand minds', as well as of enchantments much more dangerous:

> 'In secret chambers parents read, and weep,
>   My writings to their babes, no longer blind,
> And young men gather when their tyrants sleep,
>   And vows of faith each to the other bind; . . .
> And every bosom thus is rapt and shook . . .'

Self-taught as they were, Shelley's characters dabbled in alchemy almost before they knew it. The Poet of *Alastor* found himself drawn, among ancient ruins, to strange sculptured memorials and brass zodiacs. The Witch of Atlas, closeted from birth among arcane scrolls 'of some Saturnian Archimage', performed multiple miracles by 'Wisdom's wizard skill': writing unearthly dreams on the brains of the living, and keeping the dead in a state of warm suspended life in which they caught glimpses of immortality. She herself, in winter, slept within 'an inextinguishable well/ Of crimson fire', an 'innocuous liquor' of creative desire whose brimming waves were blown away like stars over the woods.

Her most impressive experiment was the making of a Hermaphrodite: a beautiful, sexless companion compounded of fire and ice. It lay dormant, like the mind of man, but at the Witch's galvanic touch it would open its eyes, spread its aethereal frost-wings, and fly. No monsters were created by alchemy in Shelley, though in one of his favourite books, the *Pharsalia* of Lucan, a corpse was raised horribly to twitching life by the Thessalian witch, and though audiences at galvanism sessions in London lecture halls could see the cadavers of murderers kick their legs and grin. He too beguiled the summer of 1816 by wondering how creatures might be put together and heated into life. But he left such things to Mary, and to Frankenstein.

In 1819 he conceived with the Gisbornes a scheme for a steamboat that would ply between Leghorn, Genoa and Marseilles. His motives were commercial, nautical and pyrotechnical; the boat obsessed him because it was forged and propelled by fire. The elements of its soul (his word) were 'the Boilers, & the Keel of the Boat, & the Cylinder', all capitalised in his excitement, as he capitalised Poet and Poem. This was his *Monstruo de fuego y agua*, a Calderón fire-creature, not blown passively by wind or breath but pushed from within by the 'self-impelling steam-wheels of the mind'. He drew such paddle-wheels all through his current notebook, on boats, on carriages and by themselves. Scrawled at the top of a page came a thought of it:

> Child of Despair & Desire
> Monster of water & fire
> Wingless sea bird, outspeeder

His purpose was autonomy and liberty, as well as cutting-edge science.

Henry Reveley, the boat's engineer, had sent him an irresistible account of its making:

> The fire was lighted in the furnace at nine, and in three hours the metal was fused. At three o'clock it was ready to cast, the fusion being remarkably rapid, owing to the perfection of the furnace. The metal was also heated to an extreme degree, boiling with fury, and seeming to dance with the pleasure of running into its proper form. The plug was struck, and a massy stream of a bluish dazzling whiteness filled the moulds in the twinkling of a shooting star.

Shelley wrote back in the same vein, as if this were a vision of the Demiurgus in the very act of creation.

> One might imagine God when he made the earth, & saw the granite mountains & flinty promontories flow into their craggy forms, & the splendour of their fusion filling millions of miles of the void space, like the tail of a comet, so looking, & so delighting in his work.

In Reveley's workshop at Leghorn Shelley found himself instantly at home, 'like some weird Archimage . . . Plotting dark spells, and devilish enginery'. Delightedly, he began to 'catalogize' Reveley's 'Great screws, and cones, and wheels, and groovèd blocks' and 'shapes of unintelligible brass'. Every object in the room held potential for magic: a dusty paintbox, an old teacup, a 'queer broken glass' with ink in it, a half-burnt match. Shelley did not know what these things were for and implied that, in Reveley's absence, he was meant to make no mischief by touching them. He did not mind and, beyond setting a 'hollow screw with cogs' afloat in a bowl of quicksilver like a paper boat, he obeyed.

Where Reveley was the *machinista*, the practical chemist and engineer, he himself was proudly the *alchemista*, able by mind- and word-magic to transform whatever he observed. 'I can make words,' he once told Medwin, 'which you cannot.'

The eventual collapse of the steamboat scheme infuriated and shattered him, and not merely because he had lost money and had been, in his opinion, betrayed by people he had supposed his friends. (Reveley simply thought the venture too ambitious for Shelley's funds.) He had failed in an experiment to fit a vessel with a soul of fire. In May 1820 he saw the half-built boat again, 'asleep under the walls', and was afraid to wake it. What he observed was a shell that would not be animated – or not by him.

Typically, he kept the idea warm. In January 1822 Williams drew from him a design for a steam-yacht to ply between Leghorn and Genoa, 'an undertaking that promises great advantages'. But the nearest Shelley came to a fire-boat was at Venice, where he would sit sometimes reading or writing in gondolas at night, 'having the little brazen lamp alight, /Unseen, uninterrupted'. The small flame burned as he floated between the upper and the lower stars.

★   ★   ★

Higher than his earthbound sight could possibly reach, the sky was filled with light and flame. The chemist in him knew this was Newton's 'most subtle Spirit', the mediating aether that surrounded the world. Electricity, magnetism, heat and light all surged through aether, as did Love. Matter could be no finer and more tenuous, nor more capable of pervading every particle of earth, air, water, and Shelley himself. In Dr Walker's lectures all Nature was kept in motion by this elementary electric fire, 'the only *essential fluid*, and probably the cause of fluidity in others'. All light, too, came from it. Macrobius (who turned up in the end-notes to Volney's *Ruins*) said this fluid made the substance of the sun and the stars, as also of men's souls. It was the agent of movement, divinity and life.

Newton had discovered through the luminous aether God's presence in everything, life-giving and expanding. Shelley, at the peak of his materialism, grappled less piously with what aether was. 'Is the electric fluid material?' he asked an elderly physician with whom he was in earnest correspondence about these things. 'Is light—is the vital principle in vegetables—in brutes—is the human soul?' He seemed to expect

305

the answer no; but this was also one of his probing trick questions. 'Matter,' he wrote around 1813,

> such as we behold it, is not inert. It is infinitely active and subtile. Light, electricity and magnetism are fluids not surpassed by thought itself in tenuity and activity: like thought they are sometimes the cause and sometimes the effect of motion; and, distinct as they are from every other class of substance, with which we are acquainted, seem to possess equal claims with thought to the unmeaning distinction of immateriality.

'Truth', he told Miss Hitchener, 'is *my* God, & *say* he is Air Water, Earth or Electricity but I think *your's* is reducible to the same simple Divinityship.'

Whichever proposition was true, it was clear that all earthly life was involved in a cycle of fire. Aethereal dew fell and condensed from its great reservoir in the sun; morning light warmed the tiny globes into vapours that slowly rose; electricity built up in thunderclouds and lightning, in a blaze, released it. Shelley, writing *Prometheus Unbound*, became that drifting dew-cloud, wrapped in 'the warm aether of the morning sun' as every man and woman would be in his new age of moral regeneration: part science, part sexual ecstasy.

> I saw not, heard not, moved not, only felt
> His presence flow and mingle through my blood
> Till it became his life, and his grew mine,
> And I was thus absorbed, until it passed,
> And like the vapours when the sun sinks down,
> Gathering again in drops upon the pines,
> And tremulous as they, in the deep night
> My being was condensed . . .

Dew began this consummation. For Shelley this was not liquid, but subtle fire: at the very least the substance the Greeks had imagined, the starry foam or spume blown off from Heaven. Spring, hovering over the Earth, shook down from her 'aetherial wings' soft sparks, not water-drops, to melt the ice and creep within the soil. Dew-globes on the grass and gossamers at dawn made a field of light that 'mocked the stars', the direct progeny of the rising sun. In winter dew made the frost-forms, the 'starry ice' that so excited him. Dews in the night woods wandered as low-trailing clouds of fire, silently restoring the energies of the Earth.

Poetry, Shelley supposed, acted in much the same way, as 'medicinal honey' made from the dews of thought. For he was physically involved in this. The fiery aether that moved in the wide universe moved also in his will and in his nerves. The subtlest parts of him were 'peopled' with hopes and intimations, 'Desires and Adorations,/ Wingèd Persuasions'. These lived in his thoughts, and far beyond them,

> Voyaging cloudlike and unpent
> Through the boundless element . . .

Their voices, 'something sadder, sweeter far than all', were what he had heard out past the water and the trees; their colours, 'skiey grain,/Orange and azure deepening into gold', were intenser, more radiant shades of the hues of human life he had seen in paintings, suffusing both figures and the sky. They filled the blue for which he longed, flashing rainbow 'smiles' like the light of stars.

He imagined such a spirit too on his own Poet's lips,

> Dreaming like a love-adept
> In the sound his breathing kept . . .

and in a lightly pencilled fragment he traced another to the depths of himself, or as close to his soul as almost made no difference.

> ~~Let me be~~ I am as a Spirit who has dwelt
> Within his heart of hearts, & I have felt
> His feelings, & have thought his thoughts, & known
> The inmost ~~meaning~~ converse of his soul, the tone
> Unheard but in the silence of his blood
> When all the pulses, in their multitude
> Image the trembling calm of summer seas
> I have untuned the golden melodies
> Of his deep soul, as with a master key
> And loosened them, & bathed myself therein
> Even as an Eagle in a thunder ~~mist~~
> Clothing his wings with lightning . . .

Such a being was much like Conscience, knowing the 'inmost skein' of Shelley's life and, with soft rebukes, loosening his temper. It was also like the Love described by Agathon in the *Symposium*, in that passage Shelley adored: 'the father of grace, and delicacy, and gentleness, and delight, and persuasion, and desire', treading 'sandalled with calm' in his heart. Yet Shelley could still be deceived, for Despair – ever slyly and assiduously in motion – so often posed as Love in the unregenerated, waiting world.

> Ah, sister! Desolation is a delicate thing:
>   It walks not on the earth, it floats not on the air,
> But treads with lulling footstep, and fans with silent wing
>   The tender hopes which in their hearts the best and gentlest
>   bear;
> Who, soothed to false repose by the fanning plumes above
>   And the music-stirring motion of its soft and busy feet,
> Dream visions of aëreal joy, and call the monster, Love,
>   And wake, and find the shadow Pain, as he whom now we
>   greet.

Inhabited by these aethereal powers – positive and negative, thrilling him to inspiration, stinging him with pain – Shelley too could build up an electrical charge, spark by spark, until his own lightning flashed loose. He longed to release it, not least to shock his readers and clear the air. The best of writers – Milton, Bacon, Byron – gathered up lightning in their wings and dispensed it as blinding, liberating light. They were eagles, fire-birds who could soar into the sun, or the light of Truth beyond the sun, and gaze on it until the scales of mortal dullness fell away from their eyes. It was impossible, Shelley wrote in *A Defence of Poetry* in 1821, 'to read the most celebrated writers of the present day without being startled by the electric life which burns within their words'. The more revolutionary the truth, the more extreme the lightning: chasms, ravines, rivers of it, splitting the whole sky.

> See! The lightnings yawn
> Deluging heaven with fire, and the lashed deeps
> Glitter and boil beneath

On good days he too was in control of the fire, an angel or daemon 'sheathing his sword in lightning' ('serpent lightning') and whirling its blade among the stars. He could be a conductor for poets whose voices were not yet understood.

> In ~~thunder & in fire~~
> ~~Thunder & lightning~~
> ~~I was spirit, struck~~
> ~~Pilot spirits clothed in~~

At this altitude, if he could reach it, there was no more faltering or falling, nor even the obscuring cloud of pessimism in which, he believed, Coleridge in his middle age wearily flew. He glided like a young eagle, free, clear-sighted, while fire-thoughts streamed from his wings and his soul-shadow, like a storm passing, flashed over the Earth. Or he was a beacon set above a raging sea to spread, if he could, light, liberty and truth to floundering sailors; straddled on his rock, he yelled 'Down with bigotry!' and laughed in exultation. More humbly, as he told Ollier in August 1818, he saw himself trying to persuade 'that prig the public . . . to desert its cherished wines' by offering a drop of dew, a tiny libation of light.

★   ★   ★

In 1812, at the age of nineteen, Shelley had looked into the sun. He discovered from Nicholson's *British Encyclopedia* that it was a 'rayless orb of fire', merely diffusing its light as it met the Earth's atmosphere, and had fed this startling fact into the text and notes of *Queen Mab*. In Davy he found, again to his surprise, that 'the solar rays producing heat are *dark*'. From Herschel's astronomical observations, the latest printed, he deduced that the sun's orb was surrounded by 'a shell as it were of phosphoric vapours, suspended many thousand miles in the atmosphere of that body', making a shining, aethereal canopy that possibly warmed and lit the sun itself.

The sun-sketches in his notebooks were, from that point of view, scientifically correct: dark solid spheres, from which flames leapt like wings. From 95 million miles away, he noted, the sun's light, either particles or vibrations, reached Earth in eight minutes seven seconds. The silver cloud that streaked the night heavens contained 'millions and millions' of suns, shining on innumerable worlds, reducing to nonsense the very idea of a Deity that looked like a man.

Yet, as a Poet, his affinity lay with the sun of myth and prophecy and with Apollo as his persona, both humanised and divine. In the Capitoline Museum in Rome he found him playing the lyre, an almost feminine figure with his legs crossed gracefully and his long hair knotted on his neck. (No one cut the locks of the sun-god, that they might stream through the sky as he rose at dawn.) He was gazing up, about to strike the strings or perhaps just having done so, on the point of singing.

The *Argonautica* of Apollonius Rhodius gave him another treasured Apollo: the god of embarkation and disembarkation, the shore and the dawn, when, as Shelley ardently described it, 'the dazzling radiance of his beautiful limbs suddenly shone over the dark Euxine'. Then, in Apollonius's words,

> beneath his feet all the island quaked, and the waves surged high on the beach . . . And they stood with heads bowed to the ground; but he, far off, passed on to the sea through the air . . .

This Apollo was the 'Far-Darter', whose bow gleamed comfort with the sunrise and whose tears, as beads of amber, strewed the tree-lined shore. The whole voyage of the Argonauts was dedicated to Apollo; it was for his gilded brightness, as well as the golden fleece, that the sailors plied their oars to the lyre songs of Orpheus, Apollo's priest.

Shelley's favourite, however, was the Apollo Belvedere: the shooter of golden, tyrant-piercing rays, and 'probably the most consummate personification of loveliness . . . that remains to us of Greek Antiquity'. His was the cast he kept at Marlow. The bow had gone, and there remained only the attitude of firing: the left arm firm, the right relaxed, the expression beautiful in its nobility and certainty of aim. Round the laurel tree at his side coiled his serpent, sacred to him. The Odes of Pindar, much cited in Greek in Shelley's notebooks, were full of the sun-power of his song: poetry as lyre music, as honey, as a victor's wreath shining with oil; poetry as the flight of an arrow or the swift, gilded race of the athlete and the charioteer.

Shelley often saw himself as a mirror or a shield on which truth glanced and blazed, as it did from the sun. Lionel was called to his work of revolution and renewal when, as a boy, 'sun-like truth' flashed on him, 'as the meteor's midnight flame/ Startles the dreamer'. Shelley's own 'mirror of intolerable light' was held up to his enemies, blinding and confounding them. He was, he told Hunt and Peacock, 'the knight of the shield of shadow': Spenser's Elfin Knight, hacking at the claws of the dragon of tyranny that clung to his sun-bright buckler. His real life, like all men's, was to a lesser or larger degree the shining back of a greater light. As the sun in the visible world – Plato again, in the *Republic* – so were the Beautiful and the Good in the intelligible world, the beacons by which men could reach the truth.

Of all Keats's poems – on which he mostly reserved judgement, believing they showed promise but bad taste – Shelley especially praised *Hyperion*, the story of Apollo's election as the new young god of the sun. He thought it 'astonishing', and 'in the very highest style of poetry'. Hyperion was a sun-god of the old guard, furious at the casting down of the Titans by the vaunting Olympian gods. But Keats's Apollo was a Shelley-child, an exile alone. The poem found him by a stream, a golden-haired boy with his golden bow, weeping gold-bright tears, though he did not know why. The goddess Mnemosyne, suddenly appearing, reminded him of the lyre she had given him; thinking of that music he remembered his own power, and knew himself a god again.

Keats had never finished *Hyperion*. His life had been extinguished first, his consumption apparently aggravated by the reviewers' bile. Shelley thought himself stronger and bolder, his shield-mirror dazzling, his arrows primed against the Critic who, in one drawing, towered over him as a urinating giant. Whatever his enemies might do or say, they would not eclipse him. The sun-god was alive in him. Like Dante, he could begin his poems with an invocation to Apollo, *Entra nel petto mio, e spira*: Enter into my breast and breathe there.

At Delphi the priestess, crouched over the vaporous ravine, felt Apollo work through her until she burst out in howling, incoherent prophecy, the voice of the god. In Aeschylus's *Agamemnon* the scorned prophetess Cassandra, in a scene Shelley loved to shout out in Greek and anno- tated in his notebooks, laboured with desperate, heaving breaths to give vent to the Deity whose truth possessed her:

> Woe, woe! O Earth! Apollo, O Apollo! . . .
> Ah, what a sudden flame comes rushing on me!
> I burn, I burn. Apollo, O Apollo!
> God of the Ways, my destroyer!

Under inspiration, Shelley told Trelawny, the pressure within himself was similar: a sort of internal combustion under which his brain simmered and boiled 'and throws off images and words faster than I can skim them off'. Only after a while, when they had cooled, could he start to

311

put them in order. ('A drunken, reeling, mystical Pythia form' was how Godwin privately described his verse, and Shelley would not have disliked that.) Apollo, Shelley thought, possessed Byron like one of his sacred swans – Plato had been another – impelling him to sing out both prophecy and poetry. But Shelley he burned.

Poets, Shelley hastened to say, were not prophets 'in the gross sense of the word'. They could not foretell the overturning of carriages, or the fall of the government of Spain. Instead, they – he – spoke with a god's voice, often astonishing themselves as well as others. They could not deny the Power that was 'seated upon the throne of their own soul', but were compelled to serve it almost despite themselves:

> For [the poet] not only beholds intensely the present as it is, and discovers those laws according to which present things ought to be ordered, but he beholds the future in the present, and his thoughts are the germs of the flower and the fruit of latest time.

Poets in this sense – seeing, ordering, telling, crying in the wilderness – were 'the unacknowledged legislators of the world'.

Above the first tentative lines of *The Revolt of Islam*, his epic revolution-poem, he drew a neat Temple of Apollo with an eagle over the cornice. Fire smoked on an altar. From the flames sprang a creature: part lion, part cat, part man in pantaloons and shoes. Its expression was furious and determined, bent on illumination. It soared – he soared – beyond the temple's columns, leaving a track like a comet. The eagle raised its wings, as if commending and dispatching him.

Under the drawing came two words: 'A vision'. Shelley had been thinking, gloomily enough, of the failure of the French Revolution. But then, suddenly,

> all became distinct & clear—
> . . .
> I stood & saw the golden dawn awaken

The sun and he worked in concert. The words that burned in him would fall on the paper, incandescent with truth. Poets, he wrote, were 'trumpets which sing to battle, and feel not what they inspire.' Yet he felt it. Though his body and mind might be mere instruments, under inspiration he became both dangerous and divine.

                    the oracular vapour is hurled up
Which lonely men drink wandering in their youth,
And call truth, virtue, love, genius, or joy,
That maddening wine of life, whose dregs they drain
To deep intoxication; and uplift,
Like Maenads who cry loud, Evoe! Evoe!
The voice which is contagion to the world.

The dictum of the Oracle at Delphi was a simple two-word command, the motto of Shelley's life: *Know thyself.* Through the sun-principle in himself, that truth-reflecting power, he intended to. But his ambitions, and his desire, could not end there.

2
Burning

Shelley might consort with gods, but the Devil also haunted him, as he had always done. To know the fire of one was to feel the fire of the other. On Earth, good and evil worked in intimate union as well as perpetual opposition. Inside him, each waged an unremitting struggle to get the upper hand.

At Field Place he had sometimes paraded as Satan, king of the fiends. He made his little sisters dress as attendants, and drew devils in the margins of *Tales of Terror* in the children's library. In the woods he set fire to trees, in a farmyard to a log-stack like a rioting labourer, 'to have a little hell of his own'. At seventeen he wrote to a friend as 'the fiend of the Sussex solitudes', the 'H+D+means Hell Devil', shrieking at midnight for his ration of gore.

Many of his boyhood experiments were to summon the Devil or to raise up Hell. Foul-smelling chemicals, tossed in a pan, were supposed to rouse him at Eton. Shelley tried to invoke him too by cursing, in the same vein as he cursed his father, and by sipping from a skull at midnight as he straddled running water. With one foot on each bank, he could ward off the Devil if he heard him rustling in the grass.

Harriet, once under his spell, was soon made 'dreadfully afraid of his supreme Majesty the Devil'. Listening to Shelley's atheistic arguments, she feared she might soon see Satan, and was terrified when his name was mentioned. She told Miss Hitchener in 1811 that she was 'no longer shackled with such idle fears'; but on the night of 26 February, two years later, the Devil apparently came calling on them.

They were at Tan-yr-allt, in the wilds of Wales, in a house set by itself beneath the mountains. They were also deeply involved in fund-raising to reclaim land from the sea at nearby Tremadoc, a scheme of radical improvement that made them suspected and disliked. For a week the weather had been rough, with lashing gales; that night a tremen-dous storm was raging. By Shelley's account, relayed to Harriet with full horrors, he heard a noise and went downstairs, pistols loaded, to see a stranger leaving through a window. The man fired at him, and missed; Shelley tried to fire back; they wrestled, Shelley fired again, and the man ran away, swearing he would be revenged. Some hours later, the rest of the household having gone back to bed, Shelley heard a noise at the window. A man thrust his arm through the glass and shot at him. The bullet pierced Shelley's flannel night-gown, narrowly missing his body. Shelley fired his own pistol and grabbed an old sword to beat the stranger off but then, losing him, set fire to the nearby woods to burn him alive.

The story was told and retold, with the assailant sometimes Robert Leeson (the owner of a local quarry and oppressor of the Tremadoc workers, threatening to shop Shelley to the government) and some-times, it seemed, no more than a phantom erupting from the air. Years later, Shelley said he still felt the pains of the attacker's knee pressing on his body. Most probably, local enemies had come to scare the nuisance-radical away. But to Shelley, at the instant he saw him, he was the Devil. Having 'shot the glass to shivers', as a neighbour, Mrs Williams, put it, 'and then bounced out on the grass', he saw Satan leaning, almost casually, against a tree. Shelley sketched him later on a wooden screen, naked, with beard and horns and a leering, sardonic smile. He then tried to burn the screen, too, to destroy him.

His father would have recognised this character. Indeed, to Shelley his father could have been this character, horns on his head, blue-smouldering with hate and violence. Yet for him the theology of devils was infinitely more complicated. Satan and God alike were projections of man's mind, nothing else. They were sappers of his will, crushers of his potential, but self-made: 'the Thought which tyrannizes thee', as he translated a line from Calderón. As such, they could sometimes be found in peculiar and tactical alliance. If God was the callous monarch, the Devil was 'the Informer, the Attorney General, and the jailor of the Celestial tribunal', commanding an army of thugs and spies like those who trailed after Shelley. He had connived with God to destroy Job and snare the soul of Faust, heaping misery on the first and tempting the second to perdition. One of

Retzsch's *Faust* etchings, so admired by Shelley, showed Mephistopheles, the Devil's familiar spirit, as a shining angel receiving God's commands, his rapt hair twisting in flames or in curiously Shelleyan horns.

For Shelley also found his own shadow in him. Satan was his self in alienation, the bad daemon twinned with the good. (The Devil seen at Tan-yr-allt may even have been his own pale face, pressed to the window glass and shattered to pieces when he fired.) This *kakadaemon* he needed to fight, shoot and burn alive, in order to bring his true self blazing into being. Yet his figure of the Devil was also Milton's in *Paradise Lost*, a type so close to his better self that he could not bring himself to hate him.

Satan had once been Lucifer, the brightest star, privy to the mysteries of Heaven. Cast out and chained on the burning lake, he still knew them. He had kept his nobility, as he had preserved, in Milton's words, the beauty of 'an Arch-Angel ruind'. He could feel and weep. And, most passionately, he refused to bow to the tyranny of God:

> What though the field be lost?
> All is not lost; th'unconquerable Will
> And study of revenge, immortal hate,
> And courage never to submit or yield:
> And what is else not to be overcome?

Milton, Shelley wrote, 'alleged no superiority of moral virtue to his God over his Devil'. In fact, the Devil was 'far superior'. Shelley could have made Satan his greatest hero-figure, rather than Prometheus, were it not for the Devil's ambition and his thirst for revenge. These made him in the end less 'poetical', as well as less ideal. Yet there was a stateliness in Satan's disobedience, a sense of reason and justice, that made him bright, rather than dark: that made him like Shelley, the light-bringer. Shelley's closing cry to enslaved mankind in his *Declaration of Rights* was Satan's, to his angels, from *Paradise Lost*: '*Awake! — arise! — or be forever fallen.*'

As the serpent, too, Shelley copied him, head erect, walking on his tail, 'with burnisht Neck of verdant Gold erect/ Amidst his circling spires', and carbuncle eyes glittering. In argument he drew himself up, that instinctive movement both Trelawny and Hunt remembered, to show his moral indignation. Death, Milton's serpent told Eve, 'whatever thing Death be', should not be feared. God 'cannot hurt ye, and be just'. As for the command not to eat the fruit of the tree, this was merely a ploy to keep man in subjection:

> 'So shall ye die perhaps, by putting off
> Human, to put on Gods, death to be wisht . . .'

These were Shelleyan words. Men and women could be gods, and the truth about death could not be known on Earth. Therefore they should eat the fruit boldly, face down their fears with fortitude, and hope.

Shelley recognised himself further in the Devil of Calderón. He translated especially those parts of *El mágico prodigioso* where the Daemon-Devil, in disguise, explained himself as a wanderer like Shelley through the labyrinths of mind and thought. Having defied God, he explained, he had forfeited everything, and would roam the world eternally like the Wandering Jew. But he would not repent, and had abandoned all thought of Heaven.

> Then I sailed
> Over the mighty fabric of the world—
> A pirate ambushed in its pathless sands,
> A lynx crouched watchfully among its caves
> And craggy shores; and I have wandered over
> The expanse of these wide wildernesses . . .

Calderón's Daemon-Devil was the self lost; Milton's Satan was the self chained by hate, pride and his own belief, amounting sometimes to despair, in the tyrant-God who tormented him. Both, if they overcame these self-imposed burdens, could be divine, as Shelley could. Only an act of will was needed.

Shelley still hoped for, dared, a direct encounter with this being. As late as 1817 he would wander at weird hours of the night in Bisham Wood, chanting again the necromantic curses needed to evoke him, or so he claimed. Satan-Shelley called Satan, challenging him to appear among the silent trees. But the Devil, he told enquirers, did not come.

So he would go to him. In the visitors' books at various Alpine resorts, having proclaimed his atheism and philanthropism, Shelley gave his destination as 'L'Enfer'. He did not jest entirely. He knew multiple hells. Most appallingly to him there was a true Hell in existence, the 'sharp fear' of it, an irrational foolishness which, like the dread of God or the Devil, kept millions in subjection:

> . . . each girt by the hot atmosphere
> Of his blind agony, like a scorpion stung
>   By his own rage upon his burning bier
> Of circling coals of fire . . .

Furiously, Shelley unravelled the horrors of this belief: that God in his infinite cruelty had devised unending tortures for his creatures while tempting them, in their frailty and ignorance, towards the sin that would condemn them. The gift of 'most merciful God' to man was an eternity of pain. By contrast Satan's gift, through the fatal apple, had been self-knowledge. Shelley's opinions, ringing in Byron's ears as they toured round Lake Geneva in the summer of 1816, turned up on the lips of Lucifer, 'Master of Spirits', in Byron's *Cain:*

> Evil springs from *him*, do not name it *mine* . . .
> One *good* gift has the fatal apple given—
> Your *reason*: —let it not be over-sway'd
> By tyrannous threats to force you into faith
> 'Gainst all external sense and inward feeling:
> Think and endure, —

Shelley kept the churchmen's Hell to bait God with, not believing it, fearing it or caring. And he could find smaller hells aplenty strewn across the universe. In his essay *On the Devil and Devils* he had cynical fun with the argument that the sun might be a Hell, swarming with devils as unconcerned about boiling as the animalculae he had seen in mutton broth, and that the countless comets might be needed as little hells too for the overflow of 'sinners' and the 'damned'. With the mind of a bigot, he could make eternal torture chambers even of the stars.

The struggle within himself was the same. He longed to pursue Beauty, Liberty and Love, but these ideals often got little purchase in him. Instead, the Devil rampaged and Hell raged, whatever names he gave them, for he had let them in. His hoped-for *imperium* over himself was often closer to the Hell of Calderón, *Desperado imperio de tí mismo*, 'Thou wild misrule of thine own anarchy', as he translated it. At Tan-yr-allt he had resisted, pushing and burning the Devil out; but at Keswick in 1811 he had opened the night door to something, a sound, a ruffian demanding more rent, and had been knocked unconscious. The Devil gained admittance then, lodging in his heart and head. When, at Pisa, he saw 'Leeson' again, his friend George Tighe advised him not to flee his fiend-pursuer but to face him boldly, 'like an Englishman'. Shelley agreed, but knew it was himself he had to face and fight. As he wrote in *A Defence of Poetry*, quoting Milton's Satan, 'The mind is its own place, and in itself/ Can make a Heaven of Hell, a Hell of Heaven.'

His damnation or salvation, therefore, lay within his own power. He brought God into the matter as a joke. 'I had rather be damned with Plato and Lord Bacon', he declared, 'than go to Heaven with Paley and Malthus.' 'If God damns me,' he told a friend,

> even by making me my own hell . . . it by no means follows that I *must* desire to be so damned. I may think it extremely disagreeable, as I do to be in an ill temper, & wish to God that God would not have damned me either in this or in any other manner— . . .

> NB. I just forgot to say that a man cannot be said to *desire* that which he possesses. How, therefore can *every man his own hell* desire to be damned when he is damned

As a Poet, Shelley moved naturally among such punished souls. Glimpsing divinity, he also met its opposite. In *Peter Bell the Third* he portrayed the young Coleridge in Hell, or rather as a guest at one of Satan's *petits-soupers* in his house in Grosvenor Square. This Coleridge was much like Shelley, a man 'fair as a maid', but touched with madness. Bravely, as the best East Indian madeira went round, he spoke to the company of poetry,

> and how
> 'Divine it was—a light—a love—
> A spirit which like wind doth blow
> As it listeth, to and fro;
> A dew rained down from God above;
>
> 'A Power which comes and goes like dream,
> And which none can ever trace—
> Heaven's light on earth—Truth's brightest beam.'
> And when he ceased there lay the gleam
> Of those words upon his face.

Divine light seemed to touch him then, illuminating him like a spirit.

But his mind was mists and shadows, groping in uncertainty; and he was still in Hell.

So too was Shelley. He stoked it high with the misery he could not master, the truths he failed to tell, the screaming rage he turned on servants, inveterate impatience. He fuelled it with ineradicable selfishness, indulged and then instantly regretted, and with every 'bare broad word' that shattered his domestic peace. Smaller, furtive, miserable things inhabited it too: the little blank-faced devils from the margins of his notebooks, or grotesque bat-winged beings that skittered, with legs and beaks trailing, on the backs of shopping lists. And then came those flames of aberrant sexual longing, his 'secret food of fires', eating at the top right-hand corner of a page:

> To thirst & find no fill—to wail and wander
> With short unsteady steps—to pause & ponder—
> To feel the blood run thro the veins, & tingle
> Where busy thoughts & blind sensation mingle;—
> To nurse the image of unfelt caresses
>   ~~dizzy~~ dazed
> Till ~~life is half-created shadow~~ imagination just possesses
>   ~~and turning~~
> The half-created shadow   ~~then to tremble~~
>   ~~and, clasping air,~~
>   ~~Feeling~~
>   ~~To find the form that dim then to grow~~
>   ~~then to borrow~~
>   all the night
> Sick

On such nights, even sleep brought no respite from the 'hell of waking time'.

He was also aware – brooding constantly, as he did, over the dark mirror of himself – that he sometimes kept both pain and inspiration dangerously locked inside. As Lionel, he hoarded like a miser this 'self-consuming treasure'; as the Maniac, raking up the coals of 'the full Hell/ Within me', he hid them like embers under the words he wrote. The gleam that would survive of him was likely to be despair. Or, in stark contrast, hope and subversion and defiance.

★   ★   ★

In August 1812 a large deal box arrived at the customs house at Holyhead, in North Wales. Broken open, it was found to be packed with sedition. Shelley, leaving Ireland after his campaign there, had filled it with all the remaining copies of his *Address to the Irish People*, his *Proposals for an Association of Philanthropists*, a ballad-satire on church and government called 'The Devil's Walk', and his *Declaration of Rights*. He was sending this 'inflammable matter' to Miss Hitchener, in tranquil Sussex, to lay a trail of insurrection.

Shelley had understood early that words could cause explosions. His 'Posthumous Fragments of Margaret Nicholson', published at Oxford, were poems supposed to have been written by the crazed washerwoman who in 1786 had tried to kill George III; these 'wild notes of liberty' cried out against war and poverty, eulogised the would-be assassins of Robespierre and once included, Hogg thought, a rhapsody addressed to the dagger of Brutus. The *Declaration of Rights*, banned from ordinary circulation, was sent aloft from Lynmouth one night in a fire balloon, becoming as it sailed away every kind of emancipating flame:

> A watch light by the patriot's lonely tomb,
> A ray of courage to the opprest and poor,
> A spark, tho' gleaming on the hovel's hearth,
> Which thro' the tyrant's gilded domes shall roar,
> A beacon in the darkness of the Earth,
> A Sun . . .

Shelley's seals in 1813 bore the mottoes 'TRUTH' and 'LIBERTY', the best of the fire-words.

The pragmatic reformer, the stirrer of minds and the enthusiast for associations were only three aspects of his political self. There was always another, burning, waiting, for the moment when other means seemed hopeless. His writings were meant to start destroying and purifying fires, the words searing individually into minds and hearts and igniting, he hoped, a roaring chain reaction. He imagined them – him – as 'one light flame' in a Norwegian forest, disregarded and trampled underfoot, snaking low among the brambles to set off a sudden conflagration among the lofty trees. Hunt saw him as one of Milton's rebel angels, holding a 'reed tipt with fire', about to unloose Satan's whole artillery against the host of Heaven.

Fire, of course, sometimes took the other side. In the back kitchen of Munday & Slatter's Printing Office, in Oxford High Street, it had consumed in mid–February 1811 almost every copy of *The Necessity of Atheism*. Shelley's 'little tract', one foolscap sheet folded in octavo and priced at sixpence, offered no resistance. Flames gnawed at 'truth', 'testimony', 'probability' and 'miracles', his elegant sentences falling to black flakes; fire licked and devoured his paragraphs on irrational belief in God. Yet if he believed in the survival of seeds of 'unextinguishable' thought, all might not be lost.

The duty of fearless enlighteners might go far beyond the writing of words. To 'produce immediate pain or disorder for the sake of future benefit' was, he believed, 'consonant . . . with the purest religion and philosophy'. He had embraced, and indeed forced on Miss Hitchener and Mary and Claire, the creed of the Illuminists, the secret Jacobin society whose code of liberty and equality was, if necessary, savagely destructive. In much this guise, Peacock had painted him as the half-mad Scythrop Glowry in *Nightmare Abbey*, 'a burnt child' – burnt by love – who stalked through the gloomy ancestral halls in a striped calico dressing gown. Scythrop was the author of a treatise called *Philosophical Gas; or, a Project for a General Illumination of the Human Mind*. In that great work, Peacock wrote,

> his meanings were carefully wrapped up in the monk's hood of transcendental technology, but filled with matter deep and dangerous, which he thought would set the whole nation in a ferment; and he awaited the result in awful expectation, as a miner who has fired a train awaits the explosion of a rock.

Shelley liked Scythrop and delighted to resemble him, but both the enlightenment and the pyrotechnics were seriously meant. In deepest Cuckfield he had 'illuminated' his uncle, making him 'warm', with *The Necessity of Atheism*. In Horsham, Keswick and Kentish Town he argued so violently against religion, 'savage and young-eyed' as Hunt described him, that his victims were traumatised and children were sent upstairs.

In 1814 he dreamed of holier warfare. He would come, an Assassin, from the murmuring valley of Bethzatanai to the slavish, corrupted city. There he would see evil for the first time with his pure, impatient eyes. Still charged with spiritual beauty, but now faced with priests, kings and lawyers, he would think these 'holy liars and parasites' mere phantasms of disordered minds, 'dreamy nothings' needing to be destroyed. And he would kill them. Pitilessly, righteously, he would drag them screaming from their beds, 'that the green and many-legged monsters

325

of the slimy grave might eat off at their leisure the lineaments of rooted malignity and detested cunning'. His 'saviour arm' would rescue the world by destroying the oppressors it imagined; his wildcat track through the city would be livid with their blood. And though ordinary men might judge him as 'among the vilest and most atrocious criminals', their opprobrium would not touch him. He would be 'secure and self-enshrined in the magnificence and pre-eminence of his conceptions, spotless as the light of heaven'.

Yet, Shelley also drew back from assassination. His hand gripped the dagger, he wrote in 1812, but his heart discarded it. Violence and revenge were oppressors' tools, a last resort only against injustice. Instead his hero-selves, armed simply with pity and 'the Spirit that lifts the slave before his Lord', fearlessly stood up to tyrants and rejected retribution. As Laon, Shelley had even stopped his revolutionist brothers from killing the tyrant's soldiers, flinging his arm before 'the mortal spear', shouting that they should forgive. The steel point tore his flesh; blood gushed out; he smiled, and yelled 'Flow thus!' He would give blood and life willingly, rather than practise hate.

In the same mode, at the end of his furious, desperate cursing of Lord Chancellor Eldon for removing his children by Harriet, Shelley grew calm. He did not hate him, for scorn and sneers and 'false cant' were Eldon's own weapons. He would not cry, for Eldon himself could weep tears like a crocodile, tears so hard that they smashed out the brains of those he purported to pity. Instead, almost shockingly, Shelley's last words wished him well.

He could be dangerous nonetheless. He had always been. His speech in Dublin in 1812 had been reported by spies to Sidmouth, the Home Secretary; once the Irish pamphlets were impounded, Sidmouth ordered him kept under observation, and told the Postmaster-General to compile a list of his correspondents. But Shelley's pamphlets did not tell half of what he believed, then or later. His letters made it plainer. 'The system of society as it exists at present', he told Hunt in 1820, 'must be over-thrown from the foundations.' His political writings, too, darkening with the dangers and repressions of the English situation after Peterloo, increasingly acknowledged that 'the last resort of resistance is undoubtedly insurrection'. In exile he still imagined his movements spied on and his letters read, as a patent threat to the state.

At times he called himself a democrat, playing delightedly with the dangerous word. He shouted once, into the face of a gentleman in Hampstead who would not help him shelter a sick woman on a winter's night, that if ever a 'convulsion' came to England, which was 'very prob-able', 'you will have your house . . . burnt over your head!' The shaken gentleman, dismissing his conduct as 'extraordinary', fled into his warm, well-lit villa; Shelley raged outside, his eyes wild and his breath smoking in the icy air, plainly intending to be the first to throw flaming brands through the windows.

As a 'republican', too, he meant that word to carry its full revolu-tionary charge. ('You know', he told Hunt, 'my passion for a republic, or any thing which approaches it.') Lulls in conversation or *longueurs* on coach journeys might be broken by Shelley, crouched on the floor, declaiming his favourite seditious lines from Shakespeare's *Richard II*:

> For God's sake, let us sit upon the ground,
> And tell sad stories of the death of kings!

An old woman in a coach once, terrified by this performance, called for the guard. Shelley, gleefully retelling the tale, would call for him too, shrieking and shrilling from the nearest flung-open window: 'Guard! Guard!'

No one came. He hoped for that. His longer poems imagined a world without officialdom or restraints, in which each man's pure conscience was his only ruler. ('Conscience', he had written in 1812, 'is a Government before which all others sink into nothingness.') This reckless indifference was not lost on readers, as John Taylor Coleridge indicated in his review of *The Revolt of Islam* for the *Quarterly*:

> Mr Shelley would abrogate our laws . . . he would abolish the right of property . . . he would overthrow the constitution . . . he would pull down our churches, level our Establishment, and burn our bibles . . .

Shelley in his fervour went much further than Paine, who envisaged only kings and nobles disappearing. He spotted crisis after crisis in England and Europe that might crush the 'evil' and 'perversion' of all present systems of government. With fierce joy, he supposed that 'we shall soon have to fight in England' and foresaw 'unimagined change'. A ring gleamed on his finger with a motto in Italian, *Il buon tempo verra*, good times will come. But not soon enough.

'The Sacred fire' would be his accomplice, raging and cleansing. In October 1814 he had signed himself off as Typhon, an Earth-born monster of Aeschylus's *Prometheus Bound*, withering up his publisher for revealing his address to his creditors: 'hissing out murder with horrid jaws, while from his eyes lighted a hideous glare, as though he would storm the sovereignty of Zeus'. In revenge, Zeus shivered Typhon to ashes with a lightning bolt; but the Shelley-monster, dormant or supposed dead, could still threaten him with 'rivers of fire' and 'hot jets of appalling, fire-breathing surge'. In Shelley's own *Prometheus Unbound* Zeus-Jupiter, surveying his cowed kingdom of the world, saw the same:

>   alone
> The soul of man, like unextinguished fire,
> Yet burns towards heaven with fierce reproach, and doubt,
> And lamentation, and reluctant prayer,
> Hurling up insurrection . . .

'I am one of those', Shelley admitted to Hunt, talking of reform, 'whom nothing will fully satisfy.'

Yet apocalypse was distant, much more so than he often wanted. The earthquakes and volcanoes of his poems were forces of history which he could do little to hasten by himself. He was morally bound to act, but felt his weakness, even as a Poet. The populist fervour of the Spanish Revolution of 1820 ('From heart to heart, from tower to tower, o'er Spain/Scattering contagious fire into the sky') was something he could only cheer on, not push forward. In that year, too, far away from restless Naples as rebellion began, he watched volcanic vapour stream 'like the standard/ Of some aetherial host' over 'oracular' woods, but could add only his faint air-voice to theirs. In December 1818 he had ridden by mule up Vesuvius with the mountain in slight eruption, hearing a river of lava creep crackling forward, watching that fire, as night closed in, turn into radiant red streams and cataracts, '& in the midst from the column of bituminous smoke shot up into the sky, fell the vast masses of rock white with the light of their intense heat, leaving behind them thro the dark vapour, trains of splendour'. But this premonition of the irresistible convulsion of the Earth left him racked with pain and aghast.

Above those volcanoes Shelley's night sky, more imagined than seen, swarmed with harbinger comets. He could be one, good or bad, wrecking or enlightening, according to taste. A passing comet, so Davy said, had destroyed the prehistoric behemoths. Shelley put a god in it, his gold hair flying, screaming 'Be not!' In a notebook of 1820–21 a tiny comet

– on closer inspection a penis and balls, retreating fast into space –
pissed a furious inky trail across his attempts, useless attempts, to write
lines for a memorial for William's grave. He had begun to write of his
other lost children, and retribution, and hate.

'Be not!' And like my words they were no more.

Grounded again, he faced the practical question of how he, a fighter,
might be ready when the moment came. He was not unarmed. From
boyhood he had taken firearms on walks, firing both at targets and
explicitly to kill. At Oxford a pair of duelling pistols went on every
outing, though they were handled with 'such inconceivable careless-
ness', Hogg said, that he sometimes removed, as a precaution, the powder
flask or flints. (Favourite targets were envelopes from Field Place, bearing
Shelley's father's parliamentary franks.) Young Thornton Hunt was
allowed to admire the pistols in their case as they were packed for Italy;
and in the 'Ode to Liberty' notebook of 1820 a pistol, evidently lying
on the open page, was drawn round carefully with ink and pencil.

The guns came out regularly, and they came out quickly. Shelley was
always 'much too ready' with his pistols, said Henry Reveley: bran-
dishing his weapon to scare away a gang of armed Italian peasants,
chasing his servant Giuseppe at gunpoint into the garden, threatening
to shoot the cur that ripped his new blue coat in Oxford. (He contented
himself, on that occasion, with furiously kicking the dog in the throat.)
In Wales he shot sick sheep, without permission, to free them from the
horrors of their scabbed and maggoty bodies. In Keswick and Marlow
his practice terrified the neighbours. Formal duels he seemed to laugh
away, but they were offered to him as to a man constantly prepared to
fire. Habit had made him a good shot, with a steady hand, a rapid aim
and a keen eye; he was often the best at Byron's shooting afternoons
in the vineyards outside Pisa, squarely hitting the pumpkin or the five-
paul piece stuck in a cane, even though, Byron said, 'he is thinking of
metaphysics rather than of firing'.

Yet, in the end, Shelley's revolution would not be made with guns.
None of his heroes handled one, since they moved in no 'real' or modern
world but in a universe idealised and set apart from time. They would
no sooner have fired a pistol than looked at a pocket watch or travelled by steam. By 1815 in any case, according to Mary, Shelley had
'begun to feel that the time for action was not ripe in England, and

329

that the pen was the only instrument wherewith to prepare the way for better things'.

His pen, therefore, was his fire-weapon. He traced it in one notebook as he drew round his gun, making sure his instrument was sharp. At other times, too frantic to trim, re-cut or dip his quill, he versified until the nib was scratching and clawing at the paper. Writing violently, he meant to have violent effect. In *The Revolt of Islam* his idyll of incest was intended, like a loud report, 'to startle the reader from the trance of ordinary life'. When writing *Adonais* for Keats, he dipped his pen 'in consuming fire for his destroyers'. His pen carried his imaginings, glowing and dangerous: again, the reed tipped with flame, or the hollow stem in which Prometheus, his hero, had first stolen fire from the gods.

★ ★ ★

After that sly theft, Prometheus had founded all the human arts that were most precious to Shelley. Language and words; music and prophetic song; the art of building in columns to admit the air, and the science of navigation by the stars. Each talent forged by Prometheus was touched by the leaping life of imagination, the fire he had stolen, approaching the divine. He was, Shelley wrote in 1819, in his preface to his greatest poem, 'the type of the highest perfection of moral and intellectual nature, impelled by the purest and truest motives to the best and noblest ends'. And though a god, rather than a man – and a Titan at that, one of the defeated race of Earth-born gods of lightning and storms – he was Shelley's exemplar.

Naturally the Olympian gods attacked him. For giving fire and liberty to men in that thin, charged reed, Jupiter had Prometheus chained to an icy ravine in the Caucasus. (Shelley, crossing the Echelles to Chambéry in March 1818, judged he saw the very scene in the 'vast rifts and caverns' and the 'walls of toppling rocks' that loomed above his carriage.) An eagle came to feed each day on Prometheus's heart; earthquakes tore open his wounds, and storms tormented him. Furies, too, mocked and infested him, the devil-aspect of the aetherial spirits who touched him – as they touched Shelley – with virtue and delight.

> [Then] we will be dread thought beneath thy brain,
> And foul desire round thine astonished heart,

330

> And blood within thy labyrinthine veins
> Crawling like agony . . .

Yet the Furies tortured him, as the Devil did, only because he believed in them. To look at them made him 'grow like what I contemplate,/ And laugh and stare in loathsome sympathy'. To curse these creatures, as he had once cursed Jupiter, was to give them life.

In Aeschylus's fragment *Prometheus Bound*, from which Shelley developed his own 'lyrical drama', Prometheus had been intended eventually to reach a pact with Jupiter. Shelley rejected 'a catastrophe so feeble'. His Prometheus would make no deals with tyrants. Instead, defiantly suffering, he would retract his anger against him, just as Shelley, saying 'I hate thee not', had withdrawn his curse on Lord Eldon. By pitying and forgiving him, he would also vanquish him.

Jupiter's phantasm, therefore, was summoned from the deep. He appeared in his robes of dark purple with his golden sceptre gripped in his hand, crying out in Prometheus's voice the curse the Titan had placed on him. Prometheus took the words back, saying 'It doth repent me.' He would purify the world, as Shelley meant to and as all men could do, by destroying with the power of love his own demons first.

His pity, he was reminded, might not be understood. His doctrine of loving enemies might be perverted, as Christ's had been. Once Prometheus had withdrawn his curse the Furies showed him Christ on the cross, despairing over a world torn apart by religion and poisoned by distortions of his words. The cross shook; Christ's bloody fingers, curled round the nails, jerked in the spasms of death. Horrified, drawn in too near, Prometheus wished 'the youth' peace. Shelley, swallowing his own disgust, implicitly did the same.

By moments he still hated the 'Galilean serpent'; but he could stomach his name, even revere it, once the trappings of established Christianity had been stripped away. Christ as the Son of God, he had written in 1812, was 'a hypocritical Daemon'. Christ as a man, on the other hand,

> stands in the foremost list of those true heroes who have died in the glorious martyrdom of liberty, and have braved torture, contempt, and poverty in the cause of suffering humanity.

Besides, Shelley noted later,

He refuses he despises pardon. he exults in the torturing flames & the insolent mockery of the oppressor. It is a triumph to him beyond all triumphs that the multitude accumulate scorn & execration on his head solely because his heart has known no measure in the love it bore them, & because the zeal which dragged him to his torments is so pure & ardent that it can make their very hatred sweet.—

This 'J.C.' Shelley paired with Socrates, an outcast from the state, and with more recent heroes. Christ's exhortation to love enemies was 'Magnificent Jacobinism . . . better than any where else', and Christ himself 'that great Reformer' who had heard the 'still, sad music of humanity', in Wordsworth's phrase, in the verses of Ecclesiastes and the Book of Job. In the 'Prologue' to *Hellas*, Christ pleaded with God the Father to promote the revolution in Greece. At times Shelley or his hero-selves became consciously Christ-like, as when Laon appealed for the life of the fallen tyrant of the Golden City until the crowd, moved by the power of good, wept and kissed his feet. Shelley felt his own head twined with pain-thorns, his tears thick as blood and his body wrapped in oiled linen, like Christ's before the resurrection. His Muse met him once, a Stranger,

> and murmured: 'Who art thou?'
> He answered not, but with a sudden hand
> Made bare his branded and ensanguined brow,
> Which was like Cain's or Christ's—oh! that it should be so!

Analysing Luke 18, where Jesus foretold that he would be delivered to the Gentiles, mocked, spat upon and killed, Shelley noted lightly: 'His prophesy [*sic*] of his death I could prophesy mine'. Years after it, perhaps, men might exalt him too 'to a divinity' for his heresies and his courage.

'*My* golden age', he had once told Miss Hitchener, proudly, 'is when the present potence will become omnipotence: this will be the millenium of Xtians.' And at that point, extraordinary as it seemed, he and Prometheus and Christ might clasp their bloodstained hands as if they were brothers.

Meanwhile, in the third act of Shelley's drama, the world changed. Evil, ugliness and falsehood drained away; the poisonous and malicious became beautiful; men and women walked freely in sincerity and sexual 'unreserve'. As in *Queen Mab* – his dreams unchanging since – the Earth became 'Of purest spirits a pure dwelling place,/Symphonious with the planetary spheres'. Even the frozen oceans of the moon flowed free, trees grew there and birds flew, as the realm of cold reason was opened to the operations of Love.

Shelley's vision was vast, his time-span aeons and his agent of transformation red floods of volcanic fire. But he saw the first signs of change already. Lightning was flashing from 'the cloud of mind' and soon the storm must break. 'The equilibrium between institutions and opinions', he wrote, 'is now restoring, or is about to be restored.' The year 1819 seemed to mark the brink of revolution in England, the moment of Shelley's hardest pushing for moral self-awareness and political change. And this was his most vital contribution.

Prometheus, he felt then, was 'the most perfect of my productions', 'the best thing I ever wrote'. He wanted it published as soon as Ollier had it, with no delay. Few might read it, fewer still might understand it (he was resigned to that, it was 'no more than 5 or 6 persons' he had written for), but he had poured into it all his hopes for the revolutionary renewal of the world. Had this been widely recognised, he knew, it would have been seized and burned as *Swellfoot the Tyrant* was the next year, the agents from the Society for the Suppression of Vice arriving swiftly on the publisher's doorstep to remove the royal satire to the bonfire. Even Hunt, one of the braver souls, might not have touched *Prometheus*, just as he drew back from the political heat of *The Mask of Anarchy* and *Peter Bell the Third*.

Shelley meant to write explanatory notes for his drama, but never did. Instead he showed particular anxiety for the proofs as they went through the press, fretting about revisions that he, in Italy, might not see and demanding 'constant information'. Despite his efforts, the 1820 printing was full of errors 'destructive of the sense'. But at least he had put his 'Ode to the West Wind' in the same volume, apocalypse and apocalypse-bringer bound up explosively together. Thrillingly, a little later, he imagined his Poet's sentence: 'guilty death'.

With luck, he would deserve it. For he was showing what man, untrammelled, had the power to do. Deliberately – and necessarily, since he was still a mortal trying to see, trying to write – he was leaving that picture only half described, so that readers would sense no limits there. First, they would be freed from all constraints social and political:

> The loathsome mask has fallen, the man remains
> Sceptreless, free, uncircumscribed, but man

> Equal, unclassed, tribeless, and nationless,
> Exempt from awe, worship, degree, the king
> Over himself . . .

And this was only the beginning. Shelley then dared man's true, rediscovered self – 'Surpassing Spirit!' as Queen Mab had cried, like a challenge, to Ianthe – to attempt a life that was 'unresting', 'unkindled', 'uncharted', 'untasted', 'unexhausted'. He offered a sphere of action that was 'wordless', 'imageless', 'undelaying', 'unascended', 'unveiled'. Only negatives could define this state of 'unimagined' being. Shelley too, still subject to death and mutability, could go no further. But the triggering impulse – that first, simple movement of selfless pity that made everything permissible and possible – was Love.

Love, then, was his weapon. It could hurt, like Eros-arrows searing into the heart, or like the death-thrust of Shelley's Assassins, whose every act was performed in its uncompromising glow. Its mandate could be unsparing, as it had been with him. Hope, self-esteem, endurance, Shelley could also invoke. But Love was subversion, from the very moment that desire, or magnetic attraction, caused the atoms to swerve defiantly aside. Love was emphatic and, once unshakeably linked to will, not only perturbing but invincible. In Shelley's awakened world it would be followed without question, each man and woman turning outwards from the self to the other, with Love flowing like electric current through their clasped, determined hands.

> Man, oh, not men! A chain of linkèd thought
> Of love and might to be divided not,
> Compelling the elements with adamantine stress—

This came close to his image of the same year, from *The Mask of Anarchy*, in which he strove to encourage in England the liberation movements that were rising in Naples and Spain and Greece. He imagined another Peterloo, in which the people would stand with folded arms in dauntless defiance of armed soldiers (or, in *A Philosophical View of Reform*, of 'the fire of the artillery, and . . . the bayonets of the charging battalions'). By gazing on evil in love, they became stronger. They could turn it to good. They would be martyred, but their courage would spur fervent imitation; the slaughter of one crowd would inspire resistance in the next, until a great wave of humanity would surge against injustice.

Rise like Lions after slumber
In unvanquishable number—
Shake your chains to earth like dew
Which in sleep had fallen on you—
Ye are many—they are few.

Shelley was mustering his sun-images: the dew fell, the lions arose.

Love, he insisted, was the law of life. Creation, motion, gravitation, magnetism, heat and electricity were all that force. He tried at times not to call it a law, with all law's connotations of thrones and domination: to live as if 'to love and live/ Be one' was his ideal, a state not of compulsion but of tenderness and zeal. 'The flame/ Of consentaneous love' was another thought, not imposed but instinctively agreed to, like the meeting lips of lovers. Love was infinite, unsatiated, ever divisible and inexhaustible; to share and divide it (as with Harriet, Mary, Claire, Emilia, Jane) was merely to increase it. In his new Promethean world, growing towards perfection, Love would be 'common as light', and light itself.

And Love was free. Love was Liberty, Liberty Love, in their highest expression one power without distinction. In Shelley's dreams man's mind, once liberated, turned naturally to the truth and light it reflected, and government withered away in sweet anarchy as each human spirit behaved the way it should. This was what had been intended for man and woman from the beginning: omnipotence of mind and will, bringing all hopes and visions into being.

He was not such an optimist, or a fool, to believe that this would last. Nothing on Earth lasted. History moved in inexorable cycles. Man's condition, though not inherently sinful, was still fallen and prey to mutability: 'unwilling dross' that could not persevere in visionary life. Prometheus would become Jupiter again. 'Infectious gloom' would spread back across the Earth, and Shelley's own demons would reassume their dominion in his heart. The revolution of the Golden City in *The Revolt of Islam*, led by Laon and Cythna as himself and Love, had failed and had been crushed by tyrant armies; his apotheosis, and hers, was in a realm of the spirit far away from men.

In *The Triumph of Life*, pausing by the dusty road as Life's chariot passed, he saw the ghost of Napoleon chained to it, his chin sunk on his breast:

And much I grieved to think how power & will
In opposition rule our mortal day—

And why God made irreconcilable
Good & the means of good . . .

The best he could predict for Earth, as Claire remembered it, was 'almost perfection'. The worst he saw with melancholy clarity: 'this dark scheme of things finishing in unfruitful death'.

Yet Shelley ended *Prometheus Unbound* with a paean to optimism. Demogorgon, the great 'gloom' itself, exhorted men 'to hope till Hope creates/ From its own wreck the thing it contemplates'. This was Shelley's 'beautiful idealism', his worked example of the power of Mind converted to Love, no matter for how brief a time. Man contained this potential, 'power in thought . . . as the tree within the seed', and with it a force for life and progress impossible even to guess at. Like some extraordinary chemical experiment, it asked only to be tried.

Those who were unfettered in Love proclaimed its power quite naturally. In Bishopsgate in 1816, as he and Mary walked in the fields at sunset, Mary's embrace of free love with him, her 'unreserve of mingled being', appeared to gild every object around her: clouds, woods, 'the points/ Of the far level grass'. For Love's force was not only moral or political. Human existence itself might be altered and overcome. Love seemed to dissolve the material particles of the body, leaving only 'One soul of interwoven flame'. This was what Shelley glimpsed and felt and what he strangely, dangerously described – as well as the burning down of houses, or the purging of the world by red volcanic fire. He made Love his law, and man's entire liberation.

⋆   ⋆   ⋆

The first phase of Promethean reform necessarily returned to the realm of alchemy. Man had to 'make bare the secrets of the Earth's deep heart'. Shelley imagined how it might be done, his Spirit of the Earth boring brightly down through the mud, rock and filth.

And from a star upon its forehead, shoot,
Like swords of azure fire, or golden spears . . .
Vast beams like spokes of some invisible wheel
Which whirl as the orb whirls, swifter than thought,

336

Filling the abyss with sun-like lightenings,
And perpendicular now, and now transverse,
Pierce the dark soil . . .

Once man had followed this path, and exploited it,

The lightning is his slave; heaven's utmost deep
Gives up her stars, and like a flock of sheep,
They pass before his eye, are numbered, and roll on!
The tempest is his steed, he strides the air;
And the abyss shouts from her depth laid bare,
Heaven, hast thou secrets? Man unveils me; I have none.

Yet lifting the veil was still hazardous. It might not be possible to glimpse the secrets of life, and survive. From at least the age of eighteen Shelley had felt the exulting danger of drawing secrets from 'the purest of fountains', as he meant to. Treading close to the source, he could sense a power 'more dreadful than death' barring his way:

They came to the fountain to draw from its stream
Waves too poisonously lovely for mortals to see;
They basked for awhile in the love-darting beam
Then perished—and perished like me . . .

Originally these waves had been 'too pure, too celestial' and silver, like Beauty's shadow. Eagerly, Shelley had bathed there. But there was also deadliness in them.

If he did not die by water, the seeker would die by fire. In Brockden Brown's *Wieland*, Shelley's favourite novel, spontaneous combustion killed the hero's father as he invoked mysterious forces in his temple–summerhouse. In Shelley's own *Queen Mab* an atheist much like himself was led to the stake, undaunted and quietly smiling. At the climax of *The Revolt of Islam* Laon and Cythna lay still, in peaceful resignation, on a giant pyre from which the flames rose steadily around them. Their followers, murmuring 'Liberty!', had lain down in the fire already. To burn would be to know what lay on the other side of death.

By 1821, when he was translating Calderón's *El mágico prodigioso* and Goethe's *Faust*, Shelley was in the almost daily company of alchemists and seekers not unlike himself. Like Calderón's hero Cyprian he would sit with his books in the 'intricate wild wilderness', desperate to know

337

the nature of God and debating with the Devil. Cyprian surrendered, offering his soul to the worst *genio* of Hell in exchange for a wand, powers, and the body of the woman he loved. But unwrapping her cloak, like Shelley with his own shade, he found Death there.

Faust too, alone in his study, surrounded by chemical equipment and with the sign of the Macrocosm displayed on the page before him, longed to delve into the mysteries of existence. As he gazed on his book the lamp faded, and red beams began to glow around him. He felt the Spirit and invoked it; a vivid flame flashed. Shelley in 1815, barely knowing German, flew to translate the scene into primitive, incantatory words.

> *The Spirit appears in the flame.*
> *Spirit.* Who calls me?
> *Faust.* (*turning away*) Horrible sight! . . . Alas! I cannot endure thee!
> *Spirit.* Thou didst implore earnestly me to see, my voice to hear, my countenance to behold. Me bent thy mighty soul-prayer: here am I. What pitiful terror seizes superman you? Where is of thy soul the flame? Where is the breast which a world in itself contains . . .? What art thou, Faust? . . .
> *Faust.* Shall I thee, Image of Fire, propitiate? I am, I am Faust—I am thy likeness!

The Spirit vanished. Faust went on searching, with Shelley beside him, now aware of his force as fire. He imagined himself soaring, the world at his feet, drinking the sun's 'everlasting light'. To be a mere worm any more, dragging in the dust, living in his 'moth-world', was unbearable. In despair, he toyed with drinking a 'certain brown juice' that offered beatitude or nothingness. When the demon Mephistopheles appeared, disguised as a travelling student, Faust eagerly debated natural philosophy with him. But this was another fire creature, red-capped and red-crested, delighting in serpent shapes – and, again, Faust's likeness. In Retzsch's etchings the two were almost identical, the devil a horned and sneering version of the man. Faust's soul was pledged to him; the price of his knowledge was death, or self-destruction.

As he read *Faust* 'over and over again' in the spring of 1822, Shelley could feel that character fusing with his own. His gloom deepened and his ideas came more rapidly, he told a friend, shot through with 'despair & a scorn of the narrow good we can attain in our present state.' He was sure those feelings showed in *Adonais* and *Hellas*; yet his own most

Faustian scene came in *The Triumph of Life*, his last, unfinished poem. There he met the shade of Rousseau on the road, and heard the story of his harrowing quest for true knowledge of himself. Rousseau had challenged 'a Shape all light' to tell him 'whence I came, and where I am, and why'.

These were Shelley's own eternal questions. He too could attempt to ask them of the dazzling Shape before him. She had come from the earthly sun 'as if she were the dawn', dew-scattering and rainbow-scarved, yet this was Beauty's mutable and mortal side, deceiving as daylight. She would offer him, as she had offered Rousseau, a crystal glass filled with 'bright Nepenthe', the herb of oblivion. And he would sip, and forget. When he had first woken on that April morning, he had been seeing visions of gold and emerald fire that came from another world. But these had already been shattered as the Shape approached him:

> 'All that was, seemed as if it had been not—
> As if the gazer's mind was strewn beneath
>   Her feet like embers, & she, thought by thought,
>
> 'Trampled its fires into the dust of death . . .'

As long as Earth held him, Shelley could only be tricked and abused like this. To know truly, as to be reborn, required Death first. In *Adonais*, he stated it categorically:

>   Die,
> If thou wouldst be with that which thou dost seek!
> Follow where all is fled!

The physical world might show man its every secret, the elements whirling at his command, as Faust and Cyprian had expected. But Rousseau's questions – Shelley's questions – were less easily answered. As Shelley wrote in his *Defence of Poetry*, for all the scientific and economic knowledge of the age, 'we want the creative faculty to imagine that which we know; we want the generous impulse to act that which we imagine; we want the poetry of life'. Selfishness, rather than Love, had become the ruling principle. As man enlarged his empire over the external world by money and war, reason and commerce, so he knew less and less of the internal one; 'and man, having enslaved the elements, remains himself a slave'.

In the first draft of the last act of *Prometheus Unbound*, the 'World within the World' tore off its veil and cried out that it had no secrets left from man. But Shelley then crossed that out, wrote 'Abyss' and underlined it strongly. The world within was still veiled. And Heaven made no reply to the taunts of the Abyss.

3
Being

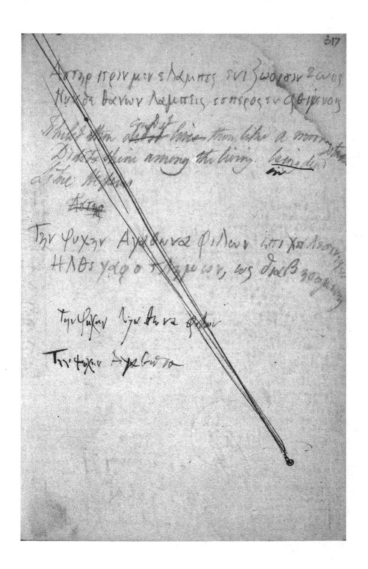

At school he was remembered exulting in the stars, as though they were lamps hung in the heavens solely for his delight. He already envisaged them strewn, in their multitudes, through a universe infinitely vast. Dr Walker's lectures evoked a time when men would travel through rivers of stars — single, double, green, blue, red, violet — in a dizzying plurality of worlds, each one covered with seas and hills and inhabited by organised life. They would find stars so distant that their light had never reached the Earth since creation. 'How much too big is this idea', the old scientist cried, 'for the human imagination!'

But not for Shelley's. Four or five years later he was there, journeying in Queen Mab's chariot through 'an immense concave,/ Radiant with million constellations, tinged/ With shades of infinite colour, / And semicircled with a belt / Flashing incessant meteors.' He moved higher and faster, systems and spheres revolving round him, unclouded sunlight breaking and sparking from his path, until he was jostled among a storm of stars.

> It was a sight of wonder: some
> Were hornèd like the crescent moon;
> Some shed a mild and silver beam
> Like Hesperus o'er the western sea;
> Some dashed athwart with trains of flame,
> Like worlds to death and ruin driven;
> Some shone like suns, and, as the chariot passed,
> Eclipsed all other light.

Walker had also suggested, to Shelley's delight, that men as spirits might make a grand tour through the heavens, progressing from planet to planet as boys passed from class to class, until they became gods.

From Herschel's observations and Nicholson's *Encyclopedia* Shelley also knew the physics of stars: how the solar system had originated in the cooling and contracting of a gaseous nebula; how nebulae, observed through proper telescopes, resolved from milky white confusion into stars; how 'inconceivably' far away the fixed stars were. (Nicholson told him the distance of Sirius from the Earth: at least 54, 224, 000,000,000 miles, calculating by the speed of light.) Those stars, though no more than 'little whitish specks of light', Shelley wrote, 'are supposed to be suns, each of them the centre of a system like ours'. Thus the Earth's sun, if he flew out high and far enough, would appear as another such pinprick, infinitesimally small.

In his student days, full of Pliny and the ancient astronomers, he imagined a sky map wriggling with the beasts of the constellations: star-studded manes and claws, fiery-scaled fish, fire-bristling bears, water poured sparkling from celestial urns. Hogg, only half cynically, thought his friend looked 'homewards' through them. All his life Shelley longed for night to come, bringing dreams and visions and reversing the 'sick', lurid heaviness of noon, 'this false Sun', so that the stars shone.

> Swiftly walk o'er the western wave,
>   Spirit of night!
> Out of the misty eastern cave
> Where, all the long and lone daylight
> Thou wovest dreams of joy and fear,
> Which make thee terrible and dear,
>   Swift be thy flight!

From Bagni di Lucca in 1818 he reported his sightings. 'The nights are for ever serene, and we see a star in the east at sunset—I think it is Jupiter—almost as fine as Venus was last summer; but it wants a certain silver and aerial radiance, and soft yet piercing splendour'. In Rome the next spring he admired 'radiant Orion' through the columns of the

Temple of Saturn, and noted how the modern buildings of the Capitol softened at sunset and star-rise. He loved to walk by starlight, alone with the constellations. Mary said he knew all their names. From his 24th birthday, in August 1816, he could observe them through a telescope made of ivory and brass: Mary's present to him, together with a fire balloon that flared and fell too fast.

The stars did not move. Their brightness was invariable, but sometimes the dross of earth and air obscured them. Intermediating clouds became 'star-inwoven', as if their shining burden were tangled in the mesh of the sky. Beauty, too, the Spirit Shelley pursued, was a star seen faintly through clouds: 'air-dissolvèd' and, like a goddess, filling the sky with fragrance interfused with light.

Despair was to lose sight of them. 'What a thing it would be', Shelley remarked to Byron once, as they gazed at the Alps across Lake Geneva, 'if all were involved in darkness at this moment, the sun and the stars to go out. How terrible the idea!' In 1816 the sky, heavy with dust from the eruption of Tambora in distant Indonesia, was sodden and overcast all summer. But four years later a fragment showed that the thought still haunted him.

> What if the suns & stars & Earth
> Which seem exempt frm death & birth—
> If all things brightest, firmest, best
> Are ~~but deciets~~
>   Were ~~visions of~~
>   Shadows of a ~~brighter~~

The brightness he left unimaginable, but the dark was not. Earth's false light faded fast. By 1814 his life with Harriet was a gloom completely unilluminated; four years later he was in that state again despite his partnership with Mary, once 'the best of living beings'. The world itself struggled in the despairing aftermath of a great revolution that had failed. He wrote of midnight darkness made deeper by 'silent lightning', of smothered hearths and black drapes falling from the sky. One star would have saved him: Love or hope, the pilot by the mast.

Through his notebooks, carelessly, he drew stars: needle-lines clustered like asterisks, single or in twos and threes. He joined their points into diamonds, triangles, crystals and concentric circles. They hung in the empty sky of the page, black on white, reversed out. His words sometimes prompted them; sometimes they simply appeared, unannounced, as if observing.

His flowers, too, were stars. He sketched narcissi as stars on the stalk, their petals spiky above the water in which their reflections shone. Up and down his margins, or in any odd space, bursts of foliage sparkled like firecrackers. On the cover of one notebook the pattern of a spiralling nebula, or the seed-threads of wild clematis, was scratched with dividers or compass points delicately into the vellum. The mimosa, himself, 'like the earliest star', had leaves as sharp as rays.

In his poems, daisies were 'constellated' and 'pearled Arcturi of the Earth'. White canopies of hawthorn, glimpsed from his boat in the spring woods, were galaxies in the dark. All flowers could be mutable daytime mirrors of the constellations: the world as it seemed to human vision, faintly copying the world that was real.

Davy in his *Chemical Philosophy* wrote that the crumbs of meteors, 'though differing in their form and appearance from any of the bodies belonging to our earth', contained silica, magnesia, sulphur, nickel and iron. Paracelsus taught that the *limus terrae*, the primordial stuff from which man was made, was not merely dust and earth but an extract of the stars. Man's imagination, once awakened to this, could then beget 'a new star' and a new Heaven. 'The starry vault', he wrote, 'imprints itself on the inner heaven of a man.' What Shelley gazed on, Shelley was.

Above a drawing of mountains and a lake he drew stars as eyes, bright and glittering as his own. Where the eyes of Earth were bandaged or opaque, these saw, and stared at their reflections in the water. A man sailed a boat to an island through a scene of vaguely threatening attention. He watched himself. Starry eyes observed the Poet, too, in *Alastor*, shining both beside him and within him, 'in the gloom of thought',

And seemed with their serene and azure smiles
To beckon him.

★   ★   ★

In the act of making poetry, he already sensed his own fire. He had no need of stoves, galvanic machines or the trickery of Mephistopheles. His own refining agent was his poetic imagination. 'Poetry', he wrote in 1821, in terms consciously alchemical,

> turns all things to loveliness; . . . it marries exultation and horror, grief and pleasure, eternity and change; it subdues to union, under its light yoke, all irreconcilable things. It transmutes all that it touches, and every form moving within the radiance of its presence is changed by wondrous sympathy to an incarnation of the spirit which it breathes; its secret alchemy turns to potable gold the poisonous waters which flow from death through life; it strips the veil of familiarity from the world and lays bare the naked and sleeping beauty, which is the spirit of its forms . . .
> It creates anew the universe . . .

Shelley called imagination 'the Sun of life', that 'lake-reflected sun' out of which his poems came. It was also the God of those poems, he told Hunt, 'the master . . . and the Spirit by which they live and are'. Being active, it was linked to the deep and remote Cause; it contained 'eternal truths'. Being creative, it brought order to the chaos of his thoughts.

Paracelsus and Spinoza had talked of man's 'natural light', by which he might understand the divinity of God. Spinoza mentioned also – Shelley marked it – 'supernatural light', by which, prophetically, a man by special election might share in that power himself. In Shelley's *Defence of Poetry*, if reason was 'analysis and dissection', imagination was 'synthesis', 'composition' and 'primary existence'. Reason was to imagination as 'the instrument to the agent, as the body to the spirit, as the shadow to the substance': as 'cold & uncertain & borrowed light' to light itself. From that pure fire at his own centre, Shelley's way of seeing and thinking shone to the farthest horizon.

His secret boyhood readings of Paracelsus had again foreshadowed this. The old alchemist believed that man, the Microcosm of the Macrocosm, was surrounded by the universe 'as a circle surrounds one point'. In Shelley's words, *Infinity within, / Infinity without*; all visible

347

creation radiating from him and, like a bright cloak, enfolding him. He, the Poet, gathered in Truth or Beauty and sent them out again as far as his powers allowed him, now synthesised and refined by his understanding soul. He himself charged the aether with electrical impulses, those dangerous or thrilling genii of hope and thought, as well as with the gentle, animating dew that fell on receptive minds. In all this, he copied the sun; but he mirrored, like the sun itself, a Sun that was purer and higher, 'a light of paradise' neither deceiving nor obscuring by shining on the things of Earth. And with that blazing potency he embraced and filled the world.

> Clasp with thy panting soul the pendulous Earth;
> As from a centre, dart thy spirit's light
> Beyond all worlds, until its spacious might
> Satiate the void circumference: then shrink
> Even to a point within our day and night . . .

Man, Shelley wrote, was 'pre-eminently an imaginative being'. Yet few drew the astonishing moral of this. As Tasso once said, there were only two creators worthy of the name, God and poets: *non c'e in mondo chi merita nome di creatore, che Dio ed il Poeta.* Shelley called this 'proud, though sublime', and often quoted it. There might be no Creator-God in his universe, but he admitted naturally the possibility of a Mind holding in conception the landscape of the world, the colours of the atmosphere and the system of the stars, 'these things not before existing', and imaging them forth, as he could. In his drafts of *A Defence of Poetry* 'Creator' slipped into upper case, God-like, when he was thinking of his Poet-self.

As a Poet, his first duty was to shadow forth Reality; his second, to open readers' eyes to that 'wonder' within themselves. It was dangerous work, using 'electric force'; in Plato's *Republic* the man who had seen Reality was not thanked, and might be killed, for leading others to see it too. For Shelley, the challenge and the power were irresistible.

> Love is like understanding, that grows bright,
> Gazing on many truths; 'tis like thy light,
> Imagination! which from earth and sky,
> And from the depths of human fantasy,
> As from a thousand prisms and mirrors, fills

348

The Universe with glorious beams, and kills
Error, the worm, with many a sun-like arrow
Of its reverberated lightning.

A calm wide eye, carefully drawn and shaded, presided over these words
as he first wrote them. He gazed and made. Like the Spirit of God, his
imagination imposed rhythm and order, 'which may be called the beautiful and the good', on chaos.

In 'Lines written among the Euganean Hills', composed in 1818, he
described the sun-power working even in his deepest despair. He had
climbed a peak in those hills and there, standing quietly, heard the rooks
herald 'the sun's uprise majestical' over the woods. At first the birds
were grey shades in the mist, sad as his thoughts; but as the sun burst
through the eastern sky he saw them soar, on purple wings starred with
'golden rain', into the upper air. He made the birds clouds, the clouds
birds, gliding and shining down the slope of the dawn. There followed
calm, encircling him

> Till all is bright, and clear, and still,
> Round the solitary hill.

He looked out. The sun, rising, lit up the whole plain of Lombardy to
its limits, the mountains and misted air. It shone – his organising, transforming self shone – on Venice, bathing it in 'aëreal gold' and turning
it from a city of sepulchres into Apollo's altar, blazing with fire from
its obelisks and domes. He, Shelley, did this. As the sun floated up the
sky towards noon, he radiated thoughts of liberty on Venice, on Padua
and over 'all between the Po/ And the eastern Alpine snow' that lay
under Austrian tyranny. At noon, his zenith, the whole landscape of
vineyards, plains and forests,

> From the curved horizon's bound
> To the point of Heaven's profound,

lay under the calming glow of his imagination, interpenetrated by his
spirit and by 'the glory of the sky':

> Be it love, light, harmony,
> Odour, or the soul of all
> Which from Heaven like dew doth fall,

349

> Or the mind which feeds this verse
> Peopling the lone universe.

In the Euganean Hills 'the frail bark of this lone being' was, for a time, beached and forgotten. In the action of imagination, self, at last, was left behind. It was burned in the fire or lost, as he explained in *A Defence of Poetry*, in the circle of ever-expanding and sympathising love.

> The great secret of morals is love; or a going out of our own nature, and an identification of ourselves with the beautiful which exists in thought, action, or person, not our own . . . The great instrument of moral good is the imagination; and poetry administers to the effect by acting upon the cause.

Even in small, passing incidents he felt this faculty at work. Walking with Byron by Lake Geneva one evening in the summer of 1816, he watched children playing ninepins on the shore. Most were diseased or deformed; but one boy was beautiful, with 'a mixture of pride and gentleness in his eyes and lips' and with 'such exquisite grace in his mien and motions as I never before saw equalled in a child'. Perhaps, Shelley reflected, these things were scarcely possible in a boy to whom he had never spoken and who had silently taken a piece of proffered money. His imagination had breathed its own visions into him, making him an angel, just as the whole scene had been bathed in the glow of the declining sun.

When he wrote of the sun, therefore, he wrote of himself. He would not have wanted the public to know it, but they would not in any case suspect it. Almost every aspect of his 'Hymn of Apollo' was also a canticle to his own imagination, making colour and form, bringing wisdom, bringing light.

> I feed the clouds, the rainbows and the flowers
>   With their aetherial colours; the moon's globe
> And the pure stars in their eternal bowers
>   Are cinctured with my power as with a robe;
> Whatever lamps on Earth or Heaven may shine
> Are portions of one spirit; which is mine.
>   . . .
> I am the eye with which the Universe
>   Beholds itself, and knows it is divine

Know thyself, the dictum of the Oracle at Delphi, was the mes[sage?] god both beyond and within. Apollo, the sun, was the ey[e?] the eye was also Shelley, staring like a totem out of his notebo[ok?] the divine Creator of the world around him. The divinity withi[n?] divinity without met, and were the same.

★   ★   ★

No fire intrigued him more than the one that was himself. He glimpsed it in others' eyes, a taper or a flame, 'far/ Like the light of an unmeasured star'. That light, in the case of lovers, 'should kindle at once & mix & melt into our own'. He felt it alive and warm, sometimes burning, on his own lips as they kissed another's. In lovemaking it seemed to consume him as if his whole self were leaping, pervading fire. At times he felt it − felt himself − stop, thrill and dissolve into the scene before him, limitless, containing the horizon. Under music's spell he sensed himself hovering at the borders of his body, feathered brightness impatient to leave. At times, with a start, he knew the shining shadow at his shoulder as his own: *The phantom is beside thee whom thou seekest.*

Doubt and waver as he might, this self he could rely on, calm, secure and pure. While his body was a mere machine, struggling towards the grave, his soul-self

> aspires to Heaven,
> Pants for its sempiternal heritage,
> And ever-changing, ever-rising still,
> Wantons in endless being.

The distinction was inevitable. In his young materialist moods he had tried not to draw it, lamenting 'the shocking absurdities' of making soul and body distinct, and 'its fatal consequences in morals'. He imagined the soul as 'intellectual particles', the finest possible, or as some kind of '*stuff*' of a higher and nobler sort. But these theories, largely drawn from Lucretius, did not take him far. Increasingly his devotion to Plato led him to see the soul as a separate essence, 'bolted' or 'glued' to the body, while everything around it obscured its light and hastened towards decay.

Plato in the *Phaedo* pictured the soul as a charioteer driving two winged horses, one nobly taking the rein, one plunging in confused disobedience. (Shelley was to drive like this in Naples, in a light *calesso*

PTO 351

with one horse harnessed and one outside the off-shaft, almost free, achieving wild speeds that brought the blood surging to his cheeks.) Diogenes Laertius concluded that Plato's soul was tripartite, with Reason in the head, Passion in the heart and Appetite in the belly, and that it enclosed the body in two circles, the circle of the Same and the circle of the Other, 'whereby he means that the motion of the soul is the motion of the universe together with the revolutions of the planets'.

As a student Shelley marked this passage particularly, together with Plato's views on the soul's immortality. The subject drew him even more than chemistry. Hogg remembered him intoning, solemnly and mysteriously, how noble metaphysics was:

> Then rising from his chair, he paced slowly about the room, with prodigious strides, and discoursed of souls with still greater animation and vehemence than he had displayed in treating of gases—of a future state—and especially of a former state—of pre-existence, obscured for a time through the suspension of consciousness—of personal identity, and also of ethical philosophy, in a deep and earnest tone of elevated morality, until he suddenly remarked that the fire was nearly out, and the candles were glimmering in their sockets . . .

Shelley's especial love in those days was the *Phaedo*, read and discussed with urgent excitement. In this the soul, distracted with longing for experience, had fallen to earthly existence from the eternal realms. Plato's *Phaedrus*, too, showed the soul – 'through all its being immortal', self-moved, infused with the very essence of life – losing its wings, drooping and falling, until it found a home in the world. In 1821, a verse from the Wisdom of Solomon caught Shelley's attention:

> For I was a witty child, & had a good Spirit—
> —Yea, rather, *being good* (as all Spirits of necessity are, the Platonist understands) I came into a body undefiled—.

The emphasis and parenthesis were Shelley's own. The history seemed taken as his own also. Plato, he wrote around 1817, had said all that could be said on the subject of the soul. To embrace his ideas, as Shelley did instinctively (though tailoring them to his own opinions and predilections), was to know his true self as that perfect being, temporarily exiled on Earth and imprisoned in the flesh.

> And early I had learned to scorn
> The chains of clay that bound a soul
> Panting to seize the wings of morn,
> And where its vital fires were born
> To soar . . .

Those lines, from 1812, were Shelley's constant conviction as a poet. As a man, he was unsure; in creation he did not question, but flamed up to his full height. In the last two years of his life he was reading the *Phaedo* and the *Phaedrus*, Plato's soul-histories, yet again in the original Greek. Each reading could convince him that this was his own past.

In the heavy stupefaction of existence his soul-self often slept, much as he pictured the electric power curled on its wings within Nature. He would stay like this, tranquil, tranquillised, until at some invisible sight or inaudible sound

> the dreaming clay
> Was lifted by the thing that dreamed below
> As smoke by fire . . .

In others he saw the 'thing' with human form, face and limbs, though almost lost in brightness. Sometimes its purity was complete. At others the tints or stains of human life still played across it, until like 'swift lightning', and with lightning's shivering charge, it fled away from mortal corruption.

Towards the end of William's brief life, in the late spring of 1819, he traced his son's soul in his 'very unusual vivacity' and in the fresh, remarkable beauty of his deep blue eyes and silken hair,

> as declining day
> Grows beautiful ere darkness

The little boy had become the 'lodestar' of his life. Conversely, when William's death had plunged Mary into misery, he glimpsed her soul 'on the hearth of pale despair', the feeble flame barely inhabiting the dreary form of the body. In the chalk portrait Hunt sent him in 1818 he looked for, and missed, 'that deepest & most earnest look with which you sometimes draw aside the inner veil of your nature when you talk with us'. Behind lay light.

Wandering seemed to be the soul's fate, at least when freed from
Earth. In *Queen Mab* Shelley tried to picture it before incarnation, in

>   that strange state
> Before the naked soul has found its home—

Two years later, recasting his poem as *The Daemon of the World*, this became

>   that strange state
>   Before the naked powers that thro' the world
>   Wander like winds have found a human home . . .

His revisions had two effects: to underline the soul's restlessness, and to
emphasise that the human form was its shelter – his shelter – only for
a time. True home was elsewhere.

In 1821, among the first drafts of *Adonais* and *Hellas* in two different
notebooks (throwing down words, deleting them, writing the words
again) Shelley tried to record a story.

>   A ~~star of Heaven has fallen upon the Earth~~ . . .
>   A burning monad of ~~eternal flame~~
>   A living atom of unquenchable eternal light
>   ~~The lightnings~~
>   ~~The sun is darkness~~
>
>   . . .
>   Pass ~~Into the Earths deep heart it past~~
>   ~~Swifter than the~~
>   ~~And like a seed~~
>   ~~To the heart~~ . . .
>   To the heart of Earth . . . the well
>   Whence ~~the~~ its pulses flow & beat
>   Unextinct in that cold source
>   ~~Like f~~ It burns ~~even as a soul of Power~~
>   ~~in a form of mortal birth~~
>   ~~even as angels soul~~
>   Guiding the sphere which is its prison
>   Like an Angel's ~~soul~~ spirit pent
>
>   . . .
>   A ray of the eternal

The fall of that fiery monad into the Earth seemed to parallel his own incarnation. For brief moments he could retrieve his power and his sense of who he was; for the rest he was an ordinary man, and the waters of forgetfulness had washed over him. The 'Shape all light', the betraying daylight, had handed him the cup of Nepenthe, no-regret, and he had drunk. He remembered nothing more.

He talked to Southey once of metempsychosis, the transmigration of souls. ('As the soul which now animates this frame was once the vivifying principle of the *infinitely* lowest link in the Chain of existence,' he said he told him, braving that hawkish stare, 'so is it ultimately destined to attain the highest.') And he kept returning, delicately, fascinated, feeling his way in the dark, to the notion of his existence before birth in a state of wisdom and enlightenment. As Plato wrote in the *Phaedrus*,

> Every soul of man has in the way of nature beheld true being: this was the condition of her passing into the form of man. But all souls do not easily recall the things of the other world; they may have seen them for a short time only, or . . . having had their hearts turned to unrighteousness through some corrupting influence, they may have lost the memory of the holy things which once they saw . . . There was a time when . . . they saw beauty shining in brightness . . . and then beheld the beatific vision . . . shining in pure light, pure ourselves and not bearing the marks of that thing we carry around and call the body, imprisoned in it like an oyster in its shell.

Hogg said that Shelley argued for this strenuously at Oxford. (He did so seven years later, too, crushed against Hogg on the swaying top of a coach from London to Marlow, reading that very passage aloud, the *Phaedrus* on Beauty.) He loved to place the immortality of the soul in an 'impregnable castle' of argument, Hogg added, and to raise himself thereby 'out of the dirt on tall stilts'. Yet Shelley too had no firm memory to help him. With the fall to Earth and the shock of incarnation, almost all of this visionary state had presumably been forgotten. He was left with 'ruin of divinest things' at which his mortal, reasoning self would ceaselessly poke and quibble. But then he would see the world, for a moment, with his Poet's eyes.

'I arose & for a space
The scene of woods & waters seemed to keep,

355

>   Though it was now broad day, a gentle trace
>   Of light diviner than the common sun
>   Sheds on the common Earth . . .'

He struggled to describe that light precisely. Though he was writing of midday, he seemed to see

>   ~~an unfading~~
>   ~~A hue of unremembered~~ ~~heaven~~ a trace
>   ~~Of light evening beams in day~~
>   ~~The sweet evening beams~~

Again and again he wrote and cancelled 'evening beams'. Something in the phrase was exact, echoing the sunset colours he had come to associate with free, ecstatic love. Yet it would not do.

His island retreat in *Epipsychidion* offered a clearer picture. The place was full of 'echoes of an antenatal dream', a web of melodious, strange sounds. Above him the air was golden and blue, spirit-colours. The rivers and ponds were 'clear as elemental diamond', reflecting beauty only as he gazed deep into them. He seemed to know the woods there, where mossy deer tracks led into caves hung with ivy and glades lit up by waterfalls; he also knew the quality of the light, coming not only from without but from within, 'like a buried lamp', or his own soul-glow within the body.

>   And every motion, odour, beam, and tone,
>   With that deep music is in unison:
>   Which is a soul within the soul—

He described this place, in a strange phrase, as 'Bright as that wandering Eden Lucifer': a country he had known, perhaps, before his fall to Earth and to experience.

At Oxford he felt sure that such memories were recoverable by instruction, or suggestion, or by snatching a baby from its mother's arms – its shawl trailing, like Wordsworth's 'clouds of glory' – and looking it squarely and longingly in the eye. He did so on Magdalen Bridge, partly as a prank, dandling the tiny swaddled soul above the reedy river. 'Can your baby', he cried, 'tell us about pre-existence, Madam?' The mother remonstrated mildly with the gowned, mortar-boarded, crazy young man; the baby smiled, but still it would not speak. So 'provokingly close', Shelley sighed as he left them, and yet so far.

Somewhere in the innocence of children lay the soul, fresh-fallen, with all its knowledge intact and not yet faded. Socrates in the *Meno* had quizzed a slave-boy on geometric propositions, finding that he could visualise without effort forms, numbers, area, multiplication and extension. Those opinions were 'stirred up afresh in the mind of that boy, as fancies are in dreaming'. The gypsy lad Shelley encountered in a lane near Oxford, silently carrying a bundle of unlawfully gathered sticks, could surely summon up the same forgotten knowledge. With only a little encouragement – a smile, an orange, a pat on the head – this boy, Shelley insisted, would unfold all the doctrines of the *Dialogues* in the dusty shade of the hedge.

With his own children Shelley seemed less sure, and did not speculate. His babies held scant interest for him, and he once leapt over his wailing toddler Percy on the doorstep without realising who he was. ('Whose child is it?' Trelawny asked him. 'Don't know,' Shelley replied.) But when infants were mild and good he delighted to play with them, down on the floor, in the world of their own imaginations. Several late notebooks were decorated with the scribbles of a very young child: Percy, perhaps, handed the pen or the pencil to see whether he could draw, from recent knowledge, perfect forms.

With nineteen-month-old Allegra, Byron's daughter by Claire, Shelley crouched to roll billiard balls across a marble floor. He was enthralled by the 'deep meaning' in her dark blue eyes and the flash of her soul, in laughter, as the balls clacked together. Three years later, visiting her in the convent to which she had been sent, he let her take his hand and tug him all over the buildings and the gardens, running and skipping 'like a mad thing'. Together they rang the bell, roused the nuns, ate sweets from a little basket and imagined Allegra in a dress of silk and gold. Though she was trapped in the shades of a prison-house, she was still relatively close to the source; hence the fresh fire of her imagination, and her preciousness to him.

He could not prove pre-existence, yet he often felt it. In November 1811 he quoted to Miss Hitchener his favourite *Curse of Kehama*:

'The *holy* flame forever burneth, From Heaven it came, to Heaven returneth—' Might there not have been a *prior* state of existence, might we not have been friends there?—This creation of soul at

357

birth is a thing *I do* not like . . . It *may* all be vanity—but I cannot think so.—

The next year, Queen Mab addressed the Spirit of Ianthe in more mysterious and intriguing terms.

> 'O Spirit! through the sense
> By which thy inner nature was apprised
> Of outward shows, vague dreams have rolled,
> And varied reminiscences have waked
> Tablets that never fade;
> All things have been imprinted there,
> The stars, the sea, the earth, the sky,
> Even the unshapeliest lineaments
> Of wild and fleeting visions . . .'

As a Poet, his first task might not be to gather new knowledge. It might be to recover what he had known before: where he had come from, who he was.

★   ★   ★

Among all the souls of the world he searched for one in particular: the match to the antiype he carried in him, the 'soul out of my soul'. Both Platonic and Hermetical philosophy taught that, in the beginning, the soul had loved its reflection in the waters of the Earth and had plunged into experience in pursuit of it. (At the very beginning of time Love had made the world this way, embracing its likeness in the depths of Chaos.) Hence Shelley's fixation with downward-gazing lights and the dark, reflecting sea.

This image was often one of sexual union: a tender Heaven-born light which, hovering by the murky pool of existence, trembled 'to mingle with its paramour'; lightning's love for 'the genii that move/ In the depths of the purple sea'; or, in his 'Epithalamium,' or marriage song, the fall itself,

> When strength & beauty, met together
> Kindle their image—like a Star
> In a sea of glassy weather—

His loves were mirrors in which he strove to see and know himself. And there was danger in this. To seek his own soul's image in the world was to risk despair, and an even steeper fall into the dark. But Shelley, despite his own warnings to himself, was impelled to seek his soul reflected. His poems were full of soul-liaisons between lovers already linked by blood and likeness, sisters and brothers. Often they were unaware of the relationship, and simply obeyed the 'dreams of flame' that insisted on their union. In his own life, family friends had remarked how like each other he and his first love, Harriet Grove, had been: more than cousins, almost twins. Perhaps this was why he had loved her. Later, he wished aloud that he and Emilia could have been twins of the same mother:

> A Lover or
> Could thy brother or a
> I love thee . . . . though to you I cannot be
> Lover or brother

Even male friendship might approach this intense intimacy of twin souls, as a letter from Hogg to his father explained after their expulsion. 'A seperation [*sic*] is impossible I may say neither length nor breadth nor height nor depth nor principalitie nor powers nor things on earth &c can seperate us . . . we are of the same age the same disposition the same pursuits the same sentiments the same principles we have read the same books we read the same books . . . We are brothers in every respect.' Shelley, meek as a 'young virgin' to Hogg, drew back from any deeper expression of male love than linking arms joyously to walk, or snuggling close to the fire with Hunt in the comfort of each other. His beloved Greeks would have gone further, in acts Shelley squeamishly tried to idealise and to abstract entirely from the body.

By contrast brother-and-sister love contained, for him, no complications. The warm, light touch of Cythna's hand in Laon's was the inevitable blending of like with like, as sweetly natural as his own small sisters sitting on his lap or snuggling, tired, in his arms. His idealised brothers and sisters loved carnally, but 'in purity'; their true union was mystical and innocent. Incest, he explained to Maria Gisborne, trying to account for his fascination with it, was 'like many other *incorrect* things a very poetical circumstance'; it might express sheer selfishness, or conversely 'the defiance of every thing for the sake of another'. It

359

might be 'the excess of love or of hate'. And a higher truth seemed to lie behind it.

While writing *The Revolt of Islam*, he had reminded himself to read certain verses from Solomon's Song:

> Thou hast ravished my heart, my sister, my spouse . . .
> A garden enclosed is my sister, my spouse . . .
> I sleep, but my heart waketh . . . Open to me, my sister, my love, my dove, my undefiled: for my head is filled with dew, and my locks with the drops of the night.

The lover addressed his own soul here, a spiritual mystery as carefully enclosed as a virgin, a garden, or a well, yet ever close to him, his holier self. Thus Cythna was Laon's 'own shadow', but purer and brighter, beside him.

In 1813, at the apogee of his love for Harriet Westbrook, Shelley called her his 'purer mind' and 'soul of my soul'. One brief year later, Mary was his soul's soul. Their moment of meeting on 28 July 1814, the elopement morning, he described with all the strange, ritualistic formality of Solomon's Song: 'I went. I saw her. She came to me.' 'How divinely sweet a task it is', he told her some months later,

> to imitate each other's excellencies—& each moment to become wiser in this surpassing love—so that constituting but one being, all real knowledge may be comprised in the maxim γνωθι σεαυτον (know thyself) . . .

'I never before', he told Hogg, 'felt the integrity of my nature, its various dependencies, & learned to consider myself as an whole accurately united.' To Harriet, explaining his new passion, he was simpler and more brutal: 'United as we are we cannot be considered separately.'

Yet the several kinds of love – physical, spiritual, intellectual – seldom combined on Earth, and Shelley had already learned to seek them in different women. In *Prince Athanase* he gave earthly love to Pandemos, the 'unworthy Venus', and spiritual love to Urania, the Muse of poetry and astronomy, 'the lady who can really reply to his soul'. Ideally, as he clumsily tried to arrange in 1814 with Harriet and Mary, he would live with both of them, husband of one and brother of the other, unlimited and prodigal in love, as love required. He saw no problem there. Indeed, he imagined a union of the disparate parts of his own self and theirs, body, mind and spirit held in balance. He was irritated and disappointed to find that, by general agreement, the plan would 'never do'.

Eventually it was not Mary, but Emilia Viviani, to whom in 1821 Shelley dedicated his longest and most ecstatic poem of soul-seeking and soul-finding. Again in their letters they had become sister and brother: *vostra sorella, mio caro fratello*. She was his *Epipsychidion*, the soul out of my soul, the soul within the soul, a word by which he meant to hint again at the flaming night torches of the epithalamium or marriage song. But her earthly identity did not matter, for the poem's core, in truth, was not about her or any woman he knew. The 'young Englishman' who had written *Epipsychidion*, in one of his several manifestations – this one crossed out, perhaps as too revealing – had 'personified the το καλόν [the Beautiful] & sought it in every form & in every opinion fell in love with it'. Yet the Beautiful was not to be personified, even as Emilia. His error, Shelley admitted, 'and I confess it is not easy for spirits cased in flesh and blood to avoid it', was to seek in a mortal image 'the likeness of what is perhaps eternal'.

Epipsychidion called forth his most explicit descriptions of the soul – his own image of 'all of wonderful, or wise, or beautiful' – incarnate in the dark of earth and water. Image after image touched but failed to fix her. This indeed was his intention; but the very proximity of his soul's soul, symbolised by 'Emily', filled him with wild confusion. He could try every simile he knew, and still not describe to others what she meant to him.

> Sweet Benediction in the eternal Curse!
> Veiled Glory of this lampless Universe!
> Thou Moon beyond the clouds! Thou living Form
> Among the dead! Thou Star above the Storm!
> Thou Wonder, and thou Beauty, and thou Terror!

Feverishly, almost incoherently, he described his search for her, from the very moment when his sighting of Beauty's shadow had hinted that the world might contain her. The journey had been one of repeated disappointment and self-delusion with every woman he had come close to; but now, imagining that he had seen her through the mists and deep water, he would set her free. Together they would escape, in the small light boat that waited, from the Earth's imprisonment; together they would enclose themselves in the island Eden he had known before his fall, 'Conscious, inseparable, one',

> Possessing and possessed by all that is
> Within that calm circumference of bliss,
> And by each other, till to love and live
> Be one . . .

Having tried to love shadows, phantoms, idols and dreams, he now reached for – almost touched – what was real.

> We shall become the same, we shall be one
> Spirit within two frames, oh! wherefore two?
> One passion in twin-hearts, which grows and grew
> Till like two meteors of expanding flame,
> Those spheres instinct with it become the same,
> Touch, mingle, are transfigured; ever still
> Burning, yet ever inconsumable:
> In one another's substance finding food,
> Like flames too pure and light and unimbued
> To nourish their bright lives with baser prey . . .

Tenderly, to the elect only, he presented the bride, 'delighting and delighted' of 'the intense, the deep, the imperishable, /Not mine but me'. Or, to invoke again the mirror-image, 'I am not thine: I am a part of *thee*.' He was made one. He was complete.

★   ★   ★

Yet Love, as he knew, also operated in another way, seeking not the perfect reflection but completion and union in difference. In Diotima's words in the *Symposium*, as he translated them,

> Love, therefore, and every thing else that desires anything, desires that which is absent and beyond his reach, that which it has not, that which is not itself . . . that which it wants . . .

His soul not only longed for what it was, its mirror-image, but for beauties and virtues it could barely apprehend, beyond the shifting veil of the world.

Shelley had glimpsed, and fallen in love with, Beauty's reflection only, 'the awful shadow of some unseen Power'. Yet in a previous existence, if Plato spoke truly, he had known what Beauty was. He was aware that Emilia's soul was also a shadow, its light shrouded in mortality. Beauty, Truth and all other absolutes − all perhaps being one, not 'disjoined' − he experienced as absence, lack, and yearning, as long as he remained imprisoned in mutability. Yet there had to be some way − in solitude, in calm, through that near-silent communion of Nature and the heart − to approach some different place, where those perfect entities would be present to him again.

Alone, in the last year of his life, he walked beside a river through the pale winter grass. He knew that he desired 'more in this world than any understand'. And yet he had never quite known what it was he loved.

> I loved . . . oh, no, I mean not one of ye,
>> Or any earthly one, though ye are dear
> As human heart to human heart may be;—
>> I loved, I know not what, but this low sphere
> And all that it contains, contains not thee
>> Thou whom seen no where, I feel every where

Up to this point he had been relatively fluent, but no longer.

> ~~Dim object of my soul's idolatry~~
> ~~Veiled~~
> Dim . . .
> ~~From~~ Heaven & Earth & all that in them are
> ~~Thou streamest~~
>> ~~In the~~
> ~~In music & even~~
> Veiled art thou like ~~the splendour~~ a storm-extinguished star

At the end of his invocation two asterisk-stars appeared again. Between them was what looked like the shape of the Earth's shadow cast in space, 'the dreary cone of our life's shade'. Three words appeared also, faintly between the lines, stumbling and hesitating into the next thought.

> and   and   ~~and~~
> And thus I went lamenting . . .

The Beauty he sought he had often expressed as unattainable and far beyond himself. His was 'the desire of the moth for the star'. He pictured it as a veiled Divinity ruling the cosmos of himself: 'this Chaos, mine and me', the tangle of earthbound Shelley and his dim, world-shadowed thoughts. From time to time, however, the remoteness was broken, and the object of his love moved close. For a moment in 1819 he caught, but could not hold, something – 'broken gleams', a burst of 'light intense' on his bewildered thought, 'Like memories of what cannot be/Within the reign of Memory'. Two years later, he tried to catch it again:

> And what is that most bright & brief Delight
> Which rushes through the touch, & through the sight
> And stands before the Spirits inmost throne,
> A naked seraph? . . . None hath ever known;—
> Its birth is darkness, and its growth desire;
> Untameable & fleet & fierce as fire
> Not to be touched but to be felt alone
> It fills the world with glory—and is gone

He also tried to describe it another way, his mind a fading coal suddenly roused to brightness by 'invisible influence, like an inconstant wind'. Hogg had seen this power visibly affecting him, his cheeks glowing, his eyes bright and his whole frame trembling as he gave himself up to contemplation.

He had no name for it. The light – the ray, the 'Power of holiest name' – sometimes flashed on his consciousness and left, but sometimes lingered. Its deep source was found, startlingly, within himself as well as far away. When he tried to address it directly he could only joke in his shyness and embarrassment, as if the men from the *Quarterly* were eavesdropping on him.

> If I love you—Listen, O ~~thou~~ embodied Ray
> Of the great ~~spirit~~ Brightness . . .
> Start not—the thing you are, is unbetrayed
> If you are human—and if but the shade
> Of some sublimer spirit. listen—o ~~Stay~~

Perhaps (they would suppose) he was addressing his mistress, perhaps 'that sweet marble monster', a hermaphrodite. Since he hardly knew himself, he meant to keep the world guessing about the thing he loved. But then – still mystifying, still mystified – he knelt to it.

Within ~~the temple~~ a cavern of ~~the mind of man~~ man's inmost
   ~~trackless~~ spirit
Is throned ~~an Idol~~ so intensely fair
That the adventurous thoughts which wander near it
Worship—and as they kneel, ~~like votaries,~~ wear
The splendour of its presence—& the light
Penetrates their dreamlike frame
Till they become charged with the strength of flame
. . .
They forever change & pass but it remains the same.

Sometimes he attempted, in scratched-out lines, to pin this Idol down
more clearly. He made it dazzling, white, cold, crowned with rays as
sharp as pine-needles or frost-grass, with its wings folded over its eyes.
Sheer light, shot through with trembling crimson ('crimson snow' he
wrote often, instinctively) prevented him from seeing more. But in lines
written out and underlined in 1820 from the Wisdom of Solomon in
the Apocrypha, he came closer. Here was divine power – Wisdom, Love,
Beauty – working in the world and in him.

> For Wisdom is more moving than any motion: she passeth & goeth through
> all things by reason of her pureness.
>   For she is the vapour of the power of God, & a pure stream flowing
> from the glory of the Almighty: therefore can no defiled thing fall ~~upon~~ into
> her.
>   For she is the brightness of the everlasting light, the unspotted mirror of
> the power of God, & the Image of his ~~brightness~~ goodness.
>   —And being but One, she can do all things; & remaining within herself
> she maketh all things new; & in all ages entering into holy Souls she
> maketh them friends of God & prophets.
>   . . .
>   To think upon her is perfection of wisdom.

He underlined 'think' twice. To apply his mind to her in contemplation was to begin to become one with her. 'And love is the keeping
of her laws.'
   This was the further, deeper love he yearned for. Once he and his
soul's soul had mingled in 'Passion's golden purity' he would be drawn
up to Dante's third Heaven, Venus's Heaven, uniting there sublimely
with Beauty and Wisdom and Love, Love's guest.

365

He could barely begin to imagine this. The being he approached – Love personified, Beauty symbolised, for as a mortal he could do no better – wore a loose robe of light through which her true form could be apprehended only as a dim, thrilling movement, like limbs through silk. She was all that stood between him and the pure divine, necessarily shielding him from what his Earth-imagination could not bear. Veil after veil could be removed, like the gauze of cloud-curtains parted by the sun, until he could see her loose hair, smell the violet-perfumes in it, sense the flowing outline of her arms and the soft glow of blood beneath the skin. Yet her own brightness still hid her from him, however close he came. The same words appeared again and again in the crossed-out confusion of the *Epipsychidion* drafts: light and fire, life and motion, love. These were all he could think of, or cling to.

He had seen such a vision before. In the last scene of the second act of *Prometheus Unbound* his heroine Asia, Love personified, was 'unveiled' yet still veiled to him, inexpressible and indescribable, almost unendurable. He had gone as far as possible, dimly seeing her, barely sensing her through the radiance and the fire, before he was lost as usual in the lower world.

> Child of Light! thy limbs are burning
>   Through the vest which seems to hide them;
> As the radiant lines of morning
>   Through the clouds ere they divide them;
> And this atmosphere divinest
> Shrouds thee whereso'er thou shinest.
>
> Fair are others; none beholds thee,
>   But thy voice sounds low and tender
> Like the fairest, for it folds thee
>   From the sight, that liquid splendour,
> And all feel, yet see thee never,
> As I feel now, lost for ever!

For as long as that moment of gazing lasted, Shelley would be regenerated. There in the third Heaven light and Love would pervade him, sweeping him up into Beauty; he would become both what he was not, and what he was.

At the very end of *Epipsychidion*, testing the limits of what he could describe, he approached that far and perilous place. But the chains of existence, yet again, held him back. He had meant to show that such love was not an end, but a beginning of man's transformation: the knowing of the self from which true revolution would come. Instead, he stood at the farthest bounds of language and on the brink of dissolution. To love was to drown. To love was to burn in ineffable light, 'as morning dew, that in the sunbeam dies'.

                    woe is me,

The ~~plumed~~ wings of words on which my ~~heart~~ Soul would ~~soar~~
    ~~pierce~~

Beyond the ~~height~~ depth of Love's rare universe
                          which upon its fiery flight

Are ~~lead~~ chains of lead ~~upon its flight of~~
    I sink

These words were not the last he wrote in his original draft. They came first, and everything that followed sprang out of his effort to return there.

To those he hoped would read his poem, he now had to explain. He had written of an ecstasy that seemed mostly corporeal and sexual. To Mary, who sniffed at 'Shelley's Italian Platonics', he was simply fooling with Emilia, or wishing to. His mystifying metaphysics, as Byron called it, was probably a cover for a history of priapic misadventure.

But this was never his purpose. As he told John Gisborne, indignantly, 'you might as well go to a ginshop for a leg of mutton, as expect any thing human or earthly from me'. He was writing in this instance not for men and women in general but for the initiated, for whom only 100 copies had been printed; and he was writing not of the world, as he explained in yet another crossed-out preface, but of 'the world as it should be'. Moreover, he added, still with mild indignation, 'the love of woman which these verses express was but the form of that universal Love which Plato taught'. Yet earthly life, and the tyranny of body and senses, seemed to mean there was no other analogy that his readers could feel as intensely, or perhaps that he himself could. The closing words of *Epipsychidion*, before the final *envoi*, were apparently the same hectic sighs of sexual release he had scattered through his little lyrics, of which he claimed to think nothing:

I pant, I sink, I tremble, I expire!

As he wrote those words, however, he was not in the body or in the world at all. He had escaped dying by a whisper and was falling, his singed wings trailing, out of the flame.

★ ★ ★

He returned to confusion. Was that consummation, fire to fire, truly death? Or was it life? It seemed clear that 'All that we see or know perishes and is changed.' Yet Shelley also had 'a spirit within him at enmity with nothingness and dissolution'. As he had told Miss Hitchener, at nineteen, 'I *will* live beyond this life. Yours yours most imperishably.' Or to put it in Diotima's words, again in his translation, 'Of necessity Love must also be the desire of immortality.'

Under what form he would continue, his rational self could not begin to say. He spoke sometimes of higher or 'more extensive' states of being, but left them vague; he had no choice. He had supposed once, in another eager letter to Miss Hitchener, 'that in a future existence [the soul] will lose all consciousness of having formerly lived elsewhere, will begin life anew, possibly under a shape of which we have now no idea'. Yet this was perhaps too whimsical. In 1819 he put the case against much as Hume had:

> It is said that it is possible we should continue to exist in some mode totally inconceivable to us at present. This is a most unreasonable presumption—to cast on the adherents of annihilation the burthen of proving the negative of a question, the affirmative of which is not supported by a single argument, and which by its very nature lies beyond the experience of the human understanding.

The case *for* got no further than a stray sentence:

> But there is another point of view from which the Universe may be considered, totally different

That point of view was not prose, but rapture. In 1821 he put that extraordinary perspective into *Hellas*. Perilously – sometimes hovering above them, sometimes jostling with them under the dark looming gates – he watched the crowds of bright immortals, 'the living and thinking beings which inhabit the planets, and to use a common and inadequate phrase, *clothe themselves in matter'*, visiting and revisiting the Earth. It was the closest he came to expressing in a published poem the soul's journey, perhaps his own: before incarnation, during it, and after.

> Worlds on worlds are rolling ever
> > From creation to decay,
> Like the bubbles on a river
> > Sparkling, bursting, borne away.
> > But they are still immortal
> > Who, through birth's orient portal
> And death's dark chasm hurrying to and fro,
> > Clothe their unceasing flight
> > In the brief dust and light
> Gathered round their chariots as they go;
> > New shapes they still may weave,
> > New gods, new laws receive,
> Bright or dim are they as the robes they last
> > On Death's bare ribs had cast.

Amid this crowd Hesperus appeared, flaring and shining, to guide the souls to a faraway place 'sinless as Eden', Paradise islands. There lay a brighter Hellas, shining in marble columns, 'a loftier Argo' rocking on the dark sea, another Orpheus singing, a new Ulysses. Yet this was not truly Greece, nor necessarily anything earthly. Shelley had described, as he admitted, 'a progressive state of more or less exalted existence, according to the degree of perfection which every distinct intelligence may have attained'. This was what he hoped for and, by his very hoping, created and saw.

He then drew back. It was intolerable to insist or 'dogmatize'. He did not know; no mortal knew. He was engaged in a 'hazardous exercise'. What he was depicting were pure idealisms of desire. Earthing himself again, he found instead his rational philosopher's voice.

That there is a true solution of the riddle, and that in our present state that solution is unattainable by us, are propositions which may be regarded as equally certain.

But this ended nothing. Shelley was too aware of the limitations of 'our present state', too astounded by the moments when he managed to go beyond it, to leave the riddle alone.

★　★　★

In mid-June of 1811, still miserable and 'maddened' after his expulsion from Oxford, Shelley told Hogg that he had watched a star from the summer-house at Field Place. Brighter than the moon, shedding 'spanglets' of light across the garden, it must have been Venus he saw, though he did not name it. In the deepening quiet it shone on him: over the lake, through the trees.

> Sweet star! . . .
> 　　　　　—art thou aught but love
> Lulling the slaves of interest to repose
> With that mild pitying gaze—oh! I cd. look
> On thy dear beam till every bond of sense
> Became unnerved—

In clearer Italian skies the evening star sprang spectacularly from the sun's last glow, winged with blue-white fire. At Baiae, after Shelley had gazed deep into the underwater world – leaning, almost diving, into the azure calm – that star lit his journey back to the shore. He sat in the small dipping boat, Venus above him. Absorbed in looking, consumed with hope and desire, he felt her light become his.

At Marlow, as he wrote *The Revolt of Islam*, Venus had especially illumined him, shining through March and April and from August to the end of October. In that poem's first canto he drew a Woman as Venus's mortal shadow, 'serene yet sorrowing', sitting by the empty sea. She was remembering a daemon-lover who had come to her dreams, a winged shape of 'speechless beauty' with golden clouds surging round him and the Morning Star blazing on his brow. Kissing her tenderly, breathing a 'wild dissolving bliss' through her body, he urged her to fight for liberty and truth, as if he were Milton's Lucifer luring away the angels to follow his defiance – or as if he were Shelley, bright-eyed, loving and subversive. Having pressed his dreams on her, he vanished.

In *Epipsychidion* Shelley explicitly colluded with the 'destined Star' to free Emilia, his soul's soul, overleaping her prison wall like Love or lightning, 'with invisible violence/Piercing its continents'. As the star rose, he proclaimed their union in light. As it set, she had fled away from the world with him.

Sometimes his light went unregarded. As Athanase, 'Like Vespers serene beam/ Piercing the rifts of ever rising clouds', he shone, softly burning, full of love he could not share. Sometimes, however, his influence might touch humankind in general. He walked then, as Lionel did, 'A spirit of unresting flame' along the brink of gloomy seas, spreading peace, like dew, in his 'sweet talk'. If men would listen to him, he was the harbinger and prophet of the principles of Liberty and Love; he showed the way, gleaming before the sun or lingering after it or, like the Morning Star for the Argonauts, releasing the liberating western breeze when he rose. In *Hellas*, bright as 'Love's folding-star', he too illumined the path to America and freedom:

> . . . like loveliness panting with wild desire
> While it trembles with fear and delight,
> Hesperus flies from awakening night
> And pants in its beauty and speed with light
> Fast-flashing, soft and bright.
> Thou beacon of love! Thou lamp of the free!
> Guide us far, far away . . .

This spirit – his spirit – 'with insolent and victorious light' struck down the crescent moon of the Turkish occupiers and made Greece free.

Yet as a star-daemon, the shadow-messenger of Truth and Love and Beauty, he could not prevail on the Earth. The 'common sun' obscured him as it rose:

> As veil by veil the silent splendour drops
> From Lucifer, amid the chrysolite
>
> Of sunrise ere it strike the mountain tops—

371

Dawn trod his brightness out. He vanished in Earth's brash, deceiving daylight as the skylark vanished, 'for ever sought, for ever lost'. Only as evening fell was his radiance visible again, Shelley's own light made apparent, shining and unchanging as the eternal sphere in which Love's star remained.

The spirit of the Morning Star fought battles frequently, light against false light, and lost most of them. That was to be expected. At the dawn of revolutionary time he had lost a fight with the Comet of evil and vengeance, almost dying in the attempt, sinking into the sea. After this, Evil in triumph changed him into a serpent on the Earth. His fall into water was a symbol of his incarnation there, not once but again and again. He crawled in the dust or floundered in the waves, his many-coloured skin showing his embrace of mutability, cursed on every side. Only his glittering eyes and his whispered spirit-talk showed the place that he had once held in Heaven.

As Love's messenger, he went on fighting and resisting. He fought with eagles, and the garish sun-bird often bore the limp reptile away. Tyrant-claws ripped his thin, lithe flesh; glittering scales fell from him. Yet still the serpent, a 'bright shadow' even in mortality, struggled for liberty. And sometimes, in that great cosmic or internal battle, the snake won, fatally weakening the eagle whose wings overshadowed the world.

In *The Revolt of Islam* Shelley's snake-self, bloodied and wearied by his struggle with the eagle, plunged into the sea again, as into earthly life; but the watching Woman, 'beautiful as morning', caught him up and placed him in her bosom, next to her heart. She sang to him in words only he and she understood. He could shed his wounded skin there and be regenerated as the Spirit of Liberty and Love, though his renewal would not be for the world to see. By moments he could appear in vision, as in *The Mask of Anarchy*, his snake-armour glittering 'brighter than the Viper's scale' and the Morning Star blazing from his helmet as he moved above the heads of the oppressed. But then, 'in a rushing light of clouds and splendour', leaving only 'a sense awakening', he would vanish away.

In the deep night quiet, Shelley could hear star-sounds: 'tingling silent-ness', or the high lute notes of the Morning Star, very far away.

> Clear, silver, icy, keen, awakening tones,
> Which pierce the sense, and live within the soul . . .

These were also, perhaps, the sounds he heard in daylight, those 'arrowy' silver sounds of Beauty absent, transfixing him.

As he floated on the Bay of Lerici, between the 'heaven beneath the water' and the Heaven above the clouds, the tinkling of Jane's guitar seemed to carry the sound

> Of some world far from ours,
> Where music & moonlight & feeling
> Are one.

That realm of highest desire, infinitely distant, was also within him, with the star-sounds and the flutter of Jane's fingers along the life-strings of his heart.

In his notebook in those last weeks, amid increasing cries of loneliness and despair, he tried several times to write a poem. It never progressed beyond a few broken images: the music of Heaven, and a star drawn out of the deep.

★   ★   ★

He had toyed with Heaven for a long time. Already in 1810, thoughts of eternity in amaranth bowers ('you see I mingle metaphysices [*sic*] with even this') had complicated his love songs. In June 1811 he told Hogg mournfully that he had been thinking of death and Heaven for four days, and speculating, as he watched the moon climb behind the chimneys of Field Place, whether only the moon would see him go there.

Of one thing he was certain: 'Those who believe that Heaven is, what earth has been, a monopoly in the hands of a favoured few, would do well to reconsider their opinion.' It was accessible to all men, and to him, whatever his father or his enemies thought. It was made or found, not earned. Yet he did not try to say where Heaven was.

As a sceptic and a Godwinian, in the years when he wore that hat most proudly, the only Heaven Shelley appeared to hope for was a steadily perfecting Earth.

> 'Oh happy Earth! reality of Heaven!
> To which those restless souls that ceaselessly
> Throng through the human universe, aspire;
> Thou consummation of all mortal hope!
>   . . .
> Genius has seen thee in her passionate dreams . . .'

Yet he knew even then that all earthly heavens were as transient as man was. He found absurd, even 'demoniacal', Wordsworth's remark that happiness was found in the world '*or not at all*'. His poetry burned with impatience to be away. Earth might be progressing, as he fervently wished, towards a 'Heaven of time', 'balancing itself on the golden wings of knowledge and of hope'; but there was also a Heaven outside time, the realm his Poet-self both intimated and longed for. After he had described 'a perfect state of society; tho still earthly' in *Queen Mab*, he told Miss Hitchener, 'I shall draw a picture of Heaven.' There – where, in his poem, Time folded dusky wings to prevent him seeing further – he would wake from the deception of life.

Laon and Cythna, burnt on the tyrant's pyre, found themselves alive. They could move and speak, in forms still endowed with sensibility, and there seemed to be a different scene around them: green banks by a river, sand at their feet. Laon, sitting up, bewildered, spoke first, in Shelley's voice:

> And is this death?—The pyre has disappeared, . . .
> The flames grow silent—slowly there is heard
>   The music of a breath-suspending song
>   Which, like the kiss of love when life is young,
> Steeps the faint eyes in darkness sweet and deep . . .

Yet he and Cythna were not lost in that ecstasy of love or death but entranced and surprised, in a new world. In the draft, Shelley tried to work out exactly where he thought they were, and with which senses, and whether human or divine:

> ~~And we are wandering through a garden~~ silent ~~wild~~
> ~~That echoes~~ voices on the wind are heard . . .

And soon a joyous ~~company we meet~~
With gentle ~~accents looks & words us two they greet~~
~~As welcome strangers; we with wonder know~~
~~They are the same~~

That scene soon broke off, as if Shelley could not sustain this image of beatified beings, or fix the nature of bodies and voices after death. Laon and Cythna were joined only by their spirit-child, a seraph who guided them in a small boat past mountains, lawns, trees and chasms that seemed to be from Paradise. At length they arrived – he arrived, the boat rocking with him under the 'hollow' sky – in the Elysian islands, 'Calm dwellings of the free and happy dead'.

Shelley had roamed often among such islands. Solitary, drifting, he would see green hills emerging from the wide ocean, oases of civilisation in the dark sweep of Time, white Alpine peaks 'islanded in the immeasurable air'. He drew them in his notebooks, too, accessible by sailing-boat to the Poet abstracted and alone. The promontories on which he wrote were islands of a sort, as were the tiny lawns he looked for in the woods. Even carriages, boats and beds could become his islands, as on his elopement with Mary, where 'we were safe . . . we felt secure . . . she was in my arms', with no pursuers visible.

In such places he could be, at last, himself alone. Temporarily safe, though lost in boundlessness, he could draw breath and recover, as in his moments of suspended, blissful calm. Assailed in 1821 by gossip, critics and enemies, he talked of taking Mary and little Percy to some 'solitary island in the sea' where, with a boat and a simple house, they would live in tranquillity and solitude. He would teach Percy Greek there, as he had once meant to teach William, and keep him unpolluted by the world. Every radical commune he vaguely tried to establish, whether at Lynmouth or in wild Wales or at Lerici, was an enclave of beauty walled away by high woods and hills. Here – at least as he idealised it – he could live in serenity, imperturbably, as Mind in its transcendence among the dazzling peaks, or as the Olympian gods beyond the clouds.

Paradise itself he did not try to describe. Instead he wrote of Eden, the 'wreck of Paradise' he had seen before falling, with its grassy hills and incense flowers and murmurs of the sea. This place, bathed in light 'from above the sun', seemed to be where he belonged, with his own soul animating and illuminating the woods and waves around him. In Plato each soul had its own star, in which it had originated and from which it had fallen to be born into the world. To be set there was at last to return to his own light, home again.

There remained the question of Heaven. In 1820, three arguing voices in his head strove to define where Heaven was and what it might be. The first saw it as the immeasurable, star-strewn container of all things and all time. The second, 'a Remoter Voice', described it as the mind's first chamber, where bewildered insect-fancies faintly climbed and dreamed of glory. But the third, 'a Louder and still Remoter Voice', saw a Heaven far more astonishing, a tiny globe of fire-dew at the centre of 'some eyed flower'. As so often, the flower was vague and unspecified; as so often, it was Shelley himself, representing Man,

> whose young leaves waken
> On an unimagined world,
> Constellated suns unshaken
> Orbits measureless, are furled
> In that frail and fading sphere . . .

His atoms had contained universes, 'sphere within sphere involving and involved'. Now the universe itself was an atom in his heart, a point of light gathering and reflecting there the light of 'ten million' imagined stars,

> To tremble, gleam, and disappear!

Heaven comprised him and he, for a moment, Heaven, with everything that shone there.

Dante in the *Paradiso* had been shown such a vision by Beatrice, who was his soul. He saw the nine glittering circles of the planetary spheres revolving round the tiny spark that lay in the depths of her eyes, a vision of Love too dazzling to be observed directly. For Dante, God was that fixed point round which the flaming circles turned. For Shelley, the circles of the spheres could radiate, some speeding, some slower, from his own inner point of ineffable brightness. In the dizzying heights or depths of himself he could fall, or soar, as far as Heaven,

                        the abode
           Of that Power which is the glass
               Wherein man his nature sees;—

And there, suddenly, was peace.

Yet this was not the end of the story. As he drafted the Prologue for
Hellas, Shelley gazed again through the mists that obscured the heavens
from him. Veil after veil might be lifted from his visions and his words,
and still their 'inmost naked beauty' would not be exposed or understood. Something still lay beyond him.

                          all on whom
           ~~Thou hast~~   oer
           ~~Thy dewy~~ secret breath has
           Thy ~~secret spirit once has shone~~
           . . .
           ~~Tell thee~~ know behold thee—tis their doom
               To be a portion every one
           Of thee—Thou art thyself alone!

Shelley did not at first say whom he was addressing. He did not need
to, but also did not want to. Further on, he tried again.

               ~~In the   the mute   thou art motion~~
                   ~~In man's spirit thou~~
                   ~~In Angels thou art love~~
                   Thou   love

And again.

               Then   thou art
               ~~Liberty~~ . . .
                   Freedom . . . yet we own
               Thou art still thyself alone.—

He seemed unable to go further. Love and Liberty, eternal, coexistent;
beyond those words there was never any more to say. The whole passage

was discarded as hopeless. Perhaps in *Adonais*, written a few months earlier, he had been explicit enough.

> The One remains, the many change and pass;
> Heaven's light forever shines, Earth's shadows fly . . .

'The One' was a rare phrase with him. If drawn to rationalise, Shelley could hazard that it was pure Being, acting in pure Freedom as pure Power, and holding in contemplation the ideas into which it modelled chaos, including the chaos of himself. But in truth it could not be defined at all. Two ruled-off lines in a notebook suggested yet another attempt:

> Oh both, oh all, oh every thing . . . yet neither
> In these proofs sense

It was not an object of sight, sound or touch, could suffer no change, had no qualities, was neither solid nor extended. It was the reverse of all Shelley could say he knew. He had approached it in the *Symposium*, the light already too bright, mocking the dark bower of laurel leaves in which he sat to draft his translation. After ascending the degrees of contemplation, Diotima had explained, he would see Supreme Beauty, 'unproduced, indestructible, neither subject to increase or decay . . . [not] like a beautiful face, or beautiful hands, or any portion of the body, not like any discourse, nor any science'. It subsisted nowhere, but was 'monoeidic' (Shelley's last-throw of a word, pure Greek) with itself: one positive among a swarm of negatives with which, as so often, he was forced to veil and delimit the deepest truth he was exploring. 'The universal Being', he wrote in his *Essay on Christianity*,

> can only be described or defined by negatives, which deny his subjection to the laws of all inferior existences. Where indefiniteness ends idolatry and anthropomorphism begin.

But by its very nature he was part of it, in whatever sense he was not included in the shadows of the Earth. His own 'aweless soul' and 'the Power unknown' he instinctively made consubstantial and coequal. Each negative he applied to his own transcendent life – 'unresting', 'uncharted', 'imageless', 'wordless' – brought him ever closer.

He had supposed his mind to be one infinitesimal part of the One Mind, and his life one passing breath of the Spirit that vivified the universe. If his imagination was divine light and fire reflected in himself, his own imagining soul might be drawn back at last to the source of it, flame rejoining flame. In *Adonais*, almost willing this apotheosis, he began to foresee what might happen to him.

> The Light whose smile kindles the Universe,
> That Beauty in which all things work and move,
> That Benediction which the eclipsing Curse
> Of birth can quench not, that sustaining Love
> Which through the web of being blindly wove
> By man and beast and earth and air and sea,
> Burns bright or dim, as each are mirrors of
> The fire for which all thirst; now beams on me,
> Consuming the last clouds of cold mortality.

He was unsure how he would keep his uniqueness, and indeed whether he would. The death of his body might mean the melting of all boundaries that distinguished him from the divine. The end was possibly some sort of exquisite immolation in which nothing of him would survive. Under every one of his elemental forms, steadily rarefying, he had anticipated this:

> I faint, I perish with my love! I grow
> Frail as a cloud whose ~~splendours~~ pale
> Under the evening's ever-changing glow:
> I die like mist upon the gale,
> And like a wave under the calm I fail.

He had imagined, more than once, that he might become 'a drop in the deep sea of Love'. Yet to be immersed in divinity was not necessarily to lose distinctness and sense, and to die. The failing wave would possibly continue, living in the sea it sought. Those who had loved would continue to love, individually and specifically, each impulse eternally surviving. And Shelley, in some way, would move among them. He had not hesitated, after all, to place Keats there, in the elegy which, he had admitted, was more about himself than about his friend.

In the closing lines of that poem, having finally convinced himself not to be afraid ('Why linger, why turn back, why shrink, my Heart?'), he sailed out towards him.

379

> ... my spirit's bark is driven
> Far from the shore, far from the trembling throng
> Whose sails were never to the tempest given;
> The massy earth and spherèd skies are riven!
> I am borne darkly, fearfully afar;
> Whilst, burning through the inmost veil of Heaven,
>   The soul of Adonais, like a star,
> Beacons from the abode where the Eternal are.

There – were he to go there – he would cast off all encumbrances. Time would become eternity; matter, spirit; darkness, light. Even fire would burn without changing. The veiled would be unveiled, and what was shadow would become Reality. He would see; and through death, as he had long suspected, he would arrive at life.

As for the Self, it would perhaps not be annihilated as much as transcended. He would realise himself through perfect surrender. As part of the One, he would become the creative love and light that 'Shelley' truly was; and that light, like the West Wind, would become him.

This was what he had desired all along, the core of his own revolution. What he had pursued he would possess. Perfect Equality, perfect Truth, perfect Justice (everything given, nothing withheld), perfect Beauty, the perfect Song. He would be himself alone, being, in utter Being. 'This world of Love, this *me*' would be subsumed in the Heaven of Love he had described to Hogg as early as 1811: 'Love, love *infinite in extent*, eternal in duration'.

Earth would follow his example, slowly. Imagination, inexorably spreading and enlightening, would increasingly blaze forth Reality in the world. Men and women would discover within themselves the power he already knew, and use it. But in order to transform the Earth – for the task could never end, and he himself could never rest – he would now work from a level infinitely higher. Having brought down divine light and beauty in poetry, he could become Light and Beauty himself – if he believed.

This was the immortal function he had ascribed to Keats, borrowing from Plato the epigraph to *Adonais* and slashing it through, diagonally from the top to the bottom of the page, with a comet or a shooting star.

> Thou wert the morning star among the living
>   Ere thy fair light had fled—

Now, having died, thou art as Hesperus, giving
New splendour to the dead.

He knew that 'the sacred few', the untameable and unconquerable, 'as soon/As they had touched the world with living flame' returned to their native light, the divine. His instinctive boyhood response to that first, fleeting intimation of his true self – the flash of silver, the school-yard tears – had been to do the same. He had longed only to soar 'sandalled with plumes of fire' towards 'the lodestar of my one desire'. But he, too, had stayed to touch the world with flame. And having fled he could reappear, Love resplendent, the Morning and the Evening Star.

In 1817 Shelley had cast himself as Prince Athanase in an idealised version of his life. 'Athanase', from the Greek, meant 'deathless'. The word was ambiguous and the work, unfinished, did not resolve it. His hero-self might be condemned to struggle for ever in his 'clay-formed dungeon', never moving higher, or might live and create eternally, a star among the stars.

Mortal still, he was not sure. He could not begin to say where Love or light sprang from. Nor, for all his constant searching, did he know what happened after death. His voyage at the end of *Adonais* was dark and fearful, not assured and calm. He had, he told Medwin and Trelawny, 'some hopes'. As long as the body enclosed him, he could do no better. His final Poet's words in his last, unfinished poem, as he stumbled by the wayside and his masks fell away, were not an affirmation but, as so often, an aching question:

Then, what is Life I cried—

The page was folded at the top. On the joining sheet, in faint outline, a boat began to appear.

Coda: The voyage out

In the afternoon he set sail. He should have left earlier, Trelawny said, but Time as usual irritated him. At some point after two o'clock on 8 July 1822 he slipped the quay at Leghorn and, with Williams, headed out to sea.

For days the air had been sultry, hanging like a lid over the water. The blue sky was implacable; no rain had fallen for weeks. On 4 June, at Lerici, electric arches formed from one arm of the bay to the other. Over the succeeding month Williams noted the strange stasis in the weather:

> June 7th A dead calm—the atmosphere hot and oppressive.
> June 10th . . . weather still threatening . . .
> June 21st Calm—the sun having excessive power
> June 27th The heat increases daily . . .

As for Shelley, he had established his compact with the place, wishing to stay 'for ever'. Time had stood still, with the rainless sky. His boat, gliding in the moonlight, and Jane's music offered him two ways to escape his chains, yet live. 'If the past and future could be obliterated,' he told John Gisborne, 'the present would content me so well that I could say with Faust to the passing moment, "Remain, thou, thou art so beautiful".'

Later in that letter, however, he gave the scene a familiar and darker twist. 'I stand, as it were, upon a precipice, which I have ascended with great, and cannot descend without *greater*, peril, and I am content if the heaven above me is calm for the passing moment.' One tiny spot of beauty was surrounded by terror.

By 1 July a fine breeze had tempted Shelley and Williams to meet Hunt in Leghorn. It blew from the west. As Shelley left Villa Magni, Mary remarked that he was 'full of spirits and joy'. Hunt thought his voice was stronger and his manner more confident, as though some of the old uncertainties had fallen away. But it was an illusion. Under the date 'June 4 / July 4'came an untidy pencil scrawl on a spare sheet of paper:

> The hours are flying
> And joys are dying
> And hope is sighing
>
> . . .
>
>   there is
> Far more to fear
> In the coming year
> Than desire can bear
>   In this

On the day of his return, four days later, the sea was strange. Oily and slow, grey as gun-metal, it curled around his hull. 'Smoke and rags', as old sailors called them, hung in the sky. Shortly after three o'clock a storm-mist came down over the water, and the sun vanished. The wind switched to the north-west, and small dark clouds scudded close to the surface of the sea. Lightning was in the vapour, grazing and shocking him. At that point he could still be seen by telescope from shore, one white and tranquil sail to leeward against a turmoil of black cloud. Not long after, as the thunder broke, fog and sea enshrouded him completely.

In an instant, the whole scene was in motion. The waves swirled, rose and foamed, flung up into a sky in which the massing clouds spread like a dense black cowl. Thunder crashed directly overhead, shaking his whole frame. Dark rain fell so hard that it bounced off the surface of the sea. It worked its way into eyes, mouth, clothes and every seam of him.

Within the weird half-light, the wind filled his sails with intoxicating breaths of air. White wings unfolded vastly from his shoulders, as if through this battering frenzy he could rise to the upper sky. A passing boat yelled an offer of help ('For God's sake reef your sails or you are lost'), but was rebuffed. A last glimpse, perhaps apocryphal, showed Williams trying to fold the sheets, struggling, and Shelley stopping him.

It might have been the sea alone that shattered and engulfed him. If not, a felucca crashed into him on the starboard quarter, perhaps as blind as he was. Their wings meshed. His mainmast snapped, and his side gave in as if it had been made of paper.

He went down instantly. Through the water he fell, down thirteen fathoms, with his notebooks, his pencils, his brass-and-ivory telescope, the crusts of bread in his jacket pockets, and £50 in Austrian dollars. He fell through forests of coral, his hair tangling with the waving weed. Nothing but foam was left behind on the surface of the sea.

At once the water began to work on him. It puckered his fair, freckled skin and turned it blue, the colour of unearthliness. After a while his limbs swelled and stiffened, as though they had absorbed the sea. A shark with a face like Castlereagh tore the white flesh slowly from his hands. By its side, a dogfish with Sidmouth's jaw chewed on the bones that protruded from his thighs. Shoals of smaller fry, massing like reviewers at the scene of a kill, delicately ate the face that had never been drawn to anyone's satisfaction.

Lightning stalked on land, alerting his friends. At Florence Henry Best saw the garden lit up by flashes and the orange trees and statues 'wrapped in flame'. Stricken with fear, he looked towards the sea. At Pisa, the clattering rain invaded Lady Mountcashell's dreams. Shelley had recently told such thrilling tales of storm and shipwreck, sitting in her drawing-room, that her nerves had been shattered and her husband had threatened to eject him. Now she saw her friend again. He came into her house looking melancholy and pale; she entreated him to sit and eat. He refused, telling her that 'I shall never eat more;

I have not a *soldo* left in the world.' When she slept again, she dreamed that he was dead.

The storm had lasted twenty minutes, no more, and every other boat had returned safe. Medwin imagined the *Don Juan* enfolded in the 'misty arms' of the wind. Other men talked of divine revenge, and wondered whether the elements had been 'commissioned' to destroy him. 'There is a solemn appeal to the thoughtful', wrote Thomas de Quincey, 'in a death of so much terrific grandeur following upon defiances of such unparalleled audacity.' Orpheus, some noted, was supposed to have died by lightning as well as laceration.

After ten days, the body was washed ashore. It could not be moved and was buried, hastily and temporarily, to conform to the Genoan quarantine laws. Loose sand covered it and an old pine root marked it, as on the mounds raised to lone, drowned strangers on the shores of ancient Greece.

The grave was too near the tide-line; the sea oozed in, invading and putrefying the flesh it had embraced. There remained of Shelley's earthly effects his black single-breasted jacket of mixed cloth, in rags; his shirt, torn at the lower sleeve; parts of his loose-fitting buff nankeen trousers; and his white silk socks, in black boots. One jacket pocket held the leather binding of a copy of Keats's *Lamia*, borrowed from Hunt (he had mislaid his own), doubled back brutally where he had thrust it away as the vessel foundered.

On 15 August the noisome body, new-exhumed with hooks and tongs, was laid out on a grate by the sea. Trelawny officiated; Hunt kept apart in his carriage, too sick and sorrowful to watch, and after a while Byron swam away. No one else was there but the Italian labourers who had dug their friend from the sand.

Wine, oil, salt and frankincense were cast on the corpse to add to the beauty and perfume of the fire. Trelawny claimed that he committed the body to the flames with incantations: 'I restore to nature through fire the elements of which this man was composed, earth, air and water;

everything is changed, but not annihilated; he is now a portion of that which he worshipped.' Byron, he said, complimented him on his pagan priestliness.

Fire licked the body slowly, disdaining the saturated flesh. It took three hours to burn with a steady phosphorescent light, fed with the lime in which the corpse had been buried. White worms of fire worked on the bones until they fell apart in ash, and blue flame hovered on the oily fluid that trickled from the heart. In the thin pan of the skull, the brains bubbled; Byron was to say later, in a moment of turmoil, that his brains were boiling 'as Shelley's did whilst you were grilling him'.

The blue sky, Hunt conjectured, seemed more than usually beautiful, filled with the 'glassy essence of vitality' rising alongside the flames. Trelawny was more worried by the winds that blew along the barren shore, threatening to disperse Shelley's dust as atoms in the air. A sea mew, or possibly a curlew, flew low across the pyre, sweeping and screaming like a phantom that would not leave the body alone.

Shelley's friends took souvenirs: the black, charred heart (or liver), pieces of the skull. In later years Trelawny would show visitors a whitened fragment of jawbone with the teeth sockets visible, wrapped in tissue paper. Other pieces of greyish bone, thin and light as shards in a kaleidoscope, were set behind glass in frames of gold and covers of tooled morocco. Fragments of the curiously small skull were handed round at parties; some ladies kissed them. Wispy curls of his hair were sewn on to pieces of paper. Most of his ashes were eventually buried in the shade of the Aurelian wall in Rome, in a spot which he had thought 'might make one in love with death'.

Mary placed the 'heart' first in a silk bag and then inside a page, folded in four, torn from her copy of *Adonais*. By 1851, when she died, only a little dust remained. It was laid in a silk-lined silver casket and kept in a shrine in the house of his descendants at Boscombe, with a red lamp burning before it as in front of his detested saints.

Shelley was not in any case there, as Mary had explained to the Hunts:

Wherever the Spirit of Beauty dwells he must be—the rustling of the trees is full of him—the waving of the tall grass—the moving shadows of the vast hills—the blue air that penetrates their ravines and rests upon their heights . . .

She saw him, too, in dreams; Hogg heard his light, quick steps still running, and Trelawny, gazing at the sea, heard his shrieking laugh again.

The boats lay scattered near where he had been. The black and red coracle was washed ashore near Viareggio, the green-and-white skiff left in pieces in the store-room at Villa Magni, the *Don Juan* put in salvage at Leghorn, its hull packed with bluish mud. Later, having been decked and sailed for a while, it was wrecked on one of the Ionian islands which had appeared to the Poet so remote and safe, like Heaven. And by a pond in London one might find a boat of folded paper not much larger than a dragonfly, inscribed with lines that had begun to blur and run:

I am not
Your obedient servant,
P. B. Shelley

Far away, serenely, Vesper glittered in the darkening sky.

Acknowledgements

Many people have helped and encouraged me with this book. First thanks should go to Dr Bruce Barker-Benfield, Senior Assistant Librarian in the Department of Special Collections at the Bodleian Library, for helping me renew my Bodleian membership and answering my questions on Shelley's notebooks with infinite courtesy and kindness. For fielding other queries and dealing with knotty points, I am most grateful to Judith Chernaik and Nora Crook. Several academics, much more conversant with Shelley and his world than I am, were kind enough to read the book in draft: Professor Nicholas Roe of the University of St Andrews, Professor Michael O'Neill of the University of Durham and Professor Janet Todd of the University of Aberdeen. Their enthusiasm was a great spur to me, though none of them is remotely to blame for my opinions or my approach.

Particular thanks should go too to Robin Wardall-Smith, archivist of University College Oxford, for keeping me abreast of the new Shelley letters discovered in 2005; to two old 'Univ' friends, Mark Studer and Andrew Lyle, for sending many useful bits and pieces from the *University College Record* and from their travels; to Professor Peter Abbs, Stoddard Martin, Andrew Miller and Fiammetta Rocco, four very busy friends, for making time to read the manuscript; to Miranda Seymour for good advice on contacts; and to Roderick Cavaliero for sending back issues of the *Keats–Shelley Bulletin*. In common with everyone who writes about Shelley, I also felt continually indebted to Shelleyan editors, scholars and biographers down the decades, from Mary Shelley onwards.

The book market, now as in the early 1800s, is not mad about metaphysics. My agent, Andrew Wylie, and my publishers, Dan Franklin at Cape and Erroll McDonald at Pantheon, deserve much gratitude for believing in this enterprise and being brave enough to back it. Joy de Menil, my great and long-suffering editor, gave her usual invaluable quotient of ruthlessness and fun. Many thanks too to Beth Humphries for her wonderfully careful copy-editing.

Lastly, heartfelt thanks to my husband Malcolm for not only putting up with the project, but positively encouraging it, though it meant many a cold supper and a lonely night, and an awful lot of (expensive) petrol consumed in Sussex, the Thames Valley, Wales and Italy. At least there were sometimes Roman sites to look at along the way.

AW

April 2007

Notes

Abbreviations

Alastor	*Alastor, or the Spirit of Solitude*
BL	British Library
BSM	Bodleian Shelley Manuscripts
c. 4	*Miscellaneous Poetry, Prose and Translations from Bodleian MS Shelley adds c. 4*, ed. E.B. Murray. BSM vol. 21 (New York and London 1995)
d. 1	*Facsimile of Bodleian MS Shelley d. 1*, 2 parts, ed. E.B. Murray. BSM vol. 4 (1988)
d. 7	*Bodleian MS. Shelley adds d.7: A Facsimile Edition*, ed. Irving Massey. BSM vol. 2 (1987)
e. 1, e. 2 and e. 3	*The 'Prometheus Unbound' Notebooks: A Facsimile of Bodleian MSS e.1, e.2, and e.3*, ed. Neil Fraistat. BSM vol. 9 (1991)
e. 4	*Bodleian Shelley MSS e. 4: A Facsimile Edition*, ed. P.M.S. Dawson. BSM vol. 3 (1987)
e. 6	*The Witch of Atlas Notebook: A Facsimile of Bodleian MSS Shelley adds e.6*, ed. Carlene A. Adamson. BSM vol. 5 (1997)
e. 7	*The Hellas Notebook: Bodleian MSS Shelley adds e.7*, ed. Donald H. Reiman and Michael Neth. BSM vol. 16 (1994)
e. 8	*Shelley's Pisan Winter Notebooks, 1820–21. A Facsimile of Shelley MSS adds e. 8*, ed. Carlene A. Adamson. BSM vol. 6 (1992)
e. 9	*Shelley's 'Devils' Notebook: Bodleian Shelley MSS adds e. 9*, ed. P.M.S. Dawson and Timothy Webb. BSM vol. 14 (1993)
e. 10	*Drafts for Laon and Cythna, Cantos V–XII: Bodleian Shelley MSS e. 10*, ed. Stephen E. Jones. BSM vol. 17 (1994)

e. 11	*The 'Julian and Maddalo' Draft Notebook: Bodleian MSS Shelley adds e. 11*, ed. Steven E. Jones. BSM vol. 15 (1990)
e. 12	*The Homeric Hymns and Prometheus Drafts Notebook: Bodleian MSS Shelley adds e. 12*, ed. Nancy Moore Goslee. BSM vol. 18 (1996)
e. 14	*Drafts for Laon and Cythna: Facsimiles of Bodleian MSS Shelley adds e. 14 and e. 19*, ed. Tatsuo Tokoo. BSM vol. 13 (1992)
e. 16	*The Geneva Notebooks of Percy Bysshe Shelley: Bodleian MSS Shelley adds e. 16 and MSS Shelley adds c. 4, folios 63, 65, 71 and 72*, ed. Michael Erkelenz. BSM vol. 11 (1992)
e. 17	*The 'Charles the First' Draft Notebook: A Facsimile of Bodleian MSS Shelley adds e. 17*, ed. Nora Crook. BSM vol. 12 (1991)
e. 18	*The 'Faust' Draft Notebook: A Facsimile of Bodleian MSS Shelley adds e. 18*, ed. Nora Crook and Timothy Webb. BSM vol. 19 (1997)
e. 19	See *e. 14* above.
e. 20	*'Shelley's Last Notebook': Bodleian MS Shelley adds. e. 20*, ed. Donald Reiman and Helene Dworzan Reiman. BSM vol. 7 (1990)
vol. 1	*Peter Bell the Third and The Triumph of Life*, ed. Donald Reiman BSM vol. 1, (1986)
CC	Claire Clairmont
CC	*The Clairmont Correspondence: Letters of Claire Clairmont, Charles Clairmont and Fanny Imlay Godwin*, ed. Marion Kingston Stocking. 2 vols (Baltimore, 1995)
CCJ	*The Journals of Claire Clairmont*, ed. Marion Kingston Stocking with David Mackenzie Stocking (Cambridge, 1968)
Chernaik	Chernaik, Judith, *The Lyrics of Shelley* (Cleveland, 1972)
Clark	*Shelley's Prose, or The Trumpet of a Prophecy*, ed. David Lee Clark (Albuquerque, 1953; reprinted London, 1988)
Contemps	*Shelley and Keats as they struck their Contemporaries*, ed. Edmund Blunden (London, 1925). Includes Thornton Hunt, 'Shelley – by one who knew him', reprinted from *Atlantic Monthly*, Feb. 1863
Dawson	Dawson, P. M. S., *The Unacknowledged Legislator: Shelley and Politics* (Oxford, 1980)
Dowden	Dowden, Edward, *The Life of Percy Bysshe Shelley*. 2 vols (London, 1886)
DP	*A Defence of Poetry*
DR	*Declaration of Rights*

EC	*Essay on Christianity*
EH	Elizabeth Hitchener
ELA	*Essays, Letters from Abroad, Translations and Fragments by Percy Bysshe Shelley*, ed. Mary Wollstonecraft Shelley. 2 vols (London, 1840)
Epip.	*Epipsychidion*
Esdaile	*The Esdaile Notebook: A Volume of Early Poems by Percy Bysshe Shelley*, ed. Kenneth Neill Cameron (London, 1964)
'Euganean Hills'	'Lines written among the Euganean Hills'
Forman	*The Prose Works of Percy Bysshe Shelley*, ed. H. Buxton Forman. 4 vols (London, 1880)
H.	*Shelley: Poetical Works*, ed. Thomas Hutchinson (Oxford, 1905; 1947 edition)
Haydon	*The Diary of Benjamin Robert Haydon*, ed. Willard Bissell Pope. 5 vols: vol. 2 (Cambridge, Mass., 1960)
HM 2111	*Shelley's 1821–1822 Huntington Notebook. A Facsimile of Huntington MS. HM 2111*, ed. Mary A. Quinn. *The Manuscripts of the Younger Romantics* (Donald Reiman, general editor), *Percy Bysshe Shelley*, vol. 7 (New York and London, 1996)
HM 2176	*Shelley's 1819–1821 Huntington Notebook. A Facsimile of Huntington MS. HM 2176*, ed. Mary A. Quinn. *The Manuscripts of the Younger Romantics, Percy Bysshe Shelley*, vol. 6 (New York and London, 1994)
HM 2177	*The Mask of Anarchy Draft Notebook: A Facsimile of Huntington MS. HM 2177*, ed. Mary A. Quinn. *The Manuscripts of the Younger Romantics, Percy Bysshe Shelley*, vol. 4 (New York and London, 1990)
Hogg	Hogg, Thomas Jefferson, *The Life of Shelley*. 2 vols (London, 1858)
HSWT	*History of a Six Weeks' Tour* (1814, published 1817)
Hunt	*The Autobiography of Leigh Hunt*, ed. Roger Ingpen. 2 vols (London, 1903)
IB	'Hymn to Intellectual Beauty'
Ingpen	Ingpen, Roger, *Shelley in England: New Facts and Letters from the Shelley–Whitton Papers*. 3 vols (London, 1917)
J&M	*Julian and Maddalo: A Conversation*
Jones	*The Letters of Percy Bysshe Shelley*, ed. Frederick L. Jones. 2 vols (Oxford, 1964)
LMG	*Letter to Maria Gisborne*

MA	*The Mask of Anarchy* (1819; published 1832)
MacFarlane	MacFarlane, Charles, *Reminiscences of a Literary Life* (London, 1917)
M/E	*The Poems of Shelley,* ed. G.M. Matthews and Kevin Everest. vol. 1, *1805–1817* (London 1989); vol. 2, *1817–1819* (London, 2000)
Medwin	Medwin, Thomas, *The Life of Percy Bysshe Shelley.* New edition with an Introduction and Commentary by H. Buxton Forman (Oxford, 1913)
Merle	Merle, Joseph, 'A Newspaper Editor's Reminiscences', Chapter IV, *Fraser's Magazine,* June 1841, pp. 699–710
MSJ	*The Journals of Mary Shelley, 1814–1844,* ed. Paula R. Feldman and Diana Scott-Kilvert. 2 vols (Oxford, 1987). Includes the joint journal kept with Shelley
MWS	Mary Wollstonecraft Shelley
MWSL	*The Letters of Mary Wollstonecraft Shelley,* ed. Betty T. Bennett. 3 vols (Baltimore, 1980–8)
NS	*Notes on the Sculptures of Rome and Florence*
NSL	Scott, W.S., ed., *New Shelley Letters* (London, 1848)
PB III	*Peter Bell the Third*
Peck	Peck, Walter Edwin, *Shelley: His Life and Work.* 2 vols (*London,* 1927)
PJ	William Godwin, *An Enquiry concerning Political Justice* (1793)
PRV	*A Proposal for Putting Reform to the Vote*
PU	*Prometheus Unbound*
PVR	*A Philosophical View of Reform*
PW	Paltock, Robert, *The Life and Adventures of Peter Wilkins,* ed. Christopher Bentley (Oxford 1973)
QM	*Queen Mab*
RAM	Samuel Taylor Coleridge, *The Rime of the Ancient Mariner* (1798)
R&H	*Rosalind and Helen:* Reiman, Donald H., *A Modern Eclogue*
RCE	'The Retrospect, Cwm Elan'
Reiman	Reiman, Donald H. *Shelley's The Triumph of Life: A Critical Study.* Illinois Studies in Lanuage and Literature, 55 (Urbana, 1965)
Reveley	Reveley, Henry, *Notes and Observations to the 'Shelley Memorials'* (1859); see *SC,* vol. 10
R of I	*The Revolt of Islam* (originally *Laon and Cythna*)

RM	Paine, Thomas, *Rights of Man* (1791–2); Everyman edition, 1930
SC	*Shelley and his Circle, 1773–1822*, ed. Kenneth Neill Cameron and Donald H. Reiman. 10 vols to date (Cambridge, Mass., 1961–2004)
SG	*Shelley's Guitar: An Exhibition of Manuscripts, First Editions and Relics, to Mark the Bicentenary of the Birth of Percy Bysshe Shelley 1792/1992*, exhibition catalogue, ed. Bruce Barker-Benfield (Oxford, 1992)
SP	'The Sensitive Plant'
Spec. Met.	*Speculations on Metaphysics* (given in Clark, c.f., as *A Treatise on Morals*)
TL	*The Triumph of Life* (Reiman's transcription)
TLP Mem.	Peacock, Thomas Love, *Memoirs of Shelley and other Essays and Reviews*, ed. Howard Mills (London, 1970)
Tre.	Trelawny, Edward John, *The Last Days of Shelley and Byron: Being the Complete Text of Trelawny's 'Recollections'*, ed. J. E. Morpurgo (London, 1952)
Tre. *Rec.*	Trelawny, Edward John, *Records of Shelley, Byron and the Author*. 2 vols (London, 1878)
WA	*The Witch of Atlas*
Walker	Walker, Adam, *Analysis of a Course of Lectures on Natural and Experimental Philosophy* (1771)
WJ	*The Journal of Edward Ellerker Williams, Companion of Shelley and Byron in 1821 and 1822*, ed. Richard Garnett (London, 1902)

Introduction

p. ix	'The poet & the man': To the Gisbornes, 19.7.21; Jones, vol. 2, p. 310
p. x	'Time and place': *DP*, Forman, vol. 3, p. 104
	'Whence I came': *TL* 398
	'Mystifying metaphysics': Byron to Trelawny, Tre. *Rec.*, vol. 1, p. 43

Prelude

p. xi	Paper boats: Hogg, vol. 1, p. 84
p. xii	Favourite of all deaths: *Contemps*, p. 17

Earth

Substance

p. 5   MacFarlane's account: MacFarlane, pp. 1–9 *passim*
p. 7   'No pleasure': Hogg, vol. 2, p. 483
          'Crimes & miseries': To Hookham, 17.12.12. Jones, vol. 1, p. 340
          Facts: To a Lady, spring of 1821. Jones, vol. 2, p. 277
          'His imagination': TLP *Mem.*, p. 24
          'Altogether incapable': Hogg, vol. 2, p. 68
          The visit to the ladies: *Ibid.*, vol. 1, p. 13
          Trelawny and sisters: Tre. *Rec.*, vol. 2, p. 21
          'Exquisitely beautiful': *An Essay on Friendship*, Hogg, vol. 1, p. 24
p. 8   'I myself also': BSM e. 8 p. 164 rev.
          Childhood: Hogg, vol. 1, pp. 19–20
p. 9   Sussex pigs: *Swellfoot the Tyrant*, esp. Act I sc.i
          Agricultural chemistry: Hogg, vol. 1, pp. 59–61
          Notes from Davy: BSM e. 6 pp. 172–1 rev.
          Potatoes and rutabaga: *Ibid.*, pp. 3–7
p. 10   No such chemical elements: Medwin, p. 28
          Lignis . . . et ignis: De rerum natura 1, 911–14
          'Unnatural and keen excitement': To Godwin, 7.12.17. Jones, vol. 1, p. 572
          'That actual world': To Godwin, 29.7.12. *Ibid.*, p. 316
p. 11   'A branch of philosophy': 6.11.12. *Ibid.*, p. 328
          Entangling his wings: BSM d. 1 f. 49v rev.
          'A mass of organized animation': To EH, 24.11.11. Jones, vol. 1, p. 193
          'I tell thee': *QM* I, 231–4, 238–41
          'Motive is to voluntary action': *QM* note to VI, 198
          'It is impossible': To EH, 16.10.11. Jones, vol. 1, p. 150
p. 12   '*The existing power*': To EH, 11.6.11. *Ibid.*, p. 101
          'REALLY feel': To EH, 28.10.11. *Ibid.*, p. 163
          'Let every seed': *QM* VII, 19–22
          Nil posse: De rerum natura 1, 155–6
          'A mass of electrified clay': To John Wedgwood, 15.12.10. See 'The Student Hoaxers: The New Shelley Letters', by Robin Darwall-Smith, *University College Record*, 14, no. 1 (2005)
p. 13   'Atom Born!': 'Ode to Heaven' 38

'I would not be': BSM e. 8 p. 112

'Wild with tears': To Byron, 24.9.17. Jones, vol. 1, p. 557

'And then they smote me': *The Lament of Tasso* VI, 162–5

p. 14   Tales to Godwin: 10.1.12. Jones, vol.1, p. 228

Athanase and tutor: BSM e. 4 f. 74r (*Prince Athanase* 130–1
219–29)

'I have known no tutor': To Godwin, 16.1.12. Jones, vol. 1,
p. 230

'Solemn vision': *Alastor* 67–8

p. 15   His conversion: IB 55–62; *R of I Dedication* 22–36

One draft: BSM e. 14 pp. 10–11

p. 16   'Far aloft . . .': *Epip.* 191–6

'Una Favola': Forman, vol. 3, pp. 83–5 (trans. 91–2)

The secret garden: Hogg, vol. 1, pp. 111–15

Wandering in Wales: RCE *passim*

p. 17   'Fine fellows these': Jones, vol. 1, p. 60n

Political background: see Dawson, Chs 1 and 2 *passim*

p. 18   'And hated it': Hogg, vol. 1, pp. 206–7

'I will not listen': 18.4.11. Jones, vol. 1, p. 65

'To cast off': Ingpen, p. 254

'A blot, a defilement': To Godwin, 10.1.12. Jones, vol. 1, p. 227

p. 19   'Obedience': 12.10.11. *Ibid.*, p. 146

Shelley and his father: Hogg, vol. 1, pp. 304–5

The music master: To E.F. Graham, ?14.5.11. Jones, vol. 1,
pp. 85–7

'Certain considerations': 16.1.12. *Ibid.*, p. 230

'*Ill, vilely*': *Ibid.*, p. 149

p. 20   'Unmeaning name': RCE 79

'Almost every one': *QM* Note to VIII, 211, 212

'Provincial Stupidity': To James T. Tisdall, 1.1.09. Jones, vol.
1, p. 3

'My object': 7.5.09. *Ibid.*, pp. 4–5

'We will all go': To Graham, 1.4.10. *Ibid.*, p. 5

Tailor's bill: Ingpen, p. 178

p. 21   'We are superior': *SC*, vol. 2, p. 737

'Oxonian society': 10.1.12. Jones, vol. 1, p. 228

£50 a year: To Hogg, 8.5.11. *Ibid.*, p. 78

'Fatuous claims': *NSL*, p. 128

p. 22   'Aristocratical sallies': Maria Gisborne cited in White, vol.
2, p. 200

Diogenes the Cynic: BSM e. 4 f. 27v
'Aristocratical': To Hunt, 3.11.19. Jones, vol. 2, p. 143
'Visionary': To EH, 26.7.11. Jones, vol. 1, p. 127
'No man . . .': *DR* XXVII–XXVIII, Forman, vol. 1, p. 397

p. 23   'Mahogany tables': To EH, 16.10.11. Jones, vol. 1, p. 150
'In me': Merle, p. 706
'You remind me': To EH, 19?.8.11. Jones, vol. 1, p. 136
Distinctions of property: *PVR*, Clark, pp. 250–1
'All is common': *EC*, Forman, vol. 2, p. 362
'Chairs tables': To EH, ?24.2.12. Jones, vol. 1, p. 257
'A system of . . . absolute perfection': *PVR*, Clark, pp. 253–4

p. 24   The blankets: Jones, vol. 1, p. 575n
Poor in France: *HSWT*, *ELA*, vol. 2, p. 16
'Moral imbecility': *EC*, Forman, vol. 2, p. 361
'A certain degree': 8.8.21. Jones, vol. 2, p. 320

p. 25   '*We* decay . . .': *Adonais* 348–51
'One mass of animated filth': 8.3.12. Jones, vol. 1, p. 268
'Stupid & shrivelled': To Peacock, 20.4.18. Jones, vol. 2, p. 9
'Spurt phiz': BSM c. 4 f. 61r

p. 26   Ianthe and the wet-nurse: White, vol. 1, p. 326
'Superhuman strength': Hogg, vol. 2, p. 2

p. 27   'Contagion of the world's slow stain': *Adonais* 356
'More delicately organized': *DP*, Forman, vol. 3, p. 142
'Thinking he was dying': To Henry Reveley, *SC*, vol. 10, p. 1134

p. 28   'Death and Love': *R of I Dedication*, 90
Mrs Ford's bill: *SC,* vol. 6, p. 326
'Yet let's be merry': *LMG* 303–5, 307

p. 29   The populace of Paris: *A Vindication of Natural Diet*, Forman, vol. 2, p. 13
Chewing the corpse: *R of I* III, 1270–6 ff.

p. 30   Proposed adoption: Merle, p.707
'A great glass of ale': TLP *Mem.*, p. 68
'The very sense of being': *QM* note to VIII, 211, 212
Food intake: *MSJ*, vol. 1, p. 142
'Those who would be free': *DR* XXX, Forman, vol. 1, p. 398
'Nearest to the Divine Nature': *EC*, Forman, vol. 2, p. 367

p. 31   'A strange melange': *c.* 19.6.11. Jones, vol. 1, p. 108
'Folly and Madness': Dawson, p. 35
'If madness 'tis . . .': 'The Sunset' 33

MacFarlane/*Queen Mab*: MacFarlane, p. 6

p. 32   'I know not': BSM e. 11 p. 1 (*Essay on Love*, Forman, vol. 2, p. 267)

'Your mind is not fitted': Hogg, vol. 2, p. 74

The mad Poet: *Alastor* 248–71

'There was a youth': *Prince Athanase*, 8–12

p. 33   'A strange fellow': BSM e. 8 p. 70

'And he/Is now gone mad': *J&M* 195, 197–8, 236–7

'How am I changed!': *R&H* 764–6

'In some degree': To Hunt, 15.8.19. Jones, vol. 2, p. 108

'Of the Maniac': *J&M* Preface

Chains

p. 37   'I never saw': To Peacock, 12.7.16. Jones, vol. 1, p. 485

'A spectre': 'The Tower of Famine' 17

Beatrice Cenci: *The Cenci* Preface

p. 38   'Confined in a damp cell': To Harriet, ?25.10.14. Jones, vol. 1, p. 410

Defence of Carlile: To Hunt as editor of the *Examiner*, 3.11.19. Jones, vol. 2, pp. 136–48

'Whose chains . . .': *QM* VI, 195–6

p. 39   Woman as 'bond-slave': *R of I* VIII, 3314

'Monkish' rules of chastity: *QM* note to V, 189 (H., p. 808)

The Dublin urchin: To EH, 10.3.12. Jones, vol. 1, p. 270

'Clothes, and fire': *MA* 221–2

p. 40   'If I know anything': To Hogg, *c.* 22.7.11. Jones, vol. 1, p. 123

'A kind of ineffable disgust': To Hogg, 8.5.11. *Ibid.*, p. 80

'One chained friend': *Epip.* 158

'Required to love': 10.1.12. Jones, vol. 1, p. 227

p. 41   'Superintending mind': To Harriet, 16.9.14. *Ibid.*, p. 395

'Love withers': *QM* note to V, 189

'Love seems inclined': To James Henry Lawrence, 17.8.12. Jones, vol. 1, p. 323

p. 42   'If I were free': 10.12.11. *Ibid.*, p. 203

'Habit & self-persuasion': 5.10.14. *Ibid.*, p. 405

'How beautiful and calm': *R of I* Dedication, 57–60

p. 43   'It is no reproach to me': 14.7.14. Jones, vol. 1, p. 390

'Are you above the world?': 14.9.14. *Ibid.*, p. 394

'I as his sister': *Ibid.*, p. 421n

'Our common treasure': To Hogg, ?26.4.15. *Ibid.*, p. 426

p. 44   The grocery list: BSM c. 4 f. 105r (*SG* no. 124, p. 150)

'A portion of herself': To the Gisbornes, 11.3.20. *SG* no. 108, p. 131

'Kiss me;—': 'Invocation to Misery' 36–40

'The quick coupled with the dead': Tre. *Rec.*, vol. 1, p. 105

p. 45   'A dead & living body': To Hogg, 4.10.14. Jones, vol. 1, p. 402

Pulses of his heart: To John Gisborne, 12.1.22. Jones, vol. 2, p. 376

'This dark and miserable abyss': *Epip.* Epigraph

The letter to Emilia: BSM e. 8 p. 20

The poem to her: BSM e. 12 p. 3

p. 46   'Bitter knowledge': To Hunt, 15.8.19. Jones, vol. 2, p. 109

'No combination': To John Gisborne, 6.11.19. *Ibid.*, p. 149

p. 47   'Of the National Debt': *SC*, vol. 6, p. 1008

Working out the debt: BSM e. 12 p. 48

'S alone looks grave': *MSJ*, p. 17 (20.8.14)

p. 48   'How many a rustic Milton': *QM* V, 137–9

'A bad man': To EH, 26.1.12. Jones, vol. 1, p. 239

Baxter's Sussex Pocket Book: See *SC,* vol. 9, pp. 67–112

'An infernal arithmetician': To Peacock, 23.1.19. Jones, vol. 2, p. 70

p. 49   Plato's equation: BSM e. 9 p. 319; e. 12 p. 8

'Anti-worldling': BSM e. 10 p. 172

'Make money cheaper': Jones, vol. 1, p. 422n

British Funds: 28.10.19. Jones, vol. 2, p. 132; 6.11.19. *Ibid.*, pp. 149–50

'My habitual . . . inability': 29.3.16. Jones, vol. 1, p. 466

p. 50   'To tie me up': To Godwin, 2.10.16. *Ibid.*, p. 509

'~~That man~~': BSM e. 7 p. 235 (1821)

p. 51   'That faery Hall!': *QM* II, 30–5

'A prejudice': To Godwin, 3.5.16. Jones, vol. 1, p. 472

The fight with the landsman: 'The Voyage' (*Esdaile* 32) 112–96

p. 52   'Dear Home': BSM e. 10 pp. 26–9

p. 53   The vicarage: TLP *Mem.*, pp. 41–2

'The trees, the bridge': To Hogg, 16.3.14. Jones, vol. 1, p. 383

p. 54   'My country dear to me': To Godwin, 3.5.16. *Ibid.*, p. 472

The Bath idyll: To Byron, 29.9.16. *Ibid.*, p. 508

'A fixed, settled, eternal home': 17.7.16. *Ibid.*, p. 491

'The shrines of the Penates': *Ibid.*, p. 490

'The curse of this life': To Peacock, 20.4.18. *Ibid.*, p. 6

p. 55   'I have . . . established myself': 11.1.22. Jones, vol. 2, p. 373

'Tranquil uniformity': To Byron, 23.4.17. Jones, vol. 1, p. 540

'A city of the dead': *MWSL*, vol. 1, p. 123

'O why do we rest': BSM e. 12 p. 148

'How like death-worms': BSM: e. 2 f. 22r

'~~Hours hours~~': BSM e. 9 p. 176

p. 56   'But I am chained to Time': *Adonais* 234

'O world, o life, o time': BSM e. 8 p. 123v rev.

Verweile doch: To John Gisborne, 18.6.22. Jones, vol. 2, p. 436

'I dare say': To Hogg, 11.2.17. Jones, vol. 1, p. 532

p. 57   'I have lost a day': Tre., pp. 73–4

The starches game: BSM d. 1 f. 104r rev.

'Perhaps the only comfort': cancelled fragment of *J&M* 630–2; HM 2176 f. 3r

p. 58   The chaos of boulders: BSM e. 9 p. 378, and see p.1

'Stones, stones, stones!': Hogg, vol. 1, p. 58

'Anchors, beaks of ships': *PU* Act IV, 289–92, 300–3

p. 59   'Philosophically false': *EC*, Forman, vol. 2, p. 369

'There's not one atom': *QM* II, 211–15

'And on the pedestal': 'Ozymandias' 9–14

p. 60   The Genius in the ruins: Volney, *Ruins of Empire*, pp. 6–14

The war scene: To Harriet, 13.8.14. Jones, vol. 1, p. 392

S.'s imaginings of Peterloo: To Hunt, 3.11.19. Jones, vol. 2, p. 136

'Blood within a living frame': *MA* 139–46

At Peterloo: 'Lines Written during the Castlereagh Administration' 1–15

p. 61   The Maremma: 'Marenghi' 87–9

'And there is no great extravagance': *QM* note to VI, 45, 46

p. 62   'Equal in rights': *RM*, pp. 12, 42

Time 'measured and created': *The Assassins*, Forman, vol. 2, p. 229

'Hardened to hope' *QM* V, 75–7

'And . . . this is the bond': Rejected lines for 'A Ballad (Young Parson Richard)', 1819

p. 63   'The town of Old Sarum': *RM*, p. 51

'Sanguine eagerness': *PRV*, Forman, vol. 2, p. 95

'Brutal and torpid': *R of I* Preface

A night in a cottage: *SC*, vol. 3, p. 347 (CC revised journal for August 1814)

'Give me a place to stand on': *QM* third epigraph

p. 64   'Shrink to your cellars': 'Song to the Men of England' 5–8, 25–32

'All . . . subdue themselves': To Horace Smith, 29.6.22. Jones, vol. 2, p. 442

'Masses of senseless clay': 'Lines Written during the Castlereagh Administration' 7–8

'Spirit, thought and love': *QM* IV, 97

'As the slow periods': *J&M* 416–19

'Thou shalt be in league': BSM e. 18 p. 160 rev (Job 5: 23)

'Fertilizing gore': *QM* note to IV, 178, 179: 'Falsehood and Vice, A Dialogue'

p. 65   'Let them ride': *MA* 319–43

The death page: BSM c. 4 f. 68r, v, and see p. 35

p. 66   'Every one does me full justice': To Mary, 16.12.16. Jones, vol. 1, p. 521

The death knell: BSM e. 8 p. 22 rev. (and d. 1 f. 108r rev.)

'Learn to make others happy': *QM* II, 64

p. 67   'The moon made thy lips pale': 'Lines' 19–20 (H., p. 527)

'Far severer anguish': 17.1.17. Jones, vol. 1, p. 530

~~'Friend had I known'~~: BSM c. 4 f. 68 (H., 'On Fanny Godwin', p. 546)

p. 68   'These are blind fancies': *R of I* IX, 3757–63

'Lured me towards sweet Death': *Epip.* 72–3

Death sewing the shroud: 'Una Favola', Forman, vol. 3, p. 85

'Is suicide wrong?': 3.1.11. Jones, vol. 1, p. 36

p. 69   'All sorts of care': 8.6.21. Jones, vol. 2, p. 296

'Careless, not to say impatient': Tre. *Rec.*, vol. 1, p. 103

'Quantities' of laudanum: *CC* 2, p. 597 (to Trelawny, 1869)

'Life's sweetest bane': *Oepidus at Colonus* (Peacock's trans.)

Mrs Godwin's account: See Peck, vol. 1, pp. 364–5

p. 70   'A double dose': 5.8.21. Jones, vol. 2, p. 314

'Poison of laurel leaves': To Hogg, *c.* 16.11.11. Jones, vol. 1, p. 184

False laurel: 'The False Laurel and the True' (H., p. 661)

Prussic Acid: 16.6.22. Jones, vol. 2, p. 433

'One poor thought': 'To St Irvyne—To Harriet ——' (*Esdaile* 58) 24

The icicle: 'On an Icicle that Clung to the Grass of a Grave'
(*Esdaile* 44), *passim*

'The wild-woods' gloomiest shade': RCE 26, 106–7

p. 71   'The babe is at peace': BSM e, 12 p. 180

'Not to be able to die': *QM* note to VII, 67

'The dead are sleeping': 'A Summer Evening Churchyard,
Lechlade, Gloucestershire' 19–24

p. 72   Severn and Shelley: William Sharp, *The Life and Letters of
Joseph Severn* (London, 1892), pp. 116–17

'Underneath the grave': 'Invocation to Misery' 41–5

'They die—the dead return not': BSM e. 16 p. 46 rev.

'I leapt in': BSM e. 8 p. 107

Masks

p. 77   Emilia's flowers: 'To Emilia Viviani', *passim* (HM 2176 f. *28v)

'Not pale, but fair': *R&H* 820

'A climber, a creeper': Hogg, vol. 2, p. 46

Thornton Hunt: *Contemps*, pp. 16–17

Lilies of the valley: SP 1, 21–4

'A little flower': 20.10.21. Jones, vol. 2, p. 361

'Yellow and blue flowers': 28.11.17. Jones, vol. 1, p. 569

The Sussex vision: 'The Question' *passim*; BSM e. 12, pp. 164–5

'Crowns of sea-buds': *R&H* 1081–3

p. 79   'All my saddest verses': 10.11.20. Jones, vol. 2, p. 246

The anemone: 'Song' ('Original Poetry by Victor & Cazire'
IV), 1–8

'O lift me from the grass!': 'The Indian Serenade' 17–18

'Upon my heart': BSM e. 12 pp. 10–11 (H., 'To Mary
Wollstonecraft Godwin' 19–22)

'Why do I drink filthy poison': BL Ashley 394 f. 106v

p. 80   'That which you call *love*': 16.1.21. Jones, vol. 2, p. 256

'Ever in love exactly': *CC*, vol. 2, p. 651

'Mary might be very much annoyed': 14.9.21. Jones, vol.
2, p. 347

'Impurity & vice': 28.10.14. Jones, vol. 1, p. 414

Masturbation: *A Discourse on the Manners of the Ancient
Greeks*, Clark, p. 222

Penis sketch: BSM c. 4 f. 201v

'That, like some maniac monk': *J&M* 424–8

Rotting flowers: SP III, 62–5 (H., p. 596)

'*Pansies* let *my* flowers be': HM 2111 f. 9r (H.,
    'Remembrance', p. 643, 20)

'The Exotic': 11.12.21. Jones, vol. 2, p. 367

p. 81   'A sweet child': SP I, 112–14

'I do not care': 8.12.16. Jones, vol. 1, p. 517

'I am . . . nothing': To Hunt, 26.8.21. Jones, vol. 2, p. 344

p. 82   *Epipsychidion* prefaces: BSM d. 1 ff.102v rev.–99v rev.

p. 83   'If you tell no one': 7.3.20. Jones, vol. 2, p. 175

'Being unwilling': Footnote to 'Henry and Louisa' (*Esdaile* 46)

'Trash': To Ollier, 11.6.21. Jones, vol. 2, p. 298

'One, whose voice': *Epip.* 256–9

'~~She was not there~~': BSM e. 8 p. 106

p. 84   'What I am and have been': To John Gisborne, 18.6.22.
        Jones, vol. 2, p. 434

Mr Peyton: *c.* 3.8.11. Jones, vol. 1, p. 131

p. 85   Elena Adelaide: For more details see Holmes, pp. 465–74

'I suppose': To the Gisbornes, 30.6.20. Jones, vol. 2, p. 206

'Everything that passes': To EH, 26. 12. 11. Jones, vol. 1, p. 213

A youth in a cap: BSM e. 10 p. 217

'Young Master Shelley': *SC*, vol. 9, p. 179; Hogg, vol. 2,
    pp. 546–8

Harlequin: To John Taaffe, 4.7.21. Jones, vol. 2, p. 307

p. 86   *Orfana anima*: BL Ashley 4086 f. 2r; *Epip.* 1

p. 87   The note of rebuff: 'To Jane: The Invitation' 33–7

Trelawny's trail: Tre., pp. 46–8

'Utterly solitary': Tre. *Rec.*, vol. 2, p. 23

'An isolated thing': 'The Solitary' (*Esdaile* 15) 1–2

'The pure and tender-hearted': *Alastor* Preface

p. 88   The still centre: *MSJ*, vol 1, p. 35 (14.10.14)

'The society of one': To Claire, 11.12.21. Jones, vol. 2, p. 368

'That common . . . talk': *PU* Act III sc. iv, 149–50

The Irish report: Forman, vol. 3, p. 370

Clearing out demons: BL Add. 37496 f. 93v

'My good genius': 29.6.22. Jones, vol. 2, p. 442

p. 89   'Killing self': BSM e. 17 p.11

'Sick to death': Jones, vol. 1, p. 34

'So much for self': 15.8.19. Jones, vol. 2, pp.108–9

'Thou makest me': BSM e. 18 p. 160 rev (Job 13:26)

'Some moon-struck sophist': *R of I* VIII, 3244–7

'The horror the *evil*': To Hogg, 8.5.11. Jones, vol. 1, p. 77

'That inward stain': *R&H* 478–80

p. 90   'Man who man would be': 'Sonnet: To the Republic of Benevento' 10–14

'To be greatly good': *DP*, Forman, vol. 3, p. 111

'The only perfect . . .': *EC*, Forman, vol. 2, p. 362

p. 91   'Indignation boiling': To Ollier, 6.6.19. Jones, vol. 2, p. 117

'A shabby stand': *LMG* 265–9

'An expression of misgiving': Hunt, Preface to *The Mask of Anarchy*, 1832 (Shelley Society reprint, ed. Wise, 1892), p. xxn

p. 92   'The indolence of scepticism': *On Life*, Forman, vol. 2, pp. 260–1

'The author to others': *DP*, Forman, vol. 3, p. 140

'An assemblage': To Hogg, 4.10.14. Jones, vol. 1, p. 403

'As to the stuff': 12.1.11. *Ibid.*, pp. 43–4

'The enthusiasm': To John Gisborne, 16.6.21. Jones, vol. 2, p. 300

'I *will* feel no more': 3.1.11. Jones, vol. 1, p. 36

'A nerve': *J&M* 449–50

'Where small talk dies': *PB III, Part the Third, Hell* 205

p. 93   'Apes of humanity': 2.3.22. Jones, vol. 2, p. 394

Shelley to Fanny: 10.12.12. Jones, vol. 1, p. 337

'I fear that': BSM e. 19 p. 39 (1817)

p. 94   'Now if they hear': Jones, vol. 1, p.165n

The recipe for medicine: *MSJ*, vol. 1, p 80

p. 95   Review of *Frankenstein*: Forman, vol. 3, p. 13

'The most filthy . . . animals': To Claire, 20.10.20. Jones, vol. 2, p. 243

On Eliza Westbrook: To Henry Reveley, *SC*, vol. 10, p. 1135; to Hogg, 16.3.14. Jones, vol. 1, p. 384

'Lean back in his chair': Dowden, vol. 2, p.173n

'A Hater': 'A Hate-Song Castlereagh and Sidmouth: Similes for two political characters of 1819' (1817)

p. 96   'By all the hate': 'To the Lord Chancellor' 53–6

'Take your eyes off!': *Ibid.* (S), pp. 32–3

The Cyclops: BSM e. 14 f. 72v

Eliza's eyes in breasts: *SC*, vol. 10, p. 1135

p. 97   'Such shapes': *WA* 134–6

Dying men's tongues: *R of I* VI, 2478–9

Shelley/Byron: Haydon, p. 485

'There is great talk': *PB III Part the Third, Hell* 172–6
The Devil, 1812: 'The Devil's Walk' *passim.* Later: *PB III, Part the First, Death* 66–75; *Part the Fourth, Sin* 93, 341

p. 98
'And this is Hell': *Ibid., Part the Third, Hell* 217–21
'Clothed with the Bible': *MA,* 22–5
'Overpowered': Medwin, p. 268

p. 99
Starting from his own company: 8.5.11. Jones, vol. 1, p. 78
'Like one': *RAM* 446–51
'Be as thou art': 'To —— (Oh there are spirits of the air)' (1816) 35
'If I do not know': TLP *Mem.*, pp. 61–2
'The most remorseless': To Peacock, 6.11.18. Jones, vol. 2, p. 47

p. 100
'Who made man': *QM* note to VI, 198
'May God . . . blast me!' To Hogg, 3.1.11. Jones, vol. 1, p. 35
'This horrid Galilean': To Hogg, 24. 4.11. *Ibid.,* p. 66
'The Atheist is a monster': *A Refutation of Deism*, Forman, vol. 2, pp. 59–60

p. 101
'A deistical coterie': To Hogg, 11.1.11. Jones, vol. 1, p. 42
'A divine little scion': To Hogg, April 1811. *Ibid.,* p. 76
The letter to Hellen: 13.12.11. *Ibid.,* p. 206
'Father, are you a Christian?': 27.9.11. *Ibid.,* p. 142
'Dragged before the tribunals': To Byron, 17.1.17. *Ibid.,* p. 530

p. 102
'I am careless': 24.9.17. *Ibid.,* p. 557
'A rare prodigy': 6.4.19. Jones, vol. 2, p. 94
Notes on atheism: BSM c. 4 ff. 1–8
List of Atheists: BSM e. 4 f. 85v
'A complete infidel': *J&M* Preface
'The Spirit that pervades': *QM* note to 1, 252, 253
'A troop of idle dirty boys': *On the Devil and Devils* (1819), Forman, vol. 2, p. 394
Shelley at dinner: Haydon, pp. 298–9

p. 103
'Very sweet & smiling': *CCJ*, p. 184 (8.11.14)
'I took up the word': Tre. *Rec.*, vol. 1, pp. 92–3
'The serpent is avoided': BSM e. 4 fos 16v, 18r
The serpent-armour: HM 2177 f. *21v

p. 104
Notes to Jane and Edward Williams: 26.1.22. Jones, vol. 2, p. 385; *c.* 18.6.22, *ibid.*, p. 437
'Wake the serpent not—': Fragment: 'Wake the serpent not' 1–4

Water

Immersion

p. 109	Letter to Kate: 18.7.03. Jones, vol 1, p. 1
p. 111	The cataract at Terni: 20.11.18. Jones, vol. 2, p. 56
	'Forever changing': To Peacock, 17/18.12.18. *Ibid.*, p. 60
	'Water of purest dew': 'Matilda Gathering Flowers' 25–39
p. 112	'A gentle rivulet': *TL*, 314–19
	'Chequered with sunbeams': 'The Voyage' (*Esdaile* 32) 160–1
	The serpent swimming: *R of I* I, 277, 294–7, 302–4
	'Like silver . . .': BSM vol.1 (*Triumph of Life*), f. 36r
p. 113	'Till, like one': *PU* Act II sc. v, 82–4
p. 114	'Yáhmani': TLP Mem., p. 37 and n.
	'Come, I will sing you': *The Cenci*, Act V sc. iii, 123–34
	'If [Love] were otherwise': Forman, vol. 3, pp. 196–7
	Walker on water: Walker, p. 43 (Hydrostatics)
	Cythna (*The Revolt of Islam*) VI, M/E, vol. 2, p. 8
p. 115	'It is a faculty': *RM*, p. 94
	'Even if blank darkness': Cancelled stanzas for *Laon and*
	'As if he were Adam': *SC*, vol. 3, p. 350
	The forest pool: 25.7.18. Jones, vol. 2, pp. 25–6
p. 116	The Maniac as water-creature: *J&M* 211–25, 274–7; Julian:
	Ibid. 21–5
	Shelley as a merman: Tre. Rec., vol. 1, pp. 164–9
p. 117	The swimming lesson: Tre., pp. 41–2
p. 118	'In . . . the chilling fogs & rain': 6.4.18. Jones, vol. 2, p. 4
	'The vast roof': Stanza for *Hellas*; BSM e. 7 pp. 11–12
	'Walking beneath': *R&H* 331–4
p. 119	'Rain—Maremma': BSM d. 1 f. 92r rev.
	'Never more comfortable': Reveley in *SC*, vol. 10, p. 1148
	Kehama's curse: *The Curse of Kehama* II, 54 ff.
p. 120	'The very deep': *RAM* Part II 123–6
	The dream: MWS letter to Maria Gisborne, Forman, vol. 4, pp. 329–31
	'Ever-changing': 'To the Moon' 5–6
p. 121	The man in the moon: Hogg, vol. 2, p. 315
	'The cold chaste Moon': *Epip.* 281–3
	'Like an image': *R&H* 836–9
	'Dead & cold': 28.10.14. Jones, vol. 1, p. 414
	'And I was laid asleep': *Epip.* 295–300; 'What frost': *Ibid.* 313–19

p. 122   'And from my fingers': 'The Magnetic Lady to her Patient' *passim*

'Less oft is peace': 'To Jane: The Recollection' 87–8

'When the faint eyes swim': *R of I* VI, 2652–5

p. 123   'The wave that died': 'The Boat on the Serchio' 108–9

'Yet now despair': 'Stanzas Written in Dejection, near Naples' 28–36

'Quick, faint kisses': *Epip.* 546–8

At Baiae: 17/18.12.18. Jones, vol. 2, p. 61

p. 124   Translating Aristeus's journey: see Webb, *Violet*, p. 335

'Their wavering limbs': *PU* Act III sc. ii, 45–7

'There was a change': *Ibid.* Act III sc. iv, 98–105

p. 125   'Whose waves': SP I, 102–5

p. 126   'Between sleep & awake': 17.10.18. Jones, vol. 2, p. 44

'heavily oh heavily': BSM e. 19 p. 50

'That morbid suspension': To Graham, 21.11.10. Jones, vol. 1, p. 22

The Villa Magni visions: Tre. *Rec.*, vol. 1, pp. 163–4; Forman, vol. 4, pp. 329–31

Mesmerism sessions: Medwin, pp. 269–70; *CCJ*, p. 196

p. 127   'To feel that I was dead': M/E, vol. 2 p. 68n (Stanza XV)

Dream notes: Forman, vol. 2, pp. 296–7; Medwin, pp. 89, 269–70

'Some imperial metropolis': BSM e. 9 pp. 20–2

p. 128   'To patch up fragments of a dream': 'Is it that in some brighter sphere' 5–6

p. 129   'Intense meditations': *ELA*, Preface, p. xvii

'Exceeding at times': To Peacock, 6.11.18. Jones, vol. 2, p. 47

'Like a harsh voice': 'Ginevra' 50–4

'Where nothing is': SP Conclusion, 124–5

p. 130   'And dreams': BSM e. 18 p. 60 rev.

'Absorbed like one': 'Ginevra' 44–5

'Ah! Why do darkling shades': 'Poems from St Irvyne', IV: 'St Irvyne's Tower' 17–20

p. 131   'Death is the veil': *PU* Act III sc. iii, 113–14

'In the dim newness': *QM* VI, 153–4

'Some say': 'Mont Blanc' III, 49–52

p. 132   '[For] thou art mine': 'Original Poetry by Victor and Cazire': XVI, 'Ghasta, or, The avenging Demon!!!' 73–4

Pseudo-writing: e.g. BSM e. 17 p. 202 rev.

p. 133   'A waking dream': *Hellas*, note 6
          An inner *camera obscura*: Medwin, pp. 17, 75
          'Which was not slumber': *TL*, 29–37, 108
          The dream while walking: To Hogg, 4.10.14. Jones vol. 1,
              pp. 402–3
p. 134   'Another yet': BSM e. 9 p. 23
          Jane Williams/Shelley: Forman, vol. 4, p. 331
          ~~'Over the desarts of'~~: HM 2177 f.*37v
p. 135   Friends in Wales: To Godwin, 25.4.12. Jones, vol. 1, p. 287
          Allegra: *WJ*, pp. 57–8
          Villa Magni visions: Tre. *Rec.*, vol. 1, pp. 163–4
          'Ere Babylon': *PU* Act I, 191–203
p. 136   The form beside him: *TL* 424–33
          'Pale Pain/ My shadow': *J&M* 324–5

Reflection

p. 139   'I saw my countenance': *R of I IV,* 1666–71
          'His eyes beheld': *Alastor* 469–74
p. 140   'Ozymandias' reflections: BSM e. 4 f. 85v
          'Whose yellow flowers': *Alastor* 406–8
          The Narcissus: HM 2177 f.*28v ('Lines to a Reviewer' H.,
              p. 625)
p. 141   'Bathed in the light': *R&H* 115–19
          Helicon or Himeros: *LMG* 316–17 and note
          Pisan shore reflections: 'To Jane: The Recollection' *passim*
          Kingfishers: *PU* Act III sc. iv, 78–83
          'Why is the reflexion': BSM e. 7 p. 236
p. 142   'It is by no means': Garnett, *Relics*, p. 89
          'Immovably unquiet': 'Evening, Ponte al Mare, Pisa' 15–16
          'Where within the surface': *WA* 513–16
p. 143   '*We move, they move*': *Spec. Met.*, Forman, vol. 2, p. 286
          'Time and place and number': *DP*, Forman, vol. 3, p. 104
          'Those divine people': To Peacock, 23.3.19. Jones, vol. 2,
              p. 89
          'Under a thin disguise of circumstance': *DP*, Forman, vol.
              3, pp. 115–16
          'I try to be': 22.10.21. Jones, vol. 2, p. 364
p. 144   'And, like unfolded flowers': 'Ode to Liberty' 54–8
          ~~'Those forms of marble'~~: BSM e. 6 p.133 rev.

'That ideal Beauty': To Maria Gisborne, 13/14.10.19. Jones, vol. 2, p. 26

'As if not dead': *R of I* X, 3998–9

In the galleries: *NS*, Forman, vol. 3, pp. 43–77 *passim*

p. 145 'Few poets': *DP*, Forman, vol. 3, p. 110

'If the reflection': BSM d. 1 back pastedown endpaper rev.

Disgusting paintings: To Peacock, 25.2.19. Jones, vol. 2, p. 80; 9.11.18, *ibid*., p. 52

p. 146 'Yet it is less the horror': 'On the Medusa of Leonardo da Vinci' *passim*, esp. II, 9–13

'Idealisms of moral excellence': To Hunt, 29.5.19. Jones, vol. 2, p. 96

'The embryon of a mighty intellect': 29.1.12. *Ibid*., p. 245

'A character moulded as I imagined': To EH, 26.11.11. Jones, vol. 1, p. 194

p. 147 'How I have loved you!': 10.11.1. *Ibid*., p. 171

Goethe: To John Gisborne, 22.10.21. Jones, vol. 2, p. 364 (*Faust* 1, *Nacht*, 281–2) (Shelley's spelling)

p. 148 One white star: *PU* Act II sc. i, 17–23

'And vesper's image': *QM* IV, 24–5

'That gaze upon themselves': BSM e. 1 f. 7v

The well: *Alastor* 457–64

'Like one beloved': 'To Jane: The Recollection' 77–80

p. 149 'Mazy depths': To Peacock, 6.4.19. Jones, vol. 2, p. 93

'Yet look on me': HM 2177 ff. 1r, 1r (a) (H: 'To ——', p. 532)

'How many a one': *Prince Athanase* 251–3

'We see dimly see': *On Love*, BSM e. 11 p. 7; Forman, vol. 2, pp. 268–9

p. 150 The interview with Southey: Hogg, vol. 2, pp. 31–3; to EH, 2.1.12, Jones, vol. 1, p. 215

p. 151 'Man's own mind is his law': *Spec. Met.*, IV; Forman, vol. 2, p. 293

Mind and its powers: *On Life*, *passim*; *ibid*., pp. 259–63

Mind as mirror: *PU* Preface

'The Soul of the Universe': To Hogg, 3.1.11. Jones, vol. 1, p. 35

'The leaf of a tree': *Ibid*.

p. 152 'Their immensity': *MSJ*, vol. 1, p. 17 (19.8.14)

'Now Heaven': *CCJ*, 8.4.18, p. 88

'The fluctuating elements': *The Assassins*, Forman, vol. 2, pp. 224–5

p. 153   'Do you . . . imagine him': 22.7.16. Jones, vol. 1, p. 499

'It breaks & rises': To Peacock, 22.7.16. *Ibid.*, pp. 498, 500

'The roar'; 'Mont Blanc' cancelled passage (H., p. 535)

Shelley on the mountain: 'Mont Blanc' IV, 134–8

p. 154   Drawing the range: BSM e. 16 p. 62

Watching the Arve: 'Mont Blanc' stanzas I–II, *passim*

The goddess in the waterfall: To Peacock, 22.7.16. *ELA*, vol. 2, pp. 80–1

On Rousseau's *Julie*: To Peacock, 12.7.16. Jones, vol. 1, p. 486

p. 155   'One sees nothing': *Julie, ou la Nouvelle Héloïse, Première Partie, Lettre XXVI*

'A sentiment of extatic wonder': 22.7.16. Jones, vol. 1, pp. 494–7

'With a sound but half its own': 'Mont Blanc' I, 6–9

'Every word and suggestion': *PU* Preface

p. 156   'One mind, the type of all': *R of I* VII, 3104–8

'The words *I, you, they*': *On Life*, Forman, vol. 2, p. 262

Mary confirming it: *ELA*, Preface, p. xiv

'On that verge': *On Life*, Forman, vol. 2, p. 262

'Great Spirit': BSM e. 4 front pastedown

p. 157   'O thou . . .': BSM e. 6 p. 33 (H., p. 661)

'A monstrous presumption': *On Life*, Forman, vol. 2, p. 262

'Day and night': 'Euganean Hills' 5–6, 19–21

'For birth but wakes': 'The Daemon of the World', 11, 539–44

p. 158   '~~What~~ And what': BSM e. 16, p. 12

'And what were thou': 'Mont Blanc' IV, 142–4

'The mind of man': *Spec. Met.* IV, Forman, vol. 2, p. 293

'Occupy, amuse': 16.1.21. Jones, vol. 2, p. 257

'Have confidence': 2.1.12. Jones, vol. 1, p. 218

'Assert yourself': 14.11.11. *Ibid.*, p. 181

p. 159   'That faculty of human nature': *Spec. Met*, Forman, vol. 2, p. 309

'It is our will . . .': *J&M* 170–5; 'We know . . .': *Ibid.*, 185–6

'A story of particular facts . . .': *DP*, Forman, vol. 3, p. 108

p. 160   'And lovely apparitions . . .': *PU* Act III sc. iii, 49–54

'Circles of life-dissolving sound': *R&H* 1166

p. 161   'There is existing in man . . .': *RM*, p. 64

'No man . . .': *DR* IX

'However slowly . . .': *PJ* Book V, ch.VIII, 218–24

p. 162   *Address to the People*: Forman, vol. 2, pp. 101–14
          Shelley's *Proposal*: *Ibid.*, pp. 87–96

p. 163   'Beside the windless . . .': *PU* Act III sc. iii, 159–66
          'Reform . . . without revolution': 20.11.16. Jones, vol. 1, p. 513
          A Philosophical View of Reform: Clark, pp. 247–61, *passim*

p. 164   'If Reform shall be begun . . .': *Ibid.*, p. 255
          'An object which is . . .': *Ibid.*, p. 254

p. 165   'It is impossible': *RM*, p. 104

Escape

p. 169   'Like some dark stream': *Prince Athanase* 100–2
          'I always go on': Tre., p. 46
          'His flashing eyes': Tre. *Rec.*, vol. 1, p. 156

p. 170   'Those millions swept . . .': *R of I* VI, 2358–61
          'The newness and energy': *Ibid.* Preface
          'Tracing general history': 19.10.11. Jones, vol. 1, p. 152
          'Thought can with difficulty . . .': *Spec. Met.* III, Forman,
              vol. 2, p. 291
          'He pants to reach . . .': 'The Solitary' (*Esdaile* 15) 17

p. 171   Peter's adventure: *PW*, pp. 73–6
          The Poet's voyage: *Alastor* 369–403, 492–570 *passim*

p. 172   'Thro the void': HM 2177 f. 36v
          'Through the shade . . .': *PU* Act II sc. iii, 56–62

p. 173   'Down down down.': BSM e. 3 f. 15v
          'The Drowned Lover': 'Poems from St Irvyne' VI, stanzas
              I and III

p. 174   The drowned Englishman: BSM d. 1 p. 29
          The inquest on Harriet Shelley: Ingpen, App.IX, pp. 648–50
          'The circumstances . . .': 17.1.17. Jones, vol. 1, p. 529
          'That time is dead': BSM e. 12 p. 30

p. 175   Pharaoh in his chariot: Jones, vol. 2, p. 128 (S. to Ollier,
              15.10.19, and note)
          'So sinks the day-star': *Lycidas* 168–71
          Sailing with Byron: 12.7.16. Jones, vol. 1, p. 483; Moore
              Works of Byron, vol. 3, p. 320

p. 176   'With the rest of the pigs': Tre. *Rec.*, vol. 1, p. 152
          'If you can't swim . . .': *J&M* 117–19
          Julie and St Preux: *Julie, Quatrième Partie, lettre XVII*

'The amorous Deep': *Adonais* 75

p. 177   'It was only a boat . . .': *HSWT*, 2.9.14: *ELA*, vol. 2, p. 39
  (Mary Shelley's spelling)

'I always find the bottom . . .': Tre. *Rec.*, vol. 1, pp. 90–1

Out with Jane: Tre., pp. 155–61

'Life and the world . . .': *On Life*, Forman, vol. 2, pp. 257–8

'How vain is it . . .': *Ibid.*, p. 259

p. 178   'Whence are we . . .': *Adonais* 184–5

'With whirlwind swiftness': *R of I* III, 1301–2

'And sinks down . . .': 'Euganean Hills' 16–18

p. 179   Visiting Avernus: To Peacock, 17/18.12.18. Jones, vol. 2, p. 61

'*This* brings me again . . .': To EH, 25.6.11. Jones, vol. 1,
  p. 116

'Yet where does [that beauty] exist': To EH. 24.11.11. *Ibid.*,
  p.192

'Perhaps the flowers . . .': 16.6.11. *Ibid.*, p. 104

p. 180   'Folded within': *Epip.* 523–4

Identity not mixed up: 24.11.11. Jones, vol. 1, p. 193

'Yet are we . . .': 10.12.11. *Ibid.*, p. 201

'The destiny of man': To Horace Smith, 29.6.22. Jones, vol.
  2, p. 442

'You have said no more . . . ?': 16.1.12. Jones, vol. 1, p. 237

p. 181   'What will befall': *MSJ*, vol. 1 pp. 6–7

The inheritance of glory: Medwin, p. 435

p. 182   The Thames trip: *CC*, vol. 1, pp. 14–15; TLP *Mem.*, p. 59

'The labyrinths': *WA* 386–7

'We have passed': *PU* Act II sc. v, 98–103

p. 183   One point of light: *Ibid.* Act II sc. iii, 82–9

'The caverns of the mind': *A Treatise on Morals*, Clark, p. 186

Cythna under the sea: *R of I* VII, 3102

The Poet's mind: *Alastor* 87–94

p. 184   The antitype: *EC*, Forman, vol. 2, p. 357

The Witch Poesy: 'Mont Blanc' II, 41–8

Asia/Panthea/Demogorgon: *PU* Act II sc. iv, *passim*

The phrase of Sophocles: HM 2177 f.*20r rev.–*19r rev.

p. 185   The two reviewers: BSM e. 8 pp. 70–1

'Shelley . . . loses—himself': *MSJ*, 26.11.16, vol. 1 p. 147

'The unquiet republic': *PU* Act IV, 398–9

p. 186   'His life beyond his limbs': 'Marenghi' 130–5

'The pleasure of believing': *J&M* 16–17

The Field Place scene: *SC*, vol. 9, p. 183

Card boats: W.M. Rossetti, 'Shelley in 1812–13', *Fortnightly Review* IX, 1 Jan–1 June 1871, p. 79

Making the coracle: *ELA*, vol. 2, p. 349

p. 187   Down the Rhine: *Ibid.*, p. 37

'A very nice little shell': To Claire, 29.4.21. Jones, vol. 2, p. 288

'As a comet': To Trelawny, 16.5.22. *Ibid.*, p. 422

p. 188   'Like some frail bark': *R&H* 815–17

'The Nautilus': 29.4.21. Jones, vol. 2, p. 288

A 'curved shell': *R of I* XII, 4630–1

'Which had no sail': *Ibid.* I, 323–7

The strange seed: *WA* 297–312, *passim*

p. 189   'I should have liked': Tre. *Rec.*, vol. 1, p. 136

Trelawny's observations: Tre. pp. 68–70

p. 190   The technical letter: 17.4.21. Jones, vol. 2, pp. 285n, 286

Old sailors: 'The Voyage' (*Esdaile* 32), note to 109

'I dreamed of nothing': undated, 1822; Jones, vol. 2, pp. 386–7

p. 191   On the little skiff: 'The Boat on the Serchio' *passim*. In draft: BSM e.17 p. 213 rev.

'Aboard! Aboard!': *Curse of Kehama* Canto XX

p. 192   'One white and tranquil sail': To Peacock, 9.11.18. Jones, vol. 2, p. 50

'Always boating': Cited in William Howitt, *Homes and Haunts of the Most Eminent British Poets*, 2 vols, vol. 1 (2nd edn, 1847), p. 455

Fleeing with Emilia: 'The Fugitives' *passim*. In draft: BSM e. 8 pp. 113–20

p. 193   'Come with me': 'To William Shelley' 5–7

Building a boat: 15.8.21. Jones, vol. 2, p. 339

'More swift': *The Faerie Queene*, Book II, Canto VI, 5

Prows: BSM vol.1 f. 45v

'My spirit': BSM e. 4 f. 34r (H., 'To Music' p. 541)

p. 194   Dante's magic ship: Jones, vol. 2, App. 1. Letter 3, p. 448

The snake in the boat: *The Assassins*, Forman, vol. 2, p. 242

The voyage in *Thalaba*: 11th Book, stanzas 33–7

p. 195   'We know not': *R of I* VI, 2587–92

Air

The shadow

p. 201 Geneva boatman: Moore, *Works of Byron*, vol. 3, p. 271
'Waft like gossamer': *R of I* XII, 4734–5
The chariot of wind: BSM e. 16 p. 38
'To rend/The veil': *QM* I, 180–4

p. 202 'We are as clouds': 'Mutability' 1–4
Shelley bolting: CC Revised Journal, Aug. 1814: *SC*, vol. 3, p. 349
The cloud: 'The Cloud' *passim*
Cloud-watching: To Peacock, 25.7.18. Jones, vol. 2, p. 25

p. 203 Words for air: HM 2176 f.15v
'A sphere': *PU* Act IV, 238–44

p. 204 'O that I may': BSM e. 12 p. 149
'There late was One': 'The Sunset' 1–6
'Given/And then withdrawn': Fragment for *Epip.*, 130–2 (H., pp. 428–9)
'How beautiful': Fragment: Thoughts come and go in Solitude 4–5
'Camaeleonic': To the Gisbornes, 13.7.21. Jones, vol. 2, p. 308
'Spite of ourselves': end Aug. 1815. Jones, vol. 1, p. 430

p. 205 'O'er the thin texture': *QM* VI, 3–5
Earth-lizards: 'An Exhortation' *passim* (H., p. 579)
'Fugitive, volatile': Hogg, vol. 2, pp. 46–7

p. 206 'Or as when a bird': BSM e. 8 pp. 165 rev., 164 rev.
The grey dressing gown: *CC*, p. 169 n. 7

p. 207 'I never looked on him': *Ibid.*, p. 180
'He was like a spirit': Hunt, p. 106
'I have but just entered': 3.1.12. Jones, vol. 1, p. 220

p. 208 Hazlitt's comments: *The Collected Works of William Hazlitt*, ed. A.R. Waller and Arnold Glover. 13 vols (London 1903), vol. 6, p. 149
Keats's opinion: Lady Jane Shelley, *Shelley Memorials from Authentic Sources, to which is added an Essay on Christianity* (London, 1859), p. 123
Peter Wilkins's wife: *PW*, pp. 106–7, 117
'S' for Shelley: BSM e. 3 title page (*SG*, no. 64a–b, p. 76)
'Which the vile slaves': RCE 62–3

p. 209 'I am not sad': BSM e. 7 pp. 144, 147

'Unconscious of the day': *Alastor* 467

'Whose flight': *Epip.* 220–1

'The wind the light the air': 16.1.21. Jones, vol. 2, p. 256

p. 210   'Pitching himself': See Timothy Webb, 'The Religion of the Heart: Leigh Hunt's Tribute to Shelley', *Keats–Shelley Review*, Autumn 1992, p. 45

The mayfly: BSM e. 16 p. 26

'The life of a man': *QM* note to VIII, 203–7

'Creatures of a day': Pindar *Pyth. Carm.* VIII, 95–7; BSM e. 6 p. 143 rev.

'Half created images': BSM e. 11 pp. 163–2 rev. (Fragment of a drama on Tasso)

p. 211   'Oh! there are spirits': 'To ——' (Untitled, 1816) 1–4, 7–12 (H., p. 525)

p. 212   'For Love walks not': Forman, vol. 3, p. 199

The page of references: BSM e. 16 p. 37

The Love daemon: Forman, vol. 3, p. 210

'To love, to be loved': *The Assassins*, Forman, vol. 2, pp. 226–7

p. 213   *Nondum amabam*: BL Ashley 394 f. 106r

'It loves': SP I, 76–7

'Always in love': To John Gisborne, 18.6.22. Jones, vol. 2, p. 434

'Will you read it': *c.* 19.and 20.6.11. Jones, vol. 1, pp. 107, 112

p. 214   The Greek youth: Forman, vol. 3, pp. 28–9

'With golden-sandalled feet . . .': *PU* Act I, 319–21

Homer's hymn: 'Hymn to Mercury' 80–105

p. 215   The magic sounds: *WJ*, p. 60 (18 May 1822)

The poem to Jane: 'To Jane, with a Guitar' *passim*

p. 216   'Kissing Agathon': BSM e. 9 pp. 316–17; e. 8 p. 146 rev.

Verses about sucking: Hogg, vol. 1, p. 267

p. 217   A friend's mistress: To Graham, 30.11.10. Jones, vol. 1, p. 23

'Wake yet a while': 'Fragment of Bion's Elegy on the Death of Adonis' 42–7

p. 218   Sweet lips: HM 2111 f. 17r rev.

In the Uffizi: To Peacock, 23.3.19. Jones, vol. 2, p. 89

'A breathless . . . voluptuousness': Forman, vol. 3, pp. 52, 59–60

p. 219   Athanase/Urania: BSM e. 4 f. 83r

The last page: BSM vol. I f. 52v

St Preux in the bedroom: *Julie, Première Partie, lettre LIV passim*

Not daring to look: 10.4.22. Jones, vol. 2, p. 407

p. 220   '[Whose] delicate brief touch': 'Marenghi' 122–3
          Mary's hair: *CCJ*, pp. 431–2
          'The fountains': 'Love's Philosophy' 1–8

p. 221   '~~Where in some labyrinth~~': BSM d. 1 f. 94v rev.
          Colours of paintings: To Peacock, 9.11.18. Jones, vol. 2,
              pp. 50, 51, 53
          'I love waves': 'Song Rarely, rarely comest thou' 33–36
              (H., p. 640)

p. 222   'Life, like a dome': *Adonais* 462–4
          'The perfect and consummate surface': *DP*, Forman,
              vol. 3, p. 136
          Queen Mab's horses: *SC*, vol. 4, pp. 85–90
          Witch of Atlas: *WA* 145–52
          'Lift not the painted veil': BSM e. 12 p. 23

p. 223   'What hast thou done': HM 2177 f.*241
          Other drafts: BSM e. 10 p. 22; e. 12 p. 23
          'Spirit of BEAUTY'. IB 13–17, 5–10

p. 224   'Facts' and 'divisions': To a Lady, Spring 1821. Jones, vol. 2,
              p. 277
          'Beauty is like remembrance': 'Time Long Past' 17–18
              (H., p. 632)

p. 225   'Perfection's germ': *QM* V, 147
          'Hence in solitude': *Essay on Love*, Forman, vol. 2, p. 269
          'When unpercipient': 'Written on a beautiful day in Spring'
              (*Esdaile* 9) 2, 5–13

p. 226   'An imaginary point': *A Discourse on the manners of the
              Ancient Greeks*; BSM e. 6 p. 46 (not in Clark)
          'When we had gone': *R of I* VI, 2644–6
          '*There is eternity*': 2.11.14. Jones, vol. 1, p. 416
          The imagined other: 27.11.14. *Ibid.*, p. 413; 7/8.11.14. *Ibid.*,
              p. 420
          'Oh my dearest love': 27.10.14. *Ibid.*, p. 412

p. 227   Thursday Evening: 3.11.14. *Ibid.*, p. 417
          'My dearest M': BSM e. 12 p. 179rev

The song

p. 231   The Muses: Tre. *Rec.*, vol. 1, p. 116
          'The greatest difference': 6.4.18. Jones, vol. 2, p. 3
          'Death's blue vault': *Alastor* 216

The great Assembly: *MA* 262–9

The Greeks in harmony: 23.1.19. Jones, vol. 2, pp. 73–5

p. 232   Reading: CC revised journal, *SC* vol. 3, pp. 346–7

The old blind man: *The Coliseum*, Forman, vol. 3, pp. 31–3

'Too often profaned': 'To ——', 1 (H., p. 645)

p. 233   'Thou art the radiance': *Prince Athanase,* fragment VI (284–93); BSM e. 4 fos 69v–r rev.

Shelley to Hogg: 12.1.11. Jones, vol. 1, pp. 44–5

p. 234   'Through wood and stream': *Adonais* 163–71

'My head is wild with weeping': BSM e. 19 p. 36

p. 235   'The god of my own heart': 2.3.22. Jones, vol. 2, p. 394

Beauty's shadow: IB *passim*

p. 236   'Thine, thine is the bond': Untitled ('I will kneel at thine altar'), *Esdaile* 42, 14–18

'An unusual spirit of resistance': Jones, vol. 1, p. 154n

'The ~~living frame~~ . . .': BSM e. 2 f. 1r

Socrates's demon: Forman, vol. 3, pp. 50n., 312

p. 237   At Pompeii: To Peacock, 23–24.1.19. Jones, vol. 2, pp. 70–75

'The emerald light': *PU* Act IV, 258

p. 238   Daubs for trees: 2.4.21. Jones, vol. 2, p. 280

'Where meeting branches': HM 2176 f. 3r rev.

p. 239   'A wind arose': *PU* Act II sc. i, 156–8

'The wind in the reeds': 'Hymn of Pan' 6–9

'Such as nor voice': 'The Aziola' 17–19

p. 240   'There is eloquence': *On Love*, Forman, vol. 2, pp. 269–70

'Until the sounds': BSM e. 11 p.155 rev. (1818) (H., p. 569)

'*Inexpressibly*': *Contemps*, p. 22

'The deep truth is imageless': *PU* Act II sc. iv, 116

p. 241   'An education of error': *On Life*, Forman, vol. 2, p. 261

'The scented gale': 4.11.14. Jones, vol. 1, p. 418

'No mood or modulation': 'Mutability' 8

The lyre suspended: *Alastor* 41–7

Harp shapes: BSM e. 2 f. 42r

p. 242   'There is a principle': *DP*, Forman, vol. 3, pp. 100–1

The veiled maid: *Alastor* 151–87

p. 243   'Some inexplicable defect': *DP*, Forman, vol. 3, p. 133

'Those soft limbs': HM 2177 f. 2v

'As dew beneath': 'To Sophia (Miss Stacey)', 19–24

Draft of 'To Constantia': BSM e. 14 fos 34v, 35r, 36 r,v

p. 244	The fallen spirit: *The Assassins*, Forman, vol. 2, pp. 234–6
	His instructions: 'With a Guitar, to Jane' 62–90 *passim*
p. 245	'And feeling ever':'Lines written in the Bay of Lerici' 15–16
	'The most removed and divine': *NS*, Forman, vol. 3, p. 76
	Hums: BSM d. 1 f. 104r rev.; HM 2176 ff. 31v–30v rev.
p. 246	~~Ni na ni na~~: *Ibid.*, f. 9v
	That 'irresistible stream': Discarded preface to *The Symposium*, Forman, vol. 3, p. 158
	'Most inadvertently': In *R of I*. See Preface
	'Swift as a spirit': *TL* 1–4
p. 247	Calderón: Quoted to Maria Gisborne, 16.11.19. Jones, vol. 2, p. 155 (Shelley's spelling)
	'All the authors': *DP*, Forman, vol. 3, pp. 106, 107
	The unheard music: BSM d. 1 fos 71v rev., 56r rev. (later *DP*, Forman, vol. 3, p. 123)
p. 248	Metrical language: *Ibid.*, p.105
	Bad words: Medwin, p. 259
	'The best word or phrase': W.M. Rossetti, 'Talks with Trelawny', *The Atheneum*, 29.7.1882
	The violet in the crucible: *DP*, Forman, vol. 3, p. 106
p. 249	'Every original language': *Ibid.*, p. 103
	'To a Skylark' first draft: BSM e. 6 p. 97 rev.
p. 250	The Poet-philosopher: *Phaedrus* 249, 255
	Poetry nothing to do with will: *DP*, Forman, vol. 3, pp. 133, 137
p. 251	Divine insanity: *Phaedrus* 245a. S. citing it: To Peacock, 16.8.18. Jones, vol. 2, p. 29
	Sipping laudanum: *LMG* 312–17
	Fountains and prisoners: To Peacock, 6.4.19. Jones, vol. 2, p. 93
	Archy and the rainbow: *Charles the First* Act I sc. ii, 413, 432–40
p. 252	'A spirit or an angel': Medwin, pp. 27–8
	'And all should cry': 'Kubla Khan' 49–54
	'Pens Ink & Paper':To Hogg, *c.* 19.6.11. Jones, vol. 1, p. 106
	'He will watch': *PU* Act I, 743–9
	'Gazing awhile': See Reiman, pp. 234, 237; Peck, vol. 2, App. J, p. 402
p. 253	'Agony & bloody sweat':To Godwin, 11.12.17. Jones, vol. 1, p. 578

'Incapable': e.g. BSM e. 7 p. 12
'*Weary*': BSM e. 14 p. 2
'Now loud': *R&H* 1105–9
The Poet as nightingale: *DP*, Forman, vol. 3, p. 109

The wind

p. 257
'And ever as he went': BSM e. 9 p. 190
'Shake the Anarch Custom's reign': *R of I Dedication*
  86–8
SINCERITY AND ZEAL: BSM e. 10

p. 258
His first favourable notice: To Hunt, 8.12.16. Jones, vol. 1,
  p. 517
'Why write I in my solitude': BSM e. 16 p. 66
'A kind of disorder': 12.7.20. Jones, vol. 2, p. 213

p. 259
'The teaching the human heart': *The Cenci* Preface
'At the high & solemn close': To John Gisborne, Nov. 1820.
  Jones, vol. 2, p. 250
Reading Homer: Hogg, vol. 2, p. 374
'To awaken in all things that are': *On Love*, Forman, vol.
  2, p. 268
'Minute & remote distinctions': 11.12.17. Jones, vol. 1,
  p. 577
Poetry as something divine: *DP*, Forman, vol. 3, p. 136
Expanding the reader's mind: *Ibid.*, p. 107

p. 260
'Every thing familiar . . .': BSM c. 4 f. 11r, v
'Dissolved into the surrounding universe': *On Life*, Forman,
  vol. 2, p. 261
The schoolboy: HM 2111, fos 8v rev. & 10v rev.
'This world of love': *Epip.* 346
'An unusually intense': *On Life*, Forman, vol. 2, p. 261

p. 261
'Impetuous boy . . .': HM 2176 f. *14r rev.
'The ocean, the glacier': *The Coliseum*, Forman, vol. 3,
  p. 36
'Self appears': *DP,* Forman, vol. 3, p. 103
Shelley and the sunset: Medwin, p. 238

p. 262
'Till mysteries': RCE 99–103
Walking with Jane: 'To Jane: The Recollection' IV *passim*
'The soul': 'To Jane: The Invitation' 24–8
'All things': *Ibid.*, 68–9

The linked rings: Forman, vol. 3, p. 263

'The sacred links': *DP*, Forman, vol. 3, p. 120

p. 263   'For the most unfailing herald': *Ibid.*, p. 143

Orpheus singing: 'Orpheus' 67–124

'If Mr Shelley desired popularity': 23.12.21. See *SC*, vol. 5, p. 167n

p. 264   'Morbidly indifferent': 14.5.21. Jones, vol. 2, p. 289

Blackwood's: Cited in David Higgins, *Romantic Genius and the Literary Magazine: Biography, Celebrity and Politics* (London, 2005), p. 19

'This was Mr Shelley's error': BSM e. 20 f. 13v

'Twenty pounds *per sheet*': *Ibid.* f. 1r

'The bigot will say': *Ibid.* f. 14r

'Better than any thing': To Claire, 8.6.21. Jones, vol. 2, p. 296

'I confess I should be surprised': To Ollier, 11.11.21. *Ibid.*, p. 365

p. 265   'The poetry of the work': Medwin, p. 310

Disgusted with writing: *Ibid.*, p. 236

'My faculties': 25.1.22. Jones, vol. 2, p. 382

'Indeed I have written nothing': 2. 3. 22. *Ibid.*, p. 394

'The spring rebels not': BSM e.18 front pastedown

'Intense and wild': MWS, note to *Hellas*

p. 266   'As to the Austrians': 18.2.21. Jones, vol. 2, p. 267

Words of Isaiah: BSM e. 9 p. 211

'Dreadfully, sweetly, swiftly': 'The Crisis, 1811' (*Esdaile* 4) 13–14

'Free and equal': *RM*, p. 12

The twig and truth: *Ibid.*, pp. 284, 151

p. 267   'And first': *PU* Act II sc. i, 48–56

An Address to the Irish People: Forman, vol. 1, pp. 326–47

p. 268   Distributing the pamphlets: To EH, 27.2.12. Jones, vol. 1, p. 263

'Passing from heart to heart': *RM*, p. 179

p. 269   The methodical society: 2.3.11, Jones, vol. 1, p. 54

'Man has a right': *Proposals for an Association of Philanthropists*, Forman, vol. 1, p. 380

'No law': *DR* XIV, Forman, vol. 1, p. 395

Meeting candidates face to face: *PVR*, Clark, pp. 254–5

'A scene of blood': 14.3.12. Jones, vol. 1, p. 270n

'Not in the slightest degree': 8.3.12. *Ibid.*, p. 268

p. 270   'It is possible': 18.3.12. *Ibid.*, p. 276

'Government has no rights': *DR*, Forman, vol. 1, pp. 393, 398

p. 271   'Might I not': To EH, 27.2.12. Jones, vol. 1, p. 264

'Heavenly medicine': 'Sonnet: On Launching some Bottles filled with *Knowledge* into the Bristol Channel' (*Esdaile* 27) 8

The balloon over Africa: Hogg, vol. 1, p. 63

'*Popular songs* wholly political': To Hunt, 1.5.20. Jones, vol. 2, p. 191

'Arise, Arise': 'An Ode, written October 1819, before the Spaniards had recovered their Liberty' 1–4

p. 272   'Liberty oh liberty!': BSM e. 12 p. 141

'Ringing through': *MA* 366–7

p. 273   The Latin lesson: Medwin, pp. 20–2

Circlets: *R&H* 797

p. 274   Poem for the *Herald*: Mac-Carthy, p. 59

The disembodied wind: 'Mary to the Sea-Wind' (*Esdaile* 30) *passim*

The gale and the flower: HM 2177 f. 2v

'Come, thou Awakener': *Ibid.* ff. 42–3

'Spirit-breathing gales': 'On leaving London for Wales' (*Esdaile* 10) 21–2, 35

'As I lay asleep': HM 2177 f. 7r

p. 275   'Bloody struggle': 6.11.19. Jones, vol. 2, pp. 149–50

p. 276   'The keen frost-wind': *QM* V, 3–4

p. 277   'By virtue I, a mortal': BSM e. 6 p. 137 rev.

The wind working in him: *Ibid.*

p. 278   *Quisquis est deus*: Natural History, Chap. 7 (5), 14

Lucan: *Pharsalia*, IX, 578–80; Forman, vol. 2, p. 345

p. 279   'Yes, in my soul's devotedness': 'A Sabbath Walk' (*Esdaile* 2) *passim*

Vico Pisano: BSM e. 9 p. 359

The altar to Pan: 2.10.21. Jones, vol. 2, p. 361

'The principle of veneration': Hogg, vol. 1, pp. 79–80

p. 280   '*There is no God*': *QM* note to VII, 13

'The interfused and overruling Spirit': *EC*, Forman, vol. 2, p. 341

Work on Spinoza: *SC* vol. 8, p. 732 ff.

Three bold Xs: *SC* vol. 4, p. 296
'O God have mercy': BSM vol. 1 f. 27v
p. 281   'Before whose breath': Prologue to *Hellas* 6–7
'There is a power': BSM e. 4 f. 11r; *EC*, Forman, vol. 2,
    pp. 343–4
'Visitations': *DP*, Forman, vol. 3, pp. 138–9; BSM d. 1 ff.
    40v, r rev.
'Footsteps': *DP*, Forman, vol. 3, p. 103; BSM d. 1, f. 89r rev.
'~~What~~ sudden': HM 2177 pp. 42–3
p. 282   That 'spirit of good within': To Maria Gisborne, 13.10.19.
    Jones, vol. 2, p. 125
'Whoever has maintained': BSM e. 4 f. 11r; Forman, vol.
    2, p. 343
'Great Spirit!': 'Ode to Naples' 149–69, 21–2
'Receiving the spirit': 20.1.21. Jones, vol. 2, p. 258
'High hope and unextinct desire': 'Ode to Naples' 168
'That sweet bondage': *QM* IX, 76
p. 283   'The breath whose might . . .': *Adonais* 487–90
'The purest and most perfect shape': *EC*, Forman, vol. 2,
    p. 348
'Sweeps through': *Adonais* 381–5
'There is a power': BSM e. 19 pp. 5–6
p. 284   Enshrining the body: To EH, 11.11.11. Jones, vol. 1, p. 173
'When the lamp': 'When the Lamp is Shattered' 1–2
'What think you the dead are': Discarded fragment of *J&M*,
    HM 2176 f. 13r
p. 285   'He is made one': *Adonais* 370–2, 379–80
'My lost William': HM 2177 f. *46r
Trelawny's question: Tre. *Rec.*, vol. 1, p. 92
Captain Kennedy's: *SC* vol. 9, pp. 182–3
p. 286   'And o'er my shoulders': 'To Constantia' 29–33
His boat from the air: BSM e. 10 p. 154; vol. 1 ff. 21v, 26v
p. 287   The soul-wings strengthening: Plato, *Phaedrus* 255
'And the ray': 'Ode to Liberty' 11–14
First draft: BSM e. 6 p. 142 rev.
'~~Unbounded~~': BSM e. 7 p. 21
p. 288   'Ah, woe is me!': *Epip.* 123–5
'As a wild swan': 'Ode to Liberty' 273–85
The spirit's warning: 'The Two Spirits: An Allegory' 1–4,
    25–32

Fire

Daring

p. 295   'Men scarcely know': *WA* 257–62
         'Most terrible, but lovely': *PU* Act II sc. iv, 67
         'Meteor-happiness': *QM* IV, 101

p. 296   'Points of lambent fire': To Peacock, 25.2.19. Jones, vol. 2,
            p. 78
         April forests: *TL* 309–10

p. 297   Fireside talks with Claire: *MSJ*, vol. 1, pp. 32–3 (7.10.14);
            CCJ, pp. 48–9
         Sleeping by the fire: Hogg, vol. 1, p. 77
         'Streaming like a meteor': *Ibid.*, p. 328. A comet: Hogg, vol.
            2, p. 112

p. 298   'And this is my distinction': HM 2176 f. 15r rev.
         The glow-worm: To Horace Smith, 21.5.22. Jones, vol. 2,
            p. 423
         A student's lamp: 'The Boat on the Serchio' 22–3
         'Thou small flame': *The Cenci* Act III sc. iii, 9–15

p. 299   'Under the dark trees': *LMG* 283–5
         Lines from Calderón: Cited to Maria Gisborne, 16.11.19.
            Jones, vol. 2, p. 155 (Shelley's spelling)
         'Hast thou . . .': Medwin, p. 244 (first two lines Medwin,
            second two Shelley)
         Concentric circles: BSM e. 8 p. 101
         To be consumed: 'The Woodman and the Nightingale' 27–9
         The fish rising: 'Lines Written in the Bay of Lerici' 45–52
         Fire experiments: Hogg, vol. 1, pp. 8–9

p. 300   Eton tricks: William Cory, 'Shelley at Eton', *Notebook of the
            Shelley Society*, Part 1, 1888, pp. 14–15
         Chemistry at Oxford: Hogg, vol. 1, pp. 69–75

p. 301   'And rein their headlong speed': *PU* Act II sc. ii, 79–82
         Transverse lightning: *LMG* 149–50
         Notes from Davy: BSM e. 6 pp. 155–72

p. 302   'Apurist': *Contemps*, p. 8
         'Like an inspired': *Alastor* 29–32

p. 303   In secret chambers: *R of I* IV, 1522–5, 1529–30
         The Witch in winter: *WA* 278–84
         'The Boilers': To Henry Reveley, 28.10.19. Jones, vol. 2,
            p. 132

p. 304   Paddle-wheels: HM 2177 fos 3r, 16r, 20r, *20v
         'Child of Despair': *Ibid.* f. 24r
         'The fire was lighted': Reveley to Shelley, 12.11.19. *ELA*,
              vol. 2, p. 251n.
         'One might imagine God': 17.11.19. Jones, vol. 2, p. 158
         Henry's workshop: *LMG* 15–105, *passim*

p. 305   'Machinista/alchemista': To the Gisbornes, 10.7.18. Jones,
              vol. 2, p. 21
         'I can make words': Medwin, p. 349
         The boat asleep: To the Gisbornes, 26.5.20. Jones, vol. 2,
              p. 203
         The steam-yacht: *WJ* (6.1.22), p. 33
         In the gondola: *J&M* 551–4
         'The only essential fluid': Walker, p. 7 (On the General
              Properties of Matter)
         'Is light?': Hogg, vol. 1, p. 271

p. 306   'Matter, such as we behold it': *A Refutation of Deism*, Forman,
              vol. 2, p. 69
         'Truth is *my* God': 5.6.11. Jones, vol. 1, p. 98
         'I saw not, heard not': *PU* Act II, sc. i, 79–86
         The starry foam: BSM e. 8 p. 13
         Dew in the night woods: SP I, 86–9

p. 307   'Medicinal honey': BSM d. 1 f. 68v–r rev.
         'Desires and Adorations': *PU* Act I, 688–9, 760–1
         'Dreaming like a love-adept': *Ibid.* 738–9
         'I am as a Spirit': BSM e. 12 p. 123

p. 308   'Ah, sister!': *PU* Act I, 772–9
         'The most celebrated writers': Forman, vol. 3, p. 144
         'See! The lightnings yawn': *R of I* I, 146–8

p. 309   'In thunder & in fire': BSM c. 4 f. 109v
         'That prig the public': 16.8.18. Jones, vol. 2, p. 31
         Notes from Davy: BSM e. 6 p. 167 rev.
         A shell of vapours: *On the Devil and Devils*, Forman, vol. 2,
              p. 403
         The sun's light reaching Earth: *QM*, note to I, 242, 243

p. 310   'The dazzling radiance': *NS*, Forman, vol. 3, p. 56
         'Beneath his feet': *Argonautica* II, 678–84
         Apollo Belvedere: *NS*, Forman, vol. 3, p. 73
         'Sun-like truth': *R&H* 617–19
         'Mirror of intolerable light': *DP*, Forman, vol. 3, p. 115

'The knight of the shield of shadow': To Peacock, 15.2.21. Jones, vol. 2, p. 261

p. 311   On Keats: To Hogg, 22.10.21, *ibid.*, p. 362; to Peacock, 8.11.20, *ibid.* p. 244; to William Gifford, editor of the *Quarterly*, Nov. 1820, *ibid.*, pp. 252–3

The critic as giant: BSM e. 20 f. 34v

A sort of internal combustion: Tre. *Rec.*, vol. 1, pp. 107–8

p. 312   'A drunken, reeling . . . form': M/E, vol. 2, p. 128n

Poets as prophets: *DP*, Forman, vol. 3, pp. 104, 144

The temple drawing: BSM c. 4 f. 2v (*SG*, no. 69, p. 84), and see p. 293

p. 313   'The oracular vapour': *PU* Act II sc. iii, 4–10

Burning

p. 317   Devilry at Field Place: Hogg, vol. 1, pp. 8, 15

Firing the log-stack: Dowden, vol. 1, p. 4

The Hell Devil: To Graham, 23.4.10. Jones, vol. 1, pp. 9–10

Harriet's fears: Dowden, vol. 1, p. 144

The Tan-yr-allt attack: best analysed in Richard Holmes, *Shelley: The Pursuit* (1974), pp. 187–97

p. 318   The devil sketch: see p. 312

'The Informer, the Attorney General': *On the Devil and Devils*, Forman, vol. 2, p. 392

p. 319   'What though the field be lost?': *Paradise Lost* I, 105–9

'Milton alleged no superiority': *DP*, Forman, vol. 3, p. 127

Satan or Prometheus: *PU* Preface

Milton's serpent: *Paradise Lost* IX, 500–2, 691–728 *passim*

p. 320   'Then I sailed': *El mágico prodigioso* sc. ii, 141–6

In Bisham Wood: Dowden, vol. 1, p. 366

p. 321   'Each girt': *R of I* XI, 4292–5

'Evil springs from *him*': *Cain* Act II sc. ii, 455–63

Sun and comets as Hells: *On the Devil and Devils*, Forman, vol. 2, pp. 402–4

'Thou wild misrule': *El mágico prodigioso* sc. III, 2

p. 322   'Like an Englishman': *SC*, vol. 9, p. 199n

'The mind is its own place': *DP*, Clark p. 295

'I had rather be damned': *PU* Preface

'If God damns me': 11.2.21. Jones, vol. 2, p. 260

'And how/Divine it was': *PB III Part the Fifth*, Grace 388–97

p. 323   'Bare broad word': *J&M* 432
         Devils on the shopping list: Bodleian Dep. c. 608/1
         'Secret food of fires': BSM e. 12 p. 7
         'To thirst': BSM e. 4 f. 34v (H. 'Igriculus Desiderii', p. 549)
         The hell of waking time: BSM e. 12 p. 36
         'The full Hell/Within me': *J&M* 351–2
p. 324   'Inflammable matter': Harriet to EH, 18.3.12. Jones, vol. 1,
            p. 279n
         'Wild notes of liberty': Hogg, vol. 1, p. 268
         'A watch light':'Sonnet to a Balloon laden with Knowledge'
            8–13
         The flame in the forest: 'Euganean Hills' 265–84
         The reed tipt with fire: Hunt, p. 103
p. 325   To 'produce immediate pain': *The Assassins*, Forman, vol. 2,
            p. 230
         Illuminating his uncle: To Hogg, 12.5.11. Jones, vol. 1, p. 83
         The Assassin in the city: Forman, vol. 2, pp. 231–3
p. 326   'The Spirit that lifts the slave': *Hellas*, 351
         Laon stopping the spear: *R of I V*, 1783–800
         Cursing Eldon: 'To the Lord Chancellor' *passim*
         'The system of society': To Hunt, 1.5.20. Jones, vol. 2, p. 191
         'The last resort': *PVR*, Clark, p. 259
         The argument in Hampstead: Hunt, pp. 272–3
p. 327   'You know my passion': 5.4.20. Jones, vol. 2, p. 180
         'Guard! Guard!': Hogg, vol. 2, pp. 305–7
         'Mr Shelley': see Holmes, *Shelley*, p. 544
         'We shall soon have to fight': To Hunt, 29.12.19. Jones, vol.
            2, p. 167
p. 328   'Hissing out murder': To Mary, 25.10.14. Jones, vol. 1, p. 411
         'Alone/The soul of man': *PU* Act III sc. i, 4–8
         'I am one of those': 14–18.11.19. Jones, vol. 2, p. 153
         'From heart to heart': 'Ode to Liberty' 3–4
         'Like the standard': Introduction to 'Ode to Naples' 45–9
         On Vesuvius: To Peacock, 17 or 18.12.18. Jones, vol. 2, p. 63
p. 329   The comet trail: BSM e. 9 p. 315
         'Be not!': *PU* Act IV, 318
         Shelley and guns: Hogg, vol. 1, pp. 79–81
         The pistol drawing: BSM e. 6 p. 44
         'Much too ready': Reveley in *SC*, vol. 10, p. 1142
         'He is thinking of metaphysics': M/B, p. 15

'The time for action was not ripe': MWS, note on the early poems (H., p. 528)

p. 330   'To startle the reader': *Laon and Cythna* Preface (omitted from *R of I* Preface). See H., p. 886

'In consuming fire': To John Gisborne, 16.6.21. Jones, vol. 2, p. 300

'The type of the highest perfection': *PU* Preface

Shelley crossing the Echelles: *MSJ*, vol. 1 p. 200 (26.3.18)

p. 331   Prometheus, the Furies, and Jupiter: *PU* Act I, *passim*

Christ as hero and demon: *QM* note to VII, 135, 136

p. 332   'He refuses he despises': BSM c. 4, f. 276v

'Magnificent Jacobinism': BSM e. 9 p. 1

'Who art thou?': *Adonais* 303–6

'His prophesy of his death': BSM e. 9 p. 7

'*My* golden age': 19.10.11. Jones, vol. 1, p. 152

p. 333   'Of purest spirits': *QM* VI, 40–1

'The equilibrium': *PU* Preface

Thoughts on *Prometheus*: To Ollier, 15.10.19, Jones, vol. 2, p. 127; to the same, 15.12.19, *ibid.*, p. 164; to John Gisborne, 26.1.22, *ibid.*, p. 388

'Guilty death': To the Gisbornes, 19.7.21. Jones, vol. 2, p. 310

'The loathsome mask': *PU* Act III sc. iv, 193–7

p. 334   'Man, oh, not men!': *Ibid.* Act IV, 394–6

'The fire of the artillery': *PVR*, Clark, p. 257

p. 335   'Rise like Lions': *MA* 151–5

To live as if 'to love . . .': *Epip.* 551–2

'The flame/Of consentaneous love': *QM* VIII, 107–8

'Common as light': *PU* Act II sc. v, 40

p. 336   'And much I grieved': *TL* 228–31

'Almost perfection': *SC*, vol. 3, p. 347 (CC revised journal, August 1814)

'This dark scheme of things': To Mary, 4.11.14. Jones, vol. 1, p. 419

'Power in thought': 'Ode to Liberty' 248

Sunset at Bishopsgate: 'The Sunset' 12–17

'One soul of interwoven flame': *R&H* 979

'And from a star': *PU* Act IV, 270–8

p. 337   'The lightning is his slave': *Ibid.*, 418–23

'They came to the fountain': 'Dares the Llama' (*Esdaile* 41) 28–31

Laon and Cythna on the pyre: *R of I* XI, 4576–84

p. 338   Shelley's 1815 translation: Forman, vol. 2, pp. 321–2

Effect of *Faust* on him: To John Gisborne, 10.4.22. Jones, vol. 2, p. 406

p. 339   'A Shape all light': *TL* 385–98

'Die,/If thou wouldst be': *Adonais* 464–6

'We want the creative faculty': Forman, vol. 3, p. 135

p. 340   The Abyss: HM 2176 f. 823v

Being

p. 343   Among the stars: *QM* I, 256–63

p. 344   From planet to planet: Medwin, p. 28

Shelley on the physics of stars: *QM* note to I, 252, 253; *On the Devil and Devils*, Forman, vol. 2, pp. 398–9

Shelley and the stars: Hogg, vol. 1, 461–3

'Swiftly walk o'er': 'To Night' 1–7

Sightings at Lucca: To Peacock, 25.7.18. Jones, vol. 2, p. 25

In Rome: To Peacock, 23.3.18. *Ibid.*, p. 86

p. 345   'What a thing it would be': *SC*, vol. 5, pp. 198–9n

'What if the suns & stars': HM 2176 f. 15v

p. 346   The spiralling nebula: BSM e. 18

'Like the earliest star': BSM e. 12 p. 143

'Pearled Arcturi': 'The Question' 10–11

Stars as eyes: BSM e. 4 f. 85v

p. 347   'And seemed': *Alastor* 490–2

Poetry as alchemy: *DP*, Forman, vol. 3, pp. 139–40

'The Sun of life': BSM d.1 f. 80v rev.

'The master . . . and the Spirit': To Hunt, 14–18.11.19. Jones, vol. 2, p. 152

'Supernatural light': *SC*, vol. 8, p. 735

'The instrument to the agent': *DP*, Forman, vol. 3, p. 100

p. 348   'Clasp with thy panting soul': *Adonais* 417–21

'An imaginative being': *Spec. Met.*, Forman, vol. 2, p. 293

Quoting Tasso: *DP*, Forman, vol. 3, p. 140 (and elsewhere)

'These things not before existing': Forman, vol. 2, p. 258

'Electric force': BSM d.1 f. 73r rev.

'Love is like understanding': *Epip.* 162–9

p. 349   The calm wide eye: BSM e. 12 p. 154

p. 350   'The great secret of morals': *DP*, Forman, vol. 3, p. 111

The boy on the shore: To Peacock, 12.7.16. Jones, vol. 1, p. 481

'I feed the clouds': 'Hymn of Apollo' 19–24, 31–2 (Chernaik version)

p. 351   The soul in eyes: *On Love*, Clark, p. 170

'The phantom is beside thee': *Epip.* 233

'Pants for its sempiternal heritage': *QM* I, 148–51

p. 352   Discoursing on metaphysics: Hogg, vol. 1, pp. 64–5

'For I was a witty child': BSM e. 8 p. 159 rev.

p. 353   'And early': RCE 57–61

'The dreaming clay': *Epip.* 338–40

'Swift lightning': see 'Ginevra' 150–7

'As declining day': HM 2177 f. *23r

'That deepest & most earnest look': 20.8.19. Jones, vol. 2, p. 111

p. 354   'That strange state': *QM* IX, 149–50; 'The Daemon of the World' II, 532–4

'A ~~star of Heaven~~ . . .': BSM e. 7 pp. 259–60; e. 20 ff. 12v, 28v

p. 355   'As the soul . . .': To EH, 2.1.12. Jones, vol. 1, p. 215

'Every soul of man . . .': *Phaedrus*, Second Discourse, 250

Hogg on Shelley and Plato: Hogg, vol. 1, pp. 193, 242

'Ruin of divinest things': 'The Daemon of the World' I, 81

'I arose . . .': *TL* 335–41

p. 356   '~~An unfading~~ . . .': BSM vol. 1, f. 40r

'And every motion': *Epip.* 430–61

'Bright as that wandering Eden': *Ibid.*, 459

On Magdalen Bridge: Hogg, vol. 1, pp. 239–40

p. 357   The gypsy boy: *Ibid.*, pp. 232–5

Leaping over Percy: Tre. *Rec.*, vol. 1, p. 110

With Allegra: *J&M* 143–57; To Mary, 15.8.21. Jones, vol. 2, pp. 334–5

'The *holy* flame': 26.11.11. Jones, vol. 1, p. 195

p. 358   'O Spirit!': *QM* VII, 49–57

'To mingle with its paramour': 'Orpheus' 12–14

'When strength & beauty': 'Epithalamium' 2–4; BSM c. 4 [p. 429]

p. 359   'Dreams of flame': *R&H* 281

Lover or brother: BSM e. 8 p. 48

'A seperation is impossible': 13.11.11. Bruce Barker-Benfield,

'Hogg–Shelley Papers of 1810–12', *Bodleian Library Record*, 14 no. 1 (October 1991), p. 21

'A young virgin': Hogg, vol. 1, p. 123

Shelley on incest: 16.11.19. Jones, vol. 2, p. 154

p. 360   Solomon's Song: BSM e. 14 p. 1

Harriet as his 'purer mind': *QM*, Dedication 'To Harriet ——', 9

'I went. I saw her': *MSJ* vol. 1, p. 6

'How divinely sweet': 28.10.14. Jones, vol. 1, p. 414

'I never before': 4.10.14. *Ibid.*, p. 403

'United as we are': 16.9.14. *Ibid.*, p. 396

p. 361   'Sweet Benediction': *Epip.* 25–9

The 'young Englishman' and Beauty: BSM d. 1 f. 101v rev.

'I confess it is not easy': To John Gisborne, 18.6.22. Jones, vol. 2, p. 434

p. 362   'Possessing and possessed': *Epip.* 549–52

'We shall become the same': *Ibid.* 573–7

'Delighting and delighted': *Ibid.* 390–4, 52

'Love therefore': *Symposium* translation: Forman, vol. 3, pp. 205, 214

p. 363   'I loved': 'The Zucca', IV, 17–24 (draft BSM e. 17 pp. 197–6 rev.)

'The dreary cone of our life's shade': *Epip.* 228

'The desire of the moth for the star': 'To ——', 13 (H., p. 645)

p. 364   'Broken gleams': BSM e. 6 p. 12

'And what is that most bright . . .': BSM c. 4 f. 10r; given by H. as a fragment associated with *Epip.*, 142–9

'If I love you': H. in a fragment associated with *Epip.* 38–44, 426–7

p. 365   'Within ~~the temple~~': BSM e. 6 p. 105 rev.; given by H. as a fragment associated with the 'Ode to Liberty', p. 610

'*For Wisdom*': BSM e. 8 pp. 161 rev., 160 rev., 163 rev., 164 rev.

p. 366   The figure: BSM e. 6 pp. 105–103 rev.

'Blind Love': 'Ode to Liberty' 264

'Child of Light!': *PU* Act II sc. v 54–65

p. 367   First words: BSM d. 1 f. 102v rev.

'You might as well go to a ginshop': 22.10.21. Jones, vol. 2, p. 363

'The world as it should be': BSM d. 1 f. 101v rev.

p. 368   'All that we see or know . . .': *On a Future State*, Forman, vol. 2, p. 278

'A spirit within him': *On Life*, Forman, vol. 2, p. 260

'Of necessity': *Symposium* translation: Forman, vol. 3, p. 215

'In a future existence': 20.6.11. Jones, vol. 1, p. 110

'It is said': *On a Future State*, Forman, vol. 2, p. 279

'But there is another point of view . . .': BSM e. 11 p. 112 rev.

'The living and thinking beings . . .': *Hellas* Preface

p. 369   'Worlds on worlds': *Hellas* 197–210

'A progressive state': *Ibid.* Preface

p. 370   The star from the summerhouse: *c.* 19.6.11. Jones, vol. 1, p. 107

The Woman and the star-spirit: *R of I* I, 478–513

p. 371   Overleaping the wall: *Epip.* 397–400

'Like Vespers serene beam': *Prince Athanase* 61–3

'Like loveliness panting': *Hellas* Semichorus II, 1036–42

'Insolent and victorious light': *Ibid.* 344

'As veil by veil': *TL* 413–14

p. 372   The snake and the Woman: *R of I*, I, 280–306 *passim*

Liberty and Love reappearing: *MA* 110–21

p. 373   'Clear, silver, icy': *PU* Act IV 190–1

'Of some world': 'To Jane, "The Keen Stars were Twinkling"' 22–4

Attempts at a poem: HM 2111 fos. 3r, 7v, 8v

'You see I mingle metaphysics': To Graham, 14.9.10. Jones, vol. 1, p. 16

Thinking of death and Heaven: *c.* 19.6.11. *Ibid.*, vol. 1, p. 108

'Those who believe': DR XXVI, Forman, vol. 1, p. 395

p. 374   'O happy Earth!': *QM* IX 1–4, 12

S on Wordsworth: To John Gisborne, 10.4.22. Jones, vol. 2, p. 406

The 'Heaven of time': *DP*, Forman, vol. 3, pp. 122–3

'A perfect state of society': 10.12.11. Jones, vol. 1, p. 201

'And is this death?': *R of I* XII, 4594–815

~~'And we are wandering'~~: BSM e. 10 pp. 203–4; M/E, vol. 2, p. 251n

p. 375   'We were safe . . .': *MSJ* vol. 1 p. 6

The solitary island: To Mary, 15.8.21. Jones, vol. 2, p. 339

Light 'from above the sun': 'To Jane: The Recollection' 19–20

p. 376 Describing Heaven: 'Ode to Heaven', *passim*; HM 2177 f. 42r–45r

p. 377 'Inmost naked beauty': *DP*, Forman, vol. 3, p. 129

'All on whom': BSM e. 7 pp. 6, 10

p. 378 'The One remains': *Adonais* 460–1

'Oh both, oh all': BSM e. 12 p. 158

'Unproduced, indestructible': *Symposium* translation, Forman, vol. 3, p. 221

'The universal Being': Forman, vol. 2, p. 345

'Aweless soul' and 'Power unknown': 'Ode to Liberty' 233

p. 379 'The Light whose smile': *Adonais* 478–86

'I faint, I perish': 'Fragment of 1821' (H., p. 660)

'A drop in the deep sea of love': 'The Sunset' 49; BSM e. 12 p. 22

'More about himself': see Hunt in Webb, 'Religion of the Heart', p. 49

p. 380 'My spirit's bark . . .': *Adonais* 487–95

'Love, love *infinite in extent*': 3.1.11. Jones, vol. 1, p. 35

The epigraph and the comet: BSM e. 9 p. 317, and see p. 339

p. 381 'The sacred few': *TL* 129–32

'The lodestar . . .': *Epip.* 217–224

Where Love sprang from: *PU* Act III sc.iv, 23

'Some hopes': Tre. *Rec.*, vol. 1, p. 119

The boat appearing: BSM vol. 1 f. 53v, and see p. 383

Coda: The voyage out

p. 385 Williams's weather notes: *WJ*, pp. 65–7, *passim*

'If the past and future . . .': 18.6.22. Jones, vol. 2, p. 436

p. 386 'The hours are flying . . .': BSM vol. 1, f 37r

The voyage and cremation: see Tre. pp. 79–90; Tre. Rec., vol. 1, pp. 201–3; Trelawny *Letters to Rossetti* (1878) *passim*; *MWSL* vol. 1 pp. 183–6 (15.8.22)

p. 387 Lady Mountcashell: Dowden, vol. 2, p. 254n; *MWSL*, vol. 1 p. 185

p. 388 Trelawny's oration: *Letters to Rossetti*, pp. 269–70

p. 389   Hunt from his carriage: Hunt, p. 101
          Pieces of bone: see BL Ashley 673
          'In love with death': *Adonais* Preface
p. 390   'Wherever the Spirit of Beauty dwells': *MWSL*, vol. 1 p. 235

Select Bibliography

Biagi, Guido. *The Last Days of Percy Bysshe Shelley* (London, 1898)

Bloom, Harold. *Shelley's Mythmaking* (New Haven, 1959)

Byron, George Noel Gordon. *Byron's Letters and Journals*, ed. Leslie A. Marchand. 13 vols (London, 1973–94)

Crook, Nora and Guiton, Derek. *Shelley's Venomed Melody* (Cambridge, 1986)

Davy, Humphry. *Elements of Chemical Philosophy* (1812); *Elements of Agricultural Chemistry* (1813)

De Quincey, Thomas. *Collected Works*, ed. David Masson. 14 vols (Edinburgh, 1890), vol. 11, pp. 354–77

Drummond, Sir William. *Academical Questions* (1805)

Elwin, Malcolm. *The Autobiography and Journals of Benjamin Robert Haydon* (London, 1950)

Foot, Paul. *Red Shelley* (London, 1980)

Forman, H. Buxton, ed. *Letters of Edward John Trelawny* (London, 1910)

Garnett, Richard. *Relics of Shelley* (London, 1862)

—— 'Shelley in Pall Mall', *Macmillan's Magazine*, 2 (June 1860), pp. 100–10

—— 'Shelley's Last Days', *Fortnightly Review*, vol. 23, Jan–June 1878, pp. 850–66

Grabo, Carl. *A Newton among Poets: Shelley's Use of Science in Prometheus Unbound* (New York, 1968)

Guiccioli, Countess Teresa. *My Recollections of Lord Byron and Those of Eye-witnesses of his Life*, trans. Hubert Jerningham (1869)

Holmes, Richard. *Shelley: The Pursuit* (London, 1974)

Hotson, Leslie, ed. *Shelley's Lost Letters to Harriet* (London, 1930)

Hunt, Leigh. *Lord Byron and Some of his Contemporaries*. 3 vols (London, 1828)

——*The Correspondence of Leigh Hunt*, edited by his eldest son. 2 vols, vol. 1 (London, 1862)

Hurst, Dorothea. *The History and Antiquities of Horsham* (Lewes, 1889)

Jones, Frederick L., ed. *Maria Gisborne and Edward E. Williams, Shelley's Friends: Their Journals and Letters* (Norman, 1951)

King-Hele, Desmond. 'The Influence of Erasmus Darwin on Shelley', *Keats–Shelley Memorial Bulletin*, 13 (1962), pp. 30–36

—— 'Shelley and Dr Lind', *ibid.*, 18 (1967), pp. 1–6

Koszul, A. H. *La Jeunesse de Shelley* (Paris, 1910)

Locock, C.D. *An Examination of the Shelley Manuscripts in the Bodleian Library* (Oxford, 1903)

Lovell, Ernest J., ed. *Medwin's Conversations of Lord Byron* (Princeton, 1966)

MacCarthy, Denis Florence. *Shelley's Early Life from Original Sources* (London, 1870)

Moore, Thomas. *The Works of Lord Byron, with his Letters and Journals and his Life.* 17 vols; vols 3 (1832), 4 (1832) and 5 (1839)

Notopoulos, James. *The Platonism of Shelley: A Study of Platonism and the Poetic Mind* (New York, 1949)

Owenson, Sydney (Lady Morgan). *The Missionary* (1811; ed. Julia M. Wright, Broadview Press, 2002)

Roe, Nicholas. *Fiery Heart: The First Life of Leigh Hunt* (London, 2004)

Rogers, Neville. *Shelley at Work: A Critical Study* (Oxford, 1962)

Rossetti, William Michael. *Memoir of Percy Bysshe Shelley* (London, 1886)

—— ed. *The Diary of John William Polidori 1816* (London, 1911)

Seymour, Miranda. *Mary Shelley* (London, 2000)

Shelley, Mary Wollstonecraft. *Frankenstein* (1818); *The Last Man* (1826); *Lodore* (1835)

Shelley-Rolls, J.C.E. and Ingpen, Roger, eds. *Verse and Prose from the Manuscripts of Percy Bysshe Shelley* (London 1934)

Tokoo, Tatsuo. *Contents of Shelley's Notebooks in the Bodleian Library*. Romantic Circles website, www.rc.umd.edu/reference/indexes/psbodleian/tokoo-home.html

Volney, Constantin. *Les Ruines, ou méditations sur les révolutions des empires* (1791)

Waller, A. R. and Glover, Arnold. *The Collected Works of William Hazlitt.* 12 vols; vols 6 (1903), 7 (1903), 10 (1904) and 12 (1904)

Wasserman, Earl. *Shelley: A Critical Reading* (Baltimore, 1971)

Webb, Timothy. *The Violet in the Crucible: Shelley and Translation* (Oxford, 1976)

——*A Voice not Understood* (Manchester, 1977)

—— 'Religion of the Heart: Leigh Hunt's Unpublished Tribute to Shelley'. *Keats–Shelley Review*, 7 (Autumn 1992), pp. 1–61

White, Newman Ivey. *Shelley.* 2 vols (New York, 1947)

Yeats, William Butler. 'The Philosophy of Shelley's Poetry', in *Ideas of Good and Evil: Essays (1896–1903)* (London, 1924)

Index

241–5, 276–8, 364; dissolution of, at death, 12–3, 65, 67–8, 278, 285, 388–9, and by love, 122–3, 225–6, 336; relation to the soul, 284, 326, 351–4, 355; astral, 127, 128, 188, 193–5, 201, 203, 204, 343, 375, 380; sidereal, 203, 305, 307, 308–9, 346, 376

Boinvilles, the, 53–4

Bracknell, Berkshire, 51, 53, 55, 134, 186

Breath, 216–9, 280–84, 303, 311, *and see* Spirit

Brockden Brown, Charles: 72, 184, 244, 337

Byron, George Gordon, Lord: first meeting with (Geneva 1816), 22, 51; in Switzerland with, 96, 297, 321, 345; tour round Lake Geneva with (July 1816), 25, 37, 175–7, 238, 321, 345, 350; sailing with, 175–6, 187, 192; in Venice with (Aug.-Sept. 1818), 33, 159, 176, 284, *and see* PBS Works, Poetry, *Julian and Maddalo*; in Pisa with (1821–2), 26, 33, 80, 159, 208, 329; at the cremation, 388; 389; views on S., x, 22, 31, 33, 49, 86, 103, 190, 329, 367; S.'s views of and ambitions for, 22, 85, 86, 91, 104, 159, 271, 298, 308, 312; S.'s letters to, 80, 102, 126, 163, 174, 264; affair with Claire (1816), 31, 88, 357; and see 54, 67, 81, 155, 183

Works: 'Cain', 321; *Childe Harold's Pilgrimage*, 171; *Don Juan*, 176; 'The Lament of Tasso', 13–14

Calderón de la Barca: 58, 247, 251, 299, 303, 318; *La vida es sueño*, 129–30; *El mágico prodigioso*, 320, 321, 337–8, 339

Carlile, Richard, 38

Castlereagh, Lord, 95, 98, 387

Caves, 16, 123, 124, 156, 276; of mind, 156, 183–5; allegory of the cave (in Plato's *Republic*), 38, 142, 147; Idol of the cave, 184–5

Cenci family, 37, 184; Beatrice, 37, 114

Chaos, 184, 232, 349, 358, 378; of himself, 84, 89, 321, 347, 349, 364, 378

Childhood, envy of, 30, 123, 126, 240, 259–61; observations of children, 39, 126, 205, 242, 350, 357

Christianity, break with, 99–100; opinions of, 99, 100, 102–3; *and see* Jesus Christ

Circles: of bees and fireflies, 298; of the skylark, 250, 253; of the wind, 273; of the spheres, 61, 203, 247, 376; of self-interest, 90, 259–62; of truth spreading, 161; linked, of poetry, 262–3; of love

spreading, 260–2, 350, 362; himself as the centre of the infinite circle, 12, 157, 259–61, 347–8; concentric circles, 299, 346

Clairmont, Charles, brother of Claire, 182

Clairmont, Claire (formerly Jane), 6, 51, 127, 152, 220; character, 43, 88; in France with S. and Mary, August 1814, 6, 43, 51, 60, 63, 110, 115; in Switzerland with them (summer 1816), 152, 153; relations with S., 43, 44, 46, 79, 84–5, 88, 158, 193–4, 213, 301, 325; her singing, 160, 193–4, 243–4, 286, 288; relations with Mary, 43, 84–5, 88; with Byron, 31, 88, 135; views of S., 69, 70, 207, 213; scared by him, 96, 103, 297; S.'s advice and remarks to, in letters, 70, 79–80, 188, 192, 209, 232, 237, 266, 336

Clairmont, Clara Alba (Allegra), C.'s illegitimate daughter by Byron, 31, 88, 135, 357

Clouds, 71, 141, 148, 201–5, 220, 231, 238, 271, 276, 284, 306, 336, 345, 366, 370, 379

Coleridge, John Taylor, 327

Coleridge, Samuel Taylor, 63, 103, 150, 309, 322–3; 'Christabel', 96; 'France: An Ode', 271; 'Kubla Khan', 252; *The Rime of the Ancient Mariner*, 99, 120, 191

Comets, 296, 304, 321, 372; S. as, 297, 312, 328–9, 380–1

Conscience, 100, 308, 327

Consciousness, 125, 129, 179, 194, 250, 260, 361, 364, 374–5

Creation: S.'s views on, 12–13; 282, 304, 348, 369; by the Witch of Atlas, 303; by himself, 155, 285, 346, 347–51, 380–1; by Love, 358

Critics: reaction to S., 185, 263–5, 327, 387; his to them, 95, 125, 140, 185, 263–5, 311

Cwm Elan, 16–17, 70, 112, 135, 174, 224–5

Cythna, heroine of *The Revolt of Islam*, 68, 183, 226, 335, 359, 360, 374–5

Daemons, 88–9, 211–2, 214, 220, 232, 236, 274, 308–9, 319, 323, 330–1, 333, 370–2

Damnation, 98, 100, 104, 321–2

Dante Alighieri: *Inferno*, 43; *Purgatorio*, 111–12, 191, 194; *Paradiso*, 147, 195, 283, 311, 365, 376; *Convito*, 157, 217–8; *Vita Nuova*, 218; the magic ship, 194

Darwin, Erasmus: 11, 14, 210, 233, 275

Davy, Humphry, 9, 203, 210, 234, 237, 301–2, 309, 328, 346

Death: as lover, 16, 45, 68–9, 83, 123, 172, 240,
    389; as horror, 25, 66–7, 68, 222, 231,
    338; as dissolution, 67–8, 77–81, 174,
    179–80, 285, 367; as life, 131, 183; and
    sleep, 123, 127, 130–1, 178; and love,
    122–3, 176, 284–5; S. exploring, 30, 56,
    65–73, 81, 130–1, 178, 179–81, 194,
    284–5, 334, 337, 339, 373, 374–5, 380–1;
    his own, 135, 180, 387–90; his own
    imagined or prefigured, 27, 28, 70, 81,
    92, 93, 175–6, 332, 337, 387; indifference
    to, 69, 100, 119, 319–20, 387; and see
    Drowning; Suicide
Demiurgus, S. as, xii, 304
Democracy: Athenian, 59, 143; French, 63, and
    see Revolution, French; S. as democrat,
    102, 326–7
Demogorgon, 172, 184, 266, 336
Devil, the, see Satan; devils, lesser, 317, 321, 323,
    330
Dew, 133, 242, 244, 281, 335, 339, 367; death-
    bringing, 70; life-bringing, 77, 306–7,
    309, 348, 349, 371; poetry as, 307, 322
Diogenes Laertius, 22, 352
Dionysus, 252, 265
Diotima (from Plato's Symposium), 212, 213, 214,
    220, 362, 368, 378
Don Juan, the, 124, 187–91, 215, 385–7, 390
Dreams, 14, 16, 32, 78, 125–31, 136, 142, 144,
    149, 162, 169, 204, 240, 266, 308, 344,
    358, 359, 362; life as, see Life S.'s own,
    120, 127–9, 131, 171–2, 288–9, 335, 370;
    himself as a dream, 129, 134–6, 147, 210,
    387–8; 'waking dreams', 126, 133–4, 135,
    151
Drowning, 119–20, 139, 172–8, 367, 387

Earth: as planet, described, 61, 247, 286; as
    grave, 12, 25, 65, 69, 70, 72–3, 297–8; as
    prison, 32, 38, 40, 52, 58, 64, 65, 67–8,
    73, 92, 215, 238, 250, 324, 339, 364; as
    mother, 17, 55, 60–1; as illusion, 129–31,
    142–3, 145, 211, 219, 222, 339, 378; in
    the Golden Age, 59; Spirit of, 336, 353;
    susceptibility to reform, 61, 63–4, 266–7,
    306–7, 328, 332–3, 335–7, 374, 380; as
    Hell, 97–8; as Heaven, 78, 332–3, 336,
    373–4
Eaton, Daniel Isaac, 38, 161
Ecclesiastes, Book of, 73, 332
Eden, 16, 81, 104, 213, 356, 361, 369, 375–6
Eldon, Lord Chancellor, 6, 95–6, 101–2, 193,
    326, 331

Electricity, 12, 94, 299–306; love as, 334, 335;
    poetry as, 308–9, 348–9
Encyclopedists, 10, 92, 150
England, state of, 38, 39, 49, 60, 62–3, 64, 98,
    118, 161–5, 261, 326; billetting of troops
    in, 47, 60, 85–6, 97; and see National
    debt, Pentridge Rising, Peterloo
    Massacre; S.'s dreams of, from abroad, 54,
    86; his hopes for, see Revolution
Equality, 22–3, 90, 143, 161, 163, 164, 268, 274,
    380; Godwin's teachings on, 14, 46, 161
Eternity, 12, 104, 153, 178, 180, 181, 225, 226,
    233, 261, 321, 351, 373, 378, 380
Eton (1804–1810), 5, 7, 17, 20, 26, 30, 31, 48,
    99, 110 114, 169, 203, 206, 287, 343;
    boating at, 110, 189, 192; bullying at, 13,
    14–15, 81, 94; chemical experiments at,
    300, 302, 317; games at, 13; medical
    experiments at, 26, 69; reading at, 14,
    130, 278, 302; and see Lind, James;
    Walker, Dr Adam
Euripides, 96, 143, 277
Eve, 26, 103, 319–20
Evening star, see Hesperus
Evil: ubiquity of, on earth, 26, 89, 98, 317,
    335–6, 350; cause of, 26, 29, 321, 335;
    annihilation of, 158–9, 325–6, 32–3, 334;
    and see Ahriman
The Examiner, 38, 81, 258, 264
Exile: in Italy, 44, 54, 60, 265, 271, 274, 301,
    326; on earth, 13, 24, 52, 55, 352; and
    see Home
Eyes: his own, 10, 96, 103, 139, 140–1, 147, 150,
    205, 325, 346, 349, 350–1; Mary's, 148;
    drawings of, 96, 148, 349; as mirrors,
    149; as labyrinths, 148–9; of mind, 147,
    149, 348

Fall, the, notions of, 26, 115, 352–3, 354–5, 356,
    358–9, 361, 375–6
Fate, 10, 184, 190, 266
Faust, 56–7, 135, 219, 318–9, 337–8, 385
Field Place, 5, 17, 18, 19, 39, 83, 302, 329, 373;
    described, 8, 30, 52, 101, 103, 109, 186,
    237, 370; S.'s behaviour at, in childhood
    and after, 20, 30, 31, 94, 100, 114, 186,
    217, 252, 299, 317; barred from, 52, 101,
    162; revisiting, 52, 85–6, 134
Finnerty, Peter, 38, 161
Florence, 79, 82, 125, 144, 145, 146, 175, 218,
    236, 387; Cascine at, 272, 275, 276
Flowers: observed, 78–83, 109–10, 185, 222,
    346; and mortality, 30, 77–81, 179–80,

213, 376; immortal, 65, 78, 296, 339, 355; as stars, 346; beneath the sea, 123–5; as simile for poetry, 78–9, 222, 250; himself as, 77, 213; as mimosa, 80–1, 346; as narcissus, 140, 346

Fossils, 58–9

France and the French, 6, 38, 39, 56, 60, 67, 115; *and see* Revolution, French

Furies, the, 97, 330–1

George III, King of England, 14, 59, 324

George IV, *see* Prince Regent

Ghosts, spectres, phantoms, 24–5, 37, 131–6, 157, 180, 181, 231, 275, 318, 325–6, 362, 387–8, 389; of Jupiter, 331; of Napoleon, 335–6; S. as, 134–6, 257, 298, 351

Gisbornes, 44, 85, 95, 204, 275, 301; steamship scheme with, 303–5; S.'s letters to John, 49, 84, 92, 143, 213, 219, 259, 338, 361, 367, 385–6; to Maria, 141, 144, 246, 251, 282, 359; and see PBS Works, Poetry, *Letter to Maria Gisborne*

God, S.'s views of, 12, 62, 89, 99, 100, 101, 102, 132, 150, 151–2, 162, 175, 176, 258, 280–1, 304, 306, 309, 318, 319–20, 321, 322, 338, 348, *and see* Atheism; God the Father, 19, 101, 102, 332; God dreamed by man, 89, 157–8, 318, 320; God as Nature, 278–9; as Breath, 281–3; S. and man as, 155–7, 278, 285, 320, 332, 344, 347, 348, 378–80; 'the god of my own heart', 235, 279

Godwin, Fanny (Fanny Imlay), step-daughter of Godwin, 65, 67, 93, 178

Godwin, Mary, see Shelley, Mary Wollstonecraft

Godwin, William, 6, 14, 19, 21, 27, 49, 150, 183, 207, 259; as S.'s mentor, 14, 17, 18, 40, 42, 46, 257, 373–4; on Irish reform, 88, 269–70; as S.'s debtor, 46, 49, 50, 234; views of S., 43, 312; S. on, 18, 46; his second wife, 69, 95

  An Enquiry Concerning Political Justice: on family allegiance, 17; on marriage and property, 40; on property and equality, 23, 46, 90; on the self and the other, 90; on the value of labour, 48; on sincerity, 85; on political action, 161–2, 164

Goethe, Johan Wolfgang von, 68, 147; *and see* Faust

Golden Age, the, 59, 61, 332

Gray, Thomas, 16, 173

Greece, dreams of, 51, 59, 140, 142–4, 231–2, 239, 375, 388; Greeks, S. on, 143–4, 295, 306, 359; himself as 'Greek', 143, 213, 214, 232; writing and speaking it, 249, 311, 378; Greek islands, dreams of, 82, 193, 390; Greek War of Independence (from 1821), 143, 266, 278, 286–7, 332, 334, 371

Grove, Harriet, 16–17, 31, 46, 68, 70, 77, 99, 114, 130, 359

Hades, 178, 179, 263

Hampden Clubs, 163

Hampstead, 93, 112, 185, 208, 326–7

Haydon, Benjamin, 102–3

Hazlitt, William, 208

Heart, his own: pictured, 26, 79, 92, 123, 243, 373, 389; as the home of the true self, 157, 225, 235, 237, 259, 279, 282, 289, 363; as heaven, 376–7

Heaven, 147, 152, 180, 185, 201, 212, 250, 262, 272, 279, 280, 295, 306, 319, 324, 351, 357; glimpses of, 141, 146, 225, 242, 252–3, 288, 373; visions of, 51, 78, 89, 238, 373–7; his mind-world reflecting, 183, 238, 376; his mind making, 183, 322, 346, 349; on earth, 78, 332–3, 336, 373–4; third Heaven, the, 365–6, 367, 373

Hell, 48, 97–9, 100, 317, 318; his own mind as, 317, 320, 321–3; scorn of, 100, 321

Herschel, William, 14, 61, 309, 344

Hesperus, 142, 148, 299, 343, 369, 371, 381, 390

History, cycles of, 16–7, 59, 60, 155, 170, 172, 266, 276, 335

Hitchener, Elizabeth, 85, 146, 158, 179–81, 317, 324, 325; their correspondence: on perfectibility, 170, 374; on sleep and death, 179; on immortality, 180, 368; on truth, 306; on the Golden Age, 332; on pre-existence, 357; on the soul, 180, 284, 355, 357–8

Hogg, Thomas Jefferson: character, 7, 146–7, 279; first meeting with S. at Oxford, 9, 298, 302; with him there, 6, 16, 21, 128, 140, 141, 160, 279, 329; on S.'s writing there, 216, 324; co-author of *The Necessity of Atheism*, 6, 17 and Harriet, 42, 147; anticipated seduction of and Mary, 43; observations and opinions of S., xii, 7, 26, 41, 58, 77, 84, 87, 110, 121, 126, 170, 185, 205, 206, 207, 267,

121, 147, 201, 204, 224; of reason, 347;
of the sun, 141, 309, 344, 350–1; sunset,
204, 261, 336, 345, 350; the 'Shape all
light', 339, 355; of the stars, 147, 224,
307, 343, 344–5, 375–6; as veil, 133,
134; as truth, 303, 308–9, 310–11;
divine, 147, 182, 356, 365, 378; of Eden,
356; in water, 147–50, 358–9, 361;
within him, 183, 184, 347, 351, 365; S.
as Light-bringer, 310–11, 319, 350,
370–2, 380–1
Lightning, 202, 209, 300, 301, 306, 307, 308–9,
333, 337, 345, 349, 353, 358, 386, 387
Lind, Dr James, 14, 31, 183, 213, 278, 302–3
Lionel, Shelley-hero of *Rosalind and Helen*,
32–3, 77, 120, 121, 191, 214, 310, 323,
371
Literary Gazette, reviews in, 31, 264–5
Locke, John, 10, 55, 91, 179
London, 40, 43, 50, 97
Love, 15, 16, 23, 28, 30, 34, 40, 45, 64, 136, 145,
156, 159, 258, 289; sexual, 39, 79–80, 83,
122–3, 220, 225–6, 323, 330, 332, 351,
367–8; homosexual, 359; and death,
122–3, 176, 284–5; as the law of life, 90,
188, 234–7, 334–6, 335, 336, 339; as god,
188, 233, 234, 247, 283; as liberty, 41, 42,
43, 45, 79, 236, 267, 279, 335, 336; as
subversion, 334, 335; Plato defining,
211–14, 220, 308, 362; S. trying to
define, 40, 79–80, 92, 150, 225, 261,
284–5, 334, 335, 358–68, 380; S. as Love-
daemon, 211–3; 'this world of love, this
me', 260, 335, 336, 367, 380; his heroines
as, *see* Asia, Cythna
Lucan, 278–9, 303
Lucifer, 319, 356, 370, 371; in Byron's 'Cain',
321
Lucretius, *De Rerum Natura*, 10–12, 58, 132, 141,
233, 274, 296, 351; S. on, 11
Luxima, 213
Lynmouth, north Devon, 50, 51–2, 58, 110, 113,
180–1, 270, 324, 375

MacFarlane, Charles, 5–6, 31
Madness, in S., 16, 27, 31–4, 116, 155, 251–2,
325, 370; in Poets generally, 251–1,
262–3, 322–3
Magnetism, law of, 234, 262, 305, 306, 334
Malthus, Thomas, 24, 222
Marlow, Buckinghamshire, S. at (Mar. 1817–Feb.
1818), 21, 24, 25, 26, 30, 38, 43–4, 51, 54,
55, 57, 62, 82, 86, 88, 118, 143, 193, 202,

205, 220, 238, 251, 258, 286, 310, 329; on
the Thames at, 50, 54, 111, 139, 140, 189,
192, 201; *and see* Bisham Wood
Matter, S. exploring nature of, 10–13, 114, 203,
222, 301, 302, 305–6
Medwin, Tom, cousin, 98, 109, 126, 133, 144,
181, 189, 207, 208, 231, 237, 248, 252,
261, 265, 271, 305, 381, 388
Memory: of home, 52–3, 55; of Beauty, 224,
355; of an ante-natal state, 355–6, 357–8;
as pain, 52–3, 80, 85; of the divine, 287,
339, 356, 364; knowledge as reminis-
cence, 356–8
Mephistopheles, 319, 338, 347
Mercury, 214–5, 244, 249, 295
Mesmerism, 27, 122, 130
Metempsychosis, 355
Meteors, 295, 296, 300, 310, 343, 346; S. as, 297,
300–1
Milton, John, 48, 259, 263, 308; *Comus*, 52, 132,
207; *Lycidas*, 115, 175; *Paradise Lost*, 78,
286, 319–20; his Satan, 319–20, 322, 370
Mind, his own: nature of, 128, 129, 143, 147,
150–1, 224; eye of, 147, 149; powers of,
41, 154–60, 250, 303–4, 336–7, 350; his
power over, 33, 158–9, 235; passivity of,
131, 147, 151, 155, 158, 250; as mirror,
140, 151, 155; as Ocean, 134–5, 156–7,
275, 282, 283; world of, described, 131,
134, 171–2, 183–5; possible persistence of,
179–81; in sleep and dreams, 126–7, 128,
131; the world as a construct of, 150–1,
154–5, 157, 159, 333–4, 336, 348; Heaven
as construct of, 183, 322, 346, 349, 376–7;
the One Mind (Universal Mind), 151,
156–7, 183, 333, 375
Miracles, 12, 132, 177
Mirrors: seeking himself in, 9, 139, 149, 323;
reflecting reality, 147–8, 149, 346, 348–9,
365; water as, 121, 139–40, 148, 149, 347;
eyes as, 148–9, 182, 376; mind as, 140,
151, 155; idealisms as, 143, 159; the lover
as mirror-image, 139, 148–9, 358–9,
361–2; the mirror within, 139, 183, 377;
S. as truth-reflecting mirror, 160,
310–11, 314, 379
Monarchy, 38–9, 59–61, 62, 89, 94, 324, 327; *and
see* George III; Prince Regent
Moon, 78, 89, 91, 112, 130, 135, 147, 201, 211,
224, 333, 373, 385; as mutability, 120–1;
as reason, 121–2; Mary and Jane as, 121,
122; moon-boats, 188; man in the
moon, 121

444

Pseudo-writing, 132
"Pure anticipated cognition", 128–9, 143–4
Pythagoras, 21

Quarterly Review, 175, 263, 264, 327, 364
Quincey, Thomas de, 388

Reality, 38, 130, 141, 160, 219, 223, 348, 362,
    380
Reason, 12–13, 100, 161, 180, 181, 251, 284,
    285, 319, 321, 325, 333, 347, 352, 355,
    369
Reform, parliamentary, 51, 52, 60, 62–3, 150,
    162–5, 269, 324; moral, 60, 63, 90,
    158–9, 241, 258–9, 263, 266, 267–8,
    270–1, 258–9, 263, 266, 267–8, 270–1,
    278, 306–7, 324–37, 367; and see
    Revolution
Religion, S.'s view on, 17, 30, 41, 53, 132, 180,
    268, 269, 325; 237, 328, 331, 334, *and see*
    Atheism, Christianity
Republics and Republicanism, 143, 164, 185, 327
Retzsch, Moritz, 219, 319, 338
Reveley, Henry, 119, 190, 304–5, 329
Revenge, 63, 64, 159; God's on man, 100, 162,
    319–20, 321; overcoming it, 64, 326,
    331–4, 372
Revolution, S.'s, 247, 258–9, 263, 266–72,
    324–36, 367; in *The Revolt of Islam*,
    14–15, 28, 29, 43, 85, 258, 276, 303; in
    England (anticipated), 49, 63–5, 162–5,
    231, 270–2, 275, 278, 324, 325, 327,
    329–30, 333, 334–5; in *Prometheus
    Unbound*, 124–5, 331–40; and the West
    Wind, 272–8, 331; volcanoes as symbols
    of, 172, 261, 267, 296, 328, 333, 336;
    American, 38, 268; French, 6, 14–15, 38,
    43, 60, 61, 159, 161, 267, 268, 269, 271,
    345 (S.'s views on, 29, 61, 63, 159, 312);
    elsewhere 61, 91, 142, 266, 271, 278,
    286, 296, 328, 334; Love effecting, 125,
    214, 267, 310, 334–6, 367; poetry
    assisting, 263, 308–9, 324, 333
Revolutions, of the Earth, 61; of atoms and
    planets, 203, 237; of the seasons, 266,
    273, 275, 276, 278, 296
Rivers: Arno, 55, 110, 117, 142, 174, 182, 185,
    190; Arve, 113, 154, 155, 182; Serchio,
    110, 125, 182, 187; Rhine, 156, 177;
    Thames, 53, 54, 71, 111, 139, 140, 149,
    182, 293; thought as, 153, 154, 155,
    169–70, 171–2, 182–4, 369, 375; time as,
    155, 369, 375

Robespierre, 29, 324
Rome, 37, 51, 52, 71, 144, 185, 239, 310;
    described, 61, 115, 251, 344; *and see*
    Baths of Caracalla, Protestant Cemetery
Rousseau, Jean-Jacques, 20, 78, 154–5, 176, 188,
    219, 221, 339

St Leonard's Forest, 8, 78, 103, 238
Satan, 98, 99, 103, 286, 315, 317–22, 324, 331; S.
    as, 99, 101, 175, 317, 319, 320; *and see*
    Mephistopheles
Scythrop Glowry (from Peacock's *Nightmare
    Abbey*), 68–9, 325
Sedition Acts, 38, 81, 161, 163, 269, 271
Self, S. exploring, 88, 89–93, 97, 182, 339;
    observed from a distance, 27, 32, 33, 50,
    264; as ghost, 134–6, 257, 338; reflected
    93, 139–40, 149, 221; idealising of,
    143–5, 181; alienation of, 99, 175, 319,
    320, 338; necessity of resisting, 89, 91–3,
    319, 323, 334, 339; persisting after death,
    179–81; the 'true self', 90, 149–50, 157,
    182, 266, 282–3, 319, 334, 380–1; the
    'purer self' as lover, 260–1; 'know
    thyself', 259, 313, 321, 351, 360, 367;
    'himself alone', 87, 90, 223, 375; 'thyself
    alone', 377
Self-portraits, written, 13–16, 32–3, 72, 77, 82,
    92, 116, 120, 139, 145, 174, 244, 276–7,
    and see Poet; self-portraits, drawn, 85, 88,
    93, 211, 237, 298, 312, 351
Senses, dominion of, 10, 92, 130, 140, 181, 183,
    321, 323, 367, 370, 378
Severn, Joseph, 72
Shadows, 131, 136, 142, 157, 172, 183, 184, 201,
    289; of reality, 129–31, 142–3, 144, 147,
    219, 347; beside him, 136, 235, 351, 360;
    himself as, 52, 129, 134, 147, 149, 210,
    309, 351, 390; pain as, 136, 308; of
    Beauty, *see* Beauty; 'shadows that were
    bright', 131, 147, 223, 310–11, 345, 351;
    'the Shadow & the God', 284
Shakespeare, 56, 72, 82, 124, 131, 151, 207, 215,
    251, 327, *and see* Ariel, Prospero
Shelley, Sir Bysshe (grandfather), 17–18, 48, 49
Shelley, Clara, daughter of S and Mary, 43, 44,
    51, 71, 113, 116, 157
Shelley, Elena Adelaide, mystery baby of S., 85
Shelley, Harriet, née Westbrook, first wife: S.'s
    first meetings with, 39–40; elopement
    with S. (Aug. 1811), 6, 18, 39, 40, 179,
    213; marriage to S.(Aug. 1811), 6, 9, 27,
    40–43, 45, 47, 52, 180; second marriage

447

449

450

182–4; as clouds, 202, 204, 306, 307; as the seed of revolutions, 267–9, 324–5, 336; wellspring of, 182–4; poetic thought, 112, 250–1, 307, 322; 'confusion of thought with the objects of thought', 133

Time, nature of, 55, 62, 143; personification of, 56, 374; burden of, 55, 56–7, 192, 323, 385; escaping from, 56, 192, 226, 375, 380; and revolutions, 164, 266; *and see* Eternity

Trance, state of, 133–4, 248, 286

Trees, 10, 51, 57, 70, 237–9, 257, 272, 307

Trelawny, Edward John, observations of S., 7, 10, 26, 61, 69, 70, 79, 103, 117, 125, 131, 140, 169, 190, 206, 285, 319, 357, 381, 390; on S. at work, 57, 87, 231, 246, 248; on S. sailing 189, 385–6; teaching him to swim, 117, 177; at his cremation, 388–9

Tremadoc, north Wales, 52, 113, 274, 318

Truth, 165, 184, 202, 380; S. on, 15, 32, 34, 90, 177, 240–1; S. and, 7, 32, 69, 257–8, 308–9, 310–13, 322, 370; fire and light of, 296, 302, 308–9; and Beauty, 142, 143

Universe, the, 125, 150, 212, 259, 281, 307, 343, 349, 368; formation of, 233–4; operations of, 11–12, 102, 203, 232; S. merging with, 259–61, 284, 307, 350–1, 375, 376, 378–9, 380; soul of, as Love, 151, 234, 380; Universal Mind, 156–8, 348–9

University College, *see* Oxford

Urania, his own Muse, 219, 332, 360

Vegetarianism, 29–31, 41, 93, 97

Veil, life as, 131, 133, 134, 145, 202, 219–23, 301–2; of sleep, 131; light as, 133, 134, 222, 366, 371–2; death as, 130; lifting it, 222–3, 301, 334, 337–8, 340, 347, 353, 362, 377, 380; Veiled Beauty, 362–8

Venice, 37, 51, 116, 159, 169, 176, 284, 305, 349

Venus, 216, 233; as star, 344, 370; Anadyomene, 145, 218; di Medici, 5; Urania, 143; the Woman 'beautiful as morning', Venus shadow, 370, 372; *and see* Hesperus, Morning Star; third Heaven of, *see* Love

Verezzi, hero of *Zastrozzi*, 29, 38

Villa Magni, near Lerici (30 April–1 July 1822), described, 51, 110, 112, 113, 114, 276; 386, 390; life at, 114, 115–6; incidents at, 116–7, 119, 126, 133, 134, 135, 245

Virgil, 41, 131, 173, 273; Fourth *Georgic*, 124

Viviani, Countess Emilia, 45–6, 68, 77, 79–80, 144, 192, 218, 246; S. escaping with, 192, 194, 220, 371; his love for her, 79–80, 144, 359, 361, 367; and *Epipsychidion*, 220, 361–2, 367

Volcanoes, 172, 261, 267, 296, 328, 333, 336; observing Vesuvius (1818), 237, 296, 328

Volney, Constantin, Count, *Ruins of Empire*, 59–60, 268, 274, 305

Voltaire, 100

Walker, Dr Adam, 114, 203, 287, 295, 305, 343

Wandering Jew, the, 71, 120, 320

Warnham: church, 8, 24, 83, 117; pond, 9, 109–10

Westbrook, Eliza, elder sister of Harriet, 39, 41, 91, 95, 96, 180, 301

Westbrook, Harriet, *see* Shelley, Harriet

West Wind, the, 120, 231, 272–8, 283, 285, 287, 371, 380; as Zephyr, 273–4, 281–2

Whitton, William, 18

Wilkins, Peter, *Adventures of*, 171, 208

Will: subduing and application of, 11, 90, 159, 161, 236–7, 282–3, 321–2; God and Devil crushing, 318, 320, 336; free will, exercise of, 276, 281, 282–3, 319

Williams, Edward, 55, 104, 110, 120, 122, 129, 135, 188, 206, 305; S. boating with, 119, 189, 190, 191, 215, 385–7; as Melchior, 191, 193

Williams, Jane, 55, 104, 110, 114, 120, 122, 127, 134, 148, 177–8, 190, 207, 218, 299, 373, 385; poems to, 83, 122, 148, 215, 244–5, 262, 373

Williams, John, manager at Tremadoc, 99 (his wife, 318)

Wisdom, 239, 303, 350, 365

Wollstonecraft, Mary, 6, 42

Wordsworth, William, 50, 78, 142, 279, 332, 356; S's views on, 30, 63, 82, 98, 234, 374

Working methods of S., 57–8, 92, 169–70, 222, 245–54, 311–2

Xenophon, *Memorabilia*, 236, 237

Zephyr, *see* West Wind

Zoroastrianism, 135–6, 153